T0281046

Lecture Notes in Computer Science

Lecture Notes in Artificial Intelligence   14343

Founding Editor

Jörg Siekmann

Series Editors

Randy Goebel, *University of Alberta, Edmonton, Canada*
Wolfgang Wahlster, *DFKI, Berlin, Germany*
Zhi-Hua Zhou, *Nanjing University, Nanjing, China*

The series Lecture Notes in Artificial Intelligence (LNAI) was established in 1988 as a topical subseries of LNCS devoted to artificial intelligence.

The series publishes state-of-the-art research results at a high level. As with the LNCS mother series, the mission of the series is to serve the international R & D community by providing an invaluable service, mainly focused on the publication of conference and workshop proceedings and postproceedings.

Georgiana Ifrim · Romain Tavenard ·
Anthony Bagnall · Patrick Schaefer ·
Simon Malinowski · Thomas Guyet ·
Vincent Lemaire
Editors

Advanced Analytics and Learning on Temporal Data

8th ECML PKDD Workshop, AALTD 2023
Turin, Italy, September 18–22, 2023
Revised Selected Papers

 Springer

Editors
Georgiana Ifrim 📵
University College Dublin
Dublin, Ireland

Anthony Bagnall 📵
University of Southampton
Southampton, UK

Simon Malinowski 📵
University of Rennes
Rennes, France

Vincent Lemaire 📵
Orange Innovation
Lannion, France

Romain Tavenard 📵
University of Rennes 2
Rennes, France

Patrick Schaefer 📵
Humboldt University of Berlin
Berlin, Germany

Thomas Guyet 📵
Claude Bernard University Lyon 1
Villeurbanne, France

ISSN 0302-9743   ISSN 1611-3349 (electronic)
Lecture Notes in Artificial Intelligence
ISBN 978-3-031-49895-4   ISBN 978-3-031-49896-1 (eBook)
https://doi.org/10.1007/978-3-031-49896-1

LNCS Sublibrary: SL7 – Artificial Intelligence

This Springer imprint is published by the registered company Springer Nature Switzerland AG
The registered company address is: Gewerbestrasse 11, 6330 Cham, Switzerland

Paper in this product is recyclable.

Preface

Workshop Description

The European Conference on Machine Learning and Principles and Practice of Knowledge Discovery in Databases (ECML PKDD) is the premier European machine learning and data mining conference and builds upon over 21 years of successful events and conferences held across Europe. This year, ECML PKDD 2023 took place in Turin, Italy, during September 18–22, 2023. The main conference was complemented by a workshop program, where each workshop was dedicated to specialized topics, cross-cutting issues, and upcoming research trends. This standalone LNAI volume includes the selected papers of the 8th International Workshop on Advanced Analytics and Learning on Temporal Data (AALTD), held at ECML PKDD 2023.

Motivation – Temporal data are frequently encountered in a wide range of domains such as bio-informatics, medicine, finance, environment, and engineering, among many others. They are naturally present in emerging applications such as motion analysis, energy efficient buildings, smart cities, social media, or sensor networks. Contrary to static data, temporal data are of complex nature; they are generally noisy, of high dimensionality, they may be non-stationary (i.e., first-order statistics vary with time) and irregular (i.e., involving several time granularities), and they may have several invariant domain-dependent factors such as time delay, translation, scale, or tendency effects. These temporal peculiarities limit the majority of standard statistical models and machine learning approaches, which mainly assume i.i.d. data, homoscedasticity, normality of residuals, etc. To tackle such challenging temporal data we require new advanced approaches at the intersection of statistics, time series analysis, signal processing, and machine learning. Defining new approaches that transcend boundaries between several domains to extract valuable information from temporal data is undeniably an important research topic that has been the subject of active research in the last decade and will continue to be so for the foreseeable future.

Workshop Topics – The aim of the AALTD workshop series[1] is to bring together researchers and experts in machine learning, data mining, pattern analysis, and statistics to share their challenges and advances in temporal data analysis. Analysis of and learning from temporal data covers a wide scope of tasks including metric learning, representation learning, unsupervised feature extraction, clustering, and classification.

For this eighth edition, the proposed workshop received papers that cover one or several of the following topics:

- Temporal data clustering
- Classification and regression of univariate and multivariate time series
- Early classification of temporal data
- Deep learning for temporal data

---

[1] https://ecml-aaltd.github.io/aaltd2023/.

- Learning representation for temporal data
- Metric and kernel learning for temporal data
- Modeling temporal dependencies
- Time series forecasting
- Time series annotation, segmentation, and anomaly detection
- Spacial-temporal statistical analysis
- Functional data analysis methods
- Data streams
- Interpretable/explainable time-series analysis methods
- Dimensionality reduction, sparsity, algorithmic complexity, and big data challenges
- Benchmarking and assessment methods for temporal data
- Applications, including bio-informatics, medical, and energy consumption, on temporal data

We also welcomed contributions that addressed aspects including, but not limited to, novel techniques, innovative applications, and techniques for the use of hybrid models.

Outcomes – AALTD 2023 was structured as a full-day workshop. We encouraged submissions of regular papers that were up to 16 pages of previously unpublished work. All submitted papers were peer-reviewed (double-blind) by two or three reviewers from the Program Committee, and selected on the basis of these reviews. AALTD 2023 received 25 submissions, among which 19 papers were accepted for inclusion in the proceedings. The papers with the highest review rating were selected for oral presentation (6 papers), and the other papers, with lower scores but still endorsed by reviewers as work of high quality, were given the opportunity to present a poster through a spotlight session and a discussion session (10 papers). Three additional papers are also included in the proceedings. These are related to the Discovery Challenge competition on "Human Activity Segmentation Challenge"[2] hosted by the ECML PKDD 2023 conference, and jointly organized with the workshop. Two papers describe the winning solutions and one paper describes and analyzes how the challenge was organized and presents its results. The workshop had an invited talk on "Convolutional Kernels for Effective and Scalable Time Series Analytics"[3] given by Geoff Webb of the Monash University Data Futures Institute, Australia[4].

We thank all the organizers, reviewers, and authors for the time and effort invested to make this workshop a success. We would also like to express our gratitude to the members of the Program Committee, the Organizing Committee of ECML PKDD 2023, and the technical staff who helped us to make AALTD 2023 a successful workshop. Sincere thanks are due to Springer for their help in publishing the proceedings. Lastly, we thank

---

[2] https://ecml-aaltd.github.io/aaltd2023/challenge.html.
[3] https://ecml-aaltd.github.io/aaltd2023/invitedtalk.html.
[4] https://research.monash.edu/en/persons/geoff-webb.

all participants and speakers at AALTD 2023 for their contributions. Their collective support made the workshop an exciting, interesting, and successful event.

November 2023

Georgiana Ifrim
Romain Tavenard
Anthony Bagnall
Patrick Schaefer
Simon Malinowski
Thomas Guyet
Vincent Lemaire

Organization

Program Committee Chairs

Anthony Bagnall	University of East Anglia, UK
Thomas Guyet	Inria, France
Georgiana Ifrim	University College Dublin, Ireland
Vincent Lemaire	Orange Innovation, France
Simon Malinowski	Université de Rennes, Inria, CNRS, IRISA, France
Patrick Schäfer	Humboldt-Universität zu Berlin, Germany
Romain Tavenard	Université de Rennes 2, France

Program Committee

Zahraa Abdallah	University of Bristol, UK
Timilehin Aderinola	University College Dublin, Ireland
Gustau Camps-Valls	Universitat de València, Spain
Pádraig Cunningham	University College Dublin, Ireland
Eoin Delaney	University College Dublin, Ireland
Maxime Devanne	Université de Haute-Alsace, France
Bhaskar Dhariyal	University College Dublin, Ireland
Rémi Emonet	Université Saint-Etienne, France
Arik Ermshaus	Humboldt-Universität zu Berlin, Germany
Germain Forestier	University of Haute Alsace, France
Dominique Gay	Université de La Réunion, France
David Guijo-Rubio	Universidad de Córdoba, Spain
Paul Honeine	Université de Rouen, France
Ali Ismail-Fawaz	Université de Haute-Alsace, France
Florian Kalinke	Karlsruhe Institute of Technology, Germany
Thach Le Nguyen	University College Dublin, Ireland
Colin Leverger	Orange Innovation, France
Brian Mac Namee	University College Dublin, Ireland
Thu Trang Nguyen	University College Dublin, Ireland
Panagiotis Papapetrou	Stockholm University, Sweden
Chang Wei Tan	Monash University, Australia

Contents

Poster Presentation

Human Activity Segmentation Challenge

Human Activity Segmentation Challenge @ ECML/PKDD'23

Arik Ermshaus[1](✉)(iD), Patrick Schäfer[1], Anthony Bagnall[2], Thomas Guyet[3],
Georgiana Ifrim[4], Vincent Lemaire[5], Ulf Leser[1], Colin Leverger[6],
and Simon Malinowski[7]

[1] Humboldt University of Berlin, Berlin, Germany
{ermshaua,patrick.schaefer,leser}@informatik.hu-berlin.de
[2] University of Southampton, Southampton, UK
a.j.bagnall@soton.ac.uk
[3] Inria, Villeurbanne, France
thomas.guyet@inria.fr
[4] University College Dublin, Dublin, Ireland
georgiana.ifrim@ucd.ie
[5] Orange Labs, Lannion, France
vincent.lemaire@orange.com
[6] Orange Innovation, Rennes, France
colin.leverger@orange.com
[7] University of Rennes 1, Rennes, France
simon.malinowski@irisa.fr

Abstract. Time series segmentation (TSS) is a research problem that focuses on dividing long multivariate sensor data into smaller, homogeneous subsequences. This task is critical for various real-world data analysis applications, such as energy consumption monitoring, climate change assessment, and human activity recognition (HAR). Despite its importance, existing methods demonstrate limited efficacy on real-world multivariate time series data. To advance the field, we organized the Human Activity Segmentation Challenge at ECML/PKDD and AALTD 2023, featuring 57 participants. Collaborating with 15 bachelor computer science students, we gathered and annotated 10.7 h of real-world human motion sensor data. The challenge required participants to segment the resulting 250 multivariate time series into an unknown number of variable-sized activities. The top-8 approaches outperformed existing baselines, but show only limited improvements, capped at 1.9% points. The segmentation of real-world mobile sensing recordings remains challenging. We release the labelled challenge data for future research.

Keywords: Ubiquitous Sensing · Human Activity Recognition · Data Mining · Unsupervised Learning · Time Series Segmentation

1 Introduction

The analysis of human behaviour can provide valuable insights into health status, fitness, or personal security [1]. This is relevant to various domains, including

G. Ifrim et al. (Eds.): AALTD 2023, LNAI 14343, pp. 3–13, 2023.
https://doi.org/10.1007/978-3-031-49896-1_1

4   A. Ermshaus et al.

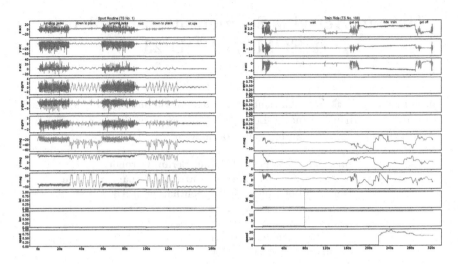

Fig. 1. Example TS of a sport routine from subject 1 (left, indoor) and a train ride from subject 1 (right, outdoor). Activity segments are coloured. Missing dimensions are displayed as empty cells.

the medical sector [2], industrial applications [3], and military operations [4]. Wearable devices, such as smartphones, have low-cost sensors that capture the dynamics of human activities in the form of long consecutive segments within temporal data, commonly known as time series (TS) [5]. Such data can be used, for instance, to detect falls in the elderly [6], or to monitor patients with dementia or mental illness [7].

To accomplish such applications, the research field of human activity recognition (HAR) implements workflows that first segment TS motion data, then learn characteristic features and finally classify individual activities [1]. Most HAR systems process fixed-length subsequences extracted from sensor measurements, as opposed to processing the entirety of a single activity [8]. This leads to heterogeneity and performance losses in many downstream tasks [7]. The automatic partitioning of multivariate sensor signals into an unknown amount of variable-sized activity segments is very challenging, and many open problems still exist, such as accurately locating activity transitions in multi-dimensional data and deciding if these are actually substantial or just emergent signal fluctuations.

The overarching task of activity segmentation is called time series segmentation (TSS), which is an unsupervised learning problem that seeks to discover variable-sized, distinguishable segments separated by change points (CPs) within TS [9,10]. TSS typically is not the final aim of data analysis, but serves as a preprocessing step to partition complex TS data for advanced analytics such as classification [11], anomaly detection [12] or motif discovery [13]. Accurate solutions need to be robust, segment a wide variety of different TS and handle imperfect and noisy multi-dimensional sensor recordings from different devices. Recently, specialized statistical methods [10] and modern data mining algorithms [14,15]

Table 1. List of motion sequences.

Motion ID	Group ID	Category	Activity Examples	Subject IDs
1	1	sport	jumping jacks, sit ups, plank, …	1,2,3,4,6,7,8
2	1	household	clear dishes, vacuum living room, push couch back, …	1,2,3,4,6,7,8
3	1	shopping	stand on escalator 1, change shoes, walk to Deichmann exit, …	1,3,4,5,6,7,8
1	2	commute	climb stairs, ride train (standing), wait for traffic lights, …	1,2,3,4,5,6,7
2	2	commute	go down stairs, wait, drive, …	1,2,3,4,5,6
3	2	sport	deep squat with arm reach, reverse plank hold, side stretch left, …	1,2,4,5,6,7

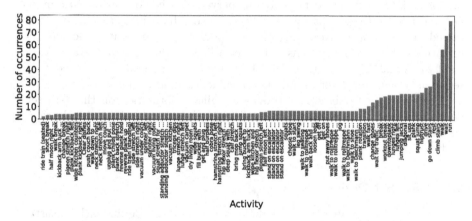

Fig. 2. Number of occurrences for single activities in the challenge data.

have been employed to address this task. However, as highlighted by the survey of Aminikhanghahi et al. [9], accuracy is still limited.

To bridge this gap, we conducted an ECML/PKDD 2023 discovery challenge in collaboration with the 8th Workshop on Advanced Analytics and Learning on Temporal Data (AALTD@ECML)[1]. The competition aimed to increase the performance of multi-modal human activity segmentation and featured 57 participants. We provided a new mobile sensing data set from a daily setting, as opposed to the typical laboratory setup with intrusive and specialized sensor devices [16,17]. We collected and annotated 10.7 hours of multi-dimensional real-world TS data using heterogenous smartphone sensors capturing 100 typical human activities performed by 15 bachelor students in 6 motion sequences. See Fig. 1 for two examples. The challenge task was to predict the amount and

---

[1] https://ecml-aaltd.github.io/aaltd2023.

locations of activity transitions in the resulting 250 multivariate TS without any training or external data. Existing algorithms which served as baselines like BinSeg [10] or ClaSP [15] score low to medium F_1 scores (24,8% to 49,6%) on these data sets. The winning solutions improve the state of the art by up to 1.9% points (pp) to 51.5%. This progress demonstrates the potential for further advancements in multivariate TSS research in general and HAR in particular. We make the labelled challenge data freely available [18] to encourage comparative evaluations in the field.

2   Challenge Data

In collaboration with 15 bachelor computer science students (see Acknowledgments), we created a multi-modal data set comprising 40 twelve-dimensional multivariate smartphone sensor recordings. These capture 6 distinct human motion sequences designed to represent pervasive behaviour in realistic indoor and outdoor settings. Data were collected using built-in smartphone sensors placed in the subjects' front right trouser pockets. We annotated the activities performed and their transitions in the recordings, resampled the data at a constant rate of 50 Hz, and segmented it to yield 250 multivariate TS. This data set serves as a benchmark for evaluating machine learning workflows.

The subsequent subsections provide detailed information on the data set's design (Subsect. 2.1), collection process (Subsect. 2.2), annotation and preprocessing workflow (Subsect.. 2.3), specifications (Subsect. 2.4), and availability (Subsect. 2.5).

2.1   Data Set Design

Two independent groups from Humboldt-Universität zu Berlin, each consisting of either 8 or 7 bachelor computer science students, recorded 3 motion sequences in 2022. These sequences covered a total of 100 activities, with the first group focusing on indoor activities and the second group targeting outdoor behaviours. The primary objective was to capture natural human behaviour. A summary of the motion sequences is provided in Table 1, and specific activity annotations are linked to individual TS.

The student cohort included 10 males and 5 females, ranging in age from 21 to 42. Further details are presented in Table 2. Within a group, each student performed up to 3 preconceived motion routines, consisting of different and partly recurring activities, the distribution of which is visualized in Fig. 2. The data collection yielded 40 multivariate recordings that were subsequently cut to create a data set of 250 multi-dimensional TS. Recordings were made using 5 different smartphones from 4 brands (Huawei, Motorola, Samsung, and Xperia) and were placed in the front right trouser pocket of (almost) all participants. The "Physics Toolbox Sensor Suite" application was employed to capture sensor data from a triaxial accelerometer, gyroscope, and magnetometer, as well as latitude, longitude, and speed when available. The resulting TS feature 12 dimensions, with 9 filled sensor data dimensions and 3 empty ones, as illustrated in

Table 2. List and characteristics of participants.

Subject ID	Group ID	Gender	Age	Size (in cm)	Weight (in kg)
1	1	M	25	180	74
2	1	F	23	155	50
3	1	M	23	179	83
4	1	M	24	167	68
5	1	F	26	166	67
6	1	F	22	180	65
7	1	F	23	170	58
8	1	F	30	172	57
1	2	M	29	183	96
2	2	M	23	183	65
3	2	M	24	182	130
4	2	M	31	180	100
5	2	M	42	171	62
6	2	M	21	186	66
7	2	M	27	186	75

Fig. 1. The empty dimensions are due to different sensors in the smartphones. To ensure continuous recording and prevent data loss in standby mode, the "Touch Protector" application was also used. This smartphone placement and sensor configuration is consistent with common practices in human activity recognition (HAR) research [19,20]. Ground truth behaviour was captured through additional recording using another smartphone or action camera.

2.2 Data Collection

The student groups conducted the data collection over several days in the fall and winter of 2022, with tasks, roles, and responsibilities delegated among smaller teams. Prior to recording, instructors briefed the subjects on the motion sequences and time commitments involved. During data collection, participants initiated sensor recording, placed the phone in their front right pocket, performed the specified motions, and then ceased recording upon completion. Additional students guided subjects through the correct motion sequences and filmed the activities to be used for annotations. All recordings were subsequently reviewed for data quality and securely stored.

The data collection process encountered several challenges. Both groups experienced data loss due to hardware failure, necessitating re-recordings. We only used uninterrupted TS in the challenge data. Organizational difficulties also arose due to illnesses among team members. In one case, a phone had to be taped onto a subject's pants due to a lack of pockets.

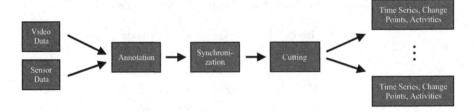

Fig. 3. The preprocessing workflow for a single recording.

2.3   Preprocessing

A basic preprocessing pipeline was applied to the challenge data, as illustrated in Fig. 3. Student groups annotated the recordings with activity labels and transitions to establish a ground truth, which is used for evaluation (Subsect. 3.3). They manually analysed the video footage in conjunction with the sensor data to do so. Subsequently, we synchronized the sensor dimensions using linear interpolation, a prerequisite for most TS analysis algorithms. A constant sample rate of 50 Hz was employed, deemed appropriate for human behaviour detection [21]. Finally, each of the 40 recordings was cut at randomly selected activity transitions to yield a data set of 250 multivariate TS, encompassing diverse problem settings.

2.4   Data Set Overview

The data set comprises 250 twelve-dimensional TS, capturing 15 participants performing up to three motion sequences each. The TS range from 7 s to 14 min in duration (median 100 s) and contain between 1 and 15 segments; 76% of TS have 5 or fewer segments (see Fig. 4, top right). Activity durations vary from half a second for waiting to 10 min for running, with generally small variances between subjects and individual executions (see Fig. 4, bottom).

Figure 1 presents two example TS from the challenge data, displaying all 12 dimensions. Activities are represented as coloured segments, and missing dimensions appear as empty cells. The sports routine (left) reveals abrupt transitions between activities, while the train ride sequence (right) shows gradual transitions and significant variations in activity duration.

2.5   Data Availability

We make all the challenge data publicly available, complete with labels, meta-information, and a Python data loader, on our website [18]. The data is licensed under CC-BY-NC-SA, allowing users to share and adapt the content, provided they give appropriate credit, use the same licence, and refrain from commercial use.

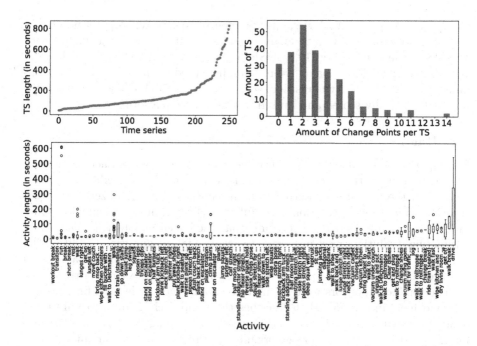

Fig. 4. Top: TS length and amount of change points. Bottom: Single activities and their lengths.

3 Challenge Organisation

We organized the contest as a discovery challenge for ECML/PKDD 2023, in collaboration with the 8th Workshop on Advanced Analytics and Learning on Temporal Data (AALTD@ECML). The competition ran from April 11 to June 11, 2023, concluding at 23:59 UTC. Registration was open until June 2, 2023. Following the competition's end, we requested the top-ranking solutions from competitors and, after a final review, released the scores on June 16, 2023. In total, the challenge attracted 57 registrations, with 17 active participants submitting 240 entries. Two winners were awarded free tickets to ECML/PKDD 2023, oral presentations of their approaches at both the conference and the workshop, as well as publications in its proceedings.

Subsequent subsections will detail the technical aspects (Subsect. 3.1), rules (Subsect. 3.2), evaluation measure (Subsect. 3.3), and competition results (Subsect. 3.4).

3.1 Technical Details

We hosted an invite-only community competition on Kaggle[2] to disseminate challenge information, data, baselines, and to maintain public and private leaderboards. Interested individuals could access the competition through an invitation

---

[2] https://www.kaggle.com/competitions/human-activity-segmentation-challenge.

link, provided upon request via a questionnaire. We supplied Jupyter notebooks featuring an exploratory data analysis and six state-of-the-art algorithms for TSS [18], including BinSeg [10], ClaSP [15], FLUSS [14], GGS [22], IGTS [23], and STRAY [24]. Participants submitted their predictions as a CSV file, containing predicted activity transitions for each of the 250 TS. These submissions were automatically scored and ranked by the Kaggle platform.

3.2 Rules

Participants had to adhere to specific rules to join the challenge. Each participant was allowed up to three daily submissions, using only reproducible and deterministic methods subject to verification on request by the organizers to prevent cheating. We deemed a solution deceitful if it relied on manually labelled annotations or machine learning algorithms that used such annotations. Only fully unsupervised solutions were permitted to ensure a fair competition. Additionally, the use of external data or metadata-based manual tuning of hyperparameters was prohibited. Parameters had to be either universally set or data-driven.

The top-3 competitors were required to submit their code for a final inspection and hand-in a report that describes their approach. Failure to fulfil these obligations resulted in forfeiture of the award and winning status, as was the case for one participant. The challenge organizers were ineligible to submit entries.

3.3 Evaluation Measure

In this challenge, participants were tasked with predicting the offsets of activity transitions for all 250 twelve-dimensional TS in our data set. Apart from the TS, sensor names, and overall sample rate, no further information was provided. Ground truth annotations, kept confidential, served as the basis for evaluating the predicted segmentations. To score submissions and generate leaderboards, the data set was randomly partitioned into public and private sets, each containing 125 TS. No stratified sampling was applied, as TSS had to be performed for single TS without training or external data. Final performance was assessed on the private set, yielding the ultimate leaderboard and rankings.

For evaluating segmentation performance, we employed a well-established benchmarking score from existing literature. Drawing inspiration from an image segmentation challenge[3], we combined classification and clustering metrics to calculate the average F_1 score across different thresholds. Specifically, for each TS, we calculated the intersection over union (IoU) between predicted and ground truth segments to yield a normalized score (higher is better). A threshold was then applied to determine sufficient overlaps, generating a confusion matrix from which the F_1 score was computed. This process was iteratively applied for multiple thresholds (ranging from 0.5 to 0.95 in steps of 0.05), and the results were averaged to generate the final normalized score. This measure was calculated for each of the 250 TS and averaged per leaderboard to measure the quality of a participant and infer the public and private rankings.

---

[3] https://www.kaggle.com/competitions/airbus-ship-detection/overview/evaluation.

Table 3. The final private leaderboard with top-10 best-ranking competitors and 3 baselines (in bold/italic). The top-8 approaches outperform the best baseline ClaSP.

Rank	F_1 Score (in %)	Participant	No. of Entries
1	51.5	gh	46
2	50.7	Koular	12
3	49.8	Panos	14
4	49.8	infoxin	15
5	49.8	kojimar	7
6	49.8	Shayekh Islam	4
7	49.8	fuge	5
8	49.8	laffrent	11
	49.6	*ClaSP*	
9	49.6	pjmathematician	16
10	49.1	ALLAccept	11
	24.8	*BinSeg*	
	23.9	*FLUSS*	

3.4   Competition Results

Table 3 displays the final rankings and F_1 scores for the top-10 competitors. The top-2 winning solutions achieved F_1 scores exceeding 50%. Both utilized the ClaSP algorithm in a multivariate setting, employing strategies for selecting relevant sensor dimensions, hyper-parameter tuning, and change point merging. Their detailed methodologies and code are available in the respective publications [25, 26]. The top-8 competitors outperformed the highest-ranking baseline, ClaSP, which scored 49.6%. However, the performance improvement, capped at 1.9 pp, highlights the inherent challenge of segmenting real-world mobile sensing data in a fully unsupervised manner.

4   Conclusion

We presented an overview and results of the Human Activity Segmentation Challenge at ECML/PKDD and AALTD 2023. The contest utilized 10.7 h of mobile sensing data recorded with 15 bachelor students, which is now publicly available for future human activity recognition research. In the challenge, 17 active participants competed, with the top-2 achieving F_1 scores over 50% for the segmentation task. However, the overall performance on this data set remains limited and requires significant improvement for TSS to be a viable component in human activity recognition workflows.

Based on this challenge, we identify several avenues for future research: (a) exploring sensor fusion within multivariate TSS, as opposed to current methods that segment TS channels independently and merge resulting change points; (b) investigating dimension selection for multivariate TSS to potentially improve accuracy; and (c) advancing domain-specific data denoising, normalization, and preprocessing, particularly to facilitate the segmentation process.

Acknowledgments. We would like to thank Jonas Albrecht, Alexandria Arnold, Leo Baur, Malte Borgmann, Simon Bosse, Sinan Genc, Alina Hartwich, Isabel Heise, Jan Evert Hinrichs, Hoai Ngoc Ho, Malte Hückelkempkes, Wei Jin, Elida Sengül, Gerrit Slomma and Katharina Winde for their work in creating, recording and annotating the motion sequences for the challenge data.

References

1. Lara, O.D., Labrador, M.A.: A survey on human activity recognition using wearable sensors. IEEE Commun. Surv. Tutor. **15**, 1192–1209 (2013)
2. Zhou, L., Fischer, E., Brahms, C.M., Granacher, U., Arnrich, B.: Duo-gait: a gait dataset for walking under dual-task and fatigue conditions with inertial measurement units. Sci. Data **10** (2023)
3. Gupta, N., Gupta, S.K., Pathak, R.K., Jain, V., Rashidi, P., Suri, J.S.: Human activity recognition in artificial intelligence framework: a narrative review. Artif. Intell. Rev. **55**, 4755–4808 (2022)
4. Mukherjee, A., Misra, S., Mangrulkar, P., Rajarajan, M., Rahulamathavan, Y.: Smartarm: a smartphone-based group activity recognition and monitoring scheme for military applications. In: IEEE International Conference on Advanced Networks and Telecommunications Systems (ANTS), pp. 1–6 (2017)
5. Ermshaus, A., Singh, S., Leser, U.: Time series segmentation applied to a new data set for mobile sensing of human activities. In: EDBT/ICDT Workshops (2023)
6. Yin, J., Yang, Q., Pan, J.J.: Sensor-based abnormal human-activity detection. IEEE Trans. Knowl. Data Eng. **20**, 1082–1090 (2008)
7. Ahad, M.A.R., Antar, A.D., Ahmed, M.: IoT sensor-based activity recognition - human activity recognition. In: Intelligent Systems Reference Library (2021)
8. Baños, O., Gálvez, J.M., Damas, M., Pomares, H., Rojas, I.: Window size impact in human activity recognition. Sensors **14**, 6474–6499 (2014)
9. Aminikhanghahi, S., Cook, D.J.: A survey of methods for time series change point detection. Knowl. Inf. Syst. **51**, 339–367 (2017)
10. Truong, C., Oudre, L., Vayatis, N.: Selective review of offline change point detection methods. Sig. Process. **167**, 107299 (2020)
11. Middlehurst, M., Schäfer, P., Bagnall, A.: Bake off redux: a review and experimental evaluation of recent time series classification algorithms. arXiv preprint arXiv:2304.13029 (2023)
12. Schmidl, S., Wenig, P., Papenbrock, T.: Anomaly detection in time series: a comprehensive evaluation. Proc. VLDB Endow. **15**, 1779–1797 (2022)
13. Schäfer, P., Leser, U.: Motiflets - simple and accurate detection of motifs in time series. Proc. VLDB Endow. **16**, 725–737 (2022)
14. Gharghabi, S., et al.: Domain agnostic online semantic segmentation for multidimensional time series. Data Min. Knowl. Disc. **33**, 96–130 (2018)
15. Ermshaus, A., Schäfer, P., Leser, U.: Clasp: parameter-free time series segmentation. Data Min. Knowl. Disc. **37**, 1262–1300 (2023)
16. Reiss, A., Stricker, D.: Introducing a new benchmarked dataset for activity monitoring. In: 2012 16th International Symposium on Wearable Computers, pp. 108–109 (2012)

17. Chavarriaga, R., et al.: The opportunity challenge: a benchmark database for on-body sensor-based activity recognition. Pattern Recognit. Lett. **34**, 2033–2042 (2013)
18. Challenge Supporting Materials (2023). https://github.com/patrickzib/human_activity_segmentation_challenge
19. Bieber, G., Voskamp, J., Urban, B.: Activity recognition for everyday life on mobile phones. In: Universal Access in Human-Computer Interaction (2009)
20. Elkader, S.A., Barlow, M., Lakshika, E.: Wearable sensors for recognizing individuals undertaking daily activities. In: Proceedings of the 2018 ACM International Symposium on Wearable Computers (2018)
21. Baños, O., et al.: Design, implementation and validation of a novel open framework for agile development of mobile health applications. Biomed. Eng. Online **14**, S6–S6 (2015)
22. Hallac, D., Nystrup, P., Boyd, S.P.: Greedy gaussian segmentation of multivariate time series. In: Advances in Data Analysis and Classification, pp. 727–751 (2019)
23. Sadri, A., Ren, Y., Salim, F.D.: Information gain-based metric for recognizing transitions in human activities. Pervas. Mob. Comput. **38**, 92–109 (2017)
24. Talagala, P.D., Hyndman, R.J., Smith-Miles, K.: Anomaly detection in high-dimensional data. J. Comput. Graph. Stat. **30**, 360–374 (2019)
25. Harańczyk, G.: Change points detection in multivariate signal applied to human activity segmentation. In: AALTD@ECML/PKDD (2023)
26. Huang, T.-J., Zhou, Q.-L., Ye, H.-J., Zhan, D.-C.: Change point detection via synthetic signals. In: AALTD@ECML/PKDD (2023)

Change Points Detection in Multivariate Signal Applied to Human Activity Segmentation

Grzegorz Harańczyk(✉)

Kraków, Poland
gharanczyk@gmail.com

Abstract. The detection of change points in multivariate signal without access to annotated data is a challenging task. The fully unsupervised approach requires the development of a robust algorithm that can effectively identify unknown a priori patterns. In this article we will present one of the solutions to "Human Activity Segmentation Challenge" ECML/PKDD'23 [4] where the task was to predict the offsets of activity transitions for multivariate time series. The described solution won the first place.

Keywords: multivariate signal segmentation · unsupervised learning · change point detection (CPD) · human activity recognition (HAR)

1 Introduction

Detecting change points is a common task when dealing with non-stationary time series and involves the identification of temporal boundaries that separate homogeneous time periods. Its importance was proven in various domains, including finance, environmental monitoring, industrial monitoring, medical condition monitoring, climate change detection, etc.

One of the popular area of application of such methods are human activity recognition (HAR) systems [1]. They are designed to automatically identify and classify human activities based on sensor data. These systems typically involve the use of wearable sensors, such as accelerometers and gyroscopes, to capture the motion and movement patterns of the human body. The data collected from these sensors is then processed and analyzed to recognize and classify different activities which later can be applied as fitness tracking, healthcare monitoring, personal security, gesture recognition etc.

Methods for change point detection can be roughly categorized as *online* [6] or *offline* [7]. Offline algorithms analyze the entire dataset as a whole and retrospectively identify points of change by examining past data. Their objective is typically to identify all the change points in a sequence in a batch processing mode. On the other hand, online (real-time algorithms) operate in parallel with the monitored process. They process each incoming data point as it becomes

G. Ifrim et al. (Eds.): AALTD 2023, LNAI 14343, pp. 14–24, 2023.
https://doi.org/10.1007/978-3-031-49896-1_2

available, aiming to detect a change point as quickly as possible after it happens, ideally prior to the arrival of subsequent data points. In this article we will focus on the offline scenario.

Traditional change point detection methods often rely on predefined assumptions or manual thresholds, making them less adaptive to complex and dynamic data. To address this challenge, unsupervised machine learning (ML) methods have gained significant attention for their ability to automatically discover change points without prior knowledge or labeled data.

2 Problem Statement

Human Activity Segmentation Challenge [4] was organized as one of Discovery Challenges during ECML PKDD 2023 conference. The objective of this challenge was to create completely unsupervised algorithms that address the time series segmentation problem. Many HAR systems currently adopt a strategy of processing fixed-length subsequences extracted from sensor measurements, rather than analyzing complete activity instances. Addressing this challenge requires the automatic partitioning of multi-variate sensor signals into variable-sized segments of activities, the number of which is unknown. Therefore the primary objective of this competition was focused on time series segmentation (TSS), an unsupervised learning problem that aims to identify homogeneous segments of variable lengths within a given time series. TSS is typically employed as a preprocessing step to partition complex time series data for advanced analytical tasks such as classification, anomaly detection, or motif discovery. However, performance in this area remains limited, especially when dealing with real-world time series data where the number of segments is not predetermined.

In order to achieve an accurate solution for the defined task, it was essential to develop robust algorithm capable of segmenting a wide range of different behaviors, while effectively handling multi-dimensional sensor recordings from different devices.

For the evaluation, the ground truth annotations of the activity transitions were used to measure the quality of predicted segmentations. Note that it was not possible to use annotations to build or tune segmentation models. Moreover, embedding human expertise about the given time series into handcrafted models was also explicitly prohibited. Parameters were supposed to be set for the entire data set or learned from the available data. It was also enforced by the validation schema (a part of the score (private score) was hidden until the end of the challenge).

2.1 Notation

In this section, we will introduce some notation that will be used later to facilitate a clearer and more precise description of our solution.

Definition 1. *A multivariate time series T is a sequence of $n \in \mathbb{N}$ real values, $T = (t_1, \ldots, t_n)$, where $t_i \in \mathbb{R}^d$ for $i = 1, \ldots, n$ that contains the observable output of d sensors over time. The values are also called observations or data points.*

Definition 2. *For a given time series T, we define a subsequence $T_{s,e}$ of T with a start offset s and an end offset e which consists of the continuous observations of T from positions s to position e (i.e., $T_{s,e} = (t_s, \ldots, t_e)$ with $1 \leq s \leq e \leq n$).*

Definition 3. *We define segmentation of time series T as set of time series subsequences S_{i_s,i_e} for $i \in I$ such that*

$$\bigcup_{i \in I} S_i = T \tag{1}$$

and

$$S_i \cap S_j = \emptyset \quad \text{for } i, j \in I \tag{2}$$

Each time series segmentation can be expressed as ordered sequence of observations of T such that $t_{i_1}, \ldots, t_{i_S}$ with $1 < i_1 < \ldots < i_S < n$. We call these observations change points.

The set of change points also determines the segmentation of the time series; hence, in this paper, we will use these terms interchangeably.

Definition 4. *We say that coverage $S_{i \in I}$ is finer than $S_{i \in J}$ if each element of $S_{i \in J}$ can be expressed as a union of elements from $S_{i \in I}$. We denote it as $S_{i \in I} \prec S_{i \in J}$*

Definition 5. *For any two time series segmentations we can define their intersection i.e.,*

$$S_{i \in I} \wedge S_{i \in J} = \{s_i \cap s_j \text{ for } (s_i, s_j) \in (S_{i \in I}, S_{j \in J})\} \tag{3}$$

It is easy to observe that $S_{i \in I} \wedge S_{i \in J} \prec S_{i \in I}$ is segmentation of time series T and

$$S_{i \in I} \wedge S_{i \in J} \prec S_{i \in I} \text{ and } S_{i \in I} \wedge S_{i \in J} \prec S_{i \in J} \tag{4}$$

In the context of human activity recognition, our objective is to perform time series segmentation on sensor signals. This segmentation yields consecutive subsequences that correspond to distinct activities, such as walking or running.

Within the specified task of Human Activity Segmentation Challenge, we are presented with time series data that already possess predefined segmentation, representing distinct activities. Our objective is to predict this segmentation accurately. In this particular setup, the initial segmentation is concealed, thus prohibiting the use of supervised machine learning methods. List of original activities is used only for method validation i.e., original segmentation $S_{i \in I}$ will be compared with predicted $\hat{S}_{i \in J}$. Note that we don't know the cardinality of the original segmentation $\#I$ so it is possible that $\#I \neq \#J$;

2.2   Dataset

A dataset of 250 twelve-dimensional multivariate time series was collected for Human Activity Segmentation Challenge. The time series were sampled at a frequency of 50 Hertz (Hz) and contain between seven seconds and fourteen minutes (median 100 s) of human motion data (with a cumulative duration of 10.7 h). Distribution of signal length was presented in Fig. 1.

The recordings were taken by students from Humboldt-Universitt zu Berlin and capture few to many potentially recurring activities from a total of one hundred different ones, each lasting for variable time durations. The acquired sensor data encompasses triaxial acceleration, gyroscope, and magnetometer readings, as well as latitude, longitude, and speed, depending on the smartphone utilized. For all time series there were always available measurement of acceleration (x-acc, y-acc, z-acc) and magnetometer measurements (x-mag, y-mag, z-mag) and either set of gyroscope measurements (x-$gyro$, y-$gyro$, z-$gyro$) or measurements of lat, lon and $speed$. So in our study, each observation in the dataset was represented by a nine-dimensional signal with sampling of 50 values collected per second. Example of such multivariate signal was presented in Fig. 2.

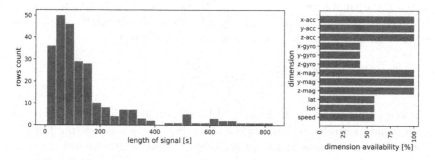

Fig. 1. Distribution of signal length and availability of a given measurement in time series.

Besides these time series, their sensor names, and the overall sample rate, no other information was provided or permitted for use. Also use of any external data and pre-trained models (as they have been trained on external data) was strictly prohibited.

2.3   Validation Procedure

As previously stated, the ground truth segmentation, representing distinct activities was not available during segmentation, only used for the external validation step. To assess the performance of a given solution predicting time series segments, the multi-threshold *F1* score was used. It is defined as follows:

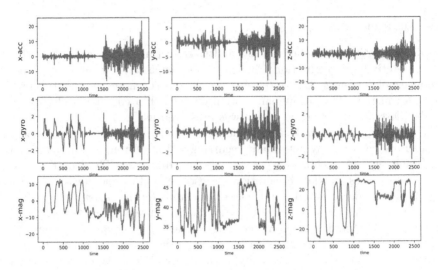

Fig. 2. Example of multivariate signal ($ts\_id = 9$).

For a given time series, we calculate the intersection over union (IoU, also called *Jaccard similarity coefficient* [5]) of overlapping predicted and ground truth segments, to obtain a normed score (higher is better).

$$IoU(S, \hat{S}) = \frac{|S \cap \hat{S}|}{|S \cup \hat{S}|} \tag{5}$$

Then we set a threshold to assess which overlaps are sufficient, from which a confusion matrix is inferred, used to calculate the $F1$ score. A true positive (TP) is counted when a single predicted segment matches a ground truth segment with an IoU above the threshold. A false positive (FP) indicates a predicted segment had no associated ground truth segment. A false negative (FN) indicates a ground truth segment had no associated predicted segment.

This computation is repeated for multiple thresholds and the results are averaged to obtain the final normalized score for a given time series:

$$\frac{1}{\#ths} \sum_{t \in ths} \frac{2TP(t)}{2TP(t) + FP(t) + FN(t)} \tag{6}$$

where set of thresholds $ths = \{0.5, 0.55, \ldots, 0.9\}$ and where $\#ths$ denotes the cardinality of the set ths.

To get the final score, this measure is calculated for each of the time series and averaged.

In our analysis, we employed a range of internal metrics, including measures of internal consistency, to evaluate the performance of our models. However, given the specific nature of the task, we also endeavored to utilize the competition scoring system as frequently as possible. After submitting segmentation for

all time series in the dataset, the value of $F1$ metric was calculated. It is important to note that utilizing the competition scoring system posed some strategic
challenges due to limitations on the number of calls to the scoring API, which
were restricted to three calls per day. Additionally, it is worth mentioning that
the scoring API provided a single value for the entire solution, encompassing
all time series in the public part of validation dataset. The score for another
part of validation dataset (private score) was not available until the end of the
competition.

3   Approach Selection

3.1   Baseline Solutions

In the initial stages, we established a set of simple baseline solutions, which were
subsequently modified to serve as benchmarks for comparing the performance of
our proposed solution. Developing these basic baselines not only facilitated the
identification of key aspects that could potentially have a significant impact on
performance but also assisted in prioritizing their importance.

Specifically, we generated a series of segmentations using a random selection
of change points, as well as a series of segmentations based on equal subsequences
with an increasing number of generated segments (see Fig. 3).

We also conducted a series of experiments that involved segmentations using
both single and multiple dimensions (see Fig. 4). These experiments not only
helped us to reduce the number of components employed in the final model but
also enabled an assessment of the performance implications associated with the
utilization of complex models.

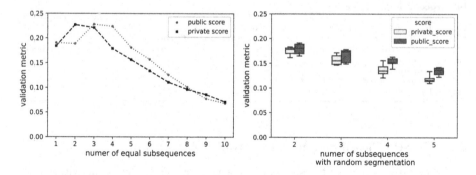

Fig. 3. Performance of simple baseline solutions - equal subsequences with increasing
number of generated segments and random segments.

3.2 General Idea

In order to maintain control over the final solution while keeping it as simple as possible, we opted to generate segmentations for one-dimensional components of given multivariate signal and subsequently aggregate them to form the final solution. Instead of utilizing all components of the multivariate signal, we selected only three components that exhibited the highest performance in one-dimensional models. Our experimentation involved exploring various methods of aggregating the results from individual components into the final solution, as well as devising a technique to reduce the final solution to prevent overfitting. Hence, the final solution consists of the following three steps (see Algorithm 1):

- generation of ClaSP change points for selected channels;
- consolidation of change points obtained from various channels;
- elimination of irrelevant change points through pruning.

Algorithm 1. Change Point Detection

 1: **function** CHANGEPOINTDETECTION($data$)
 2:    $changePoints \leftarrow \emptyset$ ▷ Initialize empty set
 3:    **for** channel $\in$ {x-acc, y-acc, z-acc} **do**   ▷ Loop over channels
 4:       $channelData \leftarrow$ extractChannelData($data$, channel)   ▷ Extract channel data
 5:       $cps \leftarrow$ ClaspProcedure($channelData$)   ▷ Apply clasp procedure
 6:       $changePoints \leftarrow changePoints \cup cps$ ▷ Merge change points
 7:    **end for**
 8:    $changePoints \leftarrow$ PruneFunction($changePoints$)   ▷ Apply prune function
 9:    **return** $changePoints$
10: **end function**

11: **procedure** CLASPPROCEDURE($channelData$)
12:    ...   ▷ Implementation details - see [2]
13: **end procedure**

14: **procedure** PRUNEFUNCTION($changePoints$)
15:    $prunedChangePoints \leftarrow \emptyset$ ▷ Initialize empty set
16:    **for** point1, point2 $\in changePoints$ **do**   ▷ Loop over change points
17:       **if** $|point1 - point2| \leq threshold$ & $point1 < point2$ **then**
18:          $prunedChangePoints \leftarrow point1$ ▷ Keep only the first change point
19:       **end if**
20:    **end for**
21:    **return** $prunedChangePoints$
22: **end procedure**

3.3 ClaSP (Classification Score Profile) Algorithm

We conducted experiments using several segmentation methods and ultimately selected the ClaSP (Classification Score Profile) algorithm to generate change points for the chosen channels. In [2], it was demonstrated that ClaSP outperforms existing state-of-the-art methods in terms of accuracy. Additionally, the evaluation of ClaSP's performance involved rigorous experimental analysis using a benchmark dataset consisting of 107 distinct data sets. Remarkably, the results indicated that ClaSP not only achieved improved accuracy but also demonstrated impressive speed and scalability.

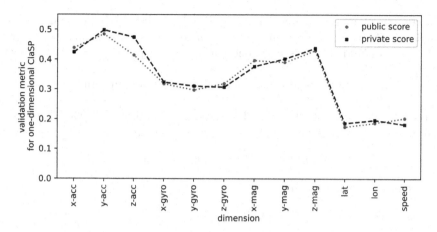

Fig. 4. Performance of ClaSP algorithm applied to single components of multivariate signal.

In our pursuit of enhancing performance, we aimed to fine-tune model parameters. In order to accomplish this, we followed the methodology outlined in Sect. 4.7 of [2] and in the article [3]. However, due to limited validation capabilities, we were unable to guarantee robustness and obtain a superior set of parameters compared to the default configuration.

3.4 Multivariate Aggregation

When combining segmentations obtained from one-dimensional time series, two primary strategies emerge as the most intuitive. The first strategy involves deeming a change point as valid for the multidimensional time series if it is valid for any of its individual dimensions. This strategy allows for variations and deviations within individual dimensions while still considering the change point as valid for the overall multidimensional time series.

The second strategy entails considering a change point as valid for a multidimensional time series only if it is deemed valid for all of its one-dimensional components. In other words, the change point should exhibit consistency across all dimensions.

Using notation from Sect. 2.1 we can express it as follows:

Scenario 1: use as a segmentation the intersection of all available one-dimensional segmentations:

$$\bigwedge_d S_{i \in I_d} = S_{i \in I_1} \wedge \ldots \wedge S_{i \in I_d} \tag{7}$$

Note that in our case finally we decided to use only measurements from accelerometers (x-acc, y-acc, z-acc), so in our case multivariate aggregation will be an intersection of these components.

Scenario 2: we define a new segmentation W such that change point $c \in W$ if and only if $c \in S_{i \in I_k}$ for each $k = 1, \ldots, d$. It can be also defined with some precision threshold, i.e., c is close enough to change point in each component segmentation.

For example, if we would get three one-dimensional segmentations:

$$\{[0, 50], [51, 100]\}, \{[0, 50], [51, 80], [81, 100]\}, \text{ and } \{[0, 50], [51, 90], [91, 100]\}$$

then Scenario 1 would give us the aggregated segmentation as

$$\{[0, 50], [51, 80], [81, 90], [91, 100]\}$$

and Scenario 2 would give us:

$$\{[0, 50], [51, 100]\}.$$

We opted to proceed with Scenario 1, wherein a change of activity in a single dimension is considered sufficient. We believe that within the context of our use case, this assumption is valid. Specifically, we posit that it is possible for an activity to change solely by altering a single component, without necessitating simultaneous changes across all dimensions.

Upon combining the one-dimensional components, we made an intriguing observation regarding the presence of numerous closely spaced change points. This phenomenon could be attributed to time shifts or delays in detecting activity changes across different components. Given the sampling frequency of 50 Hz, achieving exact alignment of change point values across all dimensions proved to be challenging. Unfortunately, the lack of access to annotated data hindered our ability to empirically validate this hypothesis. Nevertheless, in light of this observation, we made the decision to eliminate redundant change points. Remarkably, this post-processing step yielded a positive impact on the performance of our solution, further reinforcing the significance of addressing the issue of redundant change points in the context of our study.

3.5   Pruning

As previously stated, the sampling rate for all sensors was set at 50 Hz, resulting in the collection of 50 samples per second. Hence, if there is an absolute error of 50 (samples) in predicting a change point, it indicates that a discrepancy change point and the actual change point in the collected data is equal to only one second. From the other side we believe that the transition between distinct activities within the recorded signal may extend for few seconds. To address this problem, without possibility to test it with annotated data, we applied the following procedure:

For a given segmentation of time series $\{cp_i\}_{i \in I}$, in cases where the distance between two change points, denoted as cp_1 and cp_2, falls below a predefined *resolution window* w (i.e., $d(cp_1, cp_2) < w$), we adopt a selection criterion that favors retaining only cp_1. This decision is based on the assumption that cp_1 represents the initial indication of a signal change, while cp_2 and subsequent change points are likely to be observed with a delay. By prioritizing cp_1 in such scenarios, we aim to maintain consistency with the chronological order of change point occurrences, acknowledging the potential presence of temporal delays in the observed signal components.

We experimented with different lengths of resolution window, and based on performance on public validation dataset we selected the optimal value i.e., $w = 400$. The selected value turned out to be also optimal for private part of validation dataset, see Fig. 5.

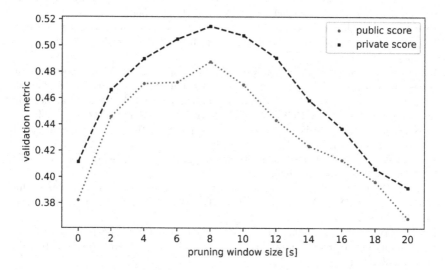

Fig. 5. Impact of pruning with a given resolution window on overall model performance.

4   Summary

We have developed a robust and effective baseline approach for segmenting multivariate signals in the field of human activity recognition. Our proposed solution demonstrates substantial superiority over defined baseline models (see Sect. 3.1). Notably, our solution achieved very good performance in the 'Human Activity Segmentation Challenge' at ECML/PKDD'23, securing the 2nd place. Furthermore, our approach demonstrated comparable performance on both the public and private parts of the validation dataset, providing evidence of its ability to avoid overfitting.

Given its performance, our baseline approach holds significant value as a simple yet robust reference point for future investigations related to the identification of human activities using multivariate signal-based methods.

The data, Python data loaders and baseline solutions can be downloaded from: github.com/patrickzib/human_activity_segmentation_challenge and the code of the described solution is available at github.com/gharanczyk/ecml_pkdd2023.

References

1. Aminikhanghahi, S., Cook, D.J.: Using change point detection to automate daily activity segmentation. In: 2017 IEEE International Conference on Pervasive Computing and Communications Workshops (PerCom Workshops), Kona, pp. 262–267 (2017). https://doi.org/10.1109/PERCOMW.2017.7917569
2. Ermshaus, A., Schäfer, P., Leser, U.: Clasp: parameter-free time series segmentation. Data Min. Knowl. Disc. **37**, 1262–1300 (2023). https://doi.org/10.1007/s10618-023-00923-x
3. Ermshaus, A., Schäfer, P., Leser, U.: Window size selection in unsupervised time series analytics: a review and benchmark. In: Guyet, T., Ifrim, G., Malinowski, S., Bagnall, A., Shafer, P., Lemaire, V. (eds.) Advanced Analytics and Learning on Temporal Data: 7th ECML PKDD Workshop, AALTD 2022, Grenoble, 19–23 September 2022, Revised Selected Papers, pp. 83–101. Springer, Cham (2023). https://doi.org/10.1007/978-3-031-24378-3_6
4. Ermshaus, A., et al.: Human activity segmentation challenge. In: ECML/PKDD 2023 Discovery Challenge (2023)
5. Jaccard, P.: Étude comparative de la distribution florale dans une portion des alpes et du jura. Bull. Soc. Vaud. Sci. Nature **37**, 547–579 (1901). https://doi.org/10.5169/SEALS-266450
6. Rauhameri, A., et al.: A comparison of online methods for change point detection in ion-mobility spectrometry data. Array **14**, 100151 (2022). https://doi.org/10.1016/j.array.2022.100151
7. Truong, C., Oudre, L., Vayatis, N.: Selective review of offline change point detection methods. Signal Process. **167**, 107299 (2020). https://doi.org/10.1016/j.sigpro.2019.107299

Change Point Detection via Synthetic Signals

Ting-Ji Huang, Qi-Le Zhou, Han-Jia Ye$^{(\boxtimes)}$, and De-Chuan Zhan$^{(\boxtimes)}$

National Key Laboratory for Novel Software Technology, Nanjing University,
Nanjing, China
{huangtj,zhouql,yehj,zhandc}@lamda.nju.edu.cn

Abstract. Detecting change points in time series data is a widely acknowledged challenge with diverse applications, in which the data obtained from measured values is often characterized by complex compositions, and the availability of real data is typically limited. However, current detection algorithms often depend on domain-specific data to achieve better performance or are restricted to analyzing single variant series, limiting their applicability. In this paper, we introduce a novel approach to change point detection that eliminates the requirement for collecting supervised data. Initially, we train a discriminant model using artificially generated synthetic signals comprising a combination of intricate patterns and random noise. This discriminant model is designed to predict the number of change points, and the synthetic data set encompasses a wide range of patterns observed in real data and offers significant advantages in terms of diversity and data volume. The trained discriminant model is then applied in conjunction with the ClaSP method for change point detection. To fully exploit multivariate series information, we propose a simple yet useful weighted-merging method that improves detection performance by aggregating change point votes within each time gap. Experimental results demonstrate the superiority of our Detection Model via Synthetic Signals (DMSS) compared to the original ClaSP method, demonstrating exceptional performance on the Human Activity Segmentation dataset.

Keywords: Change Point Detection · Synthetic Signals · Multivariate Series

1 Introduction

The exploration of time series data plays a crucial role in comprehending and predicting the intricate dynamics of real-world systems. However, the temporal nature of such data also introduces the possibility of abrupt changes or shifts in behavior, known as change points. Detecting change points in time-series data is a multifaceted and challenging problem [1]. Unlike traditional anomaly detection, which focuses on identifying outliers or deviations from a predefined norm, change-point detection aims to identify specific moments in time when the

G. Ifrim et al. (Eds.): AALTD 2023, LNAI 14343, pp. 25–35, 2023.
https://doi.org/10.1007/978-3-031-49896-1_3

statistical properties of the data undergo a fundamental shift. These shifts can manifest as sudden spikes, dips, or changes in trend, indicating a transformation in the underlying data-generating process.

Over the following decades, numerous change point detection methods have been developed [2–8]. These methods are based on diverse concepts and have the ability to recognize various types of changes in time series, such as jumps in mean and variance, correlations among different components, and more complex dependencies. Comprehensive overviews describing these algorithms can be found in various literature sources [1,9,10]. To indicate the reliability of the predicted change points, change point detection methods apply various techniques to extract relevant characteristics from each segment, such as Arc Curve [4], CUSUM statistic [3], Gaussian statistics [6], and information gain [5]. ClaSP [8] trains a binary classifier for each possible split point and utilize the accuracy to generate characteristics. These characteristics capture the properties of the segment that are indicative of different semantic classes.

However, most of the existing change point detection methods implicitly assume that all data is segmentable and the specific number of segments is usually automatically identified by heuristic algorithms, making it difficult to obtain reliable predictions. On the other hand, when there are multiple variables in a time series instead of single time series, there is lack of efficient methods to combine multiple predictions. To alleviate these two issues, we propose a novel approach called DMSS (Discriminant Model via Synthetic Signals) for detecting change points in time series. Based on the observation that real signals often consist of a certain range of recognizable patterns, our method incorporates a discriminant model trained on synthetic signals and utilizes a simple merging technique, in which the synthetic data set encompasses a wide range of patterns observed in real data and offers significant advantages in terms of diversity and data volume. We introduce a model-based method to estimate the number of change points in a series more accurately, which greatly aids subsequent segmentation tasks. We present a straightforward yet effective merging method that leverages the information from multivariate time series. Experimental results demonstrate that the proposed DMSS method outperforms the original ClaSP method on the Human Activity Segmentation data set and finally ranked the third place in HAS challenge [11].

In this paper, we will begin by describing the quality metrics and the methodology we will use to develop our algorithms. We will also present the results of our experiments and evaluate the effectiveness of our approach. Our code is available at: https://github.com/Tingji2419/MSS.

2   Related Works

Change Points Detection (CPD) has been extensively studied over the last several decades in the fields of data mining, statistics, and computer science, as it addresses a wide range of real-world problems. There are three main groups of approaches for time series segmentation: dynamic programming, heuristic, and probabilistic [12].

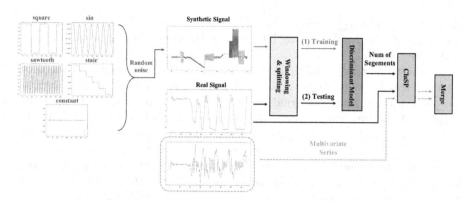

Fig. 1. The process of Detection Model via Synthetic Signals (DMSS). We first generate synthetic signals with complex patterns. The synthetic data gets multiple discrimination problems after being split by sliding windows. We train a discriminant model based on synthetic data set, which will be used to predict the number of segments of each time series in advance. After combining the discriminant model with ClaSP, we re-weight the segmentation results of each individual variable and get the final merged result, making full use of the semantic information of multiple variables.

Dynamic programming is utilized as an optimization method in conjunction with a cost function [13–15]. The fundamental technique for dynamic programming segmentation is called k-segmentation, which focuses on minimizing the variance within the segments. Heuristic approaches can be categorized into three groups: sliding window, TopDown, and BottomUp. Sliding window approaches involve sliding a window over the time series and initiating a new segment when a specified error criterion is met [16]. TopDown approaches start with a single segment and recursively partition the time series until a specific error criterion is satisfied at each step [2,3,17,18]. IGTS [5] proposes both TopDown and dynamic programming as optimization methods. On the other hand, BottomUp approaches begin with the maximum number of segments and merge them iteratively until a predefined error criterion is fulfilled. Probabilistic-based segmentation algorithms take into account the data distribution and transition times, employing methods such as Bayesian distribution [19], Hidden Markov Models [20], Gumbel distribution [7], and multivariate Gaussian distribution [6].

Apart from the aforementioned primary categories, other methods have been proposed. For example, FLUSS [4] leverages the assumption that a high probability of semantic change exists when only a few arcs intersect at a given index point. ClaSP [8] takes a unique approach by enriching a time series with a customized classification score profile using the self-supervision concepts [8].

However, many check point detection challenges, such as human activity segmentation, involve time series composed of heterogeneous data from different types of sensors. Most existing temporal segmentation methods are designed for single time series analysis. In contrast, our method extends the capabilities of ClaSP by enabling the analysis of multi-series data through a simple yet efficient merge strategy. This extension allows for more comprehensive and accurate segmentation results, taking into account the diverse information from multiple sensor streams.

Furthermore, traditional approaches for estimating the number of segments typically rely on comparing evaluation metrics on real data [5,21,22]. However, our observation is that real signals often exhibit a certain range of recognizable patterns. To address this, we generate synthetic signals that simulate real data, encompassing a wide range of patterns observed in real data sets. This synthetic data set offers significant advantages in terms of diversity and data volume.

Notably, to the best of our knowledge, there is currently no existing method for estimating the number of segments through an artificial dataset. In this regard, our proposed method stands out. By constructing a diverse synthetic dataset and training a dedicated discriminant model, we can predict the number of segments more accurately and robustly. This capability not only provides valuable insights into segment estimation but also assists subsequent methods in achieving improved performance.

In summary, while existing methods such as FLUSS and ClaSP have made notable contributions, our method expands the scope of ClaSP to analyze multi-series data and introduces a novel approach for estimating the number of segments using synthetic data. These advancements enhance the accuracy, flexibility, and applicability of segment analysis techniques, paving the way for further improvements in various domains.

3   Background

3.1   Change-Point Detection

Consider a multivariate time series $T = \{t_1, t_2, ..., t_l\}$ consisting of l observations, where each observation for a moment t is represented by a d-dimensional value $t_i \in \mathbb{R}^d$. The time series changes its behaviour at multiple moments $c_1, c_2, \ldots, c_N$.

$$\underbrace{t_1, t_2, ..., t_{c_1-1},}_{\text{Segment } g_1} \underbrace{t_{c_1}, ..., t_{c_2-1},}_{\text{Segment } g_2} t_{c_2}, ..., \underbrace{t_{c_N}, ..., t_l}_{\text{Segment } g_N}$$

The change-point detection algorithm recognizes m change-points at moments $\hat{c}_1, \hat{c}_2, \ldots, \hat{c}_M$. Let $G = \{g_1, g_2, \ldots, g_N\}$ represent the set of ground truth segments split by $c_1, c_2, \ldots, c_N$, and $P = \{p_1, p_2, \ldots, p_M\}$ denote the set of predicted segments split by $\hat{c}_1, \hat{c}_2, \ldots, \hat{c}_M$.

3.2   Quality Metrics

To evaluate the change-point detection algorithm, we computes the F1-score by comparing the predicted and ground truth segments.

We first computes the intersection over union (IoU) between two segments. Given a predicted segment p_i and a ground truth segment g_j, when the intersection between p_i and g_j is $\emptyset$, the IoU is 0, otherwise it is calculated as:

$$\text{IoU}(p_i, g_j) = \frac{\min(\text{end}(p_i), \text{end}(g_j)) - \max(\text{start}(p_i), \text{start}(g_j))}{\max(\text{end}(p_i), \text{end}(g_j)) - \min(\text{start}(p_i), \text{start}(g_j))},$$

where start(p_i) and end(p_i) represent the starting and ending moments of the predicted segment p_i, respectively. Similarly, start(g_j) and end(g_j) represent the starting and ending moments of the ground truth segment g_j.

All IoU values populate a confusion matrix for each pair of predicted and ground truth segments. The confusion matrix is a $N \times M$ matrix, where N is the number of predicted segments and M is the number of ground truth segments. Each element of the matrix represents the IoU between a predicted segment and a ground truth segment. Next, the maximum IoU value for each predicted segment is determined by taking the maximum along the rows of the confusion matrix, resulting in a vector, V of length N. V contains the highest IoU value among ground truth segment for each predicted segment.

For each predicted segment, we iterate over the thresholds in the range 0.5 to 0.95 with a step size of 0.05. Let t represent a threshold value within this range. We compare the corresponding intersection over union (IoU) value in V, denoted as V_j for the j-th predicted segment, to the threshold t. If the IoU value V_j is greater than or equal to the threshold t, the predicted segment is considered a true positive (TP). Similarly, if the IoU value V_j is less than the threshold t, the predicted segment is considered a false positive (FP):

$$TP = \sum_{j=1}^{N} \mathbb{I}(V_j \geq t), \quad FP = \sum_{j=1}^{N} \mathbb{I}(V_j < t),$$

where $\mathbb{I}(\cdot)$ represent the indicator function. To calculate the number of false negatives (FN), we subtract the true positives (TP) from the total number M of ground truth segments. We have:

$$FN = M - TP.$$

Once the values of TP, FP, and FN are computed for each threshold t, the F1-score can be calculated as:

$$\text{F1-score} = \frac{2 \times \text{precision} \times \text{recall}}{\text{precision} + \text{recall}},$$

where precision is the ratio of true positives to the sum of true positives and false positives, and recall is the ratio of true positives to the sum of true positives and false negatives.

After calculating the F1-score at each threshold, the normed score is obtained by averaging the average F1-scores across all thresholds and all time series. This normed score provides an overall measure of the change point detection algorithm's performance, with higher values indicating better performance. In summary, the metrics provide a robust evaluation of the quality of change point detection algorithms applied to the time series.

4   Proposed Methods

We first introduce a model-based method using a discriminant model to find the optimal number of change points C of a TS by training on a synthetic signals data set in advance (see Fig. 1). We assume that a TS consists of a variety of continuous signals. This assumption comes from the fact that many signal series are easily distinguishable by the human. We furthermore assume that there is only one source of the signal in the same time period. Under these two assumptions, the task of change point detection is transformed into a multiple discriminant task. Therefore, a simple idea is to first train a discriminant model to determine whether a certain subsegment has a change point.

4.1 Synthetic Signals Generation

Our research is driven by the observation that real signals frequently exhibit distinct patterns that can be recognized and analyzed. To capture the essence of these patterns, we generate synthetic signals that closely simulate real data. This synthetic data set encompasses a wide range of patterns observed in real data sets, providing significant advantages in terms of diversity and data volume. Consequently, we employ these artificially generated synthetic signals to train our discriminant model.

The utilization of synthetic signals in our approach serves two important purposes. Firstly, it alleviates the need for collecting large-scale supervised data sets, effectively minimizing the associated overhead and resource requirements. By leveraging synthetic signals, we can generate an extensive set of training samples that represent various patterns and scenarios, augmenting the effectiveness of our discriminant model. This approach contributes to the reduction of manual data labeling efforts and facilitates more efficient model training.

Furthermore, the availability of a large number of training samples enhances the classification ability of our discriminant model. The diverse nature of the synthetic data set allows the model to learn and generalize from a wide spectrum of patterns and variations, enabling it to accurately classify and distinguish between different segments in real data.

We consider the following five basic signals to compose our analog signal training set: square wave signal, sinusoidal signal, sawtooth signal, stair signal and constant signal, as shown in Fig. 1. At the same time, we also consider a variety of combination ways to construct complex signals, and add some noise to make the synthetic data set more realistic.

4.2 Discriminant Model for Change Point Detection

DMSS, the algorithm we propose in this paper, is based on change point discrimination and ClaSP [23] method, *i.e.*, it solves the change point detection problem by splitting a series into multiple discrimination problems, and then using a linear discriminant model to detect whether there exists a change point, as shown in Fig. 1.

Let $T = \{t_1, t_2, ..., t_l\}$ be a time series consisting of l observations, we first computes $l - w + 1$ overlapping windows of width w with each being split into several sub segments $x_i = \{t_i, t_{i+1}, ..., t_{i+w-1}\}$, where $i \in [0, \lfloor l/w \rfloor]$. To detect

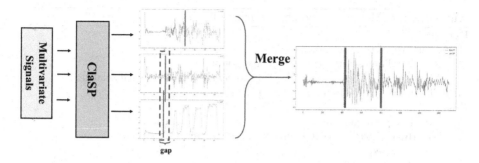

Fig. 2. Merging detected change points using three axises in Human Activity Segmentation dataset. Points within a gap will be merged by predefined weights.

change points using a logistic model, we define a binary response variable y_i, which indicates whether a change has occurred at sub segment i or not.

$$\log\left(\frac{y_i}{1-y_i}\right) = \beta_0 + \beta_1 \cdot x_i, \tag{1}$$

$$y_i = \frac{\exp(\beta_0 + \beta_1 \cdot x_i)}{1 + \exp(\beta_0 + \beta_1 \cdot x_i)}. \tag{2}$$

To obtain the number of change points in the entire time series, we can sum up the binary classification results mentioned above and take the average across all windows:

$$C = \frac{1}{L} \sum_{j \in [0,L]} \sum_{i \in [0,\lfloor l/w \rfloor]} y_i, \tag{3}$$

where $L = l - w + 1$.

The logistic regression model assumes a logistic relationship between the predictor variables and the log-odds of the binary response variable. And one important aspect to mention is that in this step, it involves, but is not limited to, the use of logistic regression. Any other binary classification or discriminant model can also be utilized. In our experiments, we employed eXtreme gradient boosting (XGBoost) [24], a boosting algorithm based on logistic regression, as an alternative approach.

4.3 Merging Multivariate Series

The original ClaSP method was primarily designed to address univariate time series problems, which limits its ability for multivariate sequences. This constraint becomes evident when considering scenarios involving multiple spatial signals associated with human body postures. For example, if the motion is confined to a single plane, relying solely on information from the y-axis would fail to capture comprehensive insights. In such cases, the incorporation of signals from the x-axis and z-axis becomes critical to accurately detect change points. Therefore, the integration of information from multiple sensors assumes paramount

Algorithm 1. Merge and Combine Change Points

Require:
1: S: Number of time sequences
2: Seq$[1 : S]$: Time sequences with change points
3: Weights$[1 : S]$: Weights corresponding to change points in each sequence
4: g: Time gap threshold for combining points
Ensure:
5: Merged_Seq: Merged time sequence
6: **procedure** MERGE_AND_COMBINE(N, Seq, Weights, g)
7:       Merged_Seq ← []
8:       **for** $i ← 1$ to S **do**
9:             combined_point ← Seq$[i][1]$
10:           combined_weight ← Weights$[i][1]$
11:           **for** $j ← 2$ to length(Seq$[i]$) **do**
12:                 **if** Seq$[i][j]$ − combined_point $> g$ **then**
13:                       Merged_Seq.$append$(combined_point)
14:                       combined_point ← Seq$[i][j]$
15:                       combined_weight ← Weights$[i][j]$
16:                 **else**
17:                       combined_weight ← combined_weight + Weights$[i][j]$
18:                 **end if**
19:           **end for**
20:           Merged_Seq.$append$(combined_point)
21:       **end for**
22:       **return** Merged_Seq
23: **end procedure**

importance in the context of change point detection, enabling a more comprehensive understanding of complex multivariate data.

To tackle this challenge, we propose a straightforward merging method based on interval weights, akin to a voting approach, as depicted in Fig. 2. Given S sequences with a time gap, denoted as g, between them, and assuming their mutual independence, we assign weights, denoted as w_i, to each sequence. Initially, we apply an individual change point detection method to each sequence. Subsequently, utilizing the assigned weights, we merge the detected change points within each segment by considering the respective weights within an interval surrounding the split points. The detailed algorithm for this merging process is defined in Algorithm 1.

5   Experiments

To evaluate the performance of various methods accurately, we conducted a series of experiments using our self-labeled Human Activity Segmentation dataset [11]. In this section, we describe the setup of our experiments, including the evaluation metric, the choice of the discriminant model, and the design of weights for merging points.

5.1 Dataset

We utilized the Human Activity Segmentation dataset [11], which is a collection of labeled human activity sequences. The challenge involved collecting and annotating 10.7 h of real-world multi-dimensional time series (TS) data. The dataset consists of 250 TS, each comprising twelve dimensions and sampled at a frequency of 50 Hertz (Hz). These TS were recorded using various smartphone sensors and captured the performance of 100 different human activities. Sixteen bachelor students participated in the data collection, showcasing diverse motion sequences during the activities. The TS data ranges from seven seconds to fourteen minutes in duration, with a median duration of 100 s. Within each TS, a varying number of potentially recurring activities are present, and each activity has its own variable time duration. The main challenge task is to predict the precise locations of activity changes without availability of ground truth labels.

5.2 Discriminant Model

For the discriminant model, we employed XGBoost [24] as a straightforward implementation. XGBoost is a popular gradient boosting algorithm known for its robustness and effectiveness in various machine learning tasks. We used the default parameters of XGBoost to ensure a fair comparison among different methods.

5.3 Merging of Points

To merge neighboring points and obtain coherent activity segments, we designed weights based on a predefined time gap, denoted as g. We set g to be 120 units of time, representing a reasonable duration for consecutive activities. The weight vector for merging points was defined as $1, 0, ..., 0$, where the first element has a weight of 1 and the remaining elements have weights of 0. This design choice ensured that only the first point within the time gap was selected, effectively merging subsequent points.

5.4 Result

Table 1 illustrates the results of our experiments, comparing the performance of our proposed method, DMSS, with the original ClaSP method [23]. DMSS achieved the highest F1-score of 0.411, outperforming the performance of ClaSP and ranked the third place in HAS challenge. These results highlight the effectiveness of our approach in accurately segmenting human activities.

Table 1. Performance on Human Activity Segmentation dataset.

Method	FLUSS	BinSeg	GSS	IGTS	STRAY	ClaSP	DMSS (ours)
F1-Score	0.214	0.263	0.152	0.141	0.227	0.395	**0.411**

6 Discussion

In this work, we propose a method for change point detection in time series based on the ClaSP method. Additionally, we train an additional discriminant model to accurately determine the number of segmentation points. To ensure sufficient training of the discriminant model, we create and utilize synthetic simulated data. Furthermore, in order to fully leverage the information from multiple sequences, we present a simple yet effective merging method based on weights and time intervals, which provides a more robust and efficient approach to segmenting time series from multiple perspectives.

Experimental results on the Human activity segmentation dataset demonstrate that our proposed DMSS (discriminant Model for Change Point Detection with Sequence Merging) method outperforms the original ClaSP method, achieving higher F1-Score. However, it should be noted that the current synthetic data used in our experiments has a relatively fixed composition of basic signal components. Future work will explore the incorporation of statistical characteristics of target signals into the generation process of the synthetic data set, aiming to enhance the realism and versatility of the simulated data.

Acknowledgments. This work is supported by National Key R&D Program of China (2022ZD0114805), NSFC (61773198, 61921006, 62006112), Collaborative Innovation Center of Novel Software Technology and Industrialization, NSF of Jiangsu Province (BK20200313).

References

1. Michele, B., et al.: Detection of Abrupt Changes: Theory and Application, vol. 104. Prentice Hall, Englewood Cliffs (1993)
2. Jushan, B.: Estimating multiple breaks one at a time. Economet. Theor. **13**(3), 315–352 (1997)
3. Piotr, F.: Wild binary segmentation for multiple change-point detection. Ann. Stat. **42**(6), 2243–2281 (2014)
4. Shaghayegh, G., Yifei, D., Michael, Y.C.-C., Kaveh, K., Liudmila, U., Eamonn, K.: Matrix profile viii: domain agnostic online semantic segmentation at superhuman performance levels. In: IEEE International Conference on Data Mining, pp. 117–126 (2017)
5. Amin, S., Yongli, R., Salim, F.D.: Information gain-based metric for recognizing transitions in human activities. Pervas. Mob. Comput. **38**, 92–109 (2017)
6. Hallac, D., Nystrup, P., Boyd, S.: Greedy gaussian segmentation of multivariate time series. Adv. Data Anal. Classif. **13**(3), 727–751 (2019)

7. Talagala, P.D., Hyndman, R.J., Smith-Miles, K.: Anomaly detection in high-dimensional data. J. Comput. Graph. Statist. **30**(2), 360–374 (2021)
8. Patrick, S., Arik, E., Ulf, L.: Clasp-time series segmentation. In: Proceedings of the 30th ACM International Conference on Information & Knowledge Management, pp. 1578–1587 (2021)
9. Aminikhanghahi, S., Cook, D.J.: A survey of methods for time series change point detection. Knowl. Inf. Syst. **51**(2), 339–367 (2017)
10. Truong, C., Oudre, L., Vayatis, N.: Selective review of offline change point detection methods. Sig. Process. **167**, 107299 (2020)
11. Arik, E., et al.: Human activity segmentation challenge. In: ECML/PKDD 2023 Discovery Challenge (2023)
12. Vana, P.: Blind Segmentation of Time-Series: A Two-Level Approach. Ph.D. thesis, Delft University of Technology (2015)
13. Johan, H., Kalle, K., Heikki, M., Johanna, T., Hannu, T.T.T.: Time series segmentation for context recognition in mobile devices. In: Proceedings of IEEE International Conference on Data Mining, pp. 203–210 (2001)
14. Heli, H.: Segmentation of Time Series and Sequences Using Basic Representations. Ph.D. thesis, Helsinki University of Technology (2007)
15. Kehagias, A., Nidelkou, E., Petridis, V.: A dynamic programming segmentation procedure for hydrological and environmental time series. Stochast. Environ. Res. Risk Assessm. **20**, 77–94 (2006)
16. Banos, O., Galvez, J.-M., Damas, M., Pomares, H., Rojas, I.: Window size impact in human activity recognition. Sensors **14**(4), 6474–6499 (2014)
17. Jing Yuan, Y., Zheng, X.X., Sun, G.: T-drive: enhancing driving directions with taxi drivers' intelligence. IEEE Trans. Knowl. Data Eng. **25**(1), 220–232 (2011)
18. Cheng, W., Zhang, X., Pan, F., Wang, W.: HICC: an entropy splitting-based framework for hierarchical co-clustering. Knowl. Inf. Syst. **46**, 343–367 (2016)
19. Prescott, A.R., MacKay David, J.C.: Bayesian online changepoint detection. CoRR (2007)
20. Taketoshi, M., Yu, N., Masamichi, S., Yushi, S., Tatsuya, H., Tomomasa, S.: Online recognition and segmentation for time-series motion with hmm and conceptual relation of actions. In: IEEE/RSJ International Conference on Intelligent Robots and Systems, pp. 3864–3870 (2005)
21. Andrew, F., Osmar R.Z.: A parameterless method for efficiently discovering clusters of arbitrary shape in large datasets. In: IEEE International Conference on Data Mining, pp. 179–186 (2002)
22. Scott Harris, R., Hess, D.R., Venegas, J.G.: An objective analysis of the pressure-volume curve in the acute respiratory distress syndrome. Am. J. Respir. Crit. Care Med. **161**(2), 432–439 (2000)
23. Ermshaus, A., Schäfer, P., Leser, U.: Clasp: parameter-free time series segmentation. Data Min. Knowl. Disc. **37**(3), 1262–1300 (2023)
24. Tianqi, C., Carlos, G.: Xgboost: a scalable tree boosting system. In: Proceedings of the 22nd ACM SIGKDD International Conference on Knowledge Discovery and Data Mining, pp. 785–794 (2016)

Oral Presentation

Clustering Time Series with k-Medoids Based Algorithms

Christopher Holder[1]([✉]), David Guijo-Rubio[1,2], and Anthony Bagnall[1]

[1] School of Computing Sciences, University of East Anglia, NR4 7TQ Norwich, UK
{c.holder,ajb}@uea.ac.uk
[2] Department of Computer Science, Universidad de Córdoba, Córdoba, Spain
dguijo@uco.es

Abstract. Time Series Clustering (TSCL) involves grouping unlabelled time series into homogeneous groups. A popular approach to TSCL is to use the partitional clustering algorithms k-means or k-medoids in conjunction with an elastic distance function such as Dynamic Time Warping (DTW). We explore TSCL using nine different elastic distance measures. Both partitional algorithms characterise clusters with an exemplar series, but use different techniques to do so: k-means uses an averaging algorithm to find an exemplar, whereas k-medoids chooses a training case (medoid). Traditionally, the arithmetic mean of a collection of time series was used with k-means. However, this ignores any offset. In 2011, an averaging technique specific to DTW, called DTW Barycentre Averaging (DBA), was proposed. Since, k-means with DBA has been the algorithm of choice for the majority of partition-based TSCL and much of the research using medoids-based approaches for TSCL stopped. We revisit k-medoids based TSCL with a range of elastic distance measures. Our results show k-medoids approaches are significantly better than k-means on a standard test suite, independent of the elastic distance measure used. We also compare the most commonly used alternating k-medoids approach against the Partition Around Medoids (PAM) algorithm. PAM significantly outperforms the default k-medoids for all nine elastic measures used. Additionally, we evaluate six variants of PAM designed to speed up TSCL. Finally, we show PAM with the best elastic distance measure is significantly better than popular alternative TSCL algorithms, including the k-means DBA approach, and competitive with the best deep learning algorithms.

Keywords: Time series · clustering · k-means · k-medoids · PAM · UCR archive

1 Introduction

Time Series Clustering (TSCL) is an unsupervised technique where a set of time series, are partitioned into "clusters", which contain time series considered to be homogeneous. By contrast, time series in different clusters are considered heterogeneous. However, there is no generally accepted definition of a cluster

© The Author(s), under exclusive license to Springer Nature Switzerland AG 2023
G. Ifrim et al. (Eds.): AALTD 2023, LNAI 14343, pp. 39–55, 2023.
https://doi.org/10.1007/978-3-031-49896-1_4

because "clusters are, in large part, in the eye of the beholder" [8]. This is because different users may have different enough needs and intentions to want a different algorithm and notion of cluster [31]. Therefore, due to the nature of the various users problems and needs, hundreds of clustering algorithms have been proposed. Many of these have been adapted to deal with time series. For instance, alternative transformation based approaches [21], deep learning based clustering algorithms [17] or statistical model based approaches [4], among others, have been proposed for TSCL. Our focus is on partitional clustering based on distance functions used to measure dissimilarity between whole time series.

Measuring dissimilarity is critical to clustering techniques in order to fulfil the objective of any clustering algorithm: it must form internally homogeneous and externally heterogeneous clusters. Measuring homogeneity usually requires a measure of dissimilarity (or similarity) between cases, commonly known as a distance measure.

In traditional clustering, this is normally a correlation based or Minkowski metric such as Euclidean Distance (ED). However, these traditional distances do not take advantage of the unique traits and characteristics of time series data. There has been a popular research topic in designing time series specific distance measures that can be used in clustering (and classification). For example, elastic distances compensate for misalignment creating a path through a cost matrix by either warping or editing time series. The most common and famous elastic distance is Dynamic Time Warping (DTW) [28]. A comparison of nine elastic distance measures [22] found there was little difference in terms of accuracy of classification accuracy when used with a nearest neighbour classifier. For TSCL, DTW is the most popular elastic distance measure, as can be observed in these works [3,10,20,26]. It is most commonly used with k-means clustering (for example [14]), which iteratively assigns cases to clusters with the nearest exemplar, or centroid. Then, the centroid is recalculated from the new membership through averaging. One popular solution for DTW based k-means is to use Dynamic Barycentre Averaging (DBA) [27] to find centroids. This involves aligning cluster members to each other with DTW, then averaging along paths. This improves k-means clustering, but at a high computational cost. An alternative to averaging to find centroids is to select instances, known as medoids, to represent cluster exemplars. The most commonly used k-medoids algorithm tries all of the current cluster members as the exemplar and chooses the one that minimises a specific clusters distance to medoid. In common with the literature, we call this algorithm alternate or alternating k-medoids, although it is sometimes referred to as Lloyds algorithm [23]. k-medoids algorithms have been used much less frequently in the TSCL literature, particularly since DBA was proposed.

Recent research [12] compared the performance of nine elastic distance measures using both k-means and a k-medoids (only using alternating k-medoids). The main conclusion of this work was that two distance functions, Move Split Merge (MSM) [34] and Time Warp Edit (TWE) [24], performed better than other distances with both clustering algorithms. A secondary conclusion was that k-medoids approach generally outperformed k-means. One key feature of k-medoids algorithms is that they require the calculation of the distance matrix between instances prior to clustering. The $O(n^2)$ space complexity can introduce an unacceptable overhead for large problems. Nevertheless, k-medoids algorithms clearly have a role to play in a large majority of TSCL studies.

Our aim is to explore k-medoids based TSCL. We assess whether k-medoids based TSCL is better than k-means based, regardless of the elastic distance function used. We then explore some of the large number of variants for k-medoids clustering that have not been used in the TSCL literature before. Finally, we compare the performance of the best k-medoids clustering approach to those of popular alternative TSCL algorithms and show them to be significantly better on the UCR archive [5]. Thus, our contributions are summarised as follows:

1. We compare the performance of k-means and standard k-medoids on 112 UCR problems using nine elastic distance measures, focussing on the clustering algorithm rather than the distance function.
2. We provide a survey of variants of k-medoids, aligned with implementations in the **aeon** toolkit[1].
3. We show that the Partition Around Medoids (PAM) [19] algorithm is significantly better than the standard k-medoids approach.
4. We evaluate the impact of a range of PAM refinements.
5. We show that PAM using MSM and TWE is significantly better than popular alternative approaches, and is not worse than the best deep learning model out of over 300 evaluated in [17].

The rest of this paper is structured as follows. Section 2 provides background information into k-medoids based clustering. Section 3 describes the set of elastic distance functions, standing out MSM and TWE. In Sect. 4, we give an overview of the experimental settings, performance measures and statistical tests used for comparing the methodologies. In Sect. 5, experimental results for the aforementioned comparisons are presented. Finally, Sect. 6 summarises our findings and highlights future work.

2 k-Medoids Based Clustering Background

k-means and k-medoids are partition based clustering algorithms and share the same basic components. Firstly, the algorithm selects time series, which we call exemplars, that are meant to characterise a cluster. This is known as the *initialisation* stage. After initialisation, there is a process of assigning membership based on distances to exemplars (the *assign* method). Then, exemplars are updated based on new cluster assignments (the *update* stage). These three steps are repeated until some convergence condition is met.

---

[1] https://github.com/aeon-toolkit/aeon/.

The iteration aims to minimise an error objective function of within class deviation, or Total Deviation (TD), given as follows:

$$TD = \sum_{i=1}^{k} \sum_{x_c \in C_i} d(x_c, e_i) \tag{1}$$

$$s = 40 + 2k \tag{2}$$

where k is the number of clusters, C_i is the set of cases in the ith cluster, d is the disimilarity measure, x_c is a case in cluster C_i and e_i is the exemplar (representative) of cluster C_i. One disadvantage of k-means for clustering is that because the exemplars are centroids (averaged cluster members), repeated calls to the distance function are required.

k-medoids clustering algorithms use instances from the train data (known as medoids) as the cluster exemplars, and hence, they can use precomputed distances. The *assign* and *update* operations can be performed independently of the time series and distance function. It is worth noting that this need for a pairwise distance matrix introduces memory overhead quadratic in train set size n, needing $O(n^2)$ distance function calls. The key algorithmic design component for k-medoids based clustering is how to choose the medoids and what objective function to use.

2.1   Alternate k-Medoids

Given a crisp cluster label to each instance, the simplest approach to choose the medoid m_i for cluster C_i is to try all current members of the cluster, and choose the one minimising the within cluster distance. At any iteration, the medoid for each cluster is chosen independently based on currently assignment, as follows:

$$m_i = \arg \min_{x_m \in C} \sum_{x_c \in C} d(x_c, x_m). \tag{3}$$

where m_i is the ith medoid, C is a set of cases, x_m and x_c are time series in C, and d is a dissimilarity measure. This alternate k-medoids is the simplest form of medoids clustering. It is closely aligned with k-means (Lloyds [23]) and gets its name because of the alternating stages of the assignment and update. The main difference between alternate k-medoids and k-means is when calculating new cluster centres, k-means computes an average whereas alternate k-medoids finds medoids.

2.2   Partition Around Medoids (PAM)

Alternating k-medoids optimises the medoid within the current cluster assignment. This may miss the opportunity for taking medoids from other clusters and it may also converge prematurely since exemplars are less likely to change than with k-means [32]. PAM [19] is an alternative approach designed to overcome these problems. PAM follows a similar structure to alternate k-medoids but uses a different evaluation function to choose new medoids. It allows cases to become medoids of clusters they did not previously belong to, and when evaluating a new candidate medoid for any cluster, the total within cluster distance of all clusters is considered.

The original PAM used a bespoke initialisation function called *build*, which is similar to the restart methods used with k-means. However, for our experiments we use random initialisation with PAM. The reason for this is outlined in Sect. 4. The *swap* stage of PAM is described in Algorithm 1.

Algorithm 1. PAM *swap*: Iterative improvement, where X is a collection of time series, n is the number of cases in X, medoids is the current set of medoids, k is the number of medoids and d is a dissimilarity measure

---

1: $init \leftarrow \text{findTD}(X, medoids)$
2: $best \leftarrow TD$
3: $cm \leftarrow medoids$
4: $continue \leftarrow true$
5: **while** continue **do**
6:     **for** $i \leftarrow 1$ to k **do**
7:         $a \leftarrow cm_i, b \leftarrow best$
8:         **for** $j \leftarrow 1$ to n **do**
9:             **if** $x_j \notin cm$ **then**
10:                 $cm_i \leftarrow x_j$
11:                 $current \leftarrow \text{findTD}(X, cm)$
12:                 **if** $current < best$ **then**
13:                     $best \leftarrow current$
14:         **if** $best = b$ **then**
15:             $cm_i = a$
16:     **if** $best = init$ **then**
17:         $continue \leftarrow false$
18: **return** $best, cm$

Function *findTD* implements Eq. 2. PAM uses a greedy algorithm that operates cluster by cluster (line 6). For each cluster, it tries all cases that are not currently medoids (lines 8–11) keeping the case that gives the lowest TD (lines 12–13). If there is no better candidate, the current medoids is retained (lines 14–15). The process terminates if the medoids have not changed (lines 16–17).

Finding the global optimum of the k-medoids problem is NP-hard [15], which is why PAM uses a greedy approximation. The algorithm requires a distance matrix ($O(n^2)$ memory) and each iteration has time complexity $O(kn^2)$. As this is both computationally and memory expensive many variations of PAM have been proposed to reduce memory, time complexity, or both.

2.3   PAM Variants

A range of refinements of the PAM algorithm have been proposed to improve PAM efficiency in both computational complexity and memory:

The Clustering LARge Applications (CLARA). [16] algorithm repeatedly applies PAM on a random subset of cases (with the recommended number being $s = 40 + 2k$). Once PAM is performed on the subset of cases and medoids obtained, the remaining cases are assigned to their closest medoid. This is repeated for multiple iterations and the iteration that has the lowest TD is returned. The time complexity is reduced to $O(k^3 + s)$.

CLARA Based on raNdomised Search (CLARANS). [25] adapts the swap operation of PAM to use a more greedy approach. This is done by only performing the first swap which results in a reduction in TD before continuing evaluation. It limits the number of attempts known as max neighbours to randomly select and check if TD is reduced. This random selection gives CLARANS an advantage when handling large datasets by avoiding local minima.

PAM Silhouette (PAMSIL). [7] adapts the PAM algorithm to minimise the Silhouette score [29] rather than the TD.

PAM Medoid Silouhette (PAMMEDSIL). [7] is a variation on PAMSIL where Silhouette score is calculated by using the medoids rather than the arithmetic mean.

FasterPAM. [32] focuses on optimising the PAM swap stage. It does this by combining optimisations made by FastPam1 [31] with a local hill-climbing approach that means any swap that reduces TD is immediately performed (eager swapping). However, while a swap is performed for any candidate that reduces TD, FasterPAM considers multiple candidates at a time in batches. The main reason for this is it allows the FasterPAM to be better parallelised. In addition FasterPAM uses the same technique for speed up that FastPam1 does by considering a swap across all medoids at once rather than a single medoid. This allows for expensive conditional logic to be moved outside the inner most loop further reducing computational time.

Faster Medoid Silhouette Clustering (FasterMSC). [18] is a variation on PAMMEDSIL that combines FasterPAM with PAMMEDSIL.

3   Elastic Distance Measures

Time series require bespoke distance functions because small offsets between series can lead to large distances between series that are conceptually similar. Elastic distances compensate for misalignment by creating a path through a cost matrix through either warping or editing time series. There have been many elastic distances proposed that attempt to align time series in different ways. We evaluate k-medoids with the nine elastic distance measures used in [12,22]. We provide a very brief overview of one of the nine elastic distances and direct the

interested reader to these other publications [12,22,33]. The distance functions
we use (with associated parameter setting) are listed in Table 1.

Table 1. Summary of distance functions, their parameters and the default values.

Algorithm	Acronym	Parameters
Dynamic Time Warping	DTW	$w = 0.2$
Derivative DTW	DDTW	$w = 0.2$
Weighted DTW	WDTW	$g = 0.05$
Weighted derivative DTW	WDDTW	$g = 0.05$
Longest Common SubSequence	LCSS	$\epsilon = 0.05$
Edit distance with Real Penalty	ERP	$g = 0.05$
Edit Distance on Real sequences	EDR	$\epsilon = 0.05$
Move Split Merge	MSM	$c = 1$
Time Warp Edit	TWE	$\nu = 0.05, \lambda = 1$

The best performing distance function according to [12] is MSM, which we
briefly review below.

3.1 Move Split Merge (MSM)

At any step, elastic distances can use one of three costs: diagonal, horizontal or
vertical, in forming an alignment. The alignment path is a series of moves across
the cost matrix. DTW assigns no explicit penalty for moving off the diagonal.
Instead, it uses an implicit penalty (long paths have longer total distance) and
a hard cut off on window size to stop large warpings. An alternative family of
distance functions are based on the concept of edit distance. An edit distance
considers a diagonal move as a match, a vertical move as an insertion and an
horizontal move as a deletion. MSM [34] follows this structure, where move is a
match (diagonal), split is a insertion (vertical) and merge is deletion (horizontal).

The move operation in MSM uses the absolute difference rather than the
squared euclidean distance for matching in DTW. The cost of the split operation
is given by cost function C (Eq. 4) with a call to $C(a_i, a_{i-1}, b_j, c)$. If the value
being inserted, b_j, is between the two values a_i and a_{i-1} being split, the cost
is a constant value c. If not, the cost is c plus the minimum deviation from the
furthest point a_i and the previous point a_{i-1} or b_j. The delete/merge is given
by $C(b_j, b_{j-1}, a_i, c)$, which is simply the same operation as split but applied to
the second series. Thus, the cost of splitting and merging values depends on the
value itself and adjacent values.

$$C(x, y, z, c) = \begin{cases} c \, \mathbf{if} \, y \leq x \leq z \, \mathbf{or} \, y \geq x \geq z \\ c + \min(|x - y|, |x - z|) \, \mathbf{otherwise.} \end{cases} \qquad (4)$$

Algorithm 2 describes how to calculate the MSM distance between two time series **a** and **b**. MSM satisfies triangular inequality and is a metric. In Algorithm 2, the first return value is the MSM distance between **a** and **b**, the second is the cost matrix used to compute the MSM distance.

4 Methodology

The different TSCL methods are compared using the whole set of 112 univariate, equal-length time series in the UCR archive [5]. Default train/test splits have been used, with data normalised to zero mean and unit standard deviation prior to the clustering stage. The training data is used to train an algorithm and the performance is assessed on the testing set. The number of clusters, k, is equal to the number of classes for classification. This choice is in line with the TSCL literature, such as [12,17].

Algorithm 2. MSM(**a** (*of length m*), **b** (*of length m*), **c** (*minimum cost*))

1: Let CM be an $m \times m$ matrix initialised to zero.
2: $CM_{1,1} = |a_1 - b_1|$
3: **for** $i \leftarrow 2$ to m **do**
4:      $CM_{i,1} = CM_{i-1,1} + C(a_i, a_{i-1}, b_1, c)$
5: **for** $i \leftarrow 2$ to m **do**
6:      $CM_{1,i} = CM_{1,i-1} + C(b_i, a_1, b+i-1, c)$
7: **for** $i \leftarrow 2$ to m **do**
8:      **for** $j \leftarrow 2$ to m **do**
9:          $move \leftarrow CM_{i-1,j-1} + |a_i - b_j|$
10:          $split \leftarrow CM_{i-1,j} + C(a_i, a_{i-1}, b_j, c)$
11:          $merge \leftarrow CM_{i,j-1} + C(b_j, b_{j-1}, a_i, c)$
12:          $CM_{i,j} \leftarrow \min(move, split, merge)$
13: **return** $CM_{m,m}, CM$

The performance of the different clusterers is evaluated using the following measures: **CLustering ACCuracy (CL-ACC)** is the number of correct predictions divided by the total number of cases. For this, each cluster is assigned to its best matching class value by taking the maximum accuracy from every permutation of cluster and class value. The **Rand Index (RI)** measures the similarity between two sets of labels such as the predicted and actual class values. An improved version known as **Adjusted Rand Index (ARI)** avoids the inflation of the RI when dealing with a high number of clusters. For this, ARI adjusts the RI based on the expected scores on a purely random model. The **Mutual Information (MI)** score uses the entropy to measure the agreement of the two clusterings or a clustering and a true labelling. Finally, **Normalised Mutual Information (NMI)** rescales MI onto $[0,1]$.

Some of the results are expressed using an adaptation of the critical difference diagram [6], replacing the post-hoc Nemenyi test with a comparison of all classifiers using pairwise Wilcoxon signed-rank tests, and cliques formed using the Holm correction [2,9].

Experiments are run with the open source python software packages `aeon`, `tslearn` [35], and `kmedoids` [30]. To enhance the reproducibility of this work, specific code and a guide to reproduce results will be available after blind review, as well as the results achieved.

The original PAM algorithm specifies a bespoke initialisation algorithm (*build*). However, we found random initilisation with ten restarts to be as effective as *build*, simpler and computationally less expensive. Given some PAM variants specify the use of random initialisation (e.g. FasterPAM) for speed, we use the same initialisation method for all algorithms in order to control factors of variation: we use random initialisation with ten restarts for all *k*-medoid and *k*-means variants.

The rationale behind using random initialisation is that random selection is likely to pick points from dense regions. The reason for rerunning the model multiple times with random initialisation and taking the best clusters (as measured by the sum of distances to their closest cluster centres) is that it reduces the chance results are skewed by poor random initial selections. Ten restarts is the most common number of restarts in the literature, and is the default value when using Lloyds algorithm in `scikit-learn`.

5 Results

The issue of which distance function is better overall is covered in depth in [12]. Our concern with these experiments is to detect differences between the two clustering algorithms over a range of distance functions. We focus first on the difference between alternate *k*-medoids and standard *k*-means in Sect. 5.1. We then evaluate a range of variants of the *k*-medoids algorithm in Sects. 5.2 and 5.3. Finally, the best *k*-medoids variant is compared against several alternative TSCL approaches in Sect. 5.4.

5.1 Alternate *k*-Medoids vs *k*-Means

Table 2 summarises the difference in performance of *k*-means and *k*-medoids clustering algorithms. The mean difference is the average difference in the metric over 112 datasets on the test data. There is no significant difference in accuracy when using ED with the two clusterers (p value $= 0.233$ with a paired T-test or 0.14 with a binomial test). *k*-medoids gives a significantly more accurate clustering for all nine elastic clusterers (test with $\alpha = 0.05$ with paired t-test, sign rank test and binomial test on wins/losses).

Figure 1 expands the data from Table 2 to show the distribution of differences for each distance measure. It shows a violin plot of the differences between alternate *k*-medoids and *k*-means for 10 distance functions in terms of NMI. It demonstrates that there is little difference when using ED. However, there is

Table 2. Differences in CL-ACC, ARI and NMI between alternate k-medoids and k-means using 10 different distance functions. A positive value indicates that k-medoids is better. W/D/L figures are for CL-ACC.

Distance	CL-ACC	ARI	NMI	k-medoids wins	k-means wins	Ties
MSM	1.54%	1.22%	1.80%	59	47	6
TWE	2.78%	3.91%	3.65%	63	45	4
ERP	3.94%	4.35%	6.34%	66	33	13
WDTW	1.33%	1.94%	2.29%	66	42	7
DTW	3.88%	4.07%	5.72%	72	31	9
ED	-0.38%	-0.38%	-0.38%	46	58	8
DDTW	7.65%	6.17%	11.68%	75	32	5
DWDTW	2.57%	1.52%	3.56%	64	38	10
LCSS	4.13%	3.55%	7.33%	73	35	4
EDR	4.50%	4.37%	7.04%	74	35	3

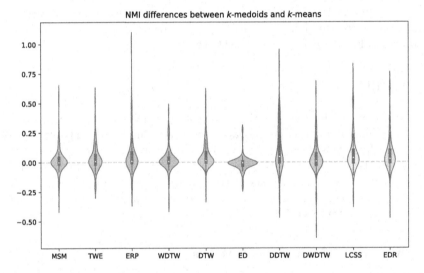

Fig. 1. Distributions of the differences between alternate k-medoids and k-means on the UCR data.

wide variation between k-medoids and k-means for the nine elastic distances, and the bulk of the distributions are positive.

These results indicate that, on average, the alternate k-medoids produces better clusters than k-means using the arithmetic mean to compute new centroids.

Table 3. Differences in CL-ACC, ARI, NMI between alternate k-medoids and PAM using 10 different distance functions. A positive value indicates that PAM is better. W/D/L figures are for CL-ACC

Distance	CL-ACC	ARI	NMI	PAM wins	k-medoids wins	Ties
MSM	1.75%	1.57%	1.56%	39	22	51
TWE	2.15%	1.51%	1.69%	59	31	22
ERP	−2.34%	-3.95%	−3.95%	40	66	6
WDTW	1.92%	2.09%	2.15%	47	35	30
DTW	2.02%	1.62%	2.03%	57	36	19
DDTW	3.81%	4.41%	4.70%	67	38	7
DWDTW	3.26%	4.10%	3.58%	60	46	6
LCSS	0.31%	−0.60%	−0.22%	57	50	5
EDR	5.73%	5.91%	6.15%	76	32	4

5.2 Alternate k-Medoids Vs PAM

The alternate technique used for the experiments in Sect. 5.1 is the simplest and easiest k-medoids algorithm. However, in standard clustering, PAM is a popular alternative and has found significantly better results than alternate k-medoids. As such we repeated the same experiments using the PAM algorithm described in Sect. 2.2 to see if the findings in standard clustering holds true for time series data. Table 3 summarises the differences between alternate k-medoids and PAM for each distance measure. With the exception of ERP, PAM significantly outperforms alternate k-medoids.

5.3 PAM Variants

PAM significantly outperforms both k-means and alternate k-medoids. However, it is computationally more expensive. In Sect. 2.3, we describe several variants of PAM meant to improve the runtime. Runtime complexity is a significant consideration when working with time series data. As such we compare six PAM variants to the original version when using MSM as a distance function. We include the following variants:

1. **clara** [16] and **clarans** [25]: subsampling techniques.
2. **fasterpam** performs eager swaps, improves time to find swaps
3. **pamsil** [7]: uses silhouette score rather than TD.
4. **pammedsil, fastermsc** [7]: use medoids silhouette score.

Figure 2 shows the average ranks of these six clusterers in terms of CL-ACC and NMI. PAM is significantly better than all variants except for fasterpam.

Figure 3 shows the distribution of the differences between PAM-MSM and the variants. As can be observed, for fasterpam most of the values are exactly 0, meaning that there is no difference to PAM for most of the datasets. Nevertheless,

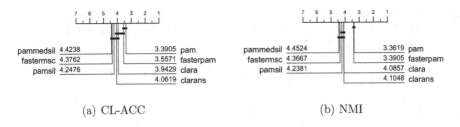

(a) CL-ACC   (b) NMI

Fig. 2. Average ranks for PAM and six variants, all of which use MSM distance.

for the remaining five variants, boxplots generally are over the 0 value, indicating that PAM is better in average.

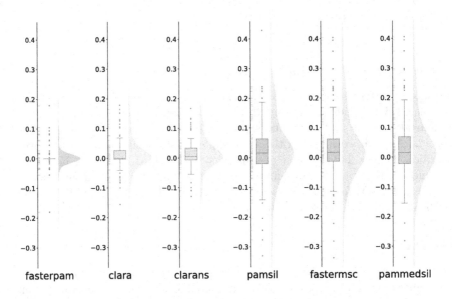

Fig. 3. Distributions of differences between PAM and the six variants. Positive values indicate PAM is better than the variant.

5.4   Elastic PAM Vs Alternative TSCL Methods

We switch from considering relative performance of variants of the same algorithm to assess the absolute performance of PAM based clustering against popular TSCL alternatives. We compare performance of the following 10 clustering algorithms.

1. k-**means-DBA**: k-means clustering with DTW barycentre averaging and DTW distance assignment [27].

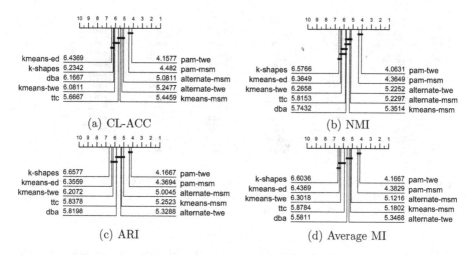

Fig. 4. Average ranks for 10 clustering algorithms using four performance measures.

2. **k-means-ED**, **k-means-MSM** and **k-means-TWE**: k-means clustering with arithmetic mean for centres, and ED, MSM and TWE distance assignment, respectively.
3. **k-shapes** clustering [26].
4. Two-step Time series Clustering (**TTC**) [1].
5. **alternate-MSM** and **alternate-TWE**: alternate k-medoids clustering with MSM and TWE distances (Lloyds algorithm).
6. **PAM-MSM** and **PAM-TWE**: PAM k-medoids clustering with MSM and TWE distances.

Figure 4 shows the average ranks for three performance measures: CL-ACC, ARI and NMI. Note that PAM-MSM and PAM-TWE form a top clique and are significantly better than the other eight algorithms. Figure 5 summarises the relative performance using a heatmap tool described in [13].

Figure 4 shows TWE and MSM outperform the other elastic distances over a ranger of clustering metrics. [12] conducted a similar experiment over the same elastic distances for k-means and alternating k-medoids models and found similar results. The reason TWE and MSM outperform other elastic distances was TWE and MSM constrain the diagonal warping with a constant cost penalty [12].

In addition from Fig. 4 k-means is outperformed by both PAM and alternating k-medoids. The reason for this is during the averaging stage of k-means the average time series computation ignores alignment of the time series and thus a poor average (centre) is obtained [11].

Finally Fig. 4 shows PAM across all our clustering metrics outperformed every other approach. The reason for this is as Sect. 2 outlines alternating only optimises the medoid from the current cluster assignment whereas PAM considers all instances as potential new medoid for a cluster which leads to better medoids being found.

Mean-Accuracy	pam-msm 0.5738	alternate-msm 0.5568	kmeans-msm 0.5406	dba 0.5396	ttc 0.5370	k-shapes 0.4781
pam-msm 0.5738	Mean-Difference r>c / r=c / r<c Wilcoxon p-value	**0.0170** **38 / 51 / 22** **0.0149**	**0.0332** **67 / 6 / 38** **0.0003**	**0.0342** **73 / 4 / 34** **0.0009**	**0.0368** **67 / 4 / 40** **0.0029**	**0.0957** **69 / 3 / 39** **≤ 1e-04**
alternate-msm 0.5568	-0.0170 22 / 51 / 38 0.0149	·	0.0162 59 / 6 / 46 0.0907	**0.0173** **70 / 6 / 35** **0.0153**	0.0198 63 / 4 / 44 0.0758	**0.0787** **61 / 4 / 46** **0.0002**
kmeans-msm 0.5406	-0.0332 38 / 6 / 67 0.0003	-0.0162 46 / 6 / 59 0.0907	·	0.0011 63 / 5 / 43 0.3578	0.0036 54 / 2 / 55 0.7262	**0.0625** **62 / 3 / 46** **0.0012**
dba 0.5396	-0.0342 34 / 4 / 73 0.0009	-0.0173 35 / 6 / 70 0.0153	-0.0011 43 / 5 / 63 0.3578	·	0.0026 53 / 8 / 50 0.8958	**0.0614** **59 / 2 / 50** **0.0035**
ttc 0.5370	-0.0368 40 / 4 / 67 0.0029	-0.0198 44 / 4 / 63 0.0758	-0.0036 55 / 2 / 54 0.7262	-0.0026 50 / 8 / 53 0.8958	·	**0.0589** **68 / 2 / 41** **0.0010**
k-shapes 0.4781	**-0.0957** **39 / 3 / 69** **≤ 1e-04**	**-0.0787** **46 / 4 / 61** **0.0002**	**-0.0625** **46 / 3 / 62** **0.0012**	**-0.0614** **50 / 2 / 59** **0.0035**	**-0.0589** **41 / 2 / 68** **0.0010**	If in bold, then p-value < 0.05

Mean-Difference scale: 0.10 / 0.05 / 0.00 / −0.05 / −0.10

Fig. 5. Summary of performance measures for six of the clusterers described in Fig. 4. Each cell shows the mean difference between algorithms, the W/D/L counts and the unadjusted p-value for a Wilcoxon sign-rank test.

Time series deep learning results are available the website associated with [17]. They provide NMI results for over 300 different clustering algorithms on the same UCR datasets we use. These are not directly comparable, since they are averaged over five runs and there may be other experimental differences. However, they can give some indication of relative performance. The best deep learning approach of the more than 300 assessed, a convolutional neural network with joint pretext loss and without clustering loss (key in their results is res_cnn_joint_None) achieved an average NMI of 0.3292. Average NMIs for PAM-TWE and PAM-MSM are 0.3366 and 0.3316, respectively.

In the context of other popular TSCL algorithms shown in Fig. 4, k-medoids based approaches perform better than other approaches. In addition, Fig. 4 highlights the strength of TWE and MSM across multiple approaches. Finally it is clear that using PAM based approaches with elastic distances yields significantly better results.

6 Conclusions

Time Series Clustering (TSCL) with k-medoids has fallen out of favour in time series machine learning research in recent years. We demonstrate that k-medoids with elastic distance measures is highly effective, particularly PAM with TWE or MSM distances. We have also demonstrated that PAM is more effective than alternate k-medoids algorithm for most elastic distances and showed that PAM-TWE and PAM-MSM are significantly better than popular TSCL alternatives, and at least as good as the best known deep learning approach. Finally, we have explored the variants of PAM that hope to address the run time and memory complexity the traditional PAM algorithm suffered from. We found that the recent FasterPAM [32] yields very similar results as PAM but achieves an O(k)-fold speedup in the swap phase, making FasterPAM a much more attractive alternative for TSCL.

In the future, we would like to further quantify the run time complexity of these clusterers. We will then investigate the possibility of creating an ensemble of elastic distances using k-medoids clusterer, similar to the elastic ensemble classifier proposed in [22]. Furthermore, we would like to perform a similar experiment with other clustering algorithms to if using TWE and MSM yields significantly better results than traditional euclidean and DTW distances.

Acknowledgments. This work is supported by the UK Engineering and Physical Sciences Research Council (EPSRC) (grant ref.: EP/W030756/1), and by "Agencia Española de Investigación (España)" (grant ref.: PID2020-115454GB-C22 / AEI / 10.13039 / 501100011033). David Guijo-Rubio's research has been subsidised by the University of Córdoba and financed by the European Union - NextGenerationEU (grant ref.: UCOR01MS). The experiments were carried out on the High Performance Computing Cluster supported by the Research and Specialist Computing Support service at the University of East Anglia. We would like to thank all those responsible for helping maintain the time series dataset archives and those contributing to open source implementations of the algorithms.

References

1. Aghabozorgi, S., Wah, T.Y.: Clustering of large time series datasets. Intell. Data Anal. **18**, 793–817 (2014)
2. Benavoli, A., Corani, G., Mangili, F.: Should we really use post-hoc tests based on mean-ranks? J. Mach. Learn. Res. **17**, 1–10 (2016)
3. Cai, B., Huang, G., Samadiani, N., Li, G., Chi, C.-H.: Efficient time series clustering by minimizing dynamic time warping utilization. IEEE Access **9**, 46589–46599 (2021)
4. Caiado, J., Maharaj, E., D'Urso, P.: Time series clustering. In: Handbook of Cluster Analysis, pp. 241–264 (2015)
5. Dau, H., et al.: The UCR time series archive. IEEE/CAA J. Automatica Sinica **6**(6), 1293–1305 (2019)
6. Demšar, J.: Statistical comparisons of classifiers over multiple data sets. J. Mach. Learn. Res. **7**, 1–30 (2006)
7. der Laan, M.V., Pollard, K., Bryan, J.: A new partitioning around medoids algorithm. J. Stat. Comput. Simul. **73**(8), 575–584 (2003)
8. Estivill-Castro, V.: Why so many clustering algorithms: a position paper. SIGKDD Explor. Newsl. **4**(1), 65–75 (2002)
9. García, S., Herrera, F.: An extension on "statistical comparisons of classifiers over multiple data sets" for all pairwise comparisons. J. Mach. Learn. Res. **9**, 2677–2694 (2008)
10. Germain, T., Truong, C., Oudre, L., Krejci, E.: Unsupervised study of plethysmography signals through dtw clustering. In: 2022 44th Annual International Conference of the IEEE Engineering in Medicine & Biology Society (EMBC), pp. 3396–3400. IEEE (2022)
11. Holder, C., Guijo-Rubio, D., Bagnall, A.: Barycentre averaging for the move-split-merge time series distance measure. In: 15th International Joint Conference on Knowledge Discovery, Knowledge Engineering and Knowledge Management (2023)
12. Holder, C., Middlehurst, M., Bagnall, A.: A review and evaluation of elastic distance functions for time series clustering. Knowl. Inform. Syst. (2023)

13. Ismail-Fawaz, A., et al.: An approach to multiple comparison benchmark evaluations that is stable under manipulation of the comparate set. arXiv preprint arXiv:2305.11921 (2023)
14. Javed, A., Lee, B. S., Rizzo, D.: A benchmark study on time series clustering. Mach. Learn. Appli. **1** (2020)
15. Kariv, O., Hakimi, S.L.: An algorithmic approach to network location problems. ii: the p-medians. SIAM J. Appli. Mathem. **37**(3), 539–560 (1979)
16. Kaufman, L., Rousseeuw, P. J.: Clustering large data sets. In: Pattern Recognition in Practice, pp. 425–437. Elsevier, Amsterdam (1986)
17. Lafabregue, B., Weber, J., Gancarski, P., Forestier, G.: End-to-end deep representation learning for time series clustering: a comparative study. Data Min. Knowl. Disc. **36**, 29–81 (2022)
18. Lenssen, L., Schubert, E.: Clustering by direct optimization of the medoid silhouette. In: Similarity Search and Applications: 15th International Conference, SISAP 2022, Bologna, Italy, Proceedings, pp. 190–204. Springer (2022). https://doi.org/10.1007/978-3-031-17849-8_15
19. Leonard Kaufman, P.J.R.: Partitioning Around Medoids (Program PAM), chapter 2, pp. 68–125. John Wiley and Sons Ltd. (1990)
20. Li, H., Liu, J., Yang, Z., Liu, R.W., Wu, K., Wan, Y.: Adaptively constrained dynamic time warping for time series classification and clustering. Inf. Sci. **534**, 97–116 (2020)
21. Li, X., Lin, J., Zhao, L.: Time series clustering in linear time complexity. Data Min. Knowl. Disc. **35**(3), 2369–2388 (2021)
22. Lines, J., Bagnall, A.: Time series classification with ensembles of elastic distance measures. Data Min. Knowl. Disc. **29**, 565–592 (2015)
23. Lloyd, S.P.: Least squares quantization in pcm. IEEE Trans. Inf. Theory **28**, 129–136 (1982)
24. Marteau, P.: Time warp edit distance with stiffness adjustment for time series matching. IEEE Trans. Pattern Anal. Mach. Intell. **31**(2), 306–318 (2009)
25. Ng, R., Han, J.: CLARANS: a method for clustering objects for spatial data mining. IEEE Trans. Knowl. Data Eng. **14**, 1003–1016 (2002)
26. Paparrizos, J., Gravano, L.: k-shape: efficient and accurate clustering of time series. In: Proceedings of the 2015 ACM SIGMOD International Conference on Management of Data, pp. 1855–1870 (2015)
27. Petitjean, F., Ketterlin, A., Gancarski, P.: A global averaging method for dynamic time warping, with applications to clustering. Pattern Recogn. **44**, 678 (2011)
28. Ratanamahatana, C., Keogh, E.: Three myths about dynamic time warping data mining. In: Proceedings of the 5th SIAM International Conference on Data Mining (2005)
29. Rousseeuw, P.J.: Silhouettes: a graphical aid to the interpretation and validation of cluster analysis. J. Comput. Appl. Math. **20**, 53–65 (1987)
30. Schubert, E., Lenssen, L.: Fast k-medoids clustering in rust and python. J. Open Source Softw. **7**(75), 4183 (2022)
31. Schubert, E., Rousseeuw, P.J.: Faster k-medoids clustering: improving the PAM, CLARA, and CLARANS algorithms. In: Amato, G., Gennaro, C., Oria, V., Radovanović, M. (eds.) SISAP 2019. LNCS, vol. 11807, pp. 171–187. Springer, Cham (2019). https://doi.org/10.1007/978-3-030-32047-8_16
32. Schubert, E., Rousseeuw, P.J.: Fast and eager k-medoids clustering: O(k) runtime improvement of the pam, clara, and clarans algorithms. Inf. Syst. **101**, 101804 (2021)

33. Shifaz, A., Pelletier, C., Petitjean, F., Webb, G.: Elastic similarity and distance measures for multivariate time series. Knowl. Inform. Syst. **65**(6) (2023)
34. Stefan, A., Athitsos, V., Das, G.: The Move-Split-Merge metric for time series. IEEE Trans. Knowl. Data Eng. **25**(6), 1425–1438 (2013)
35. Tavenard, R., et al.: Tslearn, a machine learning toolkit for time series data. J. Mach. Learn. Res. **21**(118), 1–6 (2020)

Explainable Parallel RCNN with Novel Feature Representation for Time Series Forecasting

Jimeng Shi, Rukmangadh Myana, Vitalii Stebliankin, Azam Shirali, and Giri Narasimhan[✉]

Knight Foundation School of Computing and Information Sciences, Florida International University, Miami, USA
{jshi008,rmyan001,vsteb002,ashir018,giri}@fiu.edu

Abstract. Accurate time series forecasting is a fundamental challenge in data science, as it is often affected by external covariates such as weather or human intervention, which in many applications, may be predicted with reasonable accuracy. We refer to them as *predicted future covariates*. However, existing methods that attempt to predict time series in an iterative manner with auto-regressive models end up with exponential error accumulations. Other strategies that consider the past and future in the encoder and decoder respectively limit themselves by dealing with the past and future data separately. To address these limitations, a novel feature representation strategy - *shifting* - is proposed to fuse the past data and future covariates such that their interactions can be considered. To extract complex dynamics in time series, we develop a parallel deep learning framework composed of RNN and CNN, both of which are used in a hierarchical fashion. We also utilize the *skip connection* technique to improve the model's performance. Extensive experiments on three datasets reveal the effectiveness of our method. Finally, we demonstrate the model *interpretability* using the Grad-CAM algorithm.

1 Introduction

Time series forecasting plays an essential role in many scenarios in real life. Accurate forecasting allows people to do better resource management [21] and optimization decisions [5] for critical processes. Applications include demand forecasting in retail [2], dynamic assignments of beds to patients [35], monthly inflation forecasting [1], and much more. Because of its popularity and significance, many time series forecasting methods have been explored. Traditional statistical forecasting methods, such as autoregression [8], exponential smoothing [13], and ARIMA [3], are widely utilized for univariate time series. These methods learn the temporal features (e.g., trends and seasonality) from past data and achieve good performance for univariate time series prediction. But they are ineffective to learn the complex dynamics among multivariate time

G. Ifrim et al. (Eds.): AALTD 2023, LNAI 14343, pp. 56–75, 2023.
https://doi.org/10.1007/978-3-031-49896-1_5

series, partly because of their inability to take advantage of *covariates* - independent variables that can influence the target variable, although perhaps not directly.

Good time series forecasting requires substantial amounts of historical data of the target variable(s) to learn temporal patterns. They also require the exogenous covariates to learn the dependent relationships. More importantly, in many applications, some of the covariates can be predicted with reasonable accuracy for the immediate future. We refer to such covariates from the immediate future as *predicted future covariates*. For example, in terms of the task predicting water levels in a river or canal system, a covariate of interest could be *precipitation*. And it is possible to use historical data as well as reasonably accurate predictions for the near future, which may be obtained from the weather services.

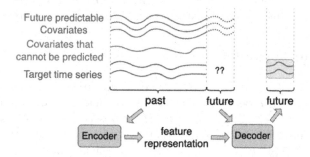

Fig. 1. Direct method using Seq2Seq models with encoder and decoder.

Existing methods employing both past and future data for time series forecasting problems are mainly divided into two categories: (1) **iterative methods** [23,25] that iteratively predict one step at a time, and (2) **direct methods** [19,31] that are trained to explicitly forecast the pre-defined horizons with sequence-to-sequence models (which originated from the speech translation domain [20]). However, they have several limitations. The iterative methods consider the prediction output from the previous time step as the input for the next time step during the model training process. Such methods suffer from error accumulation caused by the multiplication of errors.

In another direct strategy (see Fig. 1), the Seq2Seq framework - encoder and decoder [22] absorbs the historical data in the encoder and includes the predicted future covariates in the decoder. Such a strategy considers historical data and the predicted future covariates separately, probably causing the model to miss the past-future connections. Some researchers have added an attention layer [7,34] in the Seq2Seq framework to capture more local or global information, but the prediction performance improves only slightly and fails to handle the inherent constraints of the Seq2Seq model.

In this work, we aim to address the existing limitations, and our five-fold contributions are listed below:

- To avoid separately considering the past and future data, we propose a novel feature representation strategy called *shifting*, which can contextually link the past with the predicted future covariate as an integrated input. *Shifting* also makes it possible to use a single compact model to effectively combine both past and future data simultaneously.
- To improve the efficiency of the model, we introduce a parallel framework composed of RNN and CNN (ParaRCNN) to capture complex time series dynamics. Note that ParaRCNN is a single and compact model compared to the Seq2Seq architecture.
- Our model can make multi-step predictions in a one-shot manner, which can avoid error accumulation in contrast to auto-regressive models.
- We adapt the *skip connection* to facilitate improved learning since such a technique can maximize the usability of input features.
- We provide the model interpretability with the Grad-CAM algorithm to identify how each time step and feature contributes to the final predictions.

2 Problem Formulation

Let $\mathbf{Z}_{1:t}^N = (z_1^n, z_2^n, ..., z_t^n)_{n=1}^N \in R^{t \times N}$ be N univariate time series of target variables, where $z_t^n \in R$ denotes the value of the n-th target variable at time t. Let $\mathbf{X}_{1:t}^M = (x_1^m, x_2^m, \ldots, x_t^m)_{m=1}^M \in R^{t \times M}$ be M the observed time-varying covariates that are measured until time t and that cannot be predicted for the future. Finally, let $\mathbf{Y}_{1:t}^Q = (y_1^q, y_2^q, \ldots, y_t^q)_{q=1}^Q \in R^{t \times Q}$ be the Q time series for covariates measured until time t, but which can be reliably estimated for the near future; we let $\mathbf{Y}_{t+1:t+k}^Q \in R^{t \times Q}$ denote those predicted covariates k time steps into the future. We refer to these estimable variables as *future predictable covariates*. The goal of forecasting models is to compute the predicted trajectories of the target time series. We will refer to these as $\hat{\mathbf{Z}}_{t+1:t+k}^N$ (k is the forecasting length) to distinguish it from the measured target time series. The computation assumes that the input data is heterogeneous and includes the historical data (target variables $\mathbf{Z}_{1:t}^N$, observed covariates $\mathbf{X}_{1:t}^M$, historical future predictable covariates $\mathbf{Y}_{1:t}^Q$), and predicted future covariates $\mathbf{Y}_{t+1:t+k}^Q$. Note that the term "covariate" in this paper refers to those exogenous time-varying covariates rather than time itself.

3 Related Work

Traditional statistical methods learn the temporal patterns only based on historical data [3,28] of target variables themselves (see Eq. (1)). However, many approaches also aim to learn the dependent relationship between target variables and covariates, especially for the predicted future covariate [4,9,19,23,25,29,31]. Related research can be mainly categorized into iterative methods using auto-regressive models and direct strategies that use sequence-to-sequence models. We have:

$$\hat{\mathbf{Z}}_{t+i}^N = \mathbf{F}_\theta(\mathbf{Z}_{1:t}^N, \hat{\mathbf{Z}}_{t+1:t+i-1}^N), \tag{1}$$

where $\mathbf{F}_\theta(\cdot)$ is a prediction model with a set of learnable parameters θ; $\hat{\mathbf{Z}}_{t+i}^N$ is the N target variables i time step into the future for $i = 1, 2, \ldots, k$.

Iterative Methods. The iterative strategy recursively uses a one-step-ahead forecasting model [6,32] multiple times where the predicted value for the previous time step is used as the input to forecast the next time step. A typical iterative framework is the DeepAR model [25] from Amazon Research. During the training process, to predict target values $\hat{\mathbf{Z}}_t^N$ at time step t, the inputs to the network are the covariates $\mathbf{Y}_t^Q$, the target values at the previous time step $\mathbf{Z}_{t-1}^N$, and the previous network output $\mathbf{h}_{t-1}$. Note that the previous target values are known during training. During inference, measured target values $\mathbf{Z}_{t-1}^N$ are replaced by predicted target values $\hat{\mathbf{Z}}_{t-1}^N$ and then fed back to predict the next time step of $\hat{\mathbf{Z}}_{t+1}^N$ until the end of the prediction range. A mathematical formulation of such forecasting methods is given in Eq. (2) using the notation in Sect. 2. Similar approaches were adopted in [14,16,23] using different backbones. However, an inherent shortcoming of this method is that errors accumulate multiplicatively since later predictions depend on earlier predictions.

$$\hat{\mathbf{Z}}_{t+i}^N = \mathbf{F}_\theta(\mathbf{Z}_{1:t}^N, \hat{\mathbf{Z}}_{t+1:t+i-1}^N, \mathbf{X}_{1:t}^M, \mathbf{Y}_{1:t+i}^Q). \tag{2}$$

Direct Methods. The typical Seq2Seq framework for direct methods is shown in Fig 1. It deals with past and future data separately in the encoder and decoder components, respectively. The encoder model learns the feature representation of past data, which is saved as context vectors in a hidden state. The decoder model takes as input the encoder output and the additional future covariates to predict the future target values. Examples of this approach include the MQRNN model [31] that used an LSTM as the encoder to generate context vectors, which are then combined with future covariates and fed into a multi-layer perceptron (MLP) to predict the future horizon. Some efforts [7,9] have utilized a temporal attention mechanism between the encoder and the decoder. This architecture can learn the relevance of different parts of the feature representations from historical data by computing "attentional" weights. The weighted feature representations are then passed into the decoder to predict future time steps. Temporal Fusion Transformer [19] combined gated residual networks (GRNs) and an attention mechanism [30] as an additional decoder on top of the traditional encoder-decoder model. They used GRNs to filter unnecessary information and employed the additional decoder with an attention mechanism to capture long-term dependencies. Generally, the direct methods can be modeled as follows:

$$\begin{aligned} \mathbf{H}_t &= \mathbf{F}_{encoder}(\mathbf{Z}_{1:t}^N, \mathbf{X}_{1:t}^M, \mathbf{Y}_{1:t}^Q), \\ \hat{\mathbf{Z}}_{t+i}^N &= \mathbf{F}_{decoder}(\mathbf{H}_t, \mathbf{Y}_{t+1:t+i}^Q). \end{aligned} \tag{3}$$

Direct methods that use the Seq2Seq framework with the encoder and decoder in series might be prone to miss some interactions between the past and future due to separate processing styles. Moreover, the Seq2Seq framework is complicated and computationally time-consuming because of the use of two models – the encoder and the decoder. This provided the motivation for us to explore a compact model that simultaneously analyzes the measured past and the predictable future.

4   Methodology

In this section, we first illustrate the *shifting* strategy that fuses the past and future data in a structured way for an integrated feature representation. Then we present the details of the proposed model architecture and discuss how it learns from the fused data and the skip connection technique. In this paper, we define a sliding window [11] (also called rolling window [17] or look-back window [27]) of a certain length, w, as the input from the recent past, and to predict future time steps of length k.

4.1   Data Fusion with Shifting

To avoid dealing with the past and future data separately, we shift the covariates for the future period of interest (blue dotted trajectory in Fig. 2) back by s time steps, such that they are aligned and fused with all historical time series to produce distinct feature vectors. Then both the past and future data are fed into a single model together. Now the inputs are composed of all the past time series (target and covariates) aligned from time steps $t - w + 1$ to t with future predictable covariates from time steps $t - w + 1 + s$ to $t + s$. Specifically, at each time step, we obtain a 4-tuple (z_j, x_j, y_j, y_{j+s}), which is input to a state cell in the RNN (Fig. 4) or a filter kernel in the CNN (Fig. 5), thus fusing the information from the historical data (z_j, x_j, y_j) at time j and future predictable covariates y_{j+s} at time $j + s$. The above design allows both the past and future to be considered in one single component of the model at the same time. The set of target variables, $\mathbf{Z}^N_{t+1:t+k}$ are predicted in the forecasting horizon from $t + 1$ to $t + k$. The *shifting* strategy is illustrated in Fig. 2 and modelled as Eq. (4) below:

$$\hat{\mathbf{Z}}^N_{t+1:t+k} = \mathbf{G}_\theta(\mathbf{Z}^N_{t-w+1:t}, \mathbf{X}^M_{t-w+1:t}, \mathbf{Y}^Q_{t-w+1:t}, \mathbf{Y}^Q_{t-w+1+s:t+s}), \qquad (4)$$

where $\mathbf{G}_\theta(\cdot)$ is a function with learnable parameters θ; and $\mathbf{Y}^Q_{t-w+1+s:t+s}$ is the future predictable covariates along with predictions from s time steps into the future and then shifted back by s time steps (green trajectories merged with dotted blue trajectories in Fig. 2). Note that the shifted future predictable covariates $\mathbf{Y}^Q_{t-w+1+s:t+s}$ and the single unified model given by $\mathbf{G}_\theta$ in Eq. (4) differentiate our method from the previous methods discussed in Sect. 3.

4.2   Network Architectures

With the input data transformed and fused (Fig. 2, right) by the *shifting* strategy, we develop a parallel framework composed of RNN and CNN, both of which

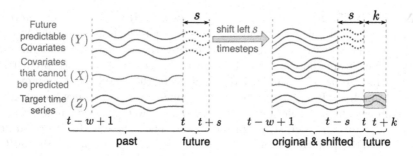

Fig. 2. Input data transformed by the *shifting* strategy. Left: Trajectories of all variables before transformation. Right: Original trajectories along with shifted future predictable covariates. Predicted output is the future k time steps of the target variables. (Color figure online)

are in a hierarchical structure. As shown in Fig. 3, both the number of filters for CNN and the number of units for RNN decrease over the layers to extract high-level time series dynamics. More specifically, since RNN and CNN learn the temporal dependency and dynamics in different mechanisms, we construct RNN and CNN in parallel, which benefits the model by capturing heterogeneous feature representations from input time series. Meanwhile, the *skip connection* technique is utilized to enhance learning since it maximizes the usability of the input features. Lastly, the fused input, the CNN output, and the RNN output are concatenated together and fed into a fully-connected layer to make the final predictions.

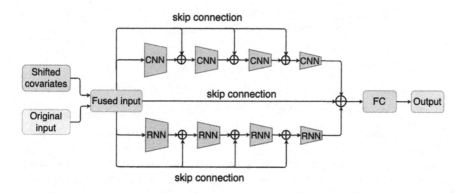

Fig. 3. Architecture of the proposed ParaRCNN model. There are 256, 128, 64, and 32 filters for CNN modules (Conv1D) and 128, 64, 32, and 16 units for RNN modules (SimpeRNN), respectively.

RNN with Shifting. Recurrent Neural Networks (RNNs) learn the temporal dependency from input features in the recent past to future one or more target variables by recurrently training and updating the transitions of an internal (hidden) state from the last time step to the current time step. To predict the future k time steps, the standard RNNs were further modified to remove the hidden states $\mathbf{h}_{t+1}, \mathbf{h}_{t+2}, .., \mathbf{h}_{t+k}$ to enable a one-shot prediction while avoiding the accumulation of prediction errors. As shown in Fig. 4, we implement the RNNs with only w hidden states in our paper. The predicted future covariates are shifted to the past by s time steps and aligned with past data by the *shifting* strategy such that the input for each hidden state $\mathbf{h}_j$ at time $t = j$ is a 4-tuple $(\mathbf{z}_j, \mathbf{x}_j, \mathbf{y}_j, \mathbf{y}_{j+s})$. Hierarchical RNNs queued in series (Fig. 3) are expected to distill the high-level features from the input time series. At last, the RNNs generate the prediction for target variables $(\mathbf{z}_{t+1}, \mathbf{z}_{t+2}, \ldots, \mathbf{z}_{t+k})$ in a one-shot manner. The hidden states are recursively computed by:

$$
\begin{aligned}
h_j &= f(\mathbf{h}_{j-1}, \mathbf{z}_j, \mathbf{x}_j, \mathbf{y}_j, \mathbf{y}_{j+s}), \\
&= tanh(\mathbf{b} + \mathbf{U}^T h_{j-1} + \mathbf{W}^T(\mathbf{z}_j, \mathbf{x}_j, \mathbf{y}_j, \mathbf{y}_{j+s})),
\end{aligned}
\tag{5}
$$

where f is an activation function (hyperbolic tangent function); $\mathbf{h}_j$ and $\mathbf{h}_{j-1}$ refer to the current and previous hidden states; $\mathbf{z}_j$, $\mathbf{x}_j$, and $\mathbf{y}_j$ represent the target time series, observed covariates, and predictable future covariates from the past w time steps; $\mathbf{y}_{j+s}$ denotes the predicted future covariates from k steps into the future; $\mathbf{U}, \mathbf{W}$ are weight matrices and $\mathbf{b}$ is the bias vector.

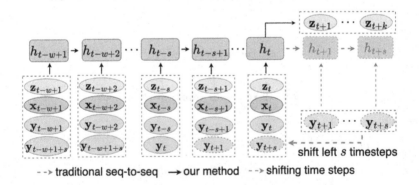

Fig. 4. The RNN architecture with the *shifting* strategy. Dashed blue ovals represent predicted future covariates. Solid ovals are historical target variables and covariates. The last row has the shifted covariates. (Color figure online)

CNN with Shifting. CNN is a popular model in the image processing field because of the powerful learning ability of *convolutional kernels* embedded inside. 2D-CNN is widely adopted to deal with images [33] by moving 2-D convolutional

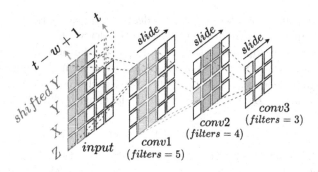

Fig. 5. CNN with 3 convolutional layers. Input includes all original variables and the shifted predicted future covariates. Each filter includes past and future information. Each row represents the convolution results with one filter.

kernels along the height and width dimension of each image. For multivariate time series, it consisted of multiple univariate time series that fundamentally are sequential in nature. Therefore, 1-D convolutional kernels (also called filters) are used in our paper to learn the temporal and cross-feature dependency [15]. We consider the multivariate time series as a matrix with the shape of (rows, columns) [36] where the rows represent the time steps, and the columns represent the features that generally equal the number of time series dimensions. We also tried 2D-CNN, and the performance was not much different from 1D-CNN, but it needs more computation resources.

As Fig. 5 shows, the shifted future predictable covariates and the original observed data are simultaneously considered by the sliding 1-D convolutional kernels. In other words, each 1-D convolutional kernel learns from the historical data (past) and the predicted data s time steps ahead (future). Such convolutional operations on both the history and predicted future input could be described by Eq. (6). Formally, a convolution operation between two convolutional layers is given by Eq. (7).

$$V_j = \sigma(K_j \circledast (\mathbf{Z}^N_{j:j+\Delta t}, \mathbf{X}^M_{j:j+\Delta t}, \mathbf{Y}^Q_{j:j+\Delta t}, \mathbf{Y}^Q_{j+s:j+\Delta t+s})), \tag{6}$$

where $\circledast$ refers to the convolution operator; K_j is a filter at the time j; Δt is the length of segmented time series for the convolution computations; σ represents the activation function; V_j is the output value at time j.

$$a^{l+1}_j = \sigma(b^l_j + \sum_{f=1}^{F^l} K^l_{jf} \circledast a^l_f), \tag{7}$$

where $\circledast$ represents the convolution operator; l indexes the layer, f indexes the filter; K_j is a filter at the time j; F^l is the number of filters used in the lth layer; σ denotes the activation function.

Skip Connection. It is used to train a deep neural network by copying and bypassing the input from the former layers to the deeper layers by matrix addition. ResNets add a skip-connection that bypasses the non-linear transformations with an identity function. For example, given a single image x_0 that is passed through subsequent convolutional layers, each layer implements a non-linear transformation $H(\cdot)$. The output of lth layer with skip connection looks as:

$$x_l = H_l(x_{l-1}) + x_{l-1}. \tag{8}$$

DenseNets [12] achieves skip connections by concatenation. In their work, for each layer, the feature maps of all preceding layers and their own feature maps are used as inputs into all subsequent layers by simple concatenation as shown in Eq. (9). There are $L(L+1)/2$ skip connections for the networks with L layers.

$$x_l = H_l(x_0, x_1, \ldots, x_{l-1}), \tag{9}$$

where $x_0, x_1, \ldots x_{l-1}$ denotes the concatenation of the feature maps produced in previous layers. It shows how the lth layer considers the feature maps of all former layers as input.

$$x_l = H_l(x_{l-1}) + x_0. \tag{10}$$

However, challenges persist with both strategies. ResNets hinder the skip connection because of the matrix addition, which needs the same dimension for both preceding and subsequent matrices. DenseNets have a more complex structure with $L(L+1)/2$ connections as it conveys all former outputs to the latter layers. U-Net models simply pass the original input once to the latter layers. In our model, we adopt L skip connections by bypassing the original input to every latter layer with concatenation (see Eq. (10) and Fig. 6d). Such a structure can facilitate the model by reusing the original input many times and learning it directly while avoiding the *vanishing gradient* issue of deeper layers [18].

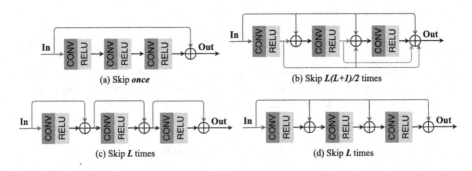

(a) Skip *once*   (b) Skip *L(L+1)/2* times

(c) Skip *L* times   (d) Skip *L* times

Fig. 6. Various strategies for skip connection. We adopt the strategy of (d) in our paper and compare it with (a) Skip *once* used in U-net [24], (b) Skip $L(L+1)/2$ times used in DenseNet [12], and (c) the benchmark strategy skipping L times.

5 Experiments

5.1 Datasets

Three real-world datasets were used for time series forecasting tasks. *Beijing PM2.5* and *Electricity price* datasets are publicly available from the Machine Learning Repository of the University of California, Irvine, and Kaggle repositories, respectively. The third one is the *Water Stage* dataset downloaded from the South Florida Water Management District (SFWMD) website.

Beijing PM2.5. It includes hourly observed data from January 1, 2010, to December 31, 2014. We consider PM2.5 as the target variable to predict, other variables such as dew, temperature, pressure, wind speed, wind direction, snow, and rain are covariates that can be predicted and can influence PM2.5 values. $PM2.5 \in [0, 671]$ $\mu g/m^3$.

Electricity Price. It has two hourly datasets from January 1, 2015, to December 31, 2018. Energy_dataset.csv includes energy demand, generation, and prices, while weather_features.csv gives the weather features temperature, humidity, etc. Electricity price is the target variable to predict, while the prior known predictable covariates are energy demand, generation, and weather features. *Electricity price* $\in [\$9.33, \$116.8]$ in this dataset.

Water Stage. This is an hourly dataset from January 1, 2010, to December 31, 2020, and includes information on water levels, the height of gate opening, water flow values through the gate, water volumes pumped at gates, and rainfall measures. The water stage is the target variable while other variables are covariates. Rainfall, gate position, and pump control are future covariates that can be predicted. *Water stage* $\in [-1.25, 4.05]$ feet in the dataset.

5.2 Training and Evaluation

Our Models. We predict $k = 24$ hours in the future with input windows of size $w = 72$ hours and predicted future covariates in the same future horizons. We consider the entire target series $\mathbf{Z}_{t+1:t+k}^N$ as the ground-truth labels in supervised learning, which can allow one-shot forecasting to avoid the error accumulation of the traditional iterative prediction. For each dataset, we selected the first 80% as the training set to train the models, and the remaining 20% was chosen as the test set to evaluate the performance. *Max-Min normalization* shown as Eq. (11) was used to squeeze the input data into $[0, 1]$ to avoid possible data bias due to the different scales. We also used *early stopping* and *L1L2 regularization* to alleviate overfitting. There are several hyperparameters in our model. We set $\{16, 32, 64, 128, 256\}$ as the candidate numbers of internal units of RNNs and filters in CNNs. $\{$1e-3, 5e-4, 1e-4, 5e-5, 1e-5$\}$ was tested as the learning rate and regularization factor. The shifting length s was validated with the range of $[1, w + k]$ (see Fig. 7). Open-source code can be accessed via the link[1].

$$x' = \frac{x - x_{min}}{x_{max} - x_{min}} \tag{11}$$

---

[1] https://github.com/JimengShi/ParaRCNN-Time-Series-Forecasting.

Algorithm 1. Model Training

Input: covariate time series: $\mathbf{X}_{1,T}, \mathbf{Y}_{1,T}$;
         target time series: $\mathbf{Z}_{1,T}$, where T is the total length of data set.
Parameter: w: sliding window length, k: forecasting length, s: shifted length.
Output: well-trained model

1:   // construct training instance pairs
2:   $D \leftarrow \emptyset$
3:   **for** each available time point $w \le t \le T - s$ **do**
4:      $S_{past} \leftarrow \{\mathbf{X}_{t-w+1,t}, \mathbf{Y}_{t-w+1,t}, \mathbf{Z}_{t-w+1,t}\}$
5:      $S_{shifted} \leftarrow \{\mathbf{Y}_{t-w+1+s,t+s}\}$
6:      $S_{target} \leftarrow \mathbf{Z}_{t+1,t+k}$
7:      put a instance pair $(\{S_{past}, S_{shifted}\}, S_{target})$ into D
8:   **end for**
9:   // train the model
10: initialize all learnable parameters θ for the model
11: **repeat**
12:     randomly selects a batch of instance pairs D_b from D
13:     model outputs $\hat{\mathbf{Z}}_{t+1,t+k}$ for each batch
14:     finds θ by minimizing the loss function in Eq. (12)
15: **until** stopping criteria is satisfied
16: **return** well-trained model with the best parameters θ

Baseline Models. DeepAR [25] iteratively predicting future time steps was viewed as one of the baseline models. Seq2Seq approaches include MQRNN [31] and Temporal Fusion Transformer (TFT) [19], which consider the past data and future covariates separately in the encoder-decoder framework. To validate the functionality of *shifting*, we also adapted baselines as a single branch in Fig. 3 (RNN or CNN) as backbones with the encoder-decoder framework (no *shifting*). We refer to them as RNN-RNN and CNN-CNN in Table 1.

All models were trained by minimizing the loss function in Eq. (12), which describes the mean square error between predicted and ground-truth values. The training process is given as Algorithm 1. The testing process is achieved by the trained model with the same data processing as the first 8 rows. Mean Absolute Errors (MAEs) and Root Mean Square Errors (RMSEs) are the metrics to evaluate the trained models. Each experiment was repeated 5 times with 5 random seeds. Table 1 reports the average results with an error bound.

$$L(\mathbf{Z}, \hat{\mathbf{Z}}) = \frac{1}{\Phi} \sum_{\phi=1}^{\Phi} [(\mathbf{Z}_{t+1,t+k}^N)^\phi - (\hat{\mathbf{Z}}_{t+1,t+k}^N)^\phi]^2. \qquad (12)$$

5.3 Hyperparameter Study

Shift Length. Figure 7 shows the MAEs and RMSEs using ParaRCNN with different shifting lengths on the Water-stage dataset, which can help us to delineate the relationship between the shifting lengths and the model performance. We observed that $k \leq s \leq w$ generates better performance.

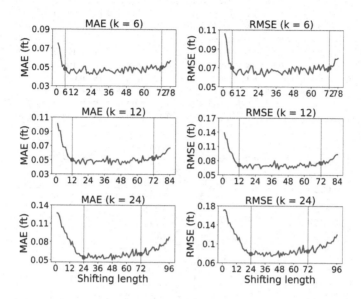

Fig. 7. MAE & RMSE for different forecasting lengths (k) and shift lengths (s). The left red point of each subplot represents the errors when $s = k$ while the right red point denotes the errors when $s = w$. ($w = 72$ hours, $k = 6, 12, 24$ h.) (Color figure online)

Model Layers. After ensuring the shifting length $s = k$, we try to analyze the best number of layers for the ParaRCNN model. We found 3 or 4 layers (see Fig. 8) perform the best for the datasets in our paper (3 layers for `Electricity` dataset, 4 layers for `Water-stage` and `PM2.5` dataset).

5.4 Prediction Results

The first 5 rows in Table 1 show the performance of the baseline models. Our models are listed in the last 5 rows. We use a single RNN architecture of RNN-RNN and apply *shifting* to it as RNN-Shift. To test the effectiveness of *skip connection*, we add it to RNN-Shift and call it RNN-Shift-SC. A similar process is applied to CNN-Shift and CNN-Shift-SC. At last, we propose ParaRCNN (see Fig. 3) by combining RNN and CNN in parallel with both *shifting* and *skip connection* techniques. Compared with baseline models in Table 1, the performance of models with *shifting* is comparable or slightly better than some baselines, while ParaRCNN achieves the best with the help of *shifting* and *skip connection*.

68   J. Shi et al.

Table 1. MAEs & RMSEs with $k = 24$ h on the test sets.

Methods	Beijing PM2.5		Electricity Price		Water Stage	
	MAE	RMSE	MAE	RMSE	MAE	RMSE
MQRNN	33.94 ± 1.14	53.13 ± 1.22	3.48 ± 0.14	4.69 ± 0.19	0.121 ± 1e-2	0.156 ± 4e-2
DeepAR	36.57 ± 0.72	57.75 ± 0.98	5.23 ± 0.12	6.59 ± 0.18	0.196 ± 9e-3	0.231 ± 1e-2
TFT	36.32 ± 0.82	60.13 ± 1.37	3.76 ± 0.16	5.52 ± 0.24	0.119 ± 7e-3	0.158 ± 9e-3
RNN-RNN	33.43 ± 0.79	52.43 ± 1.15	4.27 ± 0.15	5.72 ± 0.26	0.142 ± 4e-3	0.177 ± 8e-3
CNN-CNN	33.90 ± 0.57	53.15 ± 1.22	3.78 ± 0.14	5.08 ± 0.21	0.110 ± 8e-3	0.177 ± 9e-3
RNN-Shift	33.37 ± 0.59	52.96 ± 1.27	3.96 ± 0.13	5.23 ± 0.24	0.109 ± 1e-2	0.151 ± 9e-3
RNN-Shift-SC	31.90 ± 0.55	50.89 ± 1.09	3.49 ± 0.12	4.65 ± 0.18	0.071 ± 7e-3	0.096 ± 7e-3
CNN-Shift	33.55 ± 0.46	52.94 ± 1.11	3.85 ± 0.14	5.09 ± 0.20	0.131 ± 8e-3	0.158 ± 9e-3
CNN-Shift-SC	31.76 ± 0.43	50.61 ± 1.08	3.48 ± 0.12	4.69 ± 0.17	0.059 ± 5e-3	0.081 ± 6e-3
ParaRCNN	31.48 ± 0.36	49.97 ± 0.89	3.39 ± 0.10	4.60 ± 0.13	0.054 ± 4e-3	0.075 ± 9e-3

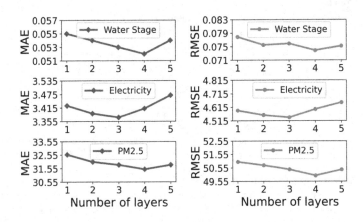

Fig. 8. Model performance vs. Number of layers ($w = 72$ h, $k = 24$ h).

5.5 Skip Connection Study

We apply *skip connection* with different strategies (see Fig. 6) to the ParaRNN model. Taking an example of L layers, there are five situations considered: (a) **One** skip in U-net [24]; (b) $\mathbf{L(L+1)/2}$ skips in DenseNet [12]; (c) **L** skips; (d) **L** skips; and (e) **No** skip connection. Figure 9 shows the performance of (e) without a skip connection is clearly much poor than others and (a-d) is roughly the same. The possible reason is that our network is a shallow one with only 4 layers. **L** and $\mathbf{L(L+1)/2}$ skips do not exist a big difference. However, the number of skip connections is indeed reduced from $\mathbf{L(L+1)/2}$ to **L**.

5.6 Model Explainability

After the model was trained, we analyzed how much each time step and feature contribute to the final outputs. With the Grad-CAM algorithm [26], we first compute the gradient of the target values with respect to the feature map activations of the concatenated layer. These gradients flow back over the input of shape (time steps × features) to obtain the neuron importance weights (see Fig. 10 in Appendix A). The water stage at S1, S25A, S25B, and S26 are target values to predict. The first 19 rows are original past input and the last 9 rows shifted covariates (shifted future covariates are from 48 to 72). It shows our model pays more attention to these future covariates since target variables in the future horizon have a dependent relationship with them. This is as described in Sect. 4.1. The water stages at different stations are more correlated because these stations are adjacent to the ocean and water stages are changing with the trend of the tide (WS_S4). We visualize each time series in Appendix B (see Figs. 11 and 12) providing better observations for readers.

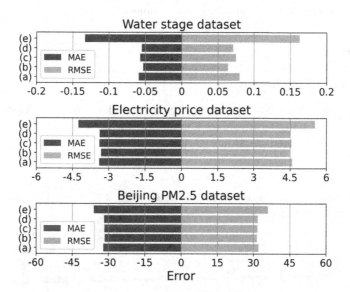

Fig. 9. MAE & RMSE for various strategies to implement *skip connection*. (a) **One** skip in U-net [24]; (b) **L(L + 1)/2** skips in DenseNet [12]; (c) **L** skips as one benchmark; (d) **L** skips we are using in our paper; and (e) **No** skip connection.

6 Discussion and Conclusions

We have demonstrated with experiments that the utilization of future covariates can enhance performance. The model explainability shows their importance from another point of view. To take the advantage of future covariates, the proposed data fusion method, *shifting*, can generate comparable or slightly better performance with a single compact model. Besides, our experiments delineate an appropriate range of the *shift* length (see Fig. 7). When $s < k$ or $s > w$, considerably lower performances occur since the models only get to utilize some of the predicted covariates from the future k time steps. However, when $s > k$, either the performance is flat or deteriorates as s is increased. We observe that $k \leq s \leq w$ generates better performance since all predicted future covariates in the forecasting horizon are included. The variations for $k \leq s \leq w$ are too small to be significant.

Skip connection can further improve the model performance. Our implementation strategy that presents the original input to each subsequent layer generated roughly the same or better performance when compared with other strategies. Our *ParaRCNN* model equipped with *shifting* and *skip connection* techniques consistently outperformed all other models in our paper.

Acknowledgements. This work is part of the I-GUIDE project, which is funded by the National Science Foundation under award number 2118329.

7   Appendix

7.1   Model Explainability

We provide the explainability of the trained model using the Water Stage dataset. The following figure shows how important each feature and each time step is for the final predictions.

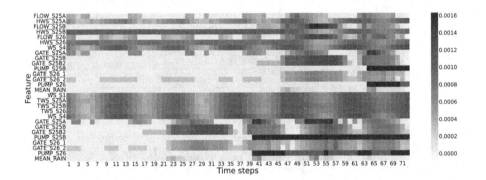

Fig. 10. Importance weights (feature vs. time step) with Grad-CAM algorithm.

7.2   Visualization of Time Series

We visualize the time series in Fig. 11 below. The unit of each feature is ignored. We refer readers to see Fig. 2 for better understanding.

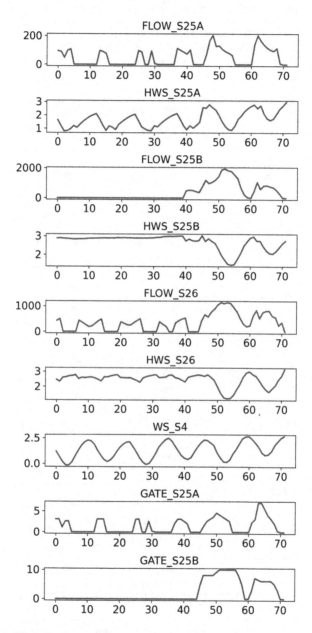

Fig. 11. Visualization of target variables and covariates from the past.

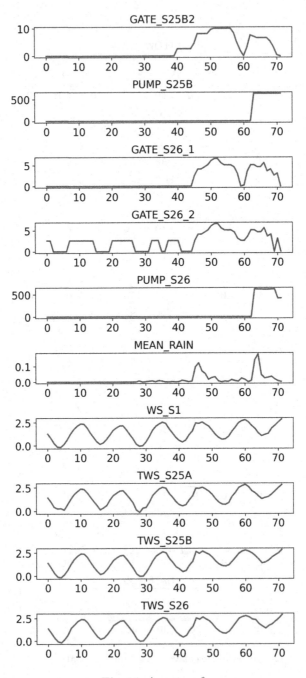

Fig. 11. (*continued*)

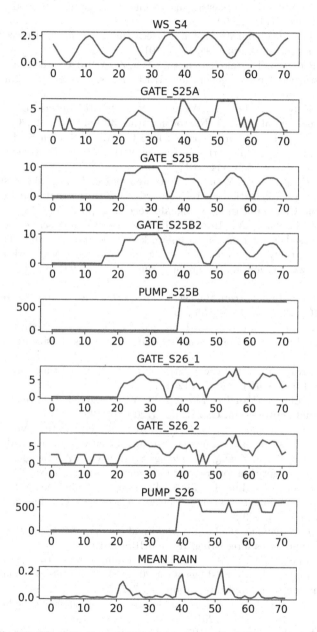

Fig. 12. Visualization of shifted future predictable covariates.

References

1. Baybuza, I.: Inflation forecasting using machine learning methods. Russian J. Money Finance **77**(4), 42–59 (2018)
2. Böse, J., et al.: Probabilistic demand forecasting at scale. In: Proceedings of the VLDB Endowment 10, pp. 1694–1705 (2017)
3. Chen, P., Pedersen, T., Bak-Jensen, B., Chen, Z.: ARIMA-based time series model of stochastic wind power generation. IEEE Trans. Power Syst. **25**(2), 667–676 (2009)
4. Chen, Y., Kang, Y., Chen, Y., Wang, Z.: Probabilistic forecasting with temporal convolutional neural network. Neurocomputing **399**, 491–501 (2020)
5. Cinar, Y., Hamid, M., Parantapa G., Eric G., Ali A., Vadim S.: Position-based content attention for time series forecasting with sequence-to-sequence RNNs. In: NeurIPS, vol. 24, pp. 533–544 (2017)
6. Dong, G., Fataliyev, K., Wang, L.: One-step and multi-step ahead stock prediction using backpropagation neural networks. In: 9th International Conference on Information, Communications & Signal Processing, pp. 1–5 (2013)
7. Du, S., Li, T., Yang, Y., Horng, S.J.: Multivariate time series forecasting via attention-based encoder-decoder framework. Neurocomputing **388**, 269–279 (2020)
8. Efendi, R., Arbaiy, N., Deris, M.: A new procedure in stock market forecasting based on fuzzy random auto-regression time series model. Inf. Sci. **441**, 113–132 (2018)
9. Fan, C., et al.: Multi-horizon time series forecasting with temporal attention learning. In: SIGKDD, pp. 2527–2535 (2019)
10. Fauvel, K., Lin, T., Masson, V., Fromont, É., Termier, A.: Xcm: an explainable convolutional neural network for multivariate time series classification. Mathematics **9**(23), 3137 (2021)
11. Gidea, M., Katz, Y.: Topological data analysis of financial time series: landscapes of crashes. Phys. A **491**, 820–834 (2018)
12. Huang, G., Liu, Z., Van Der Maaten, L., Weinberger, K.Q.: Densely connected convolutional networks. In: CVPR, pp. 4700–4708 (2017)
13. Hyndman, R., Koehler, A., Ord, J., Snyder, R.: Forecasting with exponential smoothing: the state space approach. Springer Science & Business Media (2008)
14. Lamb, A., Goyal, A., Zhang, Y., Zhang, S., Courville, A., Bengio, Y.: Professor forcing: a new algorithm for training recurrent networks. In: NeurIPS (2016)
15. Tang, W., Long, G., Liu, L., Zhou, T., Jiang, J., Blumenstein, M.: Rethinking 1d-cnn for time series classification: A stronger baseline. arXiv preprint arXiv:2002.10061 (2020)
16. Li, S., et al.: Enhancing the locality and breaking the memory bottleneck of transformer on time series forecasting. In: NeurIPS (2019)
17. Li, L., Noorian, F., Moss, D. J., Leong, P.: Rolling window time series prediction using MapReduce. In: Proceedings of the 2014 IEEE 15th International Conference on Information Reuse and Integration, pp. 757–764. IEEE (2014)
18. Li, H., Xu, Z., Taylor, G., Studer, C., Goldstein, T.: Visualizing the loss landscape of neural nets. In: NeurIPS (2018)
19. Lim, B., Arık, S.Ö., Loeff, N., Pfister, T.: Temporal fusion transformers for interpretable multi-horizon time series forecasting. Int. J. Forecast. **37**(4), 1748–1764 (2021)
20. Luong, M. T., Le, Q. V., Sutskever, I., Vinyals, O., Kaiser, L.: Multi-task sequence to sequence learning. arXiv preprint arXiv:1511.06114 (2015)

21. Niu, W., Feng, Z.: Evaluating the performances of several artificial intelligence methods in forecasting daily streamflow time series for sustainable water resources management. Sustain. Urban Areas **64**, 102562 (2021)
22. Qing, X., Jin, J., Niu, Y., Zhao, S.: Time-space coupled learning method for model reduction of distributed parameter systems with encoder-decoder and RNN. AIChE J. **66**(8), e16251 (2020)
23. Rangapuram, S., Seeger, M., Gasthaus, J., Stella, L., Wang, Y., Januschowski, T.: Deep state space models for time series forecasting. In: NeurIPS (2018)
24. Ronneberger, O., Fischer, P., Brox, T.: U-Net: convolutional networks for biomedical image segmentation. In: Navab, N., Hornegger, J., Wells, W.M., Frangi, A.F. (eds.) MICCAI 2015. LNCS, vol. 9351, pp. 234–241. Springer, Cham (2015). https://doi.org/10.1007/978-3-319-24574-4_28
25. Salinas, D., Flunkert, V., Gasthaus, J., Januschowski, T.: DeepAR: probabilistic forecasting with autoregressive recurrent networks. Int. J. Forecast. **36**(3), 1181–1191 (2020)
26. Selvaraju, R.R., Cogswell, M., Das, A., Vedantam, R., Parikh, D., Batra, D.: Gradcam: visual explanations from deep networks via gradient-based localization. In: ICCV, pp. 618–626 (2017)
27. Shi, J., Jain, M., Narasimhan, G.: Time series forecasting (tsf) using various deep learning models. arXiv preprint arXiv:2204.11115 (2022)
28. Siami-Namini, S., Tavakoli, N., Namin, A.: A comparison of ARIMA and LSTM in forecasting time series. In: 17th IEEE International Conference on Machine Learning and Applications (ICMLA), pp. 1394–1401. IEEE (2018)
29. Therneau, T., Crowson, C., Atkinson, E.: Using time dependent covariates and time dependent coefficients in the cox model. Survival Vignettes **2**(3), 1–25 (2017)
30. Vaswani, A., et al.: Attention is all you need. In: NeurIPS (2017)
31. Wen, R., Torkkola, K., Narayanaswamy, B., Madeka, D.: A multi-horizon quantile recurrent forecaster. arXiv preprint arXiv:1711.11053 (2017)
32. Yang, B., Oh, M., Tan, A.: Machine condition prognosis based on regression trees and one-step-ahead prediction. Mech. Syst. Signal Process. **22**(5), 1179–1193 (2008)
33. Yang, X., Ye, Y., Li, X., Lau, R.Y., Zhang, X., Huang, X.: Hyperspectral image classification with deep learning models. IEEE Trans. Geosci. Remote Sens. **56**(9), 5408–5423 (2018)
34. Yuan, Y., et al.: Using an attention-based LSTM encoder-decoder network for near real-time disturbance detection. IEEE J. Selected Topics Appli. Earth Observat. Remote Sensing **13**, 1819–1832 (2020)
35. Zhang, J., Nawata, K.: Multi-step prediction for influenza outbreak by an adjusted long short-term memory. Epidemiology Infect. **146**(7), 809–816 (2018)
36. Zhang, C., et al.: A deep neural network for unsupervised anomaly detection and diagnosis in multivariate time series data. In: AAAI (2019)

RED CoMETS: An Ensemble Classifier for Symbolically Represented Multivariate Time Series

Luca A. Bennett[1,2(✉)] [iD] and Zahraa S. Abdallah[1] [iD]

[1] School of Engineering Mathematics and Technology,
University of Bristol, Bristol, UK
zahraa.abdallah@bristol.ac.uk
[2] Awerian, Cambridge, UK
luca.bennett@awerian.net

Abstract. Multivariate time series classification is a rapidly growing research field with practical applications in finance, healthcare, engineering, and more. The complexity of classifying multivariate time series data arises from its high dimensionality, temporal dependencies, and varying lengths. This paper introduces a novel ensemble classifier called RED CoMETS (Random Enhanced Co-eye for Multivariate Time Series), which addresses these challenges. RED CoMETS builds upon the success of Co-eye, an ensemble classifier specifically designed for symbolically represented univariate time series, and extends its capabilities to handle multivariate data. The performance of RED CoMETS is evaluated on benchmark datasets from the UCR archive, where it demonstrates competitive accuracy when compared to state-of-the-art techniques in multivariate settings. Notably, it achieves the highest reported accuracy in the literature for the 'HandMovementDirection' dataset. Moreover, the proposed method significantly reduces computation time compared to Co-eye, making it an efficient and effective choice for multivariate time series classification.

Keywords: Time series classification · Multivariate time series · Co-eye · Symbolic representation · Ensemble classification

1 Introduction

Problems involving the classification of time series data play a crucial role in various domains, including the sciences, data mining, finance, and signal processing. Time series and their classifiers can be categorised into two types: univariate and multivariate. Despite multivariate time series classification problems being more prevalent in real-world scenarios, the literature has historically focused more on

---

L.A. Bennett—This author was with the University of Bristol while this research was undertaken but is currently affiliated with Awerian.

G. Ifrim et al. (Eds.): AALTD 2023, LNAI 14343, pp. 76–91, 2023.
https://doi.org/10.1007/978-3-031-49896-1_6

the univariate case [20]. Although recent studies have proposed promising methods to address multivariate time series classification [20], there still exists a gap, emphasising the need for accurate and efficient algorithms in this domain.

Traditional time series classifiers typically seek discriminatory features within the time series or adopt a holistic view of the entire series [2]. They often concentrate on a single representation aspect, such as shape or frequency [9]. However, time series classification problems can greatly differ in terms of training and testing sizes, dimensions, classes, series length, and class distribution. Consequently, a single approach cannot effectively handle all types of time series.

In this paper, we extend the techniques introduced by Co-eye for univariate time series classification [1], which draws inspiration from the compound eyes of insects. Co-eye utilizes two symbolic representation transformations, namely Symbolic Aggregate Approximation (SAX) [17] and Symbolic Fourier Approximation (SFA) [21], to extract discriminatory features from the time series. These transformations generate multiple "lenses" that can detect discriminatory features at various levels of granularity, capturing both fine details and broad shapes. By forming an ensemble of these lenses, Co-eye integrates different perspectives from the time and frequency domains, allowing for effective feature extraction in time series classification problems with diverse characteristics.

We propose a novel ensemble classifier for multivariate time series classification that builds upon Co-eye in two significant ways. Firstly, we enhance Co-eye's success in handling univariate problems and propose an improved approach that significantly reduces computation time without sacrificing accuracy. Secondly, we leverage this enhanced univariate approach as a foundation for a novel multivariate classifier, exploring two distinct techniques. Our proposed multivariate classifier is named RED CoMETS, which stands for Random Enhanced Co-eye for Multivariate Time Series. We evaluate RED CoMETS against state-of-the-art classifiers using datasets from the UCR archive [3], and it achieves state-of-the-art results.

The remainder of this paper is organised as follows: Sect. 2 discusses relevant prior research. Section 3 provides details on our optimized univariate foundation built upon Co-eye. Section 4 outlines the proposed extensions for multivariate classification. Section 5 presents the experimental results, specifically focusing on test accuracy. Finally, Sect. 6 concludes the paper.

2   Related Work

Co-eye leverages the Symbolic Aggregate Approximation (SAX) [17] and Symbolic Fourier Approximation (SFA) [21] techniques to construct lenses, each offering a distinct view of the time series data in both the time and frequency domains. These lenses, represented by triplets denoted as $<s, \alpha, w>$, where s indicates the choice between SAX and SFA, and α and w are the hyperparameters for alphabet size and word length, respectively, provide Co-eye with a multi-resolution perspective [1]. Through a careful "pair selection" process, Co-eye identifies the most effective set of lenses for a given classification problem.

During the classification phase, Co-eye builds a Random Forest [22] for each lens using the transformed time series. These Random Forests' outputs are combined using a dynamic voting method, allowing the most confident lenses to be matched to specific sequences and effectively extracting discriminatory features [1]. Co-eye has demonstrated competitive accuracies compared to state-of-the-art univariate classifiers when evaluated on datasets from the UCR archive [1].

The reviews by Bagnall et al. [2] and Ruiz et al. [20] provide a comprehensive overview of the strengths and weaknesses of different approaches, highlighting their performance on a range of datasets. This information is crucial in understanding the landscape of existing classifiers and identifying gaps or areas where further improvements can be made.

Dynamic Time Warping (DTW) [14] is chosen as one of the benchmark classifiers. DTW utilizes a unique distance metric in combination with the 1-nearest neighbour classifier and serves as a baseline performance measure for "good" time series classifiers. It was used as a benchmark by both Bagnall et al. [2] and Ruiz et al. [20], making it a compelling target to surpass.

Another benchmark classifier is the Multiple Representation Sequence Learner (MrSEQL) [16], which transforms time series into various symbolic representations and forms an ensemble using a SEQL classifier. While MrSEQL shares similarities with Co-eye in methodology, differences lie in the base classifier, parameterisation of symbolic representations, and voting methods [16].

ROCKET (Random Convolutional Kernel Transform) [9] is a powerful classifier that has demonstrated exceptional performance in both univariate and multivariate time series classification. ROCKET leverages random convolutional kernels to transform time series data and apply a linear classifier to make predictions. It has achieved leading accuracies across the univariate UCR archive datasets while maintaining an extremely low computation time. The effectiveness and efficiency of ROCKET make it a natural choice to benchmark against for state-of-the-art performance.

HIVE-COTE (Hierarchical Vote Collective of Transformation-based Ensembles) [18] is a heterogeneous ensemble classifier that combines multiple transformation based models. Its latest edition, HIVE-COTE 2.0 [19], is currently the best-ranked multivariate time series classifier in terms of accuracy. HIVE-COTE constructs an ensemble of diverse classifiers, including shapelet-based, interval-based, and dictionary-based classifiers, and employs a hierarchical voting strategy to make predictions. The hierarchical nature of HIVE-COTE allows it to capture different levels of temporal patterns and achieve robust performance on a wide range of time series datasets. As the leading multivariate time series classifier, HIVE-COTE serves as the "method to beat" for RED CoMETS.

In the realm of deep learning-based approaches for multivariate time series classification, InceptionTime [12] stands out. It is an ensemble of convolutional neural networks specifically designed for time series classification. InceptionTime introduces the concept of inception modules, which consist of parallel convolutional layers with different filter sizes. This design allows the network to capture diverse temporal patterns at multiple resolutions. InceptionTime has been identified by Ruiz et al. [20] as the leading deep learning-based approach for both univariate and multivariate time series classification. Their review demonstrated that InceptionTime achieved top-performing accuracy across various datasets and outperformed many traditional and state-of-the-art classifiers. Therefore, it serves as a strong baseline for comparing the performance of RED CoMETS against deep learning-based approaches.

In addition to InceptionTime, deep learning architectures such as Long Short-Term Memory (LSTM) networks and Convolutional Neural Networks (CNNs) have gained popularity in time series classification. LSTM networks, a type of recurrent neural network (RNN), are capable of capturing long-term dependencies in sequential data and have shown promising results for classifying both univariate and multivariate time series [13].

CNNs, on the other hand, are primarily known for their success in computer vision tasks, but they have also been applied to time series classification with remarkable outcomes. In the context of time series, 1D CNNs are often employed to learn hierarchical representations of input sequences by convolving filters across different time steps. This allows them to automatically extract relevant local patterns and capture higher-level representations of the data [4,24].

Deep learning-based approaches offer the advantage of automatically learning relevant features from raw time series data, obviating the need for handcrafted feature engineering. However, they often require large amounts of training data and significant computational resources for model training and optimization. Additionally, the interpretability of deep learning models can be challenging due to their black-box nature.

3 Univariate Foundation

As described in Sect. 1, we first build on the univariate classification techniques introduced by Co-eye to create a new univariate classifier as a foundation for our multivariate extensions. We adapt the learning process of Co-eye, but introduce a new pair selection method and propose three replacement voting mechanisms.

3.1 Pair Selection

Co-eye adopts a meticulous process for selecting lenses, involving two grid searches over the $\alpha - w$ parameter space for SAX and SFA, respectively. To construct an effective ensemble, each $<s, \alpha, w>$ triplet undergoes cross-validation, and pairs within a 1% margin of the highest cross-validation accuracy are chosen. However, performing an exhaustive search and cross-validation for every $<\alpha, w>$ pair can be computationally demanding, as highlighted by Abdallah and Gaber [1]. To address this bottleneck, we adopt a different approach inspired by the work of Bergstra and Bengio [7]. They suggest that random searches can yield comparable performance to grid searches for hyperparameter selection. Therefore, we incorporate random selection in our methodology.

In Co-eye, the number of pairs is not predetermined. When generating pairs randomly, it is essential to preselect the number of SAX and SFA pairs. To ensure a balanced perspective of the time series and avoid voting bias, we opt for an equal number of SAX and SFA pairs. The selection of pairs is proportional to the length of the time series, with $\lfloor p*l \rfloor$ pairs independently chosen for SAX and SFA. Here, $0 < p \leq 1$ represents the proportion of pairs, and l denotes the length of the time series. To determine the parameter space for random selection, we draw pairs uniformly from the $\alpha - w$ space defined by Abdallah and Gaber [1]. We evaluate four different values of p, namely 0.05, 0.1, 0.15, and 0.2, denoted as R5%, R10%, R15%, and R20%, respectively. These values enable us to explore the impact of different proportions of pairs on the ensemble construction process.

By adopting this approach, we aim to strike a balance between computational efficiency and lens selection effectiveness, ensuring that Co-eye can efficiently construct an ensemble of lenses while capturing diverse perspectives of the data.

3.2   Voting

To enhance accuracy and robustness, we propose three voting methods to replace Co-eye's existing dynamic voting approach. Let's consider Co-eye applied to a dataset with n classes $c_1, \ldots, c_n$ and m samples. Each base Random Forest classifier generates an $m \times n$ matrix, denoted as:

$$M_i = \begin{matrix} \text{Sample 1} \\ \vdots \\ \text{Sample } m \end{matrix} \begin{pmatrix} \overset{c_1}{P(c = c_1)} & \cdots & \overset{c_n}{P(c = c_n)} \\ \vdots & \ddots & \vdots \\ P(c = c_1) & \cdots & P(c = c_n) \end{pmatrix}. \tag{1}$$

Therefore, Co-eye produces a set of matrices, denoted as $S_M = M_1, \ldots, M_k$, where k represents the number of classifiers in the ensemble. Voting can be seen as a function on S_M, resulting in a vector of class labels for the m samples. We introduce three new voting methods based on the sum rule (SR) scheme outlined in Algorithm 1, employing different weight generation functions.

Algorithm 1. Sum Rule Scheme

1: **procedure** SUMRULE(S_M)
2:     $w \leftarrow$ getWeights()
3:     weightedMats $\leftarrow w * S_M$ ▷ Element-wise multiplication.
4:     sum $\leftarrow \sum_k$ weightedMats   ▷ Element-wise addition.
5:     **for** row in sum **do**
6:         label $\leftarrow$ max(row)
7:     **end for**
8:     **return** labels
9: **end procedure**

The first voting method is the simplest, employing uniform weights of one across the ensemble. Although efficient, we hypothesize that a more sophisticated weighting scheme could yield better results. Intuitively, matrices with higher confidence in their predictions should carry more weight. Thus, matrices with greater row-wise maximum confidences can be considered to be more confident. For a matrix $M_i \in S_M$ with m rows, the set of row-wise maxima can be defined as $R_i^{max} = \{\mathrm{row}max(j) \mid \forall j \in [m]\}$, where $\mathrm{row}max(j)$ represents the maximum value of row j in matrix M_i, and $[m] = 1, \ldots, m$. Let $\overline{R_i^{max}}$ denote the mean of the row-wise maxima. Our second voting scheme then assigns weights as $w = [\overline{R_1^{max}}, \ldots, \overline{R_k^{max}}]$.

Instead of using S_M directly for weight generation, Large et al. [15] demonstrated the effectiveness of weights determined through cross-validation. Hence, our third proposed voting method is as follows: A Random Forest is built for each $< s, \alpha, w >$ triplet, and accuracy is calculated using 5-fold cross-validation, a value supported by Burman [8]. The cross-validation accuracies are then used as weights for their respective matrices. Note that this method is significantly more computationally expensive than the other two approaches. However, unlike Co-eye's pair selection process, cross-validation is applied only to selected triplets rather than the entire $\alpha - w$ parameter space, making it computationally viable.

We refer to the three voting methods as SR Uniform, SR Mean-Max, and SR Validation, respectively.

4   Developing RED CoMETS

We anticipate that extending the multi-resolution perspectives of Co-eye, which is effective for univariate time series classification using the time and frequency domains, will be equally successful for multivariate datasets. In the literature, both forests [23] and symbolic representations [5] have achieved favourable results in this regard. To enable univariate classifiers to handle multivariate time series, we present two approaches. When combined with the univariate foundation established from Co-eye in Sect. 3, these approaches form RED CoMETS (Random Enhanced Co-eye for Multivariate Time Series).

4.1   Concatenating Approach

One intuitive approach to address multivariate time series classification is to reduce it to the more extensively studied univariate case. This can be achieved by sequentially concatenating the dimensions of a multivariate dataset. For a multivariate time series with a length of n and d dimensions, this method generates a univariate time series of length nd. Algorithm 2 demonstrates the application of this method to our univariate foundation. When utilizing the random pair selection technique described in Sect. 3.1, the number of lenses is proportional to the length of the time series. However, for computational efficiency, it was decided that if random pair selection is used, the number of lenses will be determined based on the length of the time series before concatenation, i.e., proportional to n rather than nd.

Algorithm 2. Concatenating Approach

1: **procedure** CONCATENATINGAPPROACH(TS)   ▷ TS is a multivariate dataset
2:     **for** dimension ∈ TS **do**
3:         append(concatTS, dimension)
4:     **end for**
5:     **return** UnivariateFoundation(concatTS)
6: **end procedure**

4.2   Ensembling Approach

Another approach to handling multivariate datasets is to construct an ensemble over the dimensions. This method, recommended by Ruiz et al. [20], involves building a univariate classifier for each dimension and combining their predictions for the overall classification.

Since our univariate foundation is an ensemble classifier, this leads to an ensemble of ensembles. Consequently, there are two sub-approaches depending on how the ensemble results are combined. Algorithms 3 and 4 outline these sub-approaches. Approach 1 combines the set of matrices, S_M, produced by each base classifier into a single superset $S_{all} = S_{M1} \cup S_{M2} \cup \ldots S_{Md}$, where S_{Mi} represents the set of matrices returned for the ith dimension. Voting is then applied as usual to S_{all}. Approach 2 performs voting in two stages. For each dimension, S_{Mi} is fused into a single matrix, F_i, using one of the sum rule methods outlined in Sect. 3.2. For the ith dimension, $F_i = \sum_k \boldsymbol{w} S_{Mi}$, where $\boldsymbol{w}$ is a vector of weights. Subsequently, a second round of voting is applied to the set of fused matrices across all dimensions, denoted as $S_F = \{F_i \mid \forall i \in [d]\}$, where $[d] = 1, \ldots, d$, resulting in the final classification. Different voting methods can be employed for the fusion and final classification stages.

Algorithm 3. Ensembling Approach 1

1: **procedure** ENSEMBLINGAPPROACH1(TS)   ▷ TS is a multivariate dataset
2:     **for** dimension ∈ TS **do**
3:         $S_M \leftarrow$ UnivariateFoundation(dimension)
4:         append(S_{all}, S_M)
5:     **end for**
6:     **return** vote(S_{all})
7: **end procedure**

4.3   RED CoMETS

The univariate foundation described in Sect. 3, which builds upon the innovative time series classification approach introduced by Co-eye [1], incorporates a new random pair selection process and three new voting methods. By combining the two proposed multivariate extensions from Sects. 4.1 and 4.2 with our univariate foundation, we establish a novel multivariate classifier (RED CoMETS).

Algorithm 4. Ensembling Approach 2

```
1: procedure ENSEMBLINGAPPROACH2(TS)              ▷ TS is a multivariate dataset
2:     for dimension ∈ TS do
3:         S_M ← UnivariateFoundation(dimension)
4:         F_i ← ∑_k w * S_M                        ▷ Element-wise operations
5:         append(S_F, F_i)
6:     end for
7:     return vote(S_F)
8: end procedure
```

5   Experiments and Evaluation

We evaluate our univariate foundation and RED CoMETS on univariate and multivariate datasets respectively from the UCR archive. We demonstrate that our univariate foundation is more accurate and approximately 40 times faster than Co-eye. RED CoMETS is shown to achieve accuracies comparable to the state-of-the-art classifiers outlined in Sect. 2. Our code and full results are available on GitHub[1].

5.1   Experimental Design

All of our experiments were conducted with the 111 datasets from the UCR archive [3] used by Bagnall et al. [2] and Ruiz et al. [20] in their reviews, consisting of 85 univariate and 26 multivariate datasets. This allows for comparison to the results recorded by Bagnall et al. [2] and Ruiz et al. [20] in their reviews of state-of-the-art classifiers. For consistency and to allow direct comparison, our results show the average over 30 trials on each data using 30 stratified resamples. Each resample is seeded by its sample number, such that each classifier is evaluated on identical samples and results are reproducible. Note that both SAX and SFA z-normalise the time series as their initial step. For the multivariate datasets, this means that the concatenating approach normalises the joint time series while the ensembling approach normalises each dimension independently.

We produce results for Co-eye, our univariate foundation, and RED CoMETS. Results for DTW and univariate ROCKET were taken from Bagnall et al. [2] and Dempster et al. [9] respectively. The results for DTW_D, MrSEQL, InceptionTime, and multivariate ROCKET were taken from Ruiz et al. [20]. The results for HIVE COTE-2.0 were taken from the author's website [3]. The default accuracy for predicting the majority class is also included and is taken from Bagnall et al. [2] and Ruiz et al. [20] for the univariate and multivariate datasets respectively. The voting methods proposed in Sect. 3.2 were evaluated using the R5% pair selection described in Sect. 3.1 to minimise computation time.

To compare multiple classifiers over multiple datasets, critical difference (CD) diagrams are used [10]. Current literature [6] suggests abandoning the post hoc

---

[1] https://github.com/zy18811/RED-CoMETS.

test originally suggested by Demšar [10], instead forming cliques using pairwise tests, with the Holm correction being made in the case of multiple testing. The classifiers are first ranked using the Friedman test, then grouped into cliques using pairwise Wilcoxon signed rank tests with the Holm adjustment [2,20]. Cliques represent groups of classifiers between which there is no statistically significant pairwise difference. A Python implementation produced by Fawaz et al. [11] was used to create the CD diagrams presented in this paper.

5.2 Univariate Foundation

Pair Selection. The four random pair selection methods outlined in Sect. 3.1 were evaluated on the 85 univariate datasets from the UCR archive in order to evaluate their effectiveness against Co-eye. Default accuracy, DTW, and univariate ROCKET are included as benchmarks. Figure 1 shows the test accuracy critical difference (CD) diagram for the pair selection methods. It can be seen that there are two distinct cliques containing R10%, R15%, and R20% and Co-eye and R5% respectively, with DTW found in both. Both cliques outperformed default accuracy with statistical significance. ROCKET significantly outperformed all others. R10%, R15%, and R20% all performed worse in terms of accuracy than Co-eye, and are removed from contention. There is no statistically significant pairwise difference in test accuracy between R5% and Co-eye.

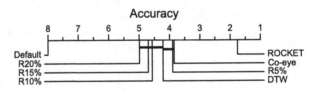

Fig. 1. Test accuracy critical difference diagram for random pair selection methods against Co-eye averaged over 30 resamples for each of the 85 univariate UCR datasets. Default accuracy, DTW, and ROCKET are included as benchmarks.

Figure 2 shows a pairwise comparison of mean train and test time between Co-eye and R5% on the 85 univariate UCR datasets. It can be seen that R5% is significantly faster than Co-eye in all cases, averaging approximately 40 times faster over the 85 datasets. As such, R5% is a pronounced improvement over Co-eye: 40 times faster with no statistically significant difference in test accuracy. For R5%, Kendall's τ coefficient was calculated between characteristics of each dataset and the associated total train and test time, with values of 0.41, 0.42, 0.33, and 0.78 for train size, test size, number of classes, and series length respectively. As one would expect, there is a positive correlation for all values, with series length as the most significant determinant of train and test time.

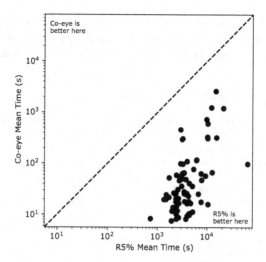

Fig. 2. Pairwise comparison of total mean train and test time between Co-eye and R5% averaged over 30 stratified resamples of the 85 univariate UCR datasets.

Voting. Section 3.2 proposed three voting methods, aiming to outperform the dynamic voting method used by Co-eye in terms of test accuracy. As done above for pair selection, the voting methods were evaluated on the 85 univariate datasets from the UCR archive with default accuracy, DTW, and univariate ROCKET as benchmarks. Figure 3 shows the test accuracy CD diagram for the voting methods. It can be seen that the three proposed voting methods all performed better than Co-eye's dynamic voting method with statistical significance. The three voting methods are cliqued, indicating no significant pairwise difference between them. As such, all three voting methods are taken forward for evaluation as part of RED CoMETS.

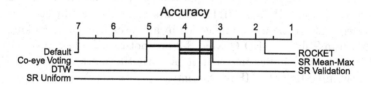

Fig. 3. Test accuracy critical difference diagram for proposed voting methods against Co-eye averaged over 30 resamples for each of the 85 univariate UCR datasets. Default accuracy, DTW, and ROCKET are included as benchmarks.

5.3   RED CoMETS

There are nine variants of RED CoMETS, which result from different combinations of a voting method and the multivariate extension. These variants are referred to by the names presented in Table 1. It is worth noting that the validation voting method is not utilised with the ensembling dimensions multivariate extension due to initial experiments demonstrating computational infeasibility.

Table 1. RED CoMETS variants.

Name	Approach	Sub-Approach	Voting Method 1	Voting Method 2
RED CoMETS-1	Concatenating	n/a	Uniform	n/a
RED CoMETS-2	Concatenating	n/a	Mean-Max	n/a
RED CoMETS-3	Concatenating	n/a	Validation	n/a
RED CoMETS-4	Ensembling	1	Uniform	n/a
RED CoMETS-5	Ensembling	1	Mean-Max	n/a
RED CoMETS-6	Ensembling	2	Uniform	Uniform
RED CoMETS-7	Ensembling	2	Uniform	Mean-Max
RED CoMETS-8	Ensembling	2	Mean-Max	Mean-Max
RED CoMETS-9	Ensembling	2	Mean-Max	Uniform

We evaluate the RED CoMETS variants against each other and the multivariate benchmarks discussed in Sect. 2 (DTW$_D$, MrSEQL, InceptionTime, ROCKET, and HIVE-COTE 2.0). When evaluated by Ruiz et al. [20], InceptionTime and MrSEQL were unable to complete all 26 datasets, with InceptionTime failing on 'EigenWorms' due to memory errors and MrSEQL failing to complete 'FaceDetection' and 'PhonemeSpectra' within the set time constraints. Likewise, all variants of RED CoMETS were unable to complete 'Eigenworms'. As such, results for these datasets will not be used in our comparison, leaving 23 datasets for evaluation. Based on the results shown in Sect. 5.2, all variants of RED CoMETS are evaluated using the R5% pair selection method. As Sect. 5.2 demonstrated no statistically significant difference between the three proposed voting methods, all nine RED CoMETS variants shown in Table 1 are evaluated.

We first analyse the nine variants of RED CoMETS. It can be seen in Fig. 4 that there is no statistically significant pairwise difference in test accuracy between the nine RED CoMETS variants, with the default accuracy being outperformed with statistical significance in all cases. However, looking at the results shown in Table 2, RED CoMETS-3 has both the highest mean accuracy and number of wins, indicating that it is both the most accurate and most reliable of the nine RED CoMETS variants.

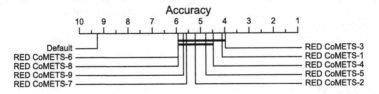

Fig. 4. Test accuracy critical difference diagram for RED CoMETS variants averaged over the 23 UCR datasets.

Table 2. Summary of RED CoMETS results showing mean accuracy across 30 resamples for each variant and multivariate dataset. The mean and number of wins are also shown. The greatest values on each row are shown in underlined bold.

Dataset	RED CoMETS-$<$N$>$ (%)								
	1	2	3	4	5	6	7	8	9
AWR	**97.73**	97.60	**97.73**	96.22	96.02	95.20	95.16	94.91	94.18
AF	30.00	29.11	29.78	28.89	28.89	**32.00**	**32.00**	31.33	31.33
BM	**98.17**	98.00	**98.17**	79.58	79.42	81.67	81.92	81.75	82.08
CR	97.08	**97.13**	**97.13**	92.59	92.73	89.31	89.31	89.58	89.68
DDG	59.60	54.47	**62.27**	20.53	19.13	20.47	20.53	19.60	19.40
EP	85.14	83.60	**85.29**	60.31	53.26	58.36	57.83	51.79	50.46
ER	**93.54**	92.38	93.51	91.23	91.19	85.68	85.63	85.88	85.79
EC	27.55	27.60	27.59	33.13	**33.36**	32.60	32.56	32.69	32.53
FM	51.93	50.30	51.60	52.20	**52.53**	52.10	52.10	52.40	52.43
HMD	54.20	54.57	**55.30**	44.36	44.68	42.40	42.40	42.81	42.99
HW	**32.73**	31.67	32.60	28.97	29.05	27.33	27.32	27.64	27.68
HB	66.44	65.38	66.50	71.02	70.98	71.02	**71.12**	70.98	71.04
LIB	**78.33**	75.93	**78.33**	73.33	72.89	58.85	58.85	57.85	57.85
LSST	15.96	05.76	**50.93**	08.90	08.07	05.35	05.21	04.03	03.71
MI	51.00	51.20	50.97	51.33	51.50	51.37	51.40	**51.57**	51.53
NATO	82.04	81.81	**82.30**	73.54	73.78	72.41	72.83	72.15	72.72
PEMS	78.30	77.59	78.30	90.98	91.89	92.08	92.49	93.14	**93.66**
PD	88.00	82.16	**88.17**	76.32	76.24	63.64	63.64	64.21	64.21
RS	**83.05**	72.74	82.87	78.60	78.82	75.46	75.70	75.61	75.77
SRS1	85.46	85.51	85.46	86.47	**86.50**	86.35	86.36	86.38	86.41
SRS2	51.89	52.02	52.00	**52.39**	52.35	52.37	52.37	52.35	52.33
SWJ	38.89	38.44	38.44	43.33	43.33	44.67	**44.89**	44.22	44.44
UW	**88.61**	88.53	88.60	84.20	84.14	81.09	80.99	80.95	80.83
Mean	66.77	64.94	**68.43**	61.67	61.34	59.64	59.68	59.30	59.26
Wins	5.5	0.5	**8**	1	3	0.5	2.5	1	1

Having identified RED CoMETS-3 as the most effective variant, we now evaluate it against the state-of-the-art methods identified in Sect. 2. It can be seen from Fig. 5 that, excluding default accuracy, RED CoMETS-3 has the lowest ranking in terms of test accuracy. However, the cliques indicate that there is no statistically significant difference in accuracy between RED CoMETS-3 and DTW$_D$, MrSEQL, and InceptionTime, demonstrating that RED CoMETS-3 is competitive with state-of-the-art multivariate classifiers.

We now further analyse the performance of RED CoMETS-3 in relation to the benchmarks, with Table 3 showing the differences in test accuracy. RED

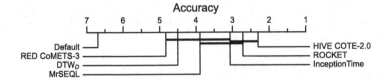

Fig. 5. Test accuracy critical difference diagram for RED CoMETS-3 against the state-of-the-art classifiers averaged over the 23 UCR datasets

CoMETS-3 was able to beat all of the benchmarks on at least four of the datasets. Both the mean and median difference in accuracy between RED CoMETS-3 and DTW_D, MrSEQL, and InceptionTime is less than 5%, concurring with Fig. 5. Looking at the maxima and minima, it can be seen that RED CoMETS-3 greatly outperforms the benchmarks on some datasets and vice versa. In fact, RED CoMETS-3 consistently outperforms the state-of-the-art benchmarks on a small number of datasets, beating all of the benchmarks on HMD, four on AF and DDG, and three on ER, SRS1, and SRS2. In other words, just six datasets account for 22 out of the 28 wins shown in Table 3. Five of these six datasets are categorised as EEG, ECG, or spectrographic. Hence, it is apparent that RED CoMETS attains its best performance on datasets with minimal phase shifting (this was also found to be the case for Co-eye by Abdallah and Gaber [1]).

Table 3. Summary of the test accuracy differences between RED CoMETS-3 and the benchmarks for the multivariate UCR datasets. Negative is better for RED CoMETS-3.

Classifier	Mean (%)	Median (%)	Max (%)	Min (%)	STD (%)	Wins	Losses
DTW_D	0.68	1.69	28.60	−24.98	10.32	9	14
MrSEQL	4.39	3.93	65.60	−33.33	18.31	6	17
InceptionTime	3.64	2.63	64.51	−65.59	21.98	5	18
ROCKET	5.09	5.25	24.06	−16.13	8.66	4	19
HIVE COTE-2.0	7.50	5.33	51.50	−15.52	13.17	4	19

HIVE COTE-2.0 and ROCKET are considered the current best within the state-of-the-art as discussed in Sect. 2. Figure 5 corroborates this, with them being ranked first and second respectively. We now compare RED CoMETS-3 against them in more detail, seeking to better understand the disparities shown in Table 3. It can be seen from Table 4 that HIVE-COTE 2.0 retains its place as the current best classifier in terms of test accuracy with both the greatest mean accuracy and number of wins. However, RED CoMETS-3 is still able to hold its own against ROCKET and HIVE-COTE 2.0, beating both of them on four of the datasets. Furthermore, the result obtained for the HMD dataset, 55.30%, is greater than any reported in the literature [3], representing a notable improvement to the state-of-the-art.

Table 4. Results for ROCKET, HIVE-COTE 2.0, and RED CoMETS-3 showing mean test accuracy across 30 resamples of each multivariate dataset. The mean and number of wins are also shown. The greatest values on each row are shown in underlined bold.

Dataset	ROCKET (%)	HIVE COTE-2.0 (%)	RED CoMETS-3 (%)
AWR	99.56	**99.58**	97.73
AF	24.89	28.22	**29.78**
BM	**99.00**	98.92	98.17
CR	**100.00**	99.95	97.13
DDG	46.13	49.87	**62.27**
EP	99.08	**99.83**	85.29
ER	98.05	**98.51**	93.51
EC	44.68	**79.09**	27.59
FM	**55.27**	55.23	51.60
HMD	44.59	39.77	**55.30**
HW	**56.67**	56.34	32.60
HB	71.76	**72.86**	66.50
LIB	90.61	**92.69**	78.33
LSST	63.15	**63.70**	50.93
MI	53.13	**53.17**	50.97
NATO	88.54	**89.20**	82.30
PEMS	**99.56**	**99.56**	88.17
PD	85.63	**99.81**	78.30
RS	92.79	**93.05**	82.87
SRS1	86.55	**87.87**	85.46
SRS2	51.35	50.46	**52.00**
SWJ	**45.56**	43.78	38.44
UW	94.43	**94.89**	88.60
Mean	73.52	**75.93**	68.43
Wins	5.5	**13.5**	4

6   Conclusion

RED CoMETS is a novel ensemble classifier for multivariate time series that builds on the success of Co-eye. In order to build a univariate foundation for our classifier, we adapted Co-eye's use of multiple symbolic representations to gain a multi-resolution perspective of both the time and frequency domains. However, we introduced a random pair selection process in order to overcome the bottleneck in Co-eye [1]. We also proposed and evaluated three new voting methods. Our adaption of Co-eye was extremely successful, achieving an approximately 40 times increase in speed and small but statistically significant gains in accuracy in comparison to Co-eye.

Two multivariate extensions were then applied to our univariate classifier. The different possible combinations of the multivariate extensions and voting methods resulted in the nine variants of RED CoMETS shown in Table 1. These were evaluated against state-of-the-art classifiers on 23 multivariate datasets from the UCR archive [3], following the methodology of Ruiz et al. [20].

RED CoMETS-3 was identified as the clear best out of the nine variants in both accuracy and reliability and was demonstrated to have no statistically significant pairwise difference in accuracy to several of the state-of-the-art benchmarks. RED CoMETS-3 was able to outperform both ROCKET and HIVE COTE-2.0, the current best-in-class, on four of the 23 datasets and achieved an accuracy greater than reported by any classifier in the literature on the 'HandMovementDirection' dataset. It was noted that RED CoMETS attains its best performance on datasets with no significant phase shifting.

There is room to further improve RED CoMETS-3 in both the R5% pair selection and SR Validation voting method. For R5%, a subset of the datasets could be used to learn the optimal bounds for the $\alpha - w$ parameter space, similar to the methodology used by Dempster et al. [9] when learning the kernel parameter space for ROCKET. SR Validation could be improved by emulating the scheme proposed by Large et al. [15] in which the weights are raised to a power in order to amplify differences between base classifiers.

References

1. Abdallah, Z.S., Gaber, M.M.: Co-eye: a multi-resolution ensemble classifier for symbolically approximated time series. Mach. Learn. **109**(11), 2029–2061 (2020). https://doi.org/10.1007/s10994-020-05887-3
2. Bagnall, A., Lines, J., Bostrom, A., Large, J., Keogh, E.: The great time series classification bake off: a review and experimental evaluation of recent algorithmic advances. Data Min. Knowl. Discov. **31**(3), 606–660 (2017). https://doi.org/10.1007/s10618-016-0483-9
3. Bagnall, A., Keogh, E., Lines, J., Bostrom, A., Large, J., Middlehurst, M.: UEA & UCR Time Series Classification Repository. www.timeseriesclassification.com
4. Bai, S., Kolter, J.Z., Koltun, V.: An empirical evaluation of generic convolutional and recurrent networks for sequence modeling. arXiv preprint arXiv:1803.01271 (2018)
5. Baydogan, M., Runger, G.: Learning a symbolic representation for multivariate time series classification. Data Min. Knowl. Discov. **29**, 1–23 (2014). https://doi.org/10.1007/s10618-014-0349-y
6. Benavoli, A., Corani, G., Mangili, F.: Should we really use post-hoc tests based on mean-ranks? J. Mach. Learn. Res. **17**(5), 1–10 (2016). http://jmlr.org/papers/v17/benavoli16a.html
7. Bergstra, J., Bengio, Y.: Random search for hyper-parameter optimization. J. Mach. Learn. Res. (2012)
8. Burman, P.: A comparative study of ordinary cross-validation, v-fold cross-validation and the repeated learning-testing methods. Biometrika **76**(3), 503 (1989). https://doi.org/10.2307/2336116

9. Dempster, A., Petitjean, F., Webb, G.I.: ROCKET: exceptionally fast and accurate time series classification using random convolutional kernels. Data Min. Knowl. Discov. **34**(5), 1454–1495 (2020). https://doi.org/10.1007/s10618-020-00701-z

10. Demšar, J.: Statistical comparisons of classifiers over multiple data sets. J. Mach. Learn. Res. **7**(1), 1–30 (2006). http://jmlr.org/papers/v7/demsar06a.html

11. Ismail Fawaz, H., Forestier, G., Weber, J., Idoumghar, L., Muller, P.A.: Deep learning for time series classification: a review. Data Min. Knowl. Discov. **33**(4), 917–963 (2019). https://doi.org/10.1007/s10618-019-00619-1

12. Ismail Fawaz, H., et al.: InceptionTime: finding AlexNet for time series classification. Data Min. Knowl. Discov. **34**(6), 1936–1962 (2020). https://doi.org/10.1007/s10618-020-00710-y

13. Karim, F., Majumdar, S., Darabi, H., Harford, S.: Multivariate LSTM-FCNs for time series classification. Neural Netw. **116**, 237–245 (2019)

14. Keogh, E.J., Pazzani, M.J.: Scaling up dynamic time warping for datamining applications. In: Proceedings of the sixth ACM SIGKDD International Conference on Knowledge Discovery and Data Mining - KDD '00, pp. 285–289. ACM Press, New York (2000). https://doi.org/10.1145/347090.347153

15. Large, J., Lines, J., Bagnall, A.: A probabilistic classifier ensemble weighting scheme based on cross-validated accuracy estimates. Data Min. Knowl. Discov. **33**(6), 1674–1709 (2019). https://doi.org/10.1007/s10618-019-00638-y

16. Le Nguyen, T., Gsponer, S., Ilie, I., O'Reilly, M., Ifrim, G.: Interpretable time series classification using linear models and multi-resolution multi-domain symbolic representations. Data Min. Knowl. Discov. **33**(4), 1183–1222 (2019). https://doi.org/10.1007/s10618-019-00633-3

17. Lin, J., Keogh, E., Wei, L., Lonardi, S.: Experiencing SAX: a novel symbolic representation of time series. Data Min. Knowl. Discov. **15**(2), 107–144 (2007). https://doi.org/10.1007/s10618-007-0064-z

18. Lines, J., Taylor, S., Bagnall, A.: Hive-cote: the hierarchical vote collective of transformation-based ensembles for time series classification. In: 2016 IEEE 16th International Conference on Data Mining (ICDM), pp. 1041–1046 (2016). https://doi.org/10.1109/ICDM.2016.0133

19. Middlehurst, M., Large, J., Flynn, M., Lines, J., Bostrom, A., Bagnall, A.: Hive-cote 2.0: a new meta ensemble for time series classification. Mach. Learn. **110**(11), 3211–3243 (2021). https://doi.org/10.1007/s10994-021-06057-9

20. Ruiz, A.P., Flynn, M., Large, J., Middlehurst, M., Bagnall, A.: The great multivariate time series classification bake off: a review and experimental evaluation of recent algorithmic advances. Data Min. Knowl. Discov. **35**(2), 401–449 (2021). https://doi.org/10.1007/s10618-020-00727-3

21. Schäfer, P., Högqvist, M.: SFA: A symbolic Fourier approximation and index for similarity search in high dimensional datasets. In: Proceedings of the 15th International Conference on Extending Database Technology - EDBT '12, p. 516. ACM Press, New York, USA (2012). https://doi.org/10.1145/2247596.2247656

22. Ho, T.K.: Random decision forests. In: Proceedings of 3rd International Conference on Document Analysis and Recognition, pp. 278–282. IEEE Computer Society Press (1995). https://doi.org/10.1109/ICDAR.1995.598994

23. Tuncel, K., Baydogan, M.: Autoregressive forests for multivariate time series modeling. Pattern Recogn. **73** (2017). https://doi.org/10.1016/j.patcog.2017.08.016

24. Wang, Z., Yan, W., Oates, T.: Time series classification from scratch with deep neural networks: a strong baseline. In: 2017 International Joint Conference on Neural Networks (IJCNN), pp. 1578–1585. IEEE (2017)

Deep Long Term Prediction for Semantic Segmentation in Autonomous Driving

Bidya Dash[1,2(✉)], Shreyas Bilagi[1], Jasmin Breitenstein[2], Volker Schomerus[1], Thorsten Bagdonat[1], and Tim Fingscheidt[2]

[1] Group Innovation, Volkswagen AG, 38440 Wolfsburg, Germany
{bidya.binayam.dash,shreyas.basavaraj.bilagi,volker.patricio.schomerus,
thorsten.bagdonat}@volkswagen.de
[2] Institute for Communications Technology, Technische Universität Braunschweig,
Schleinitzstraße 22, 38106 Braunschweig, Germany
{j.breitenstein,t.fingscheidt}@tu-bs.de

Abstract. Temporal prediction is an important function in autonomous driving (AD) systems as it forecasts how the environment will change and transform in the next few seconds. Humans have an inherited prediction capability that extrapolates a present scenario to the future. In this paper, we present a novel approach to look further into the future using a standard semantic segmentation representation and time series networks of varying architectures. An important property of our approach is its flexibility to predict an arbitrary time horizon into the future. We perform prediction in the semantic segmentation domain where inputs are semantic segmentation masks. We present extensive results and discussion on different data dimensionalities that can prove beneficial for prediction on longer time horizons (up to 2 s). We also show results of our approach on two widely employed datasets in AD research, i.e., Cityscapes and BDD100K. We report two types of mIoUs as we have investigated with self generated ground truth labels (mIoU^{seg}) for both of our dataset and actual ground truth labels (mIoU^{gt}) for a specific split of the Cityscapes dataset. Our method achieves 57.12% and 83.95% mIoU^{seg}, respectively, on the validation split of BDD100K and Cityscapes, for short-term time horizon predictions (up to 0.2 s and 0.06 s), outperforming the current state of the art on Cityscapes by 13.71% absolute. For long-term predictions (up to 2 s and 0.6 s), we achieve 37.96% and 63.65% mIoU^{seg}, respectively, for BDD100K and Cityscapes. Specifically on the validation split of Cityscapes with perfect ground truth annotations, we achieve 67.55% and 63.60% mIoU^{gt}, outperforming current state of the art by 1.45% absolute and 4.2% absolute with time horizon predictions up to 0.06 s and 0.18 s, respectively.

Keywords: Cityscapes · BDD100K · forecasting · prediction · long term prediction · semantic segmentation

© The Author(s), under exclusive license to Springer Nature Switzerland AG 2023
G. Ifrim et al. (Eds.): AALTD 2023, LNAI 14343, pp. 92–112, 2023.
https://doi.org/10.1007/978-3-031-49896-1_7

1   Introduction

Temporal prediction and forecasting has been an important task in intelligent systems and robotic decision making [2, 5]. Simple tasks like object detection and tracking have been quite well investigated with deterministic approaches such as the Kalman filter [9] and dense optical flow techniques [14]. Non-deterministic learning based approaches [1, 19, 20, 24] have proved to be better and more adapted to these tasks in the long run.

Recent advancements using image-based prediction [4, 10] and reconstruction have captured attention as an integral part in intelligent autonomous driving (AD) systems. Image-based prediction means forecasting the RGB pixels of a frame in a video sequence to their anticipated future positions in a future video frame in the pixel space. However, there are certain limitations to image-based prediction as it becomes more of a reconstruction task [4, 16] (where positions of objects are regenerated) than prediction of actual motion when using deep neural representation models. Also, the predicted RGB pixel domain provides much irrelevant information for decisions in AD scenarios, whereas, the trajectory planner in an AD system can benefit from more information than just RGB pixels for determining possible obstacles and freespace.

Here, semantic segmentation provides a relevant representation as semantically segmented maps provide concise but relevant information not only about the possible obstacles and freespace; but also an extensive distribution of semantically discrete objects with respect to their pixel occupancy in a video frame. As a result, the trajectory planner in an AD system can process more relevant information for efficient decision making. Hence, prediction of semantically segmented frames into the future proves to be much more of a sensible task than temporal prediction of RGB frames. An interesting investigation in the field of prediction of semantic segmentation masks is estimating the model's performance for longer time horizons, because it is essential for AD systems to accommodate the length that these prediction models can forecast without significant deprecation in performance.

We can summarize our main contribution as follows. First, we propose an efficient time series network with an auto regressive gradient accumulation technique for forecasting of semantic segmentation maps. The time horizon prediction during inference is independent of the training time horizon range unlike Nabavi et al. [18] where they input 4 frames as a group concurrently. Secondly, we investigate using the semantic segmentation masks only as input to our prediction method while determining which semantic segmentation representation provides the most promising results. Thirdly, we show that our prediction method outperforms the current state of the art on the Cityscapes dataset [3], and additionally we are the first to report our results on BDD100K [26] which contains scenes from all types of weather conditions and time of the day. The remainder of this work is structured as follows: We present related works in Sect. 2, followed by explaining the approaches in Sect. 3. Section 4 introduces the experimental setup including architectural details, dataset, metrics followed by implementation details. Section 5 reports the experimental results along with detailed discussion before concluding the paper in Sect. 6. We also provide a supplementary material (A) with detailed analysis of qualitative results along with a special investigation of the proposed method's behavior.

2   Related Work

Video Prediction: By introducing a 3D optical flow representation across spatial and temporal dimensions along with trilinear interpolation, Liu et al. [11] proposed an unsupervised model to predict frames for video predictions. PredNet [12] employs predictive coding with local predictions to learn future frames and also propagating the deviations from subsequent layers in an unsupervised fashion. Similarly, Walker et al. [23] propose a PixelCNN approach in addition to discretizing the hierarchy of spatiotemporal self-attention latent space in video data using VQ-VAE. Mathieu at al. [17] propose a multi-scale architecture and an adversarial training strategy along with a novel image gradient divergence loss function to enhance frame predictions over longer time horizons. Using adversarial training, retrospective cycle GANs [10] have proved to be useful for predicting video frames while enforcing the consistency of bi-directional time horizons. Guen at al. [6] propose a method where they leverage the physical knowledge described by partial differential equations dynamics to disentangle unknown complementary information in video sequences. Our work follows along the domain of prediction of frames in a video sequence using a time series network. However, in this work, we solely focus on prediction in the semantic segmentation domain for an enriched information processing that can be useful for planning future scenarios in AD systems.

Prediction in Semantic Segmentation: Luc et al. [13] came up with an autoregressive multi scale region proposal CNN based on Mathieu et al.'s [17] backbone architecture using a generative adversarial loss combined with an image gradient difference loss to predict future scenes that are semantically segmented which proves to be a reconstruction technique rather than an actual prediction. In this method, they use varying combinations of RGB frames and semantic segmentation maps together interchangeably as input rendering the input representation highly complex whereas, we investigate using the semantic segmentation masks only as input to our prediction method while determining which semantic segmentation representation provides the most promising results. Nabavi et al. [18] use a PSPNet backbone [28] and bi-directional convolutional LSTMs [22] to predict latent space embeddings in the residual layers. With increasing time horizon predictions (i.e., 1 s...2 s) into the future, these models reveal significant deviations to the ground truth. This can be attributed to the fact that the time series network used by Nabavi et al. [18] accumulates information only for a limited time span for highly dense class distributions that can be safely labeled as background (i.e., road, buildings, sidewalk, vegetation) and completely overturns the underrepresented classes distributions (i.e., pedestrian, bicycle, traffic lights). Exploiting the mutual benefits of predicting pixel annotations and dense optical flow estimations, Jin et al. [8] attempt to simultaneously model future semantic segmentation masks along with optical flow representations which proves to be quite useful for different time horizons and input resolutions. While we build on Nabavi et al.'s work [18], we get rid of the dependence of input sequence length and introduce an autoregressive frame prediction technique during inference along with predicting for longer time horizons in the future. Additionally, we report our results on BDD100K [26] dataset which is more challenging for the task of prediction.

3   Method

3.1   Prediction of Semantic Segmentation Masks

In Fig 1, we can see the details of our training methodology. There are two separate integral steps. For the first step (left, in blue), we feed in the raw RGB frames $\overline{\mathbf{x}}_t \in [0,1]^{H \times W \times C}$ where $t \in \mathcal{T} = \{1, 2, ..., T\}$, with T being the the total number of frames in the input video and t denoting the temporal frame index of the video sequence. This is fed to a standard semantic segmentation network $\mathcal{F}^{\text{semseg}}$, i.e., PSANet [29]. In Fig. 1 (left, in blue), we can see the semantic segmentation network $\mathcal{F}^{\text{semseg}}(\mathbf{x}_t; \boldsymbol{\theta}^{\text{semseg}})$ whose output is $\overline{\mathbf{y}}_t = (y_{t,i,s}) \in [0,1]^{H \times W \times S}$ where $\boldsymbol{\theta}^{\text{semseg}}$ denotes the semantic segmentation

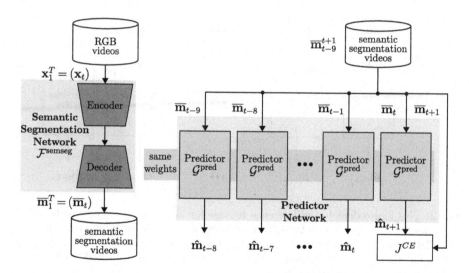

Fig. 1. The left side (in blue) depicts the step of generating pseudo ground truth semantic segmentation masks $\overline{\mathbf{m}}_1^T = \{\overline{\mathbf{m}}_1, \overline{\mathbf{m}}_2, ..., \overline{\mathbf{m}}_T\}$ from raw RGB videos as using a strong semantic segmentation network, i.e., PSANet. The right side depicts the prediction step, where a time series network receives a ten-frame mask sequence $\overline{\mathbf{m}}_{t-9}^t$ predicting $\hat{\mathbf{m}}_{t+1}$ from $\overline{\mathbf{m}}_t$ directly step by step in the semantic segmentation domain. The two steps are independent of each other and are performed one after the other with different loss representations. (Color figure online)

network's trainable parameters, $s \in \mathcal{S}$ represents the class in dataset with a total of s semantic classes and $i \in \mathcal{I} = \{1, 2, ..., H \cdot W\}$ represents the pixel indices for frames with height H and width W. The semantic segmentation network is entirely responsible for generating the semantic segmentation masks $\overline{\mathbf{m}}_t = (\overline{m}_{t,i})$ where $\overline{m}_{t,i} = \underset{s \in \mathcal{S}}{\operatorname{argmax}} \, \overline{y}_{t,i,s}$. We save these pseudo ground truth semantic segmentation masks $\overline{\mathbf{m}}_1^T$ to train our predictor network. In Fig. 1 (right, in yellow), we can see that $\overline{\mathbf{m}}_{t-9}^t = \{\overline{\mathbf{m}}_{t-9}, ..., \overline{\mathbf{m}}_{t-1}, \overline{\mathbf{m}}_t\}$ is the input sequence fed sequentially as $\overline{\mathbf{m}}_{t-9}$, $\overline{\mathbf{m}}_{t-8}$, ..., $\overline{\mathbf{m}}_t$ to the predictor network, $\mathcal{G}^{\mathrm{pred}}$ whose internal hidden states and cell states are $\mathbf{H}_t, \mathbf{C}_t$ at current time-step t. The predictor network is represented as $\mathcal{G}^{\mathrm{pred}}(\overline{\mathbf{m}}_t, \mathbf{H}_t, \mathbf{C}_t; \boldsymbol{\theta}^{\mathrm{pred}})$ whose output is $\hat{\mathbf{m}}_{t+1} = (\hat{m}_{t+1,i})$ where $\hat{m}_{t+1,i} = \underset{s \in \mathcal{S}}{\operatorname{argmax}} \, \hat{y}_{t+1,i,s}$ where $\hat{\mathbf{y}}_{t+1} \in [0, 1]^{H \times W \times S}$ denotes the normalized probabilistic output of the predictor network at timestep $t + 1$. Here, $\boldsymbol{\theta}^{\mathrm{pred}}$ denotes the predictor's trainable parameters.

The generated semantic segmentation masks from $\mathcal{F}^{\mathrm{semseg}}$ are fed as 10-frame long sequences $\overline{\mathbf{m}}_{t-9}^t = \{\overline{\mathbf{m}}_{t-9}, ..., \overline{\mathbf{m}}_{t-1}, \overline{\mathbf{m}}_t\}$ to our predictor one by one which update the intermediate hidden state representations. The loss representation $\mathcal{J}^{CE}$ (categorical cross entropy loss) is always calculated with the 10th frame prediction i.e., $\hat{\mathbf{m}}_{t+1}$ and corresponding pseudo ground truth $\overline{\mathbf{m}}_{t+1}$. Note that both training steps are performed independently of each other with different loss representations.

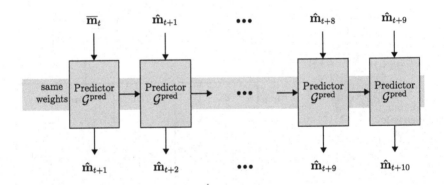

Fig. 2. This figure depicts the inference process for $\Delta t = 10$ time steps ahead using our approach. The predictor starts with the present time instant input $\overline{\mathbf{m}}_t$, generates a prediction $\hat{\mathbf{m}}_{t+1}$, uses this prediction as input to the next time step to produce $\hat{\mathbf{m}}_{t+2}$ and so on. Hence, to predict $\hat{\mathbf{m}}_{t+10}$, the model would use its own predictions $\hat{\mathbf{m}}_{t+1}$, $\hat{\mathbf{m}}_{t+2}$, ..., $\hat{\mathbf{m}}_{t+9}$ as input sequentially.

3.2   Inference Processing

We can see the inference step of our method in Fig. 2 which is at the core of our work. Hence, understanding the inference approach would give us a better idea of the proposed model's ability to look efficiently into the future. We incorporate the auto regressive approach to predict longer time horizons. The input sequence is 10 frames long represented as $\overline{\mathbf{m}}_{t-9}^{t}$ and predicts $\hat{\mathbf{m}}_{t+1}$. To predict for more than one time step ahead, this prediction $\hat{\mathbf{m}}_{t+1}$ is once again fed as input to the predictor to produce $\hat{\mathbf{m}}_{t+2}$ that is $\Delta t = 2$ time steps ahead. We choose an arbitrary length of 10 time steps to be predicted in the future and hence, this process is repeated until $\Delta t = 10$ time steps ahead.

Note that, our method only looks at the first 10 pseudo ground truth frames of a sequence ($\overline{\mathbf{m}}_{t-9}^{t}$) and can predict up to an arbitrary number of frames, Δt, into the future. This is specifically useful in AD applications where we can set the ego vehicle to warm up for a certain length of sequences and then predict into the future arbitrarily.

4 Experimental Setup

In this section, we introduce the settings for our experiments including a new architecture for defining the predictor $\mathcal{G}^{\text{pred}}$ in Subsect. 4.1. We investigate different arrangements of temporal blocks along with introducing the datasets used for our experiments and the most important metrics.

4.1 Predictor Architecture

For our predictor network $\mathcal{G}^{\text{pred}}$, we use convolutional LSTM [22] blocks along with a normalization layer to keep the training stable. We investigate three different arrangements of the convolutional LSTM blocks within $\mathcal{G}^{\text{pred}}$, which are shown in Fig. 3.

The first architecture, defined as PRED can be seen in Fig. 3(a) without the residual connections. PRED stacks up the convolutional LSTM blocks with a group normalization layer for normalizing the four intermediate activations: input gate, forget gate, cell gate and output gate. As described in Shi et al. [22], we follow the standard definition of a convolutional LSTM block which replaces the matrix-vector multiplications in the input-hidden and hidden-hidden mappings of a fully-connected LSTM [7] with convolutions, whereas keeping the general structure of the LSTM cell unchanged. The governing equations can be described as

$$
\begin{aligned}
\mathbf{I}_t &= \sigma(\mathbf{W}^{I,ih} * X_t + \mathbf{W}^{I,hh} * \mathbf{H}_{t-1} + \mathbf{B}^I) \\
\mathbf{F}_t &= \sigma(\mathbf{W}^{F,ih} * X_t + \mathbf{W}^{F,hh} * \mathbf{H}_{t-1} + \mathbf{B}^F) \\
\mathbf{O}_t &= \sigma(\mathbf{W}^{O,ih} * X_t + \mathbf{W}^{O,hh} * \mathbf{H}_{t-1} + \mathbf{B}^O) \\
\mathbf{C}_t &= \mathbf{F}_t \odot \mathbf{C}_{t-1} + \mathbf{I}_t \odot \tanh(\mathbf{W}^{C,ih} * X_t + \mathbf{W}^{C,hh} * \mathbf{H}_{t-1} + \mathbf{B}^C) \\
\mathbf{H}_t &= \mathbf{O}_t \odot \tanh(\mathbf{C}_t).
\end{aligned}
\tag{1}
$$

where $\odot$ denotes element-wise multiplication, $\sigma(\cdot)$ denotes the element-wise applied sigmoid activation. $\mathbf{I}_t, \mathbf{F}_t, \mathbf{O}_t, \mathbf{C}_t, \mathbf{H}_t$ and $\mathbf{X}_t$ are tensors for values of

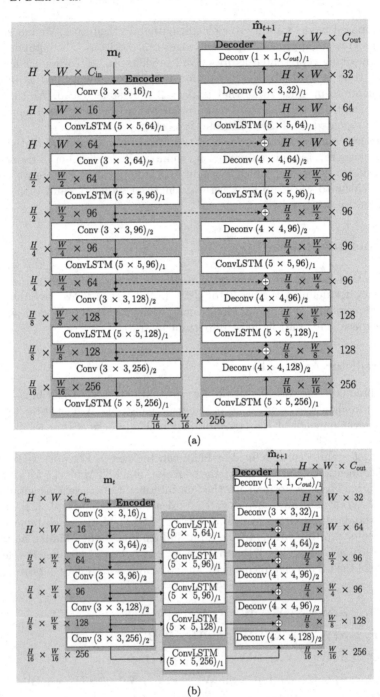

Fig. 3. (a): This figure depicts the PRED+R architecture for the predictor. By removing the residual connections (dashed lines), we obtain the PRED architecture. (b): This figure depicts the PRED+RS architecture for the predictor. Here, the ConvLSTM units are placed in the residual feature space connecting the encoders and decoders.

input gate, forget gate, output gate, cell state, hidden state and input respectively, at time step t. The tensors $\mathbf{W}^{Z,ih}$, $\mathbf{W}^{Z,hh}$ and $\mathbf{B}^Z$ where $Z \in \{I, F, O, C\}$ contain the kernel weights for input-hidden ($\mathbf{W}^{Z,ih}$), hidden-hidden ($\mathbf{W}^{Z,hh}$) mappings and bias values ($\mathbf{B}^Z$) for the input gate ($Z = I$), forget gate ($Z = F$), output gate ($Z = O$) and cell state ($Z = C$) computations respectively. For the first time step, the hidden states ($\mathbf{H}_t, \mathbf{C}_t$) are always set to zero tensors.

Every convolution layer consists of a leaky ReLU activation [15] function with a slope of -0.2. The architecture consists of an encoder part which extracts the spatio-temporal fashion with increasing receptive size for each consecutive layer. As shown in Fig. 3(a), the input and output data resolutions are denoted as $H \times W \times D$ where H, W denote the spatial resolution and D represents the channel depth of the output. Similarly, $\text{Conv}(K \times K, D_{out})_{/M}$ represents a convolutional layer with kernel size of $K \times K$, output depth of channels as D_{out} with a stride of M. The convolutional LSTM layers are denoted as $\text{ConvLSTM}(K \times K, D_{out})_{/M}$ where the denotions are same as defined before. For the decoder part in Fig. 3(a), there are corresponding deconvolutional layers with transpose convolutional LSTMs. $\text{Deconv}(K \times K, D_{out})_{/M}$ denotes a deconvolutional layer with kernel size of $K \times K$, input and output depth of channels as D_{out} with a stride of M. The convolutional LSTM layers of the decoder are denoted in the same way.

We investigate a second type of predictor architecture, PRED+R, which also can be seen in Fig. 3(a). It is similar to PRED but with the residual connections (dashed lines) after every ConvLSTM block connected in an U-Net [21] fashion with the respective group of Deconv-ConvLSTM block. This is done to overcome the generic problem of vanishing gradients as well as facilitate better flow of gradients during training phase.

Figure 3(b) shows our third proposed predictor architecture, PRED+RS. It is a more intuitive method with convolutional LSTM blocks present in between the corresponding convolution - deconvolution latent space. This can be seen in Fig. 3(b) where the convolutional LSTM units are predicting the hidden state representations in the residual connections.

4.2 Datasets

Cityscapes: The Cityscapes [3] dataset $\mathcal{D}^{CS}$ is specifically tailored for AD scenes in urban setting. The dataset contains 5000 images for semantic segmentation. The dataset is split into 2975 images for training ($\mathcal{D}^{CS}_{train}$), 500 images for validation ($\mathcal{D}^{CS}_{val}$) and 1525 images for testing ($\mathcal{D}^{CS}_{test}$). The training split and the validation split have corresponding perfect ground truths available. For each image in $\mathcal{D}^{CS}$, there exists a 30 frame long video sequence whose 20th frame annotations are available. To distinguish, we denote the dataset consisting of the entire videos as $\mathcal{D}^{CS-vid}$. This dataset accordingly contains 2975 videos for training ($\mathcal{D}^{CS-vid}_{train}$), 500 videos for validation ($\mathcal{D}^{CS-vid}_{val}$) and 1525 videos for testing ($\mathcal{D}^{CS-vid}_{test}$). Each video sequence contains 30 frames lasting 1.8 s (16.67 fps) long with a resolution of 1024×2048. Given the 16.67 fps frame rate of Cityscapes and our arbitrary choice of predicting $\Delta t = 10$ time steps in the future, our setup predicts $0.6\,$s into the future. There are $S = 19$ semantic class categories.

BDD100K: The BDD100K [26] dataset $\mathcal{D}^{BDD}$ contains randomly sampled images from 10,000 video clips with perfect semantic segmentation ground truths. This subset is split into 7000 images for training ($\mathcal{D}^{BDD}_{train}$), 1000 images for validation ($\mathcal{D}^{BDD}_{val}$) and 2000 images for testing ($\mathcal{D}^{BDD}_{test}$). For the purpose of prediction, we use the video dataset from multiple object tracking and segmentation $\mathcal{D}^{BDD-MOTS}$ subset containing 223 videos in total with 154 training $\mathcal{D}^{BDD-MOTS}_{train}$, 32 validation $\mathcal{D}^{BDD-MOTS}_{val}$ and 37 testing videos $\mathcal{D}^{BDD-MOTS}_{test}$. Each video contains about 200 frames (5 fps) lasting $40\,$s with a resolution of 720×1280. Given the 5 fps frame rate of $\mathcal{D}^{BDD-MOTS}$ and our arbitrary choice of predicting $\Delta t = 10$ time steps in the future, our setup predicts $2\,$s into the future. There are $S = 19$ semantic class categories.

4.3   Input Representations

Different types of input modalities were exploited by the model to predict future scenes using hidden state representations. Usually, most works focus only on the raw semantic segmentation masks $\overline{m}_t \in \mathcal{S}^{H \times W}$ which can be interpreted as 1-channel input [8,13,18], i.e., $\overline{m}_t \in [0,1]^{H \times W \times 1}$. This is the most prevalent input representation for prediction tasks because it is computationally less expensive and independent of predefined semantic classes in the dataset. We also conduct some investigations with 1-channel input $\overline{m}_t$ to prove our model's robustness, which are explained in detail in the supplementary material (A). However, in the process we often ignore the amount of information contained in the normalized probabilistic outputs of the semantic segmentation network, i.e., softmax activations just before the argmax function. Hence, we also conduct extensive experiments on these softmax activations as input data representations $\overline{y}_t \in [0,1]^{H \times W \times S}$, i.e., S-channel input. One advantage of using the S-channel input $\overline{y}_t$ is that all the semantic classes are equidistant to each other in the latent space. In the process, we do prove that the S-channel softmax activation $\overline{y}_t$ as input representation leads to better performance in prediction for both short-term and long-term time horizons ($\Delta t = 1, 2, 5, 10$).

4.4   Metrics

For reporting the quantitative performance of our experiments, we resort to estimating the mean intersection over union or Jaccard index. This metric is usually an indispensable estimation technique for most semantic segmentation and object detection models [25,27]. As indicated by the name, the intersection over union (IoU) is computed as area of intersection (overlap) divided by the area of union. For the application of semantic segmentation and prediction, it is more appropriate to express IoU based on sensitivity and specificity indicators.

Given the amount of true positives TP_s, false positives FP_s and false negatives FN_s for class s respectively, the IoU can be defined as

$$\text{IoU}_s = \frac{TP_s}{TP_s + FP_s + FN_s} \tag{2}$$

The overall mean performance over all the classes $\mathcal{S} = \{1, 2, ..., S\}$, i.e., mIoU can be represented as

$$\text{mIoU} = \frac{1}{S} \sum_{s=1} IoU_s \tag{3}$$

From now on, we will report two types of mIoUs: $\text{mIoU}_{\Delta t}^{\text{seg}}$, which is the mIoU between the predictions and self generated ground pseudo truth semantic segmentation masks. And $\text{mIoU}_{\Delta t}^{\text{gt}}$, which is the mIoU between the predictions and human annotated (perfect) ground truths of $\mathcal{D}_{\text{val}}^{\text{CS}-\text{vid}}$ for the 20th frame.

4.5 Implementation Details

Generating Ground Truth Annotations: As both $\mathcal{D}^{\text{BDD}-\text{MOTS}}$ and $\mathcal{D}^{\text{CS}-\text{vid}}$ do not have off-the-shelf semantically annotated masks, we create our own ground truth labels using a standard semantic segmentation model. The semantic segmentation network $\mathcal{F}^{\text{semseg}}$, i.e., PSANet [29] is trained on $\mathcal{D}_{\text{train}}^{\text{BDD}}$ and $\mathcal{D}_{\text{train}}^{\text{CS}}$ dataset first. The annotations are produced via supervised learning using human annotated ground truth semantic segmentation masks with a categorical cross entropy loss representation. For $\mathcal{D}_{\text{train}}^{\text{BDD}}$, the original image resolution is of size 720×1280 whereas for $\mathcal{D}_{\text{train}}^{\text{CS}}$, it is 1024×2048. To arrive at a unified input resolution for training, we downsample the original images to 513×1025 which is a requirement to the choice of our semantic segmentation network due to affine transformations [29]. The output of this network is again downsampled via bilinear interpolation to produce semantic segmentation masks of size 128×256. The semantic segmentation network $\mathcal{F}^{\text{semseg}}$ is trained for 1000 epochs with a batch size of 4, learning rate of 1×10^{-2} and an auxiliary weight of 0.4. This setup uses a SGD optimizer with a weight decay of 5×10^{-4}. Our implementation of the semantic segmentation network, i.e., PSANet with a ResNet50 backbone achieves an mIoU of 73.44% on $\mathcal{D}_{\text{val}}^{\text{CS}}$ and 59.84% on $\mathcal{D}_{\text{val}}^{\text{BDD}}$. The trainings were carried out on a single Tesla V100 GPU for 7 days.

Training the Predictor: The three predictor architectures (PRED, PRED+R, PRED+RS) have been trained with the same hyperparameters for 100 epochs with an early stopping for plateau conditions. The input resolution of the semantic segmentation masks is 128×256 as mentioned above as this resolution proves to be the most optimal for our predictor architecture in terms of training time, memory consumption and storage constraints. As shown in Fig. 1, the inputs are 10 frame long sequences. The sequences are fed as single mask inputs at each timestep and the predictor's hidden state representations are updated sequentially according to Eq. 1. The output is of the same size as input with a prediction time horizon of $\Delta t = 1$ timestep ahead. The batch size is set to 4 with a base learning rate of 1×10^{-3} and a learning rate scheduler with a factor of 0.5. Here, we use the Adam optimizer with a weight decay of 5×10^{-4}. The trainings were carried out on a single Tesla V100 GPU for 3 days. It is to be noted that all the reported numbers with mean and standard deviation have been averaged over 3 different seeds.

Table 1. mIoU$_{\Delta t}^{\text{seg}}$ performance for different predictor architectures on $\mathcal{D}_{\text{val}}^{\text{BDD}-\text{MOTS}}$ showing different input types as well as time horizons into the future. The best architecture per time horizon is denoted in **bold** font. Also, the best input type can be seen underlined. All the experiments have been averaged over 3 seeds except CP and OF as they are deterministic, n/a - not applicable.

Input Type	Time Horizon Δt	Methods				
		CP	OF	PRED(ours)	PRED+R(ours)	PRED+RS(ours)
1-channel	1(0.2 s)	49.32	51.75	54.96 ± 0.15	**55.20** ± 0.23	51.66 ± 0.39
	2(0.4 s)	45.39	47.15	51.62 + 0.18	**51.79** ± 0.16	48.32 ± 0.43
	5(1.0 s)	38.93	38.89	41.70 ± 0.14	**44.91** ± 0.11	41.82 ± 0.53
	10(2.0 s)	33.59	31.33	**38.41** ± 0.06	38.11 ± 0.09	35.36 ± 0.45
S-channel	1(0.2 s)	49.19	n/a	<u>57.02</u> ± 0.17	**<u>57.12</u>** ± 0.36	<u>55.33</u> ± 0.16
	2(0.4 s)	45.17	n/a	53.06 ± 0.23	**53.15** ± 0.29	51.29 ± 0.09
	5(1.0 s)	38.52	n/a	45.32 ± 0.37	**45.40** ± 0.07	43.40 ± 0.34
	10(2.0 s)	32.98	n/a	**38.16** ± 0.54	37.96 ± 0.10	36.13 ± 0.38

5   Experimental Results and Discussion

5.1   Performance on BDD100K

Comparison of the Proposed Architectures: As mentioned above, there are no semantic segmentation ground truth labels available for $\mathcal{D}^{\text{BDD}-\text{MOTS}}$. Hence, we generate our own pseudo ground truth annotations $\overline{\mathbf{m}}_t$ using PSANet. The prediction performance for the $\mathcal{D}_{\text{val}}^{BDD-MOTS}$ with the pseudo ground truths can be seen in Table 1 in terms of mIoU$_{\Delta t}^{\text{seg}}$. We compare the three proposed predictor architectures (PRED, PRED+R and PRED+RS) along with two baseline forecasting techniques based on copy-paste (CP) and optical flow (OF). Copy-paste, (CP) is simply using the last input as prediction, i.e., $\hat{\mathbf{m}}_{t+1} = \overline{\mathbf{m}}_t$. For optical flow (OF), we use Lucas et al.'s [14] dense optical flow algorithm to estimate the optical flow motion matrix $\mathbf{f}$ for each pixel which is warped to predict next frame, i.e., $\hat{\mathbf{m}}_{t+1} = \mathbf{warp}(\overline{\mathbf{m}}_t, \mathbf{f})$. The dense optical flow for S-channel inputs does not make sense as the values are simply normalized probabilistic outputs and not pixels in conventional sense. Hence, the values for dense optical flow with S-channel masks were not calculated. It can be observed that PRED+R performs consecutively better for all time horizons in both types of input representations achieving a mean mIoU$_{\Delta t}^{\text{seg}}$ performance of 57.12%, 53.15% and 45.40% for $t + 1$, $t + 2$ and $t + 5$ future time steps respectively with S-channel input. This can be explained by the fact that this model extracts the semantic information from the input semantic segmentation masks at different spatial resolutions and passes this information to the convolutional LSTM layer ahead which performs a time series probabilistic prediction. This information gets saved in the respective hidden state representation that can be used when the next frame's embeddings come into picture in the further time steps. This process is repeated until the embeddings are downsampled by 16 times. There are corresponding deconvolution layers which upsample each encoded latent feature by a factor of 2 and thus, rendering an output whose spatial resolution is exactly the same as its input. Also, it is worth mentioning that there are convolutional LSTM layers in between two consecutive de-convolution layers to extract the temporal information even while de-convolution. There are skip connections with corresponding convolutional LSTM layers of equal spatial resolution to facilitate better flow of gradients between the layer representations. These factors further enhance the performance of the predictor architecture compared to PRED+RS where the convolutional LSTM layers are placed in between corresponding convolution and de-convolution layers. Also, the PRED architecture performs quite similar to the best architecture PRED+R with slight deprecation because of the absence of residual gradient flow during backpropagation.

Table 2. mIoU$^{\text{seg}}_{\Delta t}$ performance of PRED+R on $\mathcal{D}^{\text{CS}-\text{vid}}_{\text{val}}$ showing different input types as well as time horizons into the future. The most optimal input type with the best performance can be seen in **bold font**. The experiments have been averaged over 3 seeds.

Input Type	Time Horizon Δt	Method
		PRED+R
1-channel	1(0.06 s)	83.37 ± 0.05
	2(0.12 s)	80.43 ± 0.08
	5(0.3 s)	72.37 ± 0.22
	10(0.6 s)	62.44 ± 0.51
S-channel	1(0.06 s)	**84.95 ± 0.03**
	2(0.12 s)	81.88 ± 0.07
	5(0.3 s)	73.52 ± 0.12
	10(0.6 s)	63.65 ± 0.09

It can be seen that the model performs well on the $\mathcal{D}^{\text{BDD}-\text{MOTS}}_{\text{val}}$ in Table 1 which is quite a challenging dataset given the unnormalized raw images, absence of proper lighting conditions, varying weather and diverse scenarios. In Table 1, we can see the comparison between standard baselines and our architecture on $\mathcal{D}^{\text{BDD}-\text{MOTS}}_{\text{val}}$. We can observe that PRED+R outperforms copy-paste (CP) and optical flow (OF) by 5.88% and 3.45% absolute mIoU$^{\text{seg}}_{\Delta t}$ respectively for 1-channel input and 7.93% absolute mIoU$^{\text{seg}}_{\Delta t}$ for S-channel input with copy-paste (CP) only.

Input Modalities: In Table 1, we can see that the S-channel input representation achieves an increase of 1.92%, 1.36%, 0.49% $\mathrm{mIoU}_{\Delta t}^{\mathrm{seg}}$ when compared to 1-channel inputs for PRED and PRED+R with future time horizons for $\Delta t = 1, 2, 5$, respectively. For PRED+RS, the S-channel input outperforms the 1-channel counterpart for $\Delta t = 1, 2, 5$, respectively, i.e., on an average of 3.67%, 2.97%, 1.58% $\mathrm{mIoU}_{\Delta t}^{\mathrm{seg}}$. Hence, it can be inferred that S-channel input representation performs better than the 1-channel input representation for all three predictor definitions. This can be attributed to the fact that the softmax activations, $\overline{y}_t$ (S-channel input), indeed capture better semantic sense of the scene along with the boundary definitions and probabilistic pixel motion dependencies as these are the normalized probabilistic outputs of the semantic segmentation network. The softmax activations not only contain the most likely class per pixel probability but also the less likely and false semantic-pixel information. This in turn proves to be a better alternative compared to the raw pixel class annotations (1-channel input) where the less likely pixel connotations are completely shut off in a discrete and condensed output representation.

Table 3. $\mathrm{mIoU}_{\Delta t}^{\mathrm{gt}}$ and $\mathrm{mIoU}_{\Delta t}^{\mathrm{seg}}$ performance of PRED+R and other state of the art works in the field of prediction of semantic segmentation masks on $\mathcal{D}_{\mathrm{val}}^{\mathrm{CS-vid}}$. Note that here, the one time step and three time step ahead ($\Delta t = 1, 3$) prediction is being compared and our performances are highlighted in **bold**. *Taken from Jin et al. [8], **taken from Nabavi et al. [18], − are not reported.

Model	$\Delta t = 1$		$\Delta t = 3$	
	$\mathrm{mIoU}_{\Delta t}^{\mathrm{gt}}$	$\mathrm{mIoU}_{\Delta t}^{seg}$	$\mathrm{mIoU}_{\Delta t}^{\mathrm{gt}}$	$\mathrm{mIoU}_{\Delta t}^{seg}$
S2S, Luc et al. [13]	62.60*	–	59.40*	–
Pred. Scene Parsing, Jin et al. [8]	66.10*	–	–	–
Future Sem. Seg., Nabavi et al. [18]	–	70.24**	–	58.90**
1-channel input (ours)	**67.55**	**83.95**	**63.60**	**78.28**

5.2   Performance on Cityscapes

In Table 2, we report our proposed method's performance on $\mathcal{D}_{\mathrm{val}}^{\mathrm{CS-vid}}$. We report performance only on PRED+R to save time and computation cycles, as it was clear from our experiments with the $\mathcal{D}^{\mathrm{BDD-MOTS}}$ dataset that PRED+R easily outperforms other model definitions. We achieve a mean $\mathrm{mIoU}_{\Delta t}^{\mathrm{seg}}$ performance of 84.95% and 83.37% respectively for S-channel and 1-channel input types. Here, also the S-channel input representation proves to be a better choice than the 1-channel input type for all time horizons. In Fig. 4, we also show the qualitative results of our prediction method on a sequence of Cityscapes validation split $\mathcal{D}_{\mathrm{val}}^{\mathrm{CS-vid}}$ with pseudo ground truths generated by PSANet.

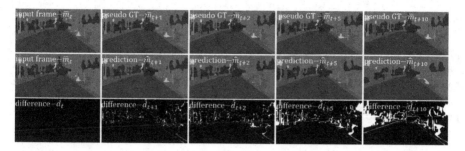

Fig. 4. Output predictions for a sequence of the Cityscapes validation split, $\mathcal{D}_{val}^{CS-vid}$. The top row depicts the pseudo ground truth $\overline{m}_t$, $\overline{m}_{t+1}$, $\overline{m}_{t+2}$, $\overline{m}_{t+5}$, $\overline{m}_{t+10}$ generated by PSANet. In the middle row, we show the input semantic segmentation $\overline{m}_t$ along with the predictions $\hat{m}_{t+1}$, $\hat{m}_{t+2}$, $\hat{m}_{t+5}$, $\hat{m}_{t+10}$ from the prediction network. The bottom row portrays the absolute difference $\hat{d}_{t+1}$, $\hat{d}_{t+2}$, $\hat{d}_{t+5}$, $\hat{d}_{t+10}$, between the ground truth and prediction frames. We also show additional qualitative results in the supplementary material (A).

5.3   Comparison with the State of the Art

Most prior work report their performance only on the benchmark Cityscapes dataset $\mathcal{D}_{val}^{CS-vid}$. Hence, to make our work comparable with previous approaches, we adapt their training styles like input resolution, input frame sequence length and re-perform the experiments to calculate performances. We input 4 frame long sequences $\overline{\mathbf{m}}_{t-3}^{t} = \{\overline{\mathbf{m}}_{t-3}, \overline{\mathbf{m}}_{t-2}, \overline{\mathbf{m}}_{t-1}, \overline{\mathbf{m}}_t\}$ and predict one time step into the future. The input masks have a spatial resolution of 256×512. This prediction is compared with the 20th human annotated ground truth frame from $\mathcal{D}_{val}^{CS-vid}$ and $\text{mIoU}_{\Delta t}^{gt}$ is calculated.

We can see in Table 3 for $\Delta t = 1$, our approach consistently outperforms Luc et al. [13] by 4.95% absolute and Jin et al. [8] by 1.45% absolute in terms of $\text{mIoU}_{\Delta t}^{gt}$. Also, our model beats Nabavi et al. [18] by 13.71% absolute in terms of $\text{mIoU}_{\Delta t}^{seg}$ when pseudo ground truth labels are taken into account. Similarly, for $\Delta t = 3$, our model beats Luc et al. [13] by 4.20% absolute in terms of $\text{mIoU}_{\Delta t}^{gt}$ and outperforms Nabavi et al. [18] by 19.38% absolute in terms of $\text{mIoU}_{\Delta t}^{seg}$.

6   Conclusion

We present a time series network using LSTM units in the convolution domain for predicting semantically segmented scenarios in the future. This would help the ego vehicle to have an excellent understanding of its maneuverability decision space in good time. Our method of using convolutional LSTMs in between feature extraction layers with residual connection proves to be a better approach for predicting dynamic and static object categories on BDD100K [26] and Cityscapes [3] datasets with the freedom to use arbitrary input sequence length and output prediction time horizons. Also, we demonstrate the usefulness of employing the

S-channel input representation over 1-channel input representation for improvement in semantic segmentation forecasting. We show results proving that our prediction method outperforms the current state of the art on the Cityscapes [3] dataset by 1.45% and 4.2% absolute mIoU$^{\text{gt}}_{\Delta t}$ with time horizon predictions up to 0.06 s and 0.18 s, respectively and also outperforming the current state of the art on Cityscapes [3] by 13.71% and 19.38% absolute mIoU$^{\text{seg}}_{\Delta t}$ with time horizon predictions up to 0.06 s and 0.18 s, and additionally we are the first to report our results on BDD100K dataset [26].

Disclaimer. The results, opinions and conclusions expressed in this publication are not necessarily those of Volkswagen Aktiengesellschaft.

A   Supplementary Material

Table 4. Re-ordering of semantic classes in BDD100K

A.1   Qualitative Results

In this section, we show the qualitative results of our method on sequences of BDD100K, $\mathcal{D}^{\text{BDD-MOTS}}_{\text{val}}$ and Cityscapes, $\mathcal{D}^{\text{CS-vid}}_{\text{val}}$. In Fig. 5, we show the qualitative results of prediction method on a sequence of $\mathcal{D}^{\text{BDD-MOTS}}_{\text{val}}$. We can observe that, for increasing time steps, i.e., $\Delta t = \{1, 2, 5, 10\}$, the prediction worsens for dynamic objects. This can be inferred from the increase in white regions in the absolute difference estimation visualizations (bottom row) defined as $\hat{\mathbf{d}}_t = |\hat{\mathbf{m}}_t - \overline{\mathbf{m}}_t|$. Also, majority of the predictions are incorrect in the boundary segregation of different classes, i.e., where car pixel occupancy meets road occupancy, where sidewalk occupancy meets road occupancy.

Specifically for the Cityscapes dataset, in Fig. 6, the predictions (middle row) are at par with their corresponding 20th frame ground truth annotations (top row) for $\Delta t = \{1, 2, 5\}$, obtained from the dataset. The semantic class boundaries are so well captured with noise supression in predictions (middle row). However, for $\Delta t = 10$, we can see that the prediction focuses more on predicting the static classes than the finer dynamic classes boundary details, i.e., visible from the missing sidewalk in the left region of $\hat{\mathbf{m}}_{t+10}$ that is visible in the ground truth annotation $\overline{\mathbf{m}}_{t+10}$ (in pink) of Fig. 6.

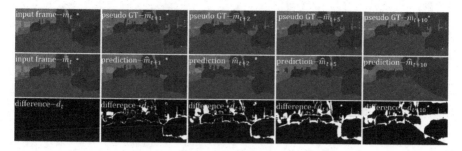

Fig. 5. Output predictions for a sequence of the BDD100K validation split, $\mathcal{D}_{\text{val}}^{\text{BDD}-\text{MOTS}}$. The top row depicts the pseudo ground truth $\overline{\mathbf{m}}_t$, $\overline{\mathbf{m}}_{t+1}$, $\overline{\mathbf{m}}_{t+2}$, $\overline{\mathbf{m}}_{t+5}$, $\overline{\mathbf{m}}_{t+10}$ generated by PSANet. In the middle row, we show the input semantic segmentation $\overline{\mathbf{m}}_t$ along with the predictions $\hat{\mathbf{m}}_{t+1}$, $\hat{\mathbf{m}}_{t+2}$, $\hat{\mathbf{m}}_{t+5}$, $\hat{\mathbf{m}}_{t+10}$ from the prediction network. The bottom row portrays the absolute difference $\hat{\mathbf{d}}_{t+1}$, $\hat{\mathbf{d}}_{t+2}$, $\hat{\mathbf{d}}_{t+5}$, $\hat{\mathbf{d}}_{t+10}$, between the ground truth and prediction frames.

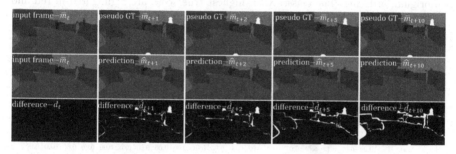

Fig. 6. Output predictions for a sequence of the Cityscapes validation split, $\mathcal{D}_{\text{val}}^{\text{CS}-\text{vid}}$. The top row depicts actual 20th frame ground truth annotations available in the dataset for $\overline{\mathbf{m}}_t$, $\overline{\mathbf{m}}_{t+1}$, $\overline{\mathbf{m}}_{t+2}$, $\overline{\mathbf{m}}_{t+5}$, $\overline{\mathbf{m}}_{t+10}$. In the middle row, we show the input semantic segmentation $\overline{\mathbf{m}}_t$ along with the predictions $\hat{\mathbf{m}}_{t+1}$, $\hat{\mathbf{m}}_{t+2}$, $\hat{\mathbf{m}}_{t+5}$, $\hat{\mathbf{m}}_{t+10}$ from the prediction network. The bottom row portrays the absolute difference $\hat{\mathbf{d}}_{t+1}$, $\hat{\mathbf{d}}_{t+2}$, $\hat{\mathbf{d}}_{t+5}$, $\hat{\mathbf{d}}_{t+10}$, between the ground truth and prediction frames.

A.2 Prediction Invariance on the Ordering of Semantic Classes

We investigate the behavior of our model when 1-channel inputs are fed to our predictor network, i.e., the generated pseudo ground truth $\overline{\mathbf{m}}_t \in \mathcal{S}^{H \times W \times 1}$ for the BDD100K dataset $\mathcal{D}^{\text{BDD}-\text{MOTS}}$. The semantic segmentation mask $\overline{\mathbf{m}}_t$ contains class indices $s \in \mathcal{S} = \{1, 2, ..., S\}$, where $S = 19$. Here, each semantic class corresponds to a specific class index s, e.g., $s = 0$ for class road, $s = 12$ for class person, etc according to the scene. For instance, if we consider a small region in a semantic segmentation mask, we usually find a certain semantic class pixels in close proximity with another semantic class pixels, i.e., class road pixels ($s = 1$) almost always occurs adjacent to class car pixels ($s = 14$) and class sidewalk pixels ($s = 2$) almost are always adjacent to class road pixels ($s = 1$) as can be seen in Fig. 7. To investigate the proposed method's performance and robustness when the original class orientation is re-ordered, we conducted some

Fig. 7. A semantic segmentation input mask $\overline{m}_t$ from $\mathcal{D}_{\text{val}}^{\text{BDD}-\text{MOTS}}$ showing different semantic classes. The left white encircled region portrays the proximal occurence of class `sidewalk` ($s = 2$) near to class `road` ($s = 1$). Similarly, the right white encircled region portrays the proximal occurrence of class `road` ($s = 1$) near to class `car` ($s = 14$).

Table 5. Confusion matrix on BDD100K: scores of all the $S = 19$ classes in BDD100K with original ordering. The classes with highest true score are highlighted in red and the cells with second highest true score are marked in light red.

Predicted Class

	road	sidewalk	building	wall	fence	pole	traffic light	traffic sign	vegetation	terrain	sky	person	rider	car	truck	bus	train	motorcycle	bicycle
road	0.97	0.01	0.00	0.00	0.00	0.00	0.00	0.00	0.00	0.00	0.00	0.00	0.00	0.01	0.00	0.00	0.00	0.00	0.00
sidewalk	0.14	0.76	0.02	0.01	0.01	0.01	0.00	0.00	0.01	0.02	0.00	0.01	0.00	0.01	0.00	0.00	0.00	0.00	0.00
building	0.00	0.00	0.90	0.00	0.01	0.01	0.00	0.00	0.03	0.00	0.02	0.00	0.00	0.01	0.00	0.00	0.00	0.00	0.00
wall	0.04	0.02	0.12	0.65	0.07	0.00	0.00	0.00	0.05	0.01	0.00	0.00	0.00	0.02	0.00	0.00	0.00	0.00	0.00
fence	0.02	0.02	0.1	0.04	0.71	0.01	0.00	0.00	0.05	0.01	0.01	0.00	0.00	0.02	0.00	0.00	0.00	0.00	0.00
pole	0.03	0.02	0.17	0.01	0.01	0.53	0.00	0.01	0.1	0.01	0.08	0.00	0.00	0.02	0.00	0.00	0.00	0.00	0.00
traffic light	0.01	0.00	0.21	0.00	0.00	0.05	0.57	0.03	0.05	0.00	0.07	0.00	0.00	0.00	0.00	0.00	0.00	0.00	0.00
traffic sign	0.00	0.00	0.13	0.00	0.01	0.02	0.00	0.75	0.05	0.00	0.03	0.00	0.00	0.00	0.00	0.00	0.00	0.00	0.00
vegetation	0.00	0.00	0.05	0.00	0.00	0.00	0.00	0.00	0.9	0.01	0.02	0.00	0.00	0.01	0.00	0.00	0.00	0.00	0.00
terrain	0.12	0.09	0.02	0.01	0.01	0.01	0.00	0.00	0.08	0.64	0.01	0.00	0.00	0.01	0.00	0.00	0.00	0.00	0.00
sky	0.01	0.00	0.04	0.00	0.00	0.00	0.00	0.00	0.03	0.00	0.92	0.00	0.00	0.00	0.00	0.00	0.00	0.00	0.00
person	0.12	0.04	0.1	0.00	0.01	0.00	0.00	0.00	0.01	0.00	0.00	0.64	0.01	0.05	0.00	0.00	0.00	0.00	0.00
rider	0.08	0.01	0.08	0.00	0.00	0.00	0.00	0.00	0.02	0.00	0.00	0.49	0.14	0.1	0.01	0.01	0.00	0.03	0.02
car	0.04	0.00	0.02	0.00	0.00	0.00	0.00	0.00	0.01	0.00	0.00	0.00	0.00	0.93	0.00	0.00	0.00	0.00	0.00
truck	0.04	0.00	0.05	0.00	0.00	0.00	0.00	0.00	0.01	0.00	0.00	0.01	0.00	0.1	0.75	0.01	0.00	0.00	0.01
bus	0.03	0.00	0.08	0.00	0.00	0.00	0.00	0.00	0.01	0.00	0.00	0.00	0.00	0.05	0.04	0.78	0.00	0.00	0.00
train	0.00	0.00	0.00	0.00	0.00	0.00	0.00	0.00	0.00	0.00	0.00	0.00	0.00	0.00	0.00	0.00	0.00	0.00	0.00
motorcycle	0.33	0.01	0.01	0.00	0.00	0.00	0.00	0.00	0.00	0.00	0.00	0.13	0.05	0.13	0.02	0.02	0.00	0.15	0.15
bicycle	0.25	0.02	0.03	0.00	0.00	0.01	0.00	0.00	0.01	0.00	0.00	0.01	0.00	0.07	0.00	0.01	0.00	0.01	0.58

Ground Truth

experiments by shuffling the class indexes in the generated pseudo ground truth frames $\overline{m}_t$. For instance, now the same scene would contain class `road` ($s = 5$) adjacent to class `car` ($s = 16$) and class `sidewalk` ($s = 9$) adjacent to class `road` ($s = 5$). Note that, the semantic classes remain the same, just the class indices are shuffled randomly. In Table 4, we can see the original class order along with the re-ordered class indices where semantic classes are marked by their actual defined colors in $\mathcal{D}^{BDD-MOTS}$. can This is an important investigation to prove that our predictor model still learns the proximal relationship between the semantic classes instead of the numerical class indices occupancy, i.e., our model perfectly learns that class road pixels are most likely to occur near class car pixels and vice-versa, irrespective of their class indices value. Hence, we performed experiments by re-ordering the class indices of $\mathcal{D}^{BDD-MOTS}$ in such a way that the classes that occurred near to each other in terms of class index distance, e.g., road $(s = 1)$ and sidewalk $(s = 2)$ are now placed further apart, e.g., road $(s = 5)$ and sidewalk $(s = 9)$ as can be seen in Table 4.

Table 5 shows the confusion matrix for the original class order of $\mathcal{D}^{BDD-MOTS}$. The confusion matrix represents how each class in the prediction is confused and interpreted with respect to all the classes present in the ground truth and vice-versa. It can be observed that, every class is predicted well with the highest score for itself (see diagonal) except class rider $(s = 13)$ which is predicted as class person $(s = 12)$ with a score of 0.49 which is obvious as rider fits into the broader category of person after all. Similarly, class motorcycle $(s = 18)$ gets confused for class road $(s = 1)$ with a score of 0.33. This could be simply attributed the fact that the class road heavily overpowers the pixel distribution in all scenes whereas the class motorcycle has very minimal occupancy in most of the scenes. Now, in Table 6, we can see the confusion matrix for the first re-ordering of classes. In Table 6, it can be observed that, the predictor still confuses class rider $(s = 17)$ for class person$(s = 11)$ with a score of 0.34 and

Table 6. Confusion matrix on BDD100K: scores of all the $S = 19$ classes in BDD100K with first re-ordering. The classes with highest true score are highlighted in red and the cells with second highest true score are marked in light red.

Ground Truth \ Predicted	pole	sky	fence	traffic sign	road	truck	train	fence	sidewalk	bicycle	person	traffic light	vegetation	building	bus	car	rider	terrain	motorcycle
pole	0.54	0.09	0.01	0.01	0.03	0.00	0.00	0.01	0.03	0.00	0.00	0.00	0.08	0.17	0.00	0.01	0.00	0.01	0.00
sky	0.00	0.92	0.00	0.00	0.01	0.00	0.00	0.00	0.00	0.00	0.00	0.00	0.00	0.03	0.04	0.00	0.00	0.00	0.00
wall	0.01	0.01	0.67	0.00	0.04	0.00	0.00	0.07	0.02	0.00	0.00	0.00	0.04	0.11	0.00	0.02	0.00	0.01	0.00
traffic sign	0.01	0.04	0.00	0.75	0.01	0.00	0.00	0.01	0.00	0.00	0.00	0.00	0.04	0.13	0.00	0.00	0.00	0.00	0.00
road	0.00	0.00	0.00	0.00	0.97	0.00	0.00	0.00	0.01	0.00	0.00	0.00	0.00	0.00	0.00	0.01	0.00	0.00	0.00
truck	0.00	0.01	0.00	0.01	0.06	0.78	0.00	0.00	0.00	0.01	0.01	0.00	0.01	0.06	0.01	0.05	0.00	0.00	0.00
train	0.00	0.00	0.00	0.00	0.00	0.00	0.00	0.00	0.00	0.00	0.00	0.00	0.00	0.00	0.00	0.00	0.00	0.00	0.00
fence	0.01	0.01	0.05	0.00	0.02	0.00	0.00	0.73	0.02	0.00	0.00	0.00	0.04	0.09	0.00	0.02	0.00	0.01	0.00
sidewalk	0.00	0.00	0.01	0.00	0.15	0.00	0.00	0.01	0.75	0.00	0.01	0.00	0.01	0.02	0.00	0.01	0.00	0.03	0.00
bicycle	0.01	0.00	0.00	0.00	0.28	0.02	0.00	0.01	0.04	0.55	0.02	0.00	0.01	0.02	0.00	0.03	0.00	0.00	0.01
person	0.00	0.00	0.00	0.00	0.13	0.00	0.00	0.01	0.04	0.01	0.63	0.00	0.01	0.1	0.00	0.04	0.02	0.00	0.00
traffic light	0.02	0.08	0.00	0.01	0.01	0.00	0.00	0.00	0.00	0.00	0.00	0.62	0.06	0.2	0.00	0.00	0.00	0.00	0.00
vegetation	0.01	0.03	0.00	0.00	0.00	0.00	0.00	0.00	0.00	0.00	0.00	0.00	0.89	0.05	0.00	0.01	0.00	0.01	0.00
building	0.01	0.02	0.00	0.00	0.00	0.00	0.00	0.01	0.00	0.00	0.00	0.00	0.03	0.90	0.00	0.01	0.00	0.00	0.00
bus	0.00	0.00	0.00	0.00	0.03	0.04	0.00	0.00	0.00	0.00	0.00	0.00	0.01	0.09	0.76	0.05	0.00	0.00	0.00
car	0.00	0.00	0.00	0.00	0.04	0.00	0.00	0.00	0.00	0.00	0.00	0.00	0.01	0.02	0.00	0.92	0.00	0.00	0.00
rider	0.00	0.00	0.00	0.00	0.1	0.01	0.00	0.00	0.01	0.01	0.34	0.00	0.02	0.1	0.00	0.11	0.24	0.02	0.02
terrain	0.00	0.00	0.01	0.00	0.13	0.00	0.00	0.01	0.07	0.00	0.00	0.00	0.07	0.02	0.00	0.02	0.00	0.66	0.00
motorcycle	0.00	0.00	0.00	0.00	0.38	0.01	0.00	0.00	0.03	0.05	0.12	0.00	0.00	0.01	0.00	0.17	0.11	0.03	0.1

Table 7. Confusion matrix on BDD100K: scores of all the $S = 19$ classes in BDD100K with second re-ordering. The classes with highest true score are highlighted in red and the cells with second highest true score are marked in light red.

Predicted Class →

Ground Truth	train	bicycle	bus	terrain	rider	sky	sidewalk	road	wall	traffic sign	motorcycle	traffic light	person	fence	building	truck	car	pole	vegetation
train	0.00	0.00	0.00	0.00	0.00	0.00	0.00	0.00	0.00	0.00	0.00	0.00	0.00	0.00	0.00	0.00	0.00	0.00	0.00
bicycle	0.00	0.50	0.04	0.00	0.00	0.00	0.02	0.29	0.00	0.00	0.01	0.00	0.01	0.01	0.03	0.04	0.04	0.00	0.01
bus	0.00	0.01	0.76	0.00	0.00	0.00	0.00	0.03	0.00	0.00	0.00	0.00	0.00	0.00	0.1	0.03	0.05	0.00	0.01
terrain	0.00	0.00	0.00	0.63	0.00	0.01	0.09	0.14	0.01	0.00	0.00	0.00	0.00	0.01	0.02	0.00	0.01	0.00	0.08
rider	0.00	0.03	0.02	0.01	0.13	0.01	0.02	0.12	0.00	0.00	0.05	0.00	0.37	0.00	0.13	0.01	0.07	0.00	0.02
sky	0.00	0.00	0.00	0.00	0.00	0.91	0.00	0.01	0.00	0.00	0.00	0.00	0.00	0.00	0.04	0.00	0.00	0.00	0.03
sidewalk	0.00	0.00	0.00	0.02	0.00	0.01	0.75	0.15	0.01	0.00	0.00	0.00	0.01	0.01	0.02	0.00	0.01	0.00	0.01
road	0.00	0.00	0.00	0.00	0.00	0.00	0.01	0.97	0.00	0.00	0.00	0.00	0.00	0.00	0.00	0.00	0.01	0.00	0.00
wall	0.00	0.00	0.00	0.01	0.00	0.00	0.02	0.04	0.66	0.00	0.00	0.00	0.00	0.07	0.12	0.00	0.02	0.00	0.05
traffic sign	0.00	0.00	0.00	0.00	0.00	0.04	0.00	0.00	0.00	0.75	0.00	0.00	0.00	0.00	0.13	0.00	0.00	0.01	0.05
motorcycle	0.00	0.08	0.01	0.00	0.04	0.00	0.02	0.38	0.00	0.01	0.17	0.00	0.16	0.00	0.01	0.01	0.11	0.00	0.00
traffic light	0.00	0.00	0.00	0.00	0.00	0.07	0.00	0.01	0.00	0.02	0.00	0.63	0.00	0.00	0.2	0.00	0.00	0.02	0.05
person	0.00	0.00	0.00	0.00	0.01	0.00	0.04	0.15	0.00	0.00	0.00	0.00	0.63	0.01	0.1	0.00	0.04	0.00	0.01
fence	0.00	0.00	0.00	0.01	0.00	0.01	0.02	0.02	0.04	0.00	0.00	0.00	0.00	0.71	0.11	0.00	0.02	0.01	0.04
building	0.00	0.00	0.00	0.00	0.00	0.02	0.00	0.00	0.00	0.00	0.00	0.00	0.00	0.01	0.91	0.00	0.01	0.01	0.03
truck	0.00	0.01	0.01	0.00	0.00	0.01	0.00	0.05	0.00	0.01	0.00	0.00	0.00	0.00	0.08	0.75	0.07	0.00	0.02
car	0.00	0.00	0.00	0.00	0.00	0.00	0.00	0.04	0.00	0.00	0.00	0.00	0.00	0.00	0.02	0.00	0.92	0.00	0.01
pole	0.00	0.00	0.00	0.01	0.00	0.08	0.02	0.03	0.01	0.01	0.00	0.00	0.00	0.01	0.17	0.00	0.02	0.5	0.12
vegetation	0.00	0.00	0.00	0.01	0.00	0.02	0.00	0.00	0.00	0.00	0.00	0.00	0.00	0.00	0.04	0.00	0.01	0.00	0.91

class motorcycle ($s = 19$) for class road ($s = 5$) with a score of 0.38. Similarly, in Table 7, we can see the confusion matrix for the second re-ordering of classes. We can see that the predictor once again interprets class rider ($s = 5$) as class person ($s = 13$) with a score of 0.37 and class motorcycle ($s = 11$) as class road ($s = 8$) with a score of 0.38. It can be inferred that the predictor regardless of class index ordering, behaves exactly the same for all the class predictions. Thus, the predictor can be safely labeled as invariant to the class ordering.

References

1. Bewley, A., Ge, Z., Ott, L., Ramos, F., Upcroft, B.: Simple online and realtime tracking. In: Proceedings of ICIP, Melbourne, VIC, Australia, pp. 3464–3468, September 2016

2. Breitenstein, J., Termöhlen, J.A., Lipinski, D., Fingscheidt, T.: Systematization of corner cases for visual perception in automated driving. In: Proceedings of IV, Las Vegas, NV, USA, pp. 986–993, October 2020

3. Cordts, M., et al.: The cityscapes dataset for semantic urban scene understanding. In: Proceedings of CVPR, Las Vegas, NV, USA, pp. 3213–3223, June 2016

4. Duwek, H.C., Shalumov, A., Tsur, E.E.: Image reconstruction from neuromorphic event cameras using Laplacian-prediction and poisson integration with spiking and artificial neural networks. In: Proceedings of CVPR - Workshops, pp. 1333–1341. Virtual, June 2021

5. Fingscheidt, T., Gottschalk, H., Houben, S. (eds.): Deep Neural Networks and Data for Automated Driving: Robustness, Uncertainty Quantification, and Insights Towards Safety. Springer, Cham (2022). https://doi.org/10.1007/978-3-031-01233-4
6. Guen, V.L., Thome, N.: Disentangling physical dynamics from unknown factors for unsupervised video prediction. In: Proceedings of ICCV, Los Alamitos, CA, USA, pp. 11471–11481, June 2020
7. Hochreiter, S., Schmidhuber, J.: Long Short-Term Memory. Neural Comput. **9**(8), 1735–1780 (1997)
8. Jin, X., et al.: Predicting scene parsing and motion dynamics in the future. In: Proceedings of the NeurIPS, Long Beach, CA, USA, December 2017
9. Kalman, R.E.: A new approach to linear filtering and prediction problems. Trans. ASME-J. Basic Eng. **82**(Series D), 35–45 (1960)
10. Kwon, Y.H., Park, M.G.: Predicting future frames using retrospective cycle GAN. In: Proceedings of CVPR, Long Beach, CA, USA, pp. 1811–1820, June 2019
11. Liu, Z., Yeh, R., Tang, X., Liu, Y., Agarwala, A.: Video frame synthesis using deep voxel flow. In: Proceedings of the ICCV, Venice, Italy, pp. 4463–4471, October 2017
12. Lotter, W., Kreiman, G., Cox, D.D.: Deep predictive coding networks for video prediction and unsupervised learning. arXiv, August 2016
13. Luc, P., Neverova, N., Couprie, C., Verbeek, J., LeCun, Y.: Predicting deeper into the future of semantic segmentation. In: Proceedings of ICCV, Venice, Italy, pp. 648–657, October 2017
14. Lucas, B.D., Kanade, T.: An iterative image registration technique with an application to stereo vision. In: Proceedings of IJCAI, Vancouver, BC, Canada, pp. 674–679, August 1981
15. Maas, A., Hannun, A., Ng, A.: Rectifier nonlinearities improve neural network acoustic models. In: Proceedings of ICML, Atlanta, Georgia (2013)
16. Mahjourian, R., Wicke, M., Angelova, A.: Geometry-based next frame prediction from monocular video. In: Proceedings of IV, pp. 1700–1707, June 2017
17. Mathieu, M., Couprie, C., LeCun, Y.: Deep multi scale video prediction beyond mean square error. In: Proceedings of ICLR, San Juan, Puerto Rico, pp. 1–14, May 2016
18. Nabavi, S.S., Rochan, M., Wang, Y.: Future semantic segmentation with convolutional LSTM. In: Proceedings of BMVC, Newcastle, UK, pp. 1–12, September 2018
19. Redmon, J., Divvala, S., Girshick, R., Farhadi, A.: You only look once: unified, real-time object detection. In: Proceedings of CVPR, Las Vegas, NV, USA, pp. 779–788, June 2016
20. Redmon, J., Farhadi, A.: YOLO9000: better, faster, stronger. In: Proceedings of CVPR, Honolulu, HI, USA, July 2017
21. Ronneberger, O., Fischer, P., Brox, T.: U-Net: convolutional networks for biomedical image segmentation. In: Navab, N., Hornegger, J., Wells, W.M., Frangi, A.F. (eds.) MICCAI 2015. LNCS, vol. 9351, pp. 234–241. Springer, Cham (2015). https://doi.org/10.1007/978-3-319-24574-4_28
22. Shi, X., Chen, Z., Wang, H., Yeung, D.Y., Wong, W.K., Woo, W.C.: Convolutional LSTM network: a machine learning approach for precipitation nowcasting. In: Proceedings of NIPS, Montreal, QC, Canada, pp. 802–810, December 2015
23. Walker, J., Razavi, A., van den Oord, A.: Predicting video with VQVAE. CoRR abs/2103.01950 (2021). https://arxiv.org/abs/2103.01950
24. Wang, Z., Zheng, L., Liu, Y., Li, Y., Wang, S.: Towards real-time multi-object tracking. In: Vedaldi, A., Bischof, H., Brox, T., Frahm, J.-M. (eds.) ECCV 2020.

LNCS, vol. 12356, pp. 107–122. Springer, Cham (2020). https://doi.org/10.1007/978-3-030-58621-8_7

25. Xie, E., Wang, W., Yu, Z., Anandkumar, A., Alvarez, J.M., Luo, P.: SegFormer: simple and efficient design for semantic segmentation with transformers. In: Proceedings of NeurIPS, pp. 12077–12090. Virtual Conference, December 2021

26. Yu, F., et al.: BDD100K: a diverse driving dataset for heterogeneous multitask learning. In: Proceedings of CVPR, Seattle, WA, USA, pp. 1–14, June 2020

27. Zhao, H., Zhang, S., Wu, G., Moura, J.M.F., Costeira, J.P., Gordon, G.J.: Adversarial multiple source domain adaptation. In: Proceedings of NeurIPS, Montréal, QC, Canada, pp. 8568–8579, December 2018

28. Zhao, H., Shi, J., Qi, X., Wang, X., Jia, J.: Pyramid scene parsing network. In: Proceedings of CVPR, Honulu, HI, USA, pp. 2881–2890, July 2017

29. Zhao, H., et al.: PSANet: point-wise spatial attention network for scene parsing. In: Ferrari, V., Hebert, M., Sminchisescu, C., Weiss, Y. (eds.) ECCV 2018. LNCS, vol. 11213, pp. 270–286. Springer, Cham (2018). https://doi.org/10.1007/978-3-030-01240-3_17

Extracting Features from Random Subseries: A Hybrid Pipeline for Time Series Classification and Extrinsic Regression

Matthew Middlehurst[(✉)] and Anthony Bagnall

School of Electronics and Computer Science, University of Southampton,
Southampton, UK
{m.b.middlehurst,a.j.bagnall}@soton.ac.uk

Abstract. In time series classification (TSC) literature, approaches which incorporate multiple feature extraction domains such as HIVE-COTE and TS-CHIEF have generally shown to perform better than single domain approaches in situations where no expert knowledge is available for the data. Time series extrinsic regression (TSER) has seen very little activity compared to TSC, but the provision of benchmark datasets for regression by researchers at Monash University and the University of East Anglia provide an opportunity to see if this insight gleaned from TSC literature applies to regression data. We show that extracting random shapelets and intervals from different series representations and concatenating the output as part of a feature extraction pipeline significantly outperforms the single domain approaches for both classification and regression. In addition to our main contribution, we provide results for shapelet based algorithms on the regression archive datasets using the RDST transform, and show that current interval based approaches such as DrCIF can find noticeable scalability improvements by adopting the pipeline format.

1 Introduction

Time series classification (TSC) is the task of predicting a categorical target variable from time series data. The field of TSC has received rapid development in recent years, in part due to the continued maintenance and expansion of the University of California, Riverside (UCR) dataset archive for TSC [9]. Time series extrinsic regression (TSER), like more traditional regression tasks for machine learning, has a continuous target variable. Both tasks differ from standard machine learning in that each data attribute takes the form of a series of ordered values, with discriminatory features found in the shape and frequency of patterns within the series.

TSER has not received the same attention in literature as TSC has, and until recently has not had a collection of datasets comparable to the UCR archive to benchmark algorithms with. A collection of 19 datasets were introduced by Tan

G. Ifrim et al. (Eds.): AALTD 2023, LNAI 14343, pp. 113–126, 2023.
https://doi.org/10.1007/978-3-031-49896-1_8

et al. from Monash University [36], recently further expanded to 63 datasets by researchers at the University of East Anglia (UEA) [19]. A few algorithms proposed for TSC have been adapted for TSER with mixed success. These algorithms are mostly simple adaptations, using an unsupervised transformation in combination with a vector classifier or regressor. On 62 datasets from the expanded TSER archive, only the Fresh Pipeline with Rotation Forest Classifier (FreshPRINCE) [27] and Diverse Representation Canonical Interval Forest (DrCIF) [29] were significantly better than a Rotation Forest (RotF) [32] benchmark using root-mean-square error (RMSE) as a performance metric [19].

For TSC problems the best approach should consider the discriminatory features present in the series, i.e. whether the presence of a pattern or its frequency is discriminatory, or if patterns are phase-dependent or phase-independent. In the absence of expert knowledge, hybrid approaches encompassing multiple feature extraction approaches have shown to perform more accurately than single domain algorithms [1,11,29,30,35]. We explore whether this improvement through incorporating multiple domains translates to TSER using a simple pipeline of unsupervised transformations from different feature domains. While hybrid algorithms such as the Hierarchical Vote Collective of Transformation-based Ensembles (HIVE-COTE) [23,29] and Time Series Combination of Heterogeneous and Integrated Embedding Forest (TS-CHIEF) [35] have already shown to perform accurately on the UCR archive compared to single domain algorithms, modifying these algorithms to accept continuous values would be a complex process which would go beyond the simple exploration we wish to present. By using unsupervised transformations, the only change made to the hybrid algorithm between tasks is the base estimator used.

Our hybrid pipeline makes use of two transformations, both of which randomly select subseries to extract features from. The algorithm selects features from the interval feature domain with a transformation based on the DrCIF ensemble, and from the shapelet feature domain using the Random Dilated Shapelet Transform (RDST). Both of these algorithms have shown to perform accurately in their feature group for TSC on the UCR archive [30]. Our pipeline involves transforming the input series into multiple representations such as first-order differences and periodograms, then extracting and concatenating features for a vector classifier using our transformations. We show that the pipeline is significantly more accurate than DrCIF and RDST on 112 UCR datasets, and that it also outperforms both algorithms on 55 regression TSER problems.

We structure the rest of this paper as follows. Section 2 discusses the background and related works. In Sect. 3 we describe our pipeline in greater detail. Section 4 discussed our experimental methodology and provides details for reproducibility, followed by Sect. 5 which presents our results on the UCR and TSER archives. In Sect. 6 we summarise our findings and conclude.

2   Background and Related Work

Both TSC and TSER are tasks where the objective is to create a function which maps input time series data to a target variable using a training set of time series and label pairs. Input case pairs $(\boldsymbol{X}, y)$ hold a time series $\boldsymbol{X}$ containing d channels $\boldsymbol{X} = \{\boldsymbol{x}_1, \boldsymbol{x}_2, \dots, \boldsymbol{x}_d\}$ with m real-valued ordered time points $\boldsymbol{x} = \{t_1, t_2, \dots, t_m\}$ and a target label y. For TSC y is a discrete class label from c possible class values, while for TSER y is a scalar value. Case pairs are grouped into datasets of n pairs $\boldsymbol{T} = \{(\boldsymbol{X}_1, \boldsymbol{y}_1), (\boldsymbol{X}_2, \boldsymbol{y}_2), \dots, (\boldsymbol{X}_n, \boldsymbol{y}_n)\}$. Datasets where the time series contains only a single channel are univariate time series problems, while those with more than a single channel are multivariate. It is not always the case that all time series in a dataset will have the same number of time points, but we restrict this work with the assumption that all series have the same length.

A comparison of TSC algorithms in 2017 [1] created a taxonomy of TSC algorithms based on the types of feature extracted, sorting the algorithms used into different domains. In 2017 there were six categories, and recent updated comparison has increased this to eight categories [30]. In the following we outline these categories, including descriptions of relevant algorithms and those we use in our Sect. 5 experiments. While we describe all categories in the following for context of the wider field and different approaches for TSC, our main interest in this study lies with interval-based approaches, shapelet-based approaches and hybrid approaches.

Distance-based algorithms make use of distance measures to compare time series, usually using a nearest-neighbour (NN) algorithm to make predictions. A popular benchmark is the elastic distance measure Dynamic Time Warping (DTW) using a 1-NN classifier or regressor. There are many elastic distances for time series proposed, which have been used individually and as part of ensembles. Proximity Forest (PF) [21,25] is a distance-based ensemble making use of different distance measures in its ensembled trees.

Dictionary-based look for the frequency of recurring patterns as a discriminatory feature. These are most commonly found through converting time series into a sequence of discrete symbolic words, forming a bag-of-words to compare cases. More recent methods run multiple configurations of word extraction techniques to form an ensemble such as the Temporal Dictionary Ensemble (TDE) [26] or as part of a pipeline with feature selection like Word Extraction for Time Series Classification (WEASEL) [33,34].

Feature-based algorithms are techniques which extract a feature vector of summary statistics to be used as part of a simple pipeline. These pipelines are mainly made up of two components, the transformation to convert the series to features, and a base estimator to build a model and make predictions using said features. An example is FreshPRINCE [27], a pipeline of the TSFresh [8] features and a rotation forest [32] which has performed as well as more complex algorithms from other domains for TSC and is a top performer on the TSER archive [19]. The iFx [17] for TSER extracts many summary statistics from different series representations and subseries as features for a Bayesian method.

Convolution-based approaches make use of many randomly initialised convolution kernels in conjunction with the linear classifier as part of a pipeline. The Random Convolutional Kernel Transform (ROCKET) [10] and its derivatives such as MultiROCKET [37] and Hydra [11] fall under this category. Our approach shares similarities with the MultiROCKET-Hydra pipeline proposed in [11], which concatenates the features of both transforms for a pipeline.

Deep learning, like other machine learning fields, is a popular topic for time series tasks. The InceptionTime [14] is currently the best performing deep learner for TSC. The version of InceptionTime we use is an ensemble of 5 networks (InceptionE) proposed in the original publication.

Interval-based approaches select phase-dependent subseries from the input series to derive features from. By selecting many subseries the goal is to derive features that may be otherwise be obscured by irrelevant activity in the series should the whole series be used. Most interval base approaches use a random forest approach [13,15,28]. The DrCIF algorithm follows this, randomly selecting multiple intervals and subsampling the Catch22 [24] features for each tree. The Randomised Supervised Time Series Forest (R-STSF) [7] breaks this mould of ensemble approaches, using a pipeline approach for its extracted intervals.

Shapelet-based algorithm find phase-independent discriminatory subseries, looking for the presence of a pattern anywhere in the time series rather than its frequency or at specific time points. Shapelet models compare extracted shapelets to series using a function $sDist()$, which finds the shorted distance from the shapelet to all subseries of the same length. The Shapelet Transform Classifier (STC) [4,22] algorithm is a pipeline algorithm which creates a feature vector of $sDist()$ values using a filtered set of shapelets and a rotation forest classifier. RDST is an algorithm based on the shapelet transform which we cover in more detail in the following section. The Multiple Representations Sequence Mine (MrSQM) [31] follows an approach of discretising series into words using multiple differently parameterised methods and uses the presence of selected subsequences in any part of the full word as features for a logistic regression model.

Hybrid algorithms incorporate two or more of the above categories in a single algorithm with the aim of leveraging the strengths of each domain included. At the time of writing the most accurate hybrid algorithm on the UCR archive is HIVE-COTE v2 [29,30], a weighed ensemble of high performance algorithms from other domains. The HC2 ensemble includes DrCIF, TDE, STC and an ensemble of ROCKET classifiers called the Arsenal. The Time Series Combination of Heterogeneous and Integrated Embedding Forest (TS-CHIEF) [35] also takes an ensemble approach to combining feature domains, but creates a homogenous forest of trees which extract hybrid features at each node rather than a heterogenous ensemble like HC2.

3   A Randomised Shapelet and Interval Transformation Pipeline

The pipeline classifier and regressor we use in our experiments is a hybrid of interval and shapelet based approaches. For brevity, we refer to this pipeline as the Randomised Interval-Shapelet Transformation (RIST) pipeline going forward. Both of these feature domains extract random subseries from the input series, but how these subseries are used and the features extracted from them differ.

For the interval half of RIST we draw from the DrCIF [29] algorithm. Instead of extracting a small amount of intervals for a single tree as part of an ensemble, we extract a larger amount of intervals in a singular step to concatenate with the shapelet transform output. For RIST we extract i intervals of random length and size. From these subseries, 30 summary statistics are extracted. These are the Catch22 [24] features used by DrCIF, as well as the mean, standard-deviation, slope, median, interquartile range, min, max, and proportion of positive values. Algorithm 1 describes the interval portion of the transformation.

Algorithm 1. Intervals(A list of n series of length m with d channels, $\boldsymbol{X}$)

Parameters: the number of intervals i
1: $\boldsymbol{X'} \leftarrow$ initialize matrix of dimensionality $n \times (i30)$
2: **for** $j \leftarrow 1$ to i **do**
3:     $b = rand(1, m - 3)$ { *interval position* }
4:     $l = rand(3, m/2)$ { *interval length* }
5:     $o = rand(1, d)$ { *interval channel* }
6:     **for** $t \leftarrow 1$ to n **do**
7:         **for** $f \leftarrow 1$ to 30 **do**
8:             $\boldsymbol{X'}_{t,(j-1)30+f} \leftarrow summaryStat(f, \boldsymbol{X}_{t,o,b:l})$
9: $\boldsymbol{X'} \leftarrow pruneIdenticalIntervals(\boldsymbol{X'})$
10: **return** $\boldsymbol{X'}$

The shapelet half of RIST leverages the RDST [20] transformation without modifications. RDST randomly selects a large number of random shapelets from the train data. Unlike the original Shapelet Transform (ST) [22] algorithm, RDST does not evaluate shapelets using information gain or any other metric to determine the quality of the shapelet to act as a filter. RDST only prunes any identical shapelets from its initial random selection. The shapelets extracted by RDST use dilation as the primary method of diversifying extracted shapelets rather than shapelet length. Using dilation in subseries is a technique which primarily used in convolution based methods such as ROCKET [10,37], but has been introduced to other algorithm domains recently [20,34]. A shapelet with a dilation value of d compares time points which are d steps apart, a d value of 1 will have no gaps between values sampled for the shapelet, while a value 2 will sample every other value.

The standard shapelet distance (sDist) method is applied by RDST. To compare a shapelet to a full time series, a sliding window is run across the series calculating the distance to all subseries of the same length as the shapelet, but with the addition of dilation. As well as taking the minimum distance from all subseries as a feature, RDST also extracts the position of the minimum distance subseries and the number of occurrences of the shapelet determined by a similarity threshold. These additional features incorporate spatial information as well as pattern occurrence information seen in dictionary based approaches into the extracted features.

When selecting its shapelets, RDST randomly initialises the dilation value of shapelet; whether the shapelet distance is z-normalised; the train case and position in the series the shapelet is extracted from; and the similarity threshold used in the shapelet occurrence feature. For multivariate time series, a two-dimensional shapelet is extracted and used to compare the distance of all channels. A simplified version of the shapelet extraction algorithm is displayed in Algorithm 2. For exact values used when selecting random shapelets, we recommended viewing the original publication or the implementation we direct to in Sect. 4.

Algorithm 2. Shapelets(A list of n series of length m with d channels, $\boldsymbol{X}$)

Parameters: the number of shapelets s

1: $\boldsymbol{X'} \leftarrow$ initialize matrix of dimensionality $n \times (s3)$
2: **for** $j \leftarrow 1$ to s **do**
3:    $dil, thr, norm \leftarrow shapeletParams()$ { *randomly select shapelet parameters* }
4:    $o \leftarrow randint(1, n)$
5:    $pos \leftarrow randint(1, m - dil10)$ { *randomly select position to extract from* }
6:    $\boldsymbol{A} \leftarrow dilatedSubseries(\boldsymbol{X}_o, pos, 11, dil)$ { *extract shapelet, always length 11* }
7:    **for** $t \leftarrow 1$ to n **do**
8:       $d \leftarrow sDist(\boldsymbol{A}, \boldsymbol{X}_t, dil, norm)$ { *distances between $\boldsymbol{A}$ and all subseries* }
9:       $\boldsymbol{X'}_{t,(j-1)3+1} \leftarrow min(\boldsymbol{d})$
10:      $\boldsymbol{X'}_{t,(j-1)3+2} \leftarrow argmin(\boldsymbol{d})$
11:      $\boldsymbol{X'}_{t,(j-1)3+3} \leftarrow occurrences(\boldsymbol{d}, thr)$
12: **return** $\boldsymbol{X'}$

Extracting intervals from different series representations has shown to improve accuracy over just extracting intervals from the base series [6,7,29]. For RIST we also extract features from different series representations by applying the series-to-series transformations used in the R-STSF algorithm, which have also seen use in many other published TSC algorithms. These are the first order differences [6,29,37], the periodogram of the series [6,15,29] and the series autoregression coefficients [7]. We run our shapelet and interval transformations on each of these series representations as well as the base series, then concatenate them for use in a feature vector classification or regression algorithm. The RIST pipeline is described in Algorithm 3.

4   Experimental Methodology and Reproducibility

We run our experiments using two time series dataset archives. Our classification experiments are run using 112 datasets from the UCR time series

Algorithm 3. RIST(A list of n cases of length m with d channels, $\boldsymbol{T} = (\boldsymbol{X}, \boldsymbol{y})$)

Parameters: the number of intervals i, the number of shapelets s, the feature vector estimator *est*

1: Let $\boldsymbol{V}$ be a $4 \times n \times d$ matrix of series with variable length, containing the base series, the periodograms, the first order differences and the autoregression coefficients
2: $\boldsymbol{X'} \leftarrow []$
3: **for** $j \leftarrow 1$ to $|\boldsymbol{V}|$ **do**
4:     $\boldsymbol{I} \leftarrow Intervals(\boldsymbol{V}_j, i)$
5:     $\boldsymbol{X'} \leftarrow \boldsymbol{X'} + \boldsymbol{I}$ { *concatenate feature vectors* }
6:     $\boldsymbol{S} \leftarrow Shapelets(\boldsymbol{V}_j, s)$
7:     $\boldsymbol{X'} \leftarrow \boldsymbol{X'} + \boldsymbol{S}$ { *concatenate feature vectors* }
8: $est.buildEstimator(\boldsymbol{X'}, \boldsymbol{y})$

archive[1] [9]. We exclude all datasets from the archive which contain unequal length series or series with missing values from our selection. All classification datasets used are univariate, containing a single channel time series for each case. For our extrinsic regression experiments, we use 55 datasets out of the 63 total from the TSER repository[2] [36] and datasets from a proposed extension[3] [19]. The NewsHeadlineSentiment; PPGDalia-equal-length; VentilatorPressure; AustraliaRainfall; NewsTitleSentiment; BIDMC32SpO2; BIDMC32HR; and BIDMC32RR datasets are excluded solely due to time constraints. The TSER archive includes both univariate and multivariate datasets, of which we use both to supplement the low volume of univariate datasets. With the inclusion of multivariate TSER datasets it is sensible to ask why the UEA archive of multivariate TSC datasets [2] is not included. We again exclude these due to time constraints in the running of our experiments, but note that many of the algorithms including our proposed one are multivariate capable and these datasets should be explored in future work.

We present the performance of an algorithm on a dataset as an average over 5 resamples. Both UCR and TSER archives provide a default train and test split, which we use for the first resample. The remaining runs are resampled randomly from the provided split in a stratified manner for the UCR datasets, and fully random for the TSER data. Each algorithm and data resample random number generation is seeded using the resample index to help ensure reproducibility.

For comparison of multiple classifiers over multiple datasets, an adaptation of the critical difference diagram [12] is used. The post-hoc Nemenyi test is replaced using pairwise Wilcoxon signed-rank tests using our averaged scores. Cliques are formed using the Holm correction, following recommendations from [3,16]. We compare our classification algorithms using accuracy, and our regression algorithms using RMSE following [19,36].

---

[1] https://www.timeseriesclassification.com/dataset.php.

[2] http://tseregression.org/.

[3] https://tsml-eval.readthedocs.io/en/latest/publications/2023/
tser_archive_expansion/tser_archive_expansion.html.

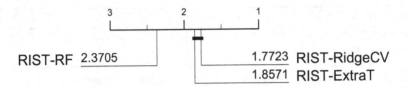

Fig. 1. Accuracy critical difference diagram for RIST with different base classifiers. Displays the average accuracy rank averaged over 5 resamples on 112 UCR datasets.

All the tools to run our experiments are available through the *tsml-eval*[4] package, primarily using implementations from the *aeon*[5] toolkit. More details on reproducing our experiments and results files can be found on the companion webpage[6].

5   Results

In the following, we present summarised results for RIST and relevant algorithms for both archives. For RIST we set the number of intervals extracted to $i = (sqrt(m) * sqrt(d) * 15 + 5)$ and the number of shapelets to $s = (sqrt(m) * 200 + 5)$. Both of these are functions of the dataset series length and number of dimensions, taking into account that the series length may change per series representation.

Prior to our main results, we show results for different base estimators used in RIST, showing that this selection can have a large impact on overall results. The base estimators we compare include a linear Ridge estimator using cross-validation (RidgeCV) which is a commonly used base classifier for TSC [10,20, 37]. Also compared are a Random Forest (RF) [5] which is a well known and popular baseline, and the Extra Trees (ExtraT) [18] algorithm, another random tree base ensemble used by R-STSF [7].

5.1   112 UCR Archive Classification Datasets

Figure 1 compares the RIST transform using different feature vector classifiers. Both the ridge and extra trees classifiers show no significant difference when used as a base. As the extra trees classifier was quicker at 7 min on average to process the UCR datasets against the 10 min of the ridge classifier, we use that as our base. Figure 2 shows a pairwise diagram comparing the average accuracy of the extra trees classifier against the ridge classifier for all datasets. Despite using the same seeded transformation, the difference in accuracy between both algorithms can be quite large for some datasets.

---

[4] https://github.com/time-series-machine-learning/tsml-eval.
[5] https://www.aeon-toolkit.org/.
[6] https://tsml-eval.readthedocs.io/en/latest/publications/2023/rist_pipeline/rist_pipeline.html.

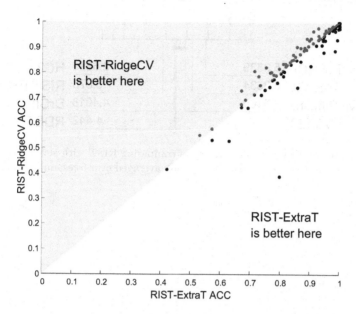

Fig. 2. Scatter plot of RIST using an extra trees and ridge base classifier. Compares the average accuracy over 5 resamples for each of the 112 UCR archive datasets. RIST-RidgeCV Win/Draw/Loss 60/8/44.

We compare RIST against other TSC algorithms in Fig. 3. Similar to the RDST and R-STSF pipelines, we include a single domain interval pipeline which just our interval transformer and an extra trees classifier to help gauge the impact of the pipeline structure vs ensemble structure of DrCIF. The simple RIST pipeline concatenating transform outputs significantly outperforms both DrCIF and RDST, the algorithms the transforms are based on. The only algorithm which it performs significantly worse than in our comparison is HC2, another hybrid containing more feature domains and more complex algorithms.

A comparison of runtime against accuracy rank is shown in Fig. 4. RIST is not as fast as RDST, R-STSF or ROCKET, but compares favourably to more complex algorithms. While HC2 is significantly more accurate than RIST, it is also close to 40 times slower to build on average. The interval transformation pipeline we included shows no significant difference in performance to DrCIF and is an order of magnitude faster than DrCIF. To achieve similar scalability improvements using the ensemble structure, the amount of DrCIF trees built and intervals extracted would have to be significantly reduced, which is likely to impact performance considerably.

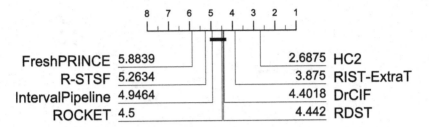

Fig. 3. Accuracy critical difference diagram comparing RIST with seven classification algorithms. Displays the average accuracy rank averaged over 5 resamples on 112 UCR datasets.

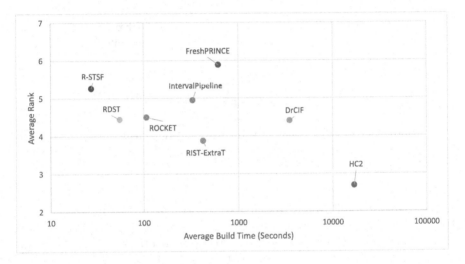

Fig. 4. A comparison of classifiers accuracy rank and build time averaged over 112 UCR problems. The build time is on a log scale.

5.2   55 TSER Archive Datasets

In our previous experiments we show that a combination of shapelet and interval features from RIST outperforms the single domain classifiers the features are derived from on the UCR archive. We now experiment to see if this is the case for the newly introduced TSER archive as well.

Figure 5 compares different base regressors for RIST as we previously did for classification. While for the classification task the random forest classifier was significantly worse, the random forest regressor has seemingly swapped position with the ridge regressor. In previous comparisons on the TSER archive, ROCKET which also uses a ridge regressor performed below expectations considering its success in classification [19]. It is possible that the selection of base estimator could play a part in this underperformance. Of the two best performing base regressors, the extra trees algorithms is faster to build on the TSER

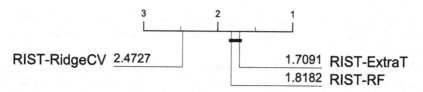

Fig. 5. RMSE critical difference diagram for RIST with different base regressors. Displays the average RMSE rank averaged over 5 resamples on 55 TSER datasets.

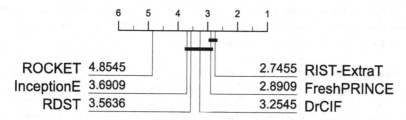

Fig. 6. RMSE critical difference diagram comparing RIST with five regression algorithms. Displays the average RMSE rank averaged over 5 resamples on 55 TSER datasets.

archive. For this reason and to keep consistency with the classification version, we use it as a base for our regression experiments.

A critical difference diagram comparing RIST and competitive TSER algorithms on the 55 datasets is shown in Fig. 6. RDST was not included in previous publications experimenting with the TSER archive, and places middle of the pack in a clique with inception time, DrCIF and FreshPRINCE. RIST shows no significant difference to FreshPRINCE, but once again performs significantly better than both DrCIF and RDST. While there are other factors at play which could contribute to this increased performance, we believe it is likely that the same assumption regarding the performance of hybrid approaches in TSC also applies to TSER given the similarity of the presented results for both tasks for RIST, DrCIF and RDST.

6   Conclusions

We have shown that a transformation extracting random interval and shapelet subseries from different series representation can outperform individual interval and shapelet feature domain algorithms. While showing that hybrid algorithms have increased performance on the UCR archive is not new, RIST is much faster and simpler than other suggested hybrid approaches. The RIST transformation is fully unsupervised and can be easily applied to both classification and regression tasks. Our experiments show that the performance of RIST carries over to the TSER archive, presenting an early hybrid approach for TSER.

Given the performance of RIST for TSER, there is likely scope for further improvement by developing more sophisticated hybrid approaches for the task.

HC2 outperforms RIST for classification, and as algorithms continue to be developed for the task a similar ensemble approach over multiple feature domains may find success as well.

While only briefly covered in our results, formatting the interval transform as a pipeline rather than an ensemble for the DrCIF algorithm resulted in significant scalability improvements. Even with the addition of the shapelet features, RIST is still much faster than the ensemble. This follows the approach of numerous recent algorithms, which produce a mass of features and leave a vector estimator to select the useful ones. While faster, a drawback of this approach is that it could be costly in terms of memory to perform these large transforms and require all features to be stored in memory at a single point.

Acknowledgements. This work is supported by the UK Engineering and Physical Sciences Research Council (EPSRC) grant number EP/W030756/1. The experiments were carried out on the High Performance Computing Cluster supported by the Research and Specialist Computing Support service at the University of East Anglia (UEA). We would like to thank all those responsible for helping maintain the time series dataset archives and those contributing to open source implementations of the algorithms.

References

1. Bagnall, A., Lines, J., Bostrom, A., Large, J., Keogh, E.: The great time series classification bake off: a review and experimental evaluation of recent algorithmic advances. Data Min. Knowl. Disc. **31**(3), 606–660 (2017)
2. Bagnall, A., et al.: The UEA multivariate time series classification archive. arXiv preprint arXiv:1811.00075 (2018)
3. Benavoli, A., Corani, G., Mangili, F.: Should we really use post-hoc tests based on mean-ranks? J. Mach. Learn. Res. **17**, 1–10 (2016)
4. Bostrom, A., Bagnall, A.: Binary shapelet transform for multiclass time series classification. Trans. Large-Scale Data Knowl. Centered Syst. **32**, 24–46 (2017)
5. Breiman, L.: Bagging predictors. Mach. Learn. **24**(2), 123–140 (1996)
6. Cabello, N., Naghizade, E., Qi, J., Kulik, L.: Fast and accurate time series classification through supervised interval search. In: IEEE International Conference on Data Mining (2020)
7. Cabello, N., Naghizade, E., Qi, J., Kulik, L.: Fast, accurate and interpretable time series classification through randomization. arXiv preprint arXiv:2105.14876 (2021)
8. Christ, M., Braun, N., Neuffer, J., Kempa-Liehr, A.W.: Time Series FeatuRe Extraction on basis of Scalable Hypothesis tests (tsfresh-A Python package). Neurocomputing **307**, 72–77 (2018)
9. Dau, H., et al.: The UCR time series archive. IEEE/CAA J. Automatica Sinica **6**(6), 1293–1305 (2019)
10. Dempster, A., Petitjean, F., Webb, G.: ROCKET: exceptionally fast and accurate time series classification using random convolutional kernels. Data Min. Knowl. Disc. **34**, 1454–1495 (2020)
11. Dempster, A., Schmidt, D.F., Webb, G.I.: HYDRA: competing convolutional kernels for fast and accurate time series classification. arXiv preprint arXiv:2203.13652 (2022)

12. Demšar, J.: Statistical comparisons of classifiers over multiple data sets. J. Mach. Learn. Res. **7**, 1–30 (2006)

13. Deng, H., Runger, G., Tuv, E., Vladimir, M.: A time series forest for classification and feature extraction. Inf. Sci. **239**, 142–153 (2013)

14. Fawaz, H., et al.: InceptionTime: finding AlexNet for time series classification. Data Min. Knowl. Disc. **34**(6), 1936–1962 (2020)

15. Flynn, M., Large, J., Bagnall, T.: The contract random interval spectral ensemble (c-RISE): the effect of contracting a classifier on accuracy. In: Pérez García, H., Sánchez González, L., Castejón Limas, M., Quintián Pardo, H., Corchado Rodríguez, E. (eds.) HAIS 2019. LNCS (LNAI), vol. 11734, pp. 381–392. Springer, Cham (2019). https://doi.org/10.1007/978-3-030-29859-3_33

16. García, S., Herrera, F.: An extension on "statistical comparisons of classifiers over multiple data sets" for all pairwise comparisons. J. Mach. Learn. Res. **9**, 2677–2694 (2008)

17. Gay, D., Bondu, A., Lemaire, V., Boullé, M.: Interpretable feature construction for time series extrinsic regression. In: Karlapalem, K., et al. (eds.) PAKDD 2021. LNCS (LNAI), vol. 12712, pp. 804–816. Springer, Cham (2021). https://doi.org/10.1007/978-3-030-75762-5_63

18. Geurts, P., Ernst, D., Wehenkel, L.: Extremely randomized trees. Mach. Learn. **63**, 3–42 (2006)

19. Guijo-Rubio, D., Middlehurst, M., Arcencio, G., Silva, D.F., Bagnall, A.: Unsupervised feature based algorithms for time series extrinsic regression. arXiv preprint arXiv:2305.01429 (2023)

20. Guillaume, A., Vrain, C., Elloumi, W.: Random dilated shapelet transform: a new approach for time series shapelets. In: El Yacoubi, M., Granger, E., Yuen, P.C., Pal, U., Vincent, N. (eds.) Pattern Recognition and Artificial Intelligence: Third International Conference, ICPRAI 2022, Paris, France, 1–3 June 2022, Proceedings, Part I, pp. 653–664. Springer, Cham (2022). https://doi.org/10.1007/978-3-031-09037-0_53

21. Herrmann, M., Tan, C.W., Salehi, M., Webb, G.I.: Proximity Forest 2.0: a new effective and scalable similarity-based classifier for time series. arXiv preprint arXiv:2304.05800 (2023)

22. Lines, J., Davis, L., Hills, J., Bagnall, A.: A shapelet transform for time series classification. In: Proceedings of the 18th ACM SIGKDD International Conference on Knowledge Discovery and Data Mining (2012)

23. Lines, J., Taylor, S., Bagnall, A.: Time series classification with HIVE-COTE: the hierarchical vote collective of transformation-based ensembles. ACM Trans. Knowl. Discov. Data **12**(5), 1–36 (2018)

24. Lubba, C., Sethi, S., Knaute, P., Schultz, S., Fulcher, B., Jones, N.: Catch22: canonical time-series characteristics. Data Min. Knowl. Disc. **33**(6), 1821–1852 (2019)

25. Lucas, B., et al.: Proximity forest: an effective and scalable distance-based classifier for time series. Data Min. Knowl. Disc. **33**(3), 607–635 (2019)

26. Middlehurst, M., Large, J., Cawley, G., Bagnall, A.: The temporal dictionary ensemble (TDE) classifier for time series classification. In: Hutter, F., Kersting, K., Lijffijt, J., Valera, I. (eds.) ECML PKDD 2020. LNCS (LNAI), vol. 12457, pp. 660–676. Springer, Cham (2021). https://doi.org/10.1007/978-3-030-67658-2_38

27. Middlehurst, M., Bagnall, A.: The FreshPRINCE: a simple transformation based pipeline time series classifier. In: El Yacoubi, M., Granger, E., Yuen, P.C., Pal, U., Vincent, N. (eds.) Pattern Recognition and Artificial Intelligence, ICPRAI 2022.

LNCS, vol. 13364, pp. 150–161. Springer, Cham (2022). https://doi.org/10.1007/978-3-031-09282-4_13

28. Middlehurst, M., Large, J., Bagnall, A.: The canonical interval forest (CIF) classifier for time series classification. In: IEEE International Conference on Big Data, pp. 188–195 (2020)

29. Middlehurst, M., Large, J., Flynn, M., Lines, J., Bostrom, A., Bagnall, A.: HIVE-COTE 2.0: a new meta ensemble for time series classification. Mach. Learn. **110**, 3211–3243 (2021)

30. Middlehurst, M., Schäfer, P., Bagnall, A.: Bake off redux: a review and experimental evaluation of recent time series classification algorithms. arXiv preprint arXiv:2304.13029 (2023)

31. Nguyen, T.L., Ifrim, G.: Fast time series classification with random symbolic subsequences. In: Guyet, T., Ifrim, G., Malinowski, S., Bagnall, A., Shafer, P., Lemaire, V. (eds.) International Workshop on Advanced Analytics and Learning on Temporal Data, vol. 13812, pp. 50–65. Springer, Cham (2022). https://doi.org/10.1007/978-3-031-24378-3_4

32. Rodriguez, J.J., Kuncheva, L.I., Alonso, C.J.: Rotation forest: a new classifier ensemble method. IEEE Trans. Pattern Anal. Mach. Intell. **28**(10), 1619–1630 (2006)

33. Schäfer, P., Leser, U.: Fast and accurate time series classification with WEASEL. In: Proceedings of the ACM Conference on Information and Knowledge Management, pp. 637–646 (2017)

34. Schäfer, P., Leser, U.: Weasel 2.0 - a random dilated dictionary transform for fast, accurate and memory constrained time series classification. arXiv preprint arXiv:2301.10194 (2023)

35. Shifaz, A., Pelletier, C., Petitjean, F., Webb, G.I.: TS-CHIEF: a scalable and accurate forest algorithm for time series classification. Data Min. Knowl. Discov. **34**(3), 742–775 (2020)

36. Tan, C.W., Bergmeir, C., Petitjean, F., Webb, G.: Time series extrinsic regression. Data Min. Knowl. Discov. **35**, 1032–1060 (2021)

37. Tan, C.W., Dempster, A., Bergmeir, C., Webb, G.: MultiRocket: multiple pooling operators and transformations for fast and effective time series classification. Data Min. Knowl. Discov. **36**, 1623–1646 (2022)

ShapeDBA: Generating Effective Time Series Prototypes Using ShapeDTW Barycenter Averaging

Ali Ismail-Fawaz[1(✉)], Hassan Ismail Fawaz[1,4], François Petitjean[2],
Maxime Devanne[1], Jonathan Weber[1], Stefano Berretti[3], Geoffrey I. Webb[2],
and Germain Forestier[1,2]

[1] IRIMAS, Universite de Haute-Alsace, Mulhouse, France
{ali-el-hadi.ismail-fawaz,hassan.ismail-fawaz,maxime.devanne,
jonathan.weber,germain.forestier}@uha.fr
[2] Department of Data Science and Artificial Intelligence, Monash University,
Melbourne, Australia
{francois.petitjean,geoff.webb,germain.forestier}@monash.edu
[3] MICC, University of Florence, Florence, Italy
stefano.berretti@unifi.it
[4] Ericsson Research, Massy, France
hassan.ismail.fawaz@ericsson.com

Abstract. Time series data can be found in almost every domain, ranging from the medical field to manufacturing and wireless communication.
Generating realistic and useful exemplars and prototypes is a fundamental data analysis task. In this paper, we investigate a novel approach
to generating realistic and useful exemplars and prototypes for time
series data. Our approach uses a new form of time series average, the
ShapeDTW Barycentric Average. We therefore turn our attention to
accurately generating time series prototypes with a novel approach. The
existing time series prototyping approaches rely on the Dynamic Time
Warping (DTW) similarity measure such as DTW Barycentering Average (DBA) and SoftDBA. These last approaches suffer from a common
problem of generating out-of-distribution artifacts in their prototypes.
This is mostly caused by the DTW variant used and its incapability of
detecting neighborhood similarities, instead it detects absolute similarities. Our proposed method, ShapeDBA, uses the ShapeDTW variant of
DTW, that overcomes this issue. We chose time series clustering, a popular form of time series analysis to evaluate the outcome of ShapeDBA
compared to the other prototyping approaches. Coupled with the k-
means clustering algorithm, and evaluated on a total of 123 datasets from
the UCR archive, our proposed averaging approach is able to achieve new
state-of-the-art results in terms of Adjusted Rand Index.

Keywords: Time Series · Clustering · Dynamic Time Warping · Time
Series Averaging · ShapeDTW

G. Ifrim et al. (Eds.): AALTD 2023, LNAI 14343, pp. 127–142, 2023.
https://doi.org/10.1007/978-3-031-49896-1_9

1   Introduction

Time series data can now be seen in many real life problems. This data is starting to be of interest in many research fields. For instance time series can be found in medical data such as ECG signals, in human motion data, in satellite images, etc. Generating exemplars and prototypes for time series data is an essential problem that could be used in many areas. For example, time series averaging is being used to generate synthetic data in order to augment the training data and boost supervised models [5,11] or used to make the classification task more accurate [16]. Time series prototyping can also be used for explainability [6].

One challenge when prototyping time series data is evaluation, which is addressed in most of the cases using clustering, a fundamental machine learning tool in data analysis. Clustering is a machine learning unsupervised problem that aims to discover a set of clusters in the data that should correspond to the same distribution and the previously unseen class label. Clustering for time series data has been very much addressed in the literature [1,13]. Varying from machine learning tools such as k-means and k-medoids [7] to the usage of deep learning [12]. Unlike other data types, basic machine learning clustering algorithms need to be adapted to the case of temporal data. For instance, the k-means algorithm aims to minimize a distance between the samples in a cluster and the centroid of this cluster. This distance is usually the Euclidean distance, but the implicit assumption using such metric is that the input samples are made of independent feature points. However, this is not the case in time series data, where each feature point, referred to as time stamp, is dependent with all other time stamps. This is referred to as a temporal correlation, which obligates the definition of a replacement of the Euclidean distance in the k-means algorithm. For this reason, time series similarity measures such as DTW and SoftDTW have been used instead and showed a significant improvement over the usage of the Euclidean distance.

A further issue with the naive way of using the k-means algorithm, is the averaging phase to define the clusters' centroids. The averaging method used in the k-means algorithm is the arithmetic mean, which presents the same problem as the Euclidean distance. For this reason, a novel averaging method was proposed that uses the DTW similarity measure in order to produce a meaningful centroid. This technique, DBA, showed to perform significantly better than other naive approaches. The problem of finding a meaningful average for time series data presents much more challenges than defining the similarity metric. This is due to the challenge in defining what an average time series does represent. However, finding a meaningful average presents a much higher impact on the performance of the k-means algorithm than defining the similarity measure. For these reasons, we address the clustering problem by producing a more respectful averaging algorithm for time series data.

The defined averaging techniques for time series data until now suffer from a common problem of generating out-of-distribution artifacts (see Fig. 3). This problem occurs because these averaging techniques do not look into the neighborhood of each time stamp in the time series data. Instead, the averaging occurs after aligning each time stamp of the centroid with the ones in the time series dataset. In this work, we propose incorporating ShapeDTW [20] into the DBA algorithm in order to overcome this issue. ShapeDTW is a DTW variant that manages to avoid aligning two time stamp that have closer values but in a significantly different neighborhood. This last case study occurs often in time series data and is the main reason, to the best of our knowledge, for the existence of the generated artifacts. The ShapeDTW similarity measure coupled with DBA, i.e., the proposed ShapeDBA algorithm, is coupled with the k-means algorithm in order to apply clustering on time series data.

The contributions of this work are:

- Proposing a novel averaging algorithm ShapeDBA based on ShapeDTW;
- Extensive experiments on the UCR archive showing that ShapeDBA achieves state-of-the-art performance following the Adjusted Rand Index metric;
- Efficient implementation of ShapeDTW resulting in ShapeDBA being faster than SoftDBA.

2   Related Work

Definitions The following definitions will be used throughout the rest of the paper:

- Univariate Time Series (UTS) $\mathbf{x} = \{x_0, x_1, \ldots, x_{L-1}\}$ is a sequence of length L made of correlated data points equally separated in time.
- A TSC dataset $\mathcal{D} = \{(\mathbf{x}_i, y_i)\}_{i=0}^{N-1}$ is a collection of N time series with their corresponding labels y.
- A Time Series Average (TSA) $\mathbf{x}_{avg} = \{x_0, x_1, \ldots, x_{L-1}\}$ is a time series of length L that represents the average of a part of $\mathcal{D}$.

2.1   Time Series Similarity

Euclidean Distance (ED). The naive solution to define a similarity is by using the Euclidean Distance (ED). This metric defined in (1) supposes that the two time series are aligned on the time axis, which is not the case most of the times.

$$ED(\mathbf{x}_1, \mathbf{x}_2) = \sqrt{\sum_{t=0}^{L-1} (x_{1,t} - x_{2,t})^2}. \tag{1}$$

Another limitation that this similarity measure presents is that both time series should have the same length. In case of unequal length samples in the dataset, the problem should be addressed as dicussed in [18] such as padding, uniform scaling, etc.

Dynamic Time Warping (DTW). The following measure [14] is a more general formulation of the ED that is: (a) independent of the time series length, and (b) aligns the two time series on the time axis. The formulation of the DTW is presented in (2).

$$DTW(\mathbf{x}_1, \mathbf{x}_2) = \min_{\pi \in \mathcal{M}(\mathbf{x}_1, \mathbf{x}_2)} (\sum_{(i,j) \in \pi} |x_{1,i} - x_{2,j}|^q)^{1/q}, \tag{2}$$

with $\mathcal{M}(\mathbf{x}_1, \mathbf{x}_2)$ being the set of all possible alignment paths on the time axis between $\mathbf{x}_1$ and $\mathbf{x}_2$. The parameter q is the order of the Minkovski distance used, if $q = 2$ then the distance is set to be Euclidean. The hypothesis in this case is that $\mathbf{x}_1$ and $\mathbf{x}_2$ have different lengths, L_1 and L_2, respectively. The goal of DTW is to find the optimal path π of length L_π that minimizes the loss in (2). Some conditions should be applied on the optimal path as listed below:

- $\pi_0 = (0,0)$;
- $\pi_{L_\pi - 1} = (L_1 - 1, L_2 - 1)$;
- The elements of the path should be a strictly increasing sequence in the indices i and j of π.

Soft Dynamic Time Warping (SoftDTW). One issue of the DTW measure is its non-differentiability. For this reason, in [3] the Soft Dynamic Time Warping (SoftDTW) was proposed, which is differentiable. This differentiability exists because of the replacement of the hard min function in (2) by the softer version as seen in (3):

$$softmin^\gamma(x_0, \ldots, x_{L-1}) = -\gamma . \log(\sum_{i=0}^{L-1} e^{-x_i/\gamma}). \tag{3}$$

where the parameter γ controls the smoothness of the *softmin* function. The smaller the value of γ, the closer the *softmin* function is to the hard min.

Shape Dynamic Time Warping (ShapeDTW). In [20], a different version of DTW was proposed that, instead of aligning all the time series at the same time, aligns transformations of sub-sequences of the time series. This is done in order to preserve the fact that the alignment between two time stamps of two different time series takes into consideration the structure of their neighborhoods. For the mathematical definition of ShapeDTW, let us assume $\mathcal{F}$ is a descriptor function, x_1 and x_2 two univariate time series of lengths L_1 and L_2, respectively. The first step is to extract the sub-sequences of length l from x_1 and x_2 denoted by $\mathcal{X}_1$ and $\mathcal{X}_2$ represented as two multivariate time series of shape (L_1, l) and (L_2, l), respectively. The second step is to extract the descriptors from the sub-sequences using $\mathcal{F}$ and produce $\mathcal{D}_1 = \mathcal{F}(X_1)$ and $\mathcal{D}_2 = \mathcal{F}(\mathcal{X}_2)$ of shapes (L_1, d) and (L_2, d), respectively, where d is the target dimension. The ShapeDTW measure comes down to the following optimization problem:

$$ShapeDTW(x_1, x_2) = \min_{\pi \in \mathcal{M}(x_1, x_2)} (\sum_{(i,j) \in \pi} |\mathcal{D}_{1,i} - \mathcal{D}_{2,j}|^q)^{1/q} \tag{4}$$

The above definition can simply be adapted to multivariate time series as mentioned in the original work [20] by extracting multivariate sub-sequences and applying the descriptors on each dimension independently or by finding a suitable multivariate descriptor function.

2.2 Time Series Averaging - Clustering

Time Series Clustering. Given a time series dataset, usually an unlabeled one, the goal of the clustering algorithm is to learn how to group time series samples that should belong to the same class label together. A well known clustering algorithm is the k-means one, which learns how to group time series samples given their distance to a cluster's centroid. For this reason, a definition of a time series cluster centroid should be defined.

Dynamic Time Warping Barycenter Averaging (DBA). To define an average of a collection of time series, in [17] the usage of DTW measure was proposed in order to find the optimal average that takes into consideration the misalignment between the samples of this collection. In other words, given two time series, the DBA algorithm defines for each time stamp its barycenter by taking the average of all the aligned values. DBA has proven to be very effective in clustering using the k-means algorithm.

Soft Dynamic Time Warping Barycenter Averaging (SoftDBA). In [3], authors also proposed the replacement of DTW in the DBA algorithm by using SoftDTW instead. Our proposed approach, called SoftDBA, is shown to work better than DBA in clustering and classification.

3 Proposed Approach

3.1 Shape Dynamic Time Warping Barycenter Averaging (ShapeDBA)

ShapeDBA follows the same methodology of DBA and SoftDBA that is averaging over the aligned time stamps. The key difference of ShapeDBA is the usage of the ShapeDTW [20] aligning method of time series data. The ShapeDBA algorithm can be summarized in the following steps:

- **Step 1**: Initialize the average time series, for example choose a random selection of the time series set in question;
- **Step 2**: Find the aligned points of each time stamp of the average series with all the samples of the data. We call the time stamps of all the samples aligned with a given time stamp t of the average series as $assoc_t = \{assoc_{t_0}, assoc_{t_1}, \ldots, assoc_{t_{A-1}}\}$, where A is the number of associated time stamps with t;

- **Step 3**: For each time stamp t of the average series, the resulting average is the *barycenter* of $assoc_t$.
  Where $barycenter(assoc_{t_0}, assoc_{t_1}, \ldots, assoc_{t_{A-1}}) = \frac{1}{A} \sum_{i=0}^{A-1} assoc_{t_i}$;
- Repeat from Step 2 until convergence.

3.2   Clustering with ShapeDBA

The k-means clustering algorithm in machine learning can be used with any time series averaging technique, coupled with any time series similarity measure. The averaging method, i.e., ShapeDBA for instance, is used to find the centroids of each cluster during the training phase. The similarity measure is then used to calculate the distance of each series in the data to the centroid of each cluster.

In the rest of this paper, we refer to the following coupling for applying the k-means clustering algorithm:

- DBA: the DBA as an averaging method coupled with the DTW as a similarity measure;
- MED: the arithmetic mean as an averaging technique coupled with the Euclidean Distance (ED) as a similarity measure; MED finds iteratively the arithmetic average series, as in DBA, without taking into consideration the temporal alignment between the prototype and the samples;
- SoftDBA: the SoftDBA as an averaging method coupled with the SoftDTW as a similarity measure;
- ShapeDBA: the ShapeDBA as an averaging method coupled with the Shape-DTW as a similarity measure.

3.3   Implementation Efficiency

The ShapeDTW algorithm comes down to applying the original DTW similarity measure on the transformed input time series. In the univariate case coupled with the 'identity' descriptor of each neighborhood [20], the transformed time series is a multivariate version. For each time stamp, its neighborhood is added as a Euclidean vector to form a multivariate time series. When applying the DTW similarity measure on this transformed series, the algorithm is simply computing the Euclidean distance between the channel vectors of a pair of time stamps. This creates a computational waste when sliding the reach window as illustrated in Fig. 1. This problem only occurs when the descriptor is set to be the identity transformation.

To avoid this issue, the Euclidean pairwise distance between the two time series in question is computed as a first step. This distance matrix is then padded with its edges values $reach/2$ times. We then slide a window of height and width equal to the time series lengths on this Euclidean distance matrix. The direction of the sliding window is over the second diagonal of the distance matrix. The results captured on the sliding window are accumulated in a zero-initialized matrix. After accumulating all the information into the new distance matrix, we apply the DTW algorithm on the new matrix. This implementation saves time by avoiding unnecessary computations. A summary of this efficient implementation of the ShapeDTW can be seen in Fig. 2.

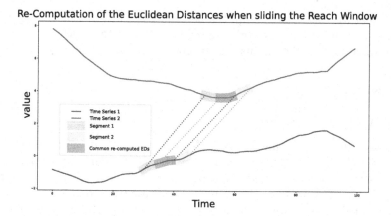

Fig. 1. Computation of the ShapeDTW measure between two time series. It can be observed that the common area between the two sliding window is re-computed.

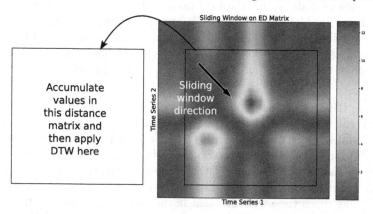

Fig. 2. A more efficient implementation of the ShapeDTW measure when the descriptor is set to be the identity. Instead of applying the DTW on the multivariate transformation of the time series, a window slides on the ED matrix between the two time series. The captured frames are accumulated in another zero-initialized matrix on which the DTW algorithm is then applied.

3.4 Reach Value Control

The hyperparameter of ShapeDTW, called "reach", controls the length of the neighborhood of each time stamp to be used for the alignment. This value makes the ShapeDTW algorithm a general definition that includes two similarity measures: the DTW and the Euclidean distance. For instance, on the one hand, if the reach value is set to 1, the algorithm will behave just as the original DTW similarity measure. This is due to the fact that the length of the neighborhood of each time stamp will be set to 1 leading to taking into consideration only this time stamp. On the other hand, if the reach is large enough, i.e., ∞, the ShapeDTW algorithm will behave just as the Euclidean distance. This is due to the fact that for each time stamp, the neighborhood length will be larger than the time series itself. In this work, we set the value of the reach to 30 given it was the value used in the original paper [20].

4   Results

4.1   Experimental Setup

Datasets. All the experiments were conducted on 123 datasets of the UCR archive [4]. The total number of datasets in the UCR archive since 2018 is 128, but five datasets were excluded from the experiments given the large length of the time series. This was crucial given the quadratic time complexity of most of the executed algorithms with respect to the time series length. All of the datasets were Z-normalized in order to have a zero mean and unit standard deviation for each time series. The clustering algorithms are trained on the combination of the train test splits for all the 123 datasets used in the experiments. It is important to note that some datasets of the UCR archive are simply another train test split of an exiting dataset. This does not occur much, which would mean that the clustering algorithm is done on the same dataset more than one time. The source code of this work is publicly available for reproducibility[1].

Removing Bias. A typical problem in non-deterministic estimators in machine learning is the biased performance to a given initial setup. This problem occurs in many problems such as deep learning where the performance can be biased to an initialization of the weights. In this clustering task, the bias in performance comes down to the initialization of the clusters before the k-means algorithm starts its optimization. To avoid this bias, we do the same experiments five different times, each time with different initial clusters and present the average performance on each dataset. However, this may raise the issue of fairness among multiple clustering algorithms experimented with. This is due to the probable second bias of a method to a specific five initial clusters. To fix this bias as well, in this work the same initial clusters are used over the five experiments for all clustering algorithms. Given that for clustering experiments using k-means and k-shape need the initial clusters, which are usually randomly selected, it would create an issue if not all algorithms use the same initial clusters. For this reason, we made sure that for all the experiments done, for the same dataset, all of the clustering variants used the same initial clusters. This was done with five different initial clusters and the average performance is presented in order to remove any variance in the results.

4.2   Qualitative Evaluation of DBA Variants

Given a set of time series example from the GunPointMaleVersusFemale dataset of the UCR archive, we can generate the average time series to compare and

---

[1] https://github.com/MSD-IRIMAS/ShapeDBA.

analyse the limitation of each technique. In Fig. 3, the generated average time series is presented from a set of samples from the GunPointMaleVersusFemale dataset. It can be seen that for the naive way of averaging, using the Euclidean distance, i.e., Arithmetic Mean, differs from all other approaches by the shifting issue. In other words, the Arithmetic Mean does not take into consideration the time warping and miss-aligned information between the samples of the example set.

Comparing other alignment techniques with ShapeDBA, the TSA almost is placed in the same time interval. The difference between warping methods is that DBA and SoftDBA present additional artifacts in the shape. This results in a TSA that includes some small peaks (red circles in Fig. 3) that do not appear in the original set of time series. ShapeDBA avoids generating this kind of artifacts given the usage of shapeDTW. ShapeDTW's advantage is to avoid aligning a time stamp with an outlier, which is obtained thanks to the ability of the method of aligning time stamp in specific sub-sequence of the time series. This advantage leads ShapeDBA to generate a prototype that is more likely to be randomly selected from the dataset distribution.

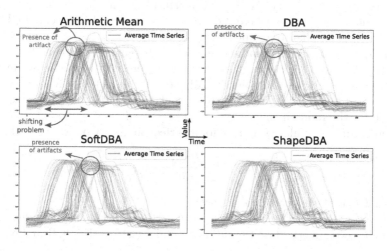

Fig. 3. A qualitative evaluation of the proposed average technique compared to other approaches on a GunPoint dataset. The ShapeDBA algorithm is the only approach to not generate out-of-distribution artifacts. (Color figure online)

4.3 Quantitative Evaluation

Competitor. In this work, we compare the proposed method to other time series averaging techniques as detailed in Sect. 3.2. The state-of-the-art model for time series clustering is k-shape [15]. This algorithm is an improvement over the k-means algorithm on time series data by using a Shape Based Distance (SBD) that uses the cross-correlation between two time series instead of an alignment measure. Until now, to the best of our knowledge, k-shape is the state-of-the-art and most efficient clustering method on time series data.

Adjusted Rand Index (ARI). The Adjusted Rand Index (ARI) [9] is a new fixed version of the original Rand Index (RI) defined in (5). Given the true labels of the time series dataset $\mathbf{y}$ and the predicted labels by the clustering algorithm $\hat{\mathbf{y}}$, the RI is calculated as follows:

$$RI(\mathbf{y}, \hat{\mathbf{y}}) = \frac{TP + TN}{TP + FP + FN + TN}, \tag{5}$$

where, TP and TN stand, respectively, for True Positive and True Negative, while FP and FN stand for False Positive and False Negative, respectively.

The RI counts the number of pairs that are present in the intersection of both sets of true and predicted labels as well as the number of pairs that exist in the difference of these two sets. This metric, however, presents a limitation: a high RI should indicate that the two clusters in question are almost identical, which is not always the case. The RI may favor high identical clusters without taking into consideration the case where the intersection was randomly generated. This is due to the fact that the expected value of the RI is not constant between two random clusters. This random chance can be generated when the number of clusters becomes high enough that the probability of a pair to be in both clusters is large. For this reason, the Adjusted Rand Index (ARI) is proposed with a scaled version that takes into account this randomness by setting the value 0.0 for the random chance. The ARI presented in (6) is bounded between -0.5 indicating no similarity and 1.0 for a perfect similarity between the clusters.

$$ARI(\mathbf{y}, \hat{\mathbf{y}}) = \frac{RI(\mathbf{y}, \hat{\mathbf{y}}) - E[RI]}{1.0 - E[RI]}, \tag{6}$$

where $E[RI]$ is the expected value of RI.

We present in the following three different ways to compare the performance of each clustering method on the total of 123 datasets of the UCR archive.

One-vs-One Comparison: In this approach, we present a scatter plot of all the pairwise comparisons between k-means with ShapeDBA and the approaches in the literature. Each point visualized in Fig. 4 represents one dataset, the x-axis presents the ARI value on this dataset using a method from the literature and the y-axis the ARI value using ShapeDBA. The Win-Tie-Loss count is presented in the legend of each One-vs-One scatter plot as well as a p-value. This latter p-value is produced using the Wilcoxon Signed Rank Test [19]. If this p-value is larger than the threshold 0.05, than the difference in performance between the comparates in question is not considered statistically significant.

It is clear from Figs. 4a, 4b, and 4c that the usage of ShapeDBA as an averaging method in k-means is significantly better than the baseline, i.e., ED and DBA with k-means and significantly better than the state-of-the-art k-shape.

From Fig. 4d it can be seen that even though ShapeDBA presents more wins compared to SoftDBA, the difference in performance is still not significantly different. In what follows, we show however that ShapeDBA is way faster than SoftDBA.

Analysing Outliers. Some unique outliers from the One-vs-One scatter plots are clear to favor either ShapeDBA or the other approaches. For instance, compared to *k*-shape, ShapeDBA does not perform well (low ARI) on two datasets: ShapeletSim and ECGFiveDays. On the one hand, given knowledge on the UCR archive datasets, we believe that no correct conclusion can be found on Shapelet-Sim given that this dataset is simply a simulation of random data. On the other hand, the ECGFiveDays dataset presented in Fig. 5 is a unique example to show case the disadvantage of ShapeDBA.

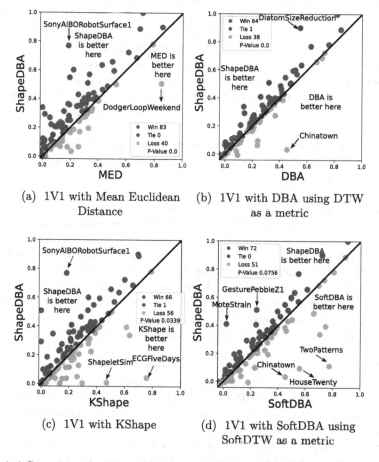

(a) 1V1 with Mean Euclidean Distance

(b) 1V1 with DBA using DTW as a metric

(c) 1V1 with KShape

(d) 1V1 with SoftDBA using SoftDTW as a metric

Fig. 4. 1v1 Comparison between using *k*-means with ShapeDBA-ShapeDTW and other approaches from the literature using the Adjusted Rand Index clustering metric.

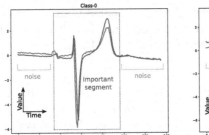
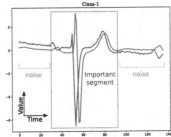

Fig. 5. Two examples from each class taken from the ECGFiveDays dataset of the UCR archive. Most time stamps of this dataset represent noise and the important neighborhood of the time stamp is just in the middle of the whole time series.

This dataset is mostly made of noisy time stamps with an information compressed in the important segments placed in the middle of the time series as seen in Fig. 5. For this reason, ShapeDTW will be adding noise in the optimization steps. A clear winner on the SonyAIBORobotSurface1 dataset, however, is ShapeDBA compared to k-shape with almost a 0.6 difference in the ARI. After analysing this dataset, still no hard conclusions can be found but this is not a special case for ShapeDBA given that MED, DBA and SoftDBA perform better than k-shape on this dataset. Suggesting that it is k-shape underperforming on this dataset.

Comparing ShapeDBA to DBA, it seems as if ShapeDBA has an advantage over the DiatomSizeReduction dataset, which suffers from the lack of training samples with only four samples per class label.

Critical Difference Diagram (CDD): A technique to compare multiple estimators by reducing the metrics on multiple datasets into a one dimensional view. This one dimensional view is presented by using the average rank of each method on the total of the 123 datasets used. The best performing clustering approach is the one with the lowest rank as for instance ShapeDBA in Fig. 6. The CDD used in this work utilizes, as proposed in [2], the Wilcoxon Signed-Rank Test [19] coupled with the Holm multiple test correction [8] in order to generate the cliques. If a clique links a set of comparates in the CDD, this represents that the differences in performance between this set of comparates is not statistically significant.

Multi-Comparison Matrix (MCM) : was proposed in [10] arguing that CDD has some limitations that can miss-lead the interpretation of the results. First, one important issue with CDD as mentioned in [10] is the instability of the average rank. For instance the average rank can easily be manipulated by the addition or removal of some comparates. For this reason, MCM proposes the usage of a descriptive statistics that does not change with this addition and removal of comparates. This statistics is the average performance on the total of the 123 datasets used, in our case it is the average ARI over these datasets for each clustering approach. Second, a common issue of the CDD is the usage

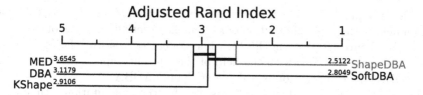

Fig. 6. Critical Difference Diagram showing the average rank of the ARI score over the datasets of the UCR archive.

of the multiple test correction, which is unstable to the addition and removal of comparates. Finally, a major limitation with only using the CDD is the lack of pairwise comparison information. The MCM proposed in [10] overcomes these three problems by using the average performance instead of the average rank to order the comparates, not applying a multiple test correction for the produced Wilcoxon p-values and presenting the pairwise comparisons between comparates. The MCM in Fig. 7 shows that SoftDBA is the winning approach given the average ARI with not much difference with the average ARI of ShapeDBA that comes in second place. A full pairwise and multi-comparates comparison between all clustering techniques discussed in this work on the ARI metric is presented in Fig. 10.

In what follows, we did a computational runtime comparison between all approaches. We show that although ShapeDBA does not outperform in significant manner SoftDBA, it is however faster.

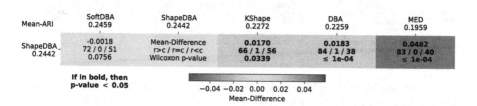

Fig. 7. A Multi-Comparison Matrix showing the proposed approach's performance compared to other approaches using a tool that is stable to the addition/removal of new classifiers.

Computational Runtime. Given that all experiments were conducted on the same machine with the same environment, fairness in time computation comparison stands here. By keeping track of the total computation time for each clustering approach, averaged over five initialization, we can apply the same comparison techniques as for the ARI. In Fig. 8, the CDD of the computational runtime is presented. Given that in the case of runtime, the lower the time the better, and to keep the ordering of the average rank as lower is better, we multiplied the values of the computational time by -1. It is clear from the CDD plot that the fastest approach is k-shape and the slowest one is SoftDBA. The reason behind the fast computation of k-shape is essentially because of the usage of the Fast Fourier Transform (FFT), while doing the cross-correlation between the time series. However, with the help of the efficient implementation used in ShapeDBA, the computation is way faster than SoftDBA.

For ARI, we generated the MCM as well for the computational time comparison in Fig. 9. On average of 123 datasets, ShapeDBA is 1.7 times faster than SoftDBA with 109 wins for ShapeDBA in terms of computational runtime. It is important to note that in this case of MCM, the Win-Tie-Loss count considers the lower the better.

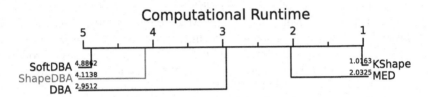

Fig. 8. Critical Difference Diagram showing the average rank of the duration (in seconds) of the k-means algorithm over the datasets of the UCR archive.

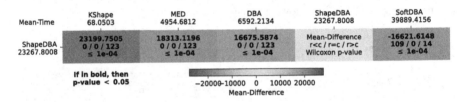

Fig. 9. A Multi-Comparison Matrix showing the proposed approach's duration (in seconds) compared to other approaches using a tool that is stable to the addition/removal of new classifiers.

5   Conclusion

In this work, we addressed the problem of Time Series Averaging (TSA) using elastic distances. We proposed a novel TSA approach, ShapeDBA, based on the similarity measure ShapeDTW similarity measure. We showed that ShapeDBA has the ability to preserve the shape of the true dataset distribution instead of producing spikes artifacts as other approaches. To quantitatively evaluate the proposed approached, we provided extensive experiments on the UCR archive using the k-means clustering algorithm. We show that in terms of the Adjusted Rand Index metric, our approach achieves state-of-the-art performance, while

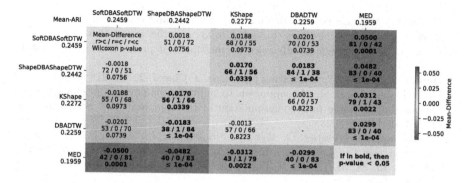

Fig. 10. A Multi-Comparison Matrix showing the full One-vs-One comparison and the multi-comparates comparison between all the time series clustering approaches used and proposed in this work.

being much faster than SoftDBA that represents the current elastic state-of-the-art averaging technique. This last observation is beneficial to help deploy time series averaging techniques in real life problems. Finally, to avoid computation waste in our proposed ShapeDBA algorithm, we present a dynamic programming detailed implementation of the algorithm.

Acknowledgements. This work was supported by the ANR DELEGATION project (grant ANR-21-CE23-0014) of the French Agence Nationale de la Recherche. The authors would like to acknowledge the High Performance Computing Center of the University of Strasbourg for supporting this work by providing scientific sup- port and access to computing resources. Part of the computing resources were funded by the Equipex Equip@Meso project (Programme Investissements d'Avenir) and the CPER Alsacalcul/Big Data. The authors would also like to thank the creators and providers of the UCR Archive.

References

1. Aghabozorgi, S., Shirkhorshidi, A.S., Wah, T.Y.: Time-series clustering-a decade review. Inf. Syst. **53**, 16–38 (2015)
2. Benavoli, A., Corani, G., Mangili, F.: Should we really use post-hoc tests based on mean-ranks? J. Mach. Learn. Res. **17**(1), 152–161 (2016)
3. Cuturi, M., Blondel, M.: Soft-DTW: a differentiable loss function for time-series. In: International Conference on Machine Learning, pp. 894–903. PMLR (2017)
4. Dau, H.A., et al.: The UCR time series archive. IEEE/CAA J. Automatica Sinica **6**(6), 1293–1305 (2019)
5. Forestier, G., Petitjean, F., Webb, G., Dau, H.A., Keogh, E.: Generating synthetic time series to augment sparse datasets. In: IEEE International Conference on Data Mining (ICDM), pp. 865–870 (2017). https://doi.org/10.1109/ICDM.2017.106
6. Gee, A.H., Garcia-Olano, D., Ghosh, J., Paydarfar, D.: Explaining deep classification of time-series data with learned prototypes. In: CEUR Workshop Proceedings, vol. 2429, p. 15. NIH Public Access (2019)

7. Holder, C., Middlehurst, M., Bagnall, A.: A review and evaluation of elastic distance functions for time series clustering. arXiv preprint arXiv:2205.15181 (2022)
8. Holm, S.: A simple sequentially rejective multiple test procedure. Scand. J. Stat. **6**, 65–70 (1979)
9. Hubert, L., Arabie, P.: Comparing partitions. J. Classif. **2**, 193–218 (1985)
10. Ismail-Fawaz, A., et al.: An approach to multiple comparison benchmark evaluations that is stable under manipulation of the comparate set. arXiv preprint arXiv:2305.11921 (2023)
11. Ismail Fawaz, H., Forestier, G., Weber, J., Idoumghar, L., Muller, P.A.: Data augmentation using synthetic data for time series classification with deep residual networks. In: ECML/PKDD Workshop on Advanced Analytics and Learning on Temporal Data (2018)
12. Lafabregue, B., Weber, J., Gançarski, P., Forestier, G.: End-to-end deep representation learning for time series clustering: a comparative study. Data Min. Knowl. Disc. **36**(1), 29–81 (2022)
13. Liao, T.W.: Clustering of time series data-a survey. Pattern Recogn. **38**(11), 1857–1874 (2005)
14. Müller, M.: Dynamic time warping. In: Information Retrieval for Music and Motion, pp. 69–84 (2007)
15. Paparrizos, J., Gravano, L.: k-Shape: efficient and accurate clustering of time series. In: Proceedings of the 2015 ACM SIGMOD International Conference on Management of Data, pp. 1855–1870 (2015)
16. Petitjean, F., Forestier, G., Webb, G., Nicholson, A., Chen, Y., Keogh, E.: Dynamic time warping averaging of time series allows faster and more accurate classification. In: IEEE International Conference on Data Mining (ICDM), pp. 470–479 (2014). https://doi.org/10.1109/ICDM.2014.27
17. Petitjean, F., Ketterlin, A., Gançarski, P.: A global averaging method for dynamic time warping, with applications to clustering. Pattern Recogn. **44**(3), 678–693 (2011)
18. Tan, C.W., Petitjean, F., Keogh, E., Webb, G.I.: Time series classification for varying length series. arXiv preprint arXiv:1910.04341 (2019)
19. Wilcoxon, F.: Individual comparisons by ranking methods. In: Kotz, S., Johnson, N.L. (eds.) Breakthroughs in Statistics. Springer Series in Statistics: Methodology and Distribution, pp. 196–202. Springer, New York (1992). https://doi.org/10.1007/978-1-4612-4380-9_16
20. Zhao, J., Itti, L.: ShapeDTW: shape dynamic time warping. Pattern Recogn. **74**, 171–184 (2018)

Poster Presentation

Temporal Performance Prediction for Deep Convolutional Long Short-Term Memory Networks

Laura Fieback[1]([✉]) [iD], Bidya Dash[1] [iD], Jakob Spiegelberg[1] [iD],
and Hanno Gottschalk[2] [iD]

[1] Volkswagen AG, Berliner Ring 2, 38440 Wolfsburg, Germany
{laura.fieback,bidya.binayam.dash,jakob.spiegelberg}@volkswagen.de
[2] Mathematical Modeling of Industrial Life Cycles, Institute of Mathematics,
TU Berlin, Berlin, Germany
gottschalk@math.tu-berlin.de

Abstract. Quantifying predictive uncertainty of deep semantic segmentation networks is essential in safety-critical tasks. In applications like autonomous driving, where video data is available, convolutional long short-term memory networks are capable of not only providing semantic segmentations but also predicting the segmentations of the next timesteps. These models use cell states to broadcast information from previous data by taking a time series of inputs to predict one or even further steps into the future. We present a temporal postprocessing method which estimates the prediction performance of convolutional long short-term memory networks by either predicting the intersection over union of predicted and ground truth segments or classifying between intersection over union being equal to zero or greater than zero. To this end, we create temporal cell state-based input metrics per segment and investigate different models for the estimation of the predictive quality based on these metrics. We further study the influence of the number of considered cell states for the proposed metrics.

Keywords: Uncertainty quantification · Video frame prediction ·
Semantic segmentation

1   Introduction

Retrieving information from images is an important task for scene understanding. Semantic image segmentation is a common approach to gain knowledge about image content by assigning each pixel a label from a predefined label space using neural networks. In safety-critical applications like autonomous driving [11] or medical diagnostics [28], information about the reliability of a prediction is indispensable for decision making. While most approaches to uncertainty quantification focus on a single frame only, temporal information is often available as

Fig. 1. Visualization of the meta regression task. Ground truth semantic segmentation (bottom left), predicted semantic segmentation via ConvLSTM (bottom right), true IoU_{adj} of prediction and ground truth per segment, where green colors represent high values of IoU_{adj} and red colors represent low values (top left), predicted IoU_{adj} via meta regression (top right). (Color figure online)

in the case of video data. To leverage on this, we build on the meta classification and regression approach from [23] and [17]. The method introduced in [23] provides a postprocessing framework to predict the performance of a segmentation network based on its softmax output, i.e., to predict the intersection over union IoU (also known as Jaccard index [13]) per segment from metrics derived from its aggregated softmax outputs (meta regression) or classifying between $IoU = 0$ and $IoU > 0$ (meta classification). Figure 1 provides a visualization of the meta regression task. Note that this approach can be equipped with any pixel-wise uncertainty measure. In [17], the approach of [23] is extended to time series metrics using a light-weight tracking algorithm. In this work, we investigate temporal metrics retrieved from convolutional long short-term memory networks (ConvLSTMs). Long short-term memory networks (LSTMs) [9] take time series as inputs to make predictions for future timesteps. Thus, the metrics presented in this work express uncertainties in single frames by taking account of temporal information from LSTM outputs. Moreover, we use the light-weight tracking algorithm from [17] to investigate the power of LSTM meta models. This is the first work that conducts meta classification and regression by considering LSTM-based temporal metrics and meta models. Note that our procedure requires a semantic segmentation LSTM network and a video stream of input data.

In our experiments, we predict the performance of a ConvLSTM network [26] trained on the VIsual PERception (VIPER) dataset [21]. This network takes a time series of semantic segmentations as input to predict the segmentation for the next timestep. We achieve meta classification accuracy of 96.15%($\pm$0.17%) and

Area Under Receiver Operating Characteristic ($AUROC$) of 95.04%($\pm$0.22%). The best meta classification results using time series temporal metrics are obtained by our proposed LSTM meta model. For meta regression, we obtain R^2 values of 74.31%($\pm$0.33%).

The remainder of this work is organized as follows. An overview over related work in the field of uncertainty quantification and object tracking is provided in Sect. 2. In Sect. 3, we introduce the temporal metrics for time-dynamic uncertainty quantification followed by the light-weight tracking algorithm in Sect. 4. In Sect. 5 we describe the meta classification and regression method for time-dynamic performance prediction. Finally, we present our numerical results in Sect. 6.

2   Related Work

2.1   Uncertainty Quantification

Modern neural networks tend to be overconfident in their predictions [8,19]. Temperature scaling [8] and Dirichlet calibration [15] are scaling methods to calibrate the model's confidence estimates. Another common approach to quantify model uncertainty are Bayesian models [18]. Different methods have been established to conduct Bayesian inference via variational approximations like [4] and [5]. In [11], the sampling procedure is simulated based on temporal information in video data. Besides, Monte Carlo dropout [7] is widely used to approximate Bayesian neural networks. In [16], deep ensembles are proposed to quantify predictive uncertainty based on the variance of the ensemble prediction. Other approaches like [22] and [10] propose to model predictive uncertainty based on gradients. In [23], a meta learning approach for semantic segmentation networks is introduced for false positive detection (meta classification) and performance prediction in terms of IoU (meta regression). In [25] and [17], this work is extended by adding resolution dependent uncertainty and temporal metrics, respectively. In [6], performance metrics for video object segmentation and tracking are introduced.

2.2   Object Tracking

Most works in the field of object tracking refer to the task of multi-object tracking, that is, tracking multiple objects in videos by means of bounding boxes [3,20]. Tracking-by-detection [1] is a common approach for this task, which separates objects from the background. The approaches in [27] and [2] are based on segmentation and perform tracking using fully-convolutional Siamese networks and particle filters, respectively. Video panoptic segmentation [14] combines the task of semantic segmentation and object tracking at the same time. Recent works in this field [12,14] propose end-to-end architectures to fulfill both tasks simultaneously. In [17], a tracking algorithm is introduced which builds up on a semantic segmentation and matches segments of the same class based on their overlap in consecutive video frames.

3   Segment-Wise Dispersion and Temporal Metrics

We build input metrics for the meta classification and regression task based on the output of our ConvLSTM video frame prediction model. The aim of our model is to predict the semantic segmentation of the next timestep given a video sequence of previous segmentations. Semantic segmentation can be viewed as a pixel-wise classification task, where each pixel z of an input image x is classified as a label $y \in C = \{y_1, \ldots, y_c\}$ with c possible output labels. The network's softmax output $f_z(y|x, w)$ can be interpreted as a probability distribution over the output labels $y \in C = \{y_1, \ldots, y_c\}$ given the input image x and the network weights w. The predicted class for a pixel z is then given by the largest softmax value, i.e.,

$$\hat{y}_z(x, w) = \operatorname*{argmax}_{y \in C} f_z(y|x, w). \tag{1}$$

The degree of randomness in a network's softmax output can be quantified using dispersion measures. Thus, we build metrics for the meta classification and regression task based on uncertainty heatmaps representing pixel-wise dispersion measure as proposed in [25]. We consider the entropy

$$E_z(x, w) = -\frac{1}{\log(c)} \sum_{y \in C} f_z(y|x, w) \log f_z(y|x, w), \tag{2}$$

the variation ratio

$$V_z(x, w) = 1 - \max_{y \in C} f_z(y|x, w), \tag{3}$$

as well as the probability margin

$$M_z(x, w) = 1 - \max_{y \in C} f_z(y|x, w) + \max_{y \in C \backslash \hat{y}_z} f_z(y|x, w). \tag{4}$$

Note that, for better comparison, these quantities have been normalized to the interval $[0, 1]$.

Let $\hat{S}_x = \{\hat{y}_z(x, w) | z \in x\}$ denote the predicted semantic segmentation for an image x and $\hat{\mathcal{K}}_x$ the set of all predicted segments k in x, i.e., the set of all connected components of pixels z' with the same predicted class c', that is, $\hat{y}_{z'} = c'$ for all pixels z'. The segment-wise dispersion metrics based on the pixel-wise uncertainty heatmaps introduced above are defined as

$$\bar{D} = \frac{1}{S} \sum_{z \in k} D_z(x, w), \tag{5}$$

where $D_z \in \{E_z, V_z, M_z\}$ and $S = |\{z \in k\}|$ denotes the segment size, i.e., the number of pixels contained in k. As proposed in [23], we define segment-wise inner dispersion metrics and boundary dispersion metrics, since we typically observe high values of D_z for boundary pixels. To this end, let $k_{in} \subset k$ denote the set of all inner pixels of segment k, where a pixel $z \in k$ is called an inner pixel of k if all eight neighboring pixels are an element of k, and let $k_{bd} = k \backslash k_{in}$

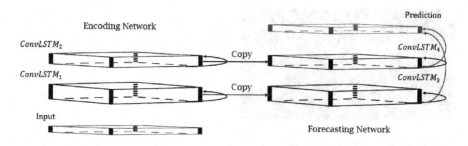

Fig. 2. Depiction of a ConvLSTM block with shared hidden states and cell states between the encoding and forecasting network (from [26]). Here, both networks consist of two ConvLSTM cells, respectively. $ConvLSTM_1$ and $ConvLSTM_3$ share the same states as well as $ConvLSTM_2$ and $ConvLSTM_4$.

denote the set of boundary pixels of segment k. We obtain further segment-wise dispersion metrics by averaging the pixel-wise uncertainty heatmaps over all inner pixels and boundary pixels by analogy with Eq. (5) yielding the inner and boundary dispersion metrics $\bar{D}_{in}$ and $\bar{D}_{bd}$, respectively, as well as S_{in} and S_{bd}. Based on these metrics, we obtain the respective relative metrics $\tilde{S} = S/S_{bd}$, $\tilde{S}_{in} = S_{in}/S_{bd}$, $\tilde{D} = \bar{D}\tilde{S}$ and $\tilde{D}_{in} = \bar{D}_{in}\tilde{S}_{in}$ with $D \in \{E, V, M\}$. Our set of metrics further contains the geometric center

$$\bar{k} = (\bar{k}_1, \bar{k}_1) = \frac{1}{S} \sum_{z \in k} (z_1, z_1),\tag{6}$$

where z_1 and z_2 are the vertical and horizontal coordinates of pixel z as well as the mean class probabilities for each class $y \in C = \{y_1, \dots, y_c\}$,

$$P(y|k) = \frac{1}{S} \sum_{z \in k} f_z(y|x, w).\tag{7}$$

This results in the following set of metrics (see [17])

$$\begin{aligned}
U = &\{\bar{D}, \bar{D}_{in}, \bar{D}_{bd}, \tilde{D}, \tilde{D}_{in} \mid D \in \{E, V, M\}\} \cup \{\bar{k}\} \\
&\cup \{S, S_{in}, S_{bd}, \tilde{S}, \tilde{S}_{in}\} \cup \{P(y|k) \mid y = y_1, \dots, y_c\}.
\end{aligned}\tag{8}$$

We use these metrics as a baseline in our tests and define additional metrics based on the cell states of our ConvLSTM video frame prediction model. Our model consists of $l = 10$ ConvLSTM blocks (see Fig. 2) using ten previous semantic segmentations x_{t-i}, $i = 1, \dots, 10$, of a video to predict the semantic segmentation of the next video frame $\hat{x}_t$. Note that every ConvLSTM block itself consists of an encoding network and a forecasting network, where both networks consist of the same number of convolutional LSTM cells with shared hidden states and cell states (see Fig. 2). The shared hidden states and cell states between both networks are the same states, which are broadcasted to the next ConvLSTM

Fig. 3. Prediction error between ground truth and predicted semantic segmentation mask via ConvLSTM (left), where black areas correspond to correctly predicted pixels and white areas to misclassified pixels, and pixel-wise temporal cell state-based heatmap C_z^9 (right).

block. In our model, the last convolutional LSTM cell of the forecasting network of each ConvLSTM block outputs states of the same height and width as the model's prediction with 64 features. Thus, for every ConvLSTM block, we focus on the cell state of the last convolutional LSTM cell and define the mean cell state $\bar{C}^i$, $i = 1, \ldots, 10$, of block i as the mean over the 64 features. Based on this, we build temporal heatmaps from the stability of the mean cell state $\bar{C}^i$ over i ConvLSTM blocks. To this end, we define the stability of cell state j for an image x, a pixel z and network weights w as

$$C_z^j (x, w) = |\bar{C}_z^1 (x, w) - \bar{C}_z^{j+1} (x, w)|, \ j = 1, \ldots, 9. \qquad (9)$$

Figure 3(right) shows a temporal heatmap obtained from C_z^9, that is, the stability of cell state $j = 9$. As for the uncertainty heatmaps introduced above, we define segment-wise temporal metrics based on the temporal heatmaps as

$$\bar{T} = \frac{1}{S} \sum_{z \in k} T_z (x, w), \qquad (10)$$

with $T_z \in \{C_z^j, \ j = 1, \ldots, 9\}$. With the notation above, we define our proposed set of metrics for $m = 1, \ldots, 9$ as

$$V_m = U \cup CS_m, \qquad (11)$$

where

$$CS_m = \{\bar{T}, \bar{T}_{in}, \bar{T}_{bd}, \tilde{T}, \tilde{T}_{in} \mid T \in \{C^j, \ j = 1, \ldots, m\}\}. \qquad (12)$$

Note that all of these metrics can be calculated from our model output without any knowledge of the ground truth.

4   Tracking Algorithm

For the investigation of LSTM meta models, we apply the tracking algorithm proposed in [17]. This algorithm builds on a video sequence of semantic segmentations and performs tracking based on the overlap of segments of the same class in consecutive frames. It does not require additional training. Within this procedure, every segment is assigned a tracking id. To this end, let $\{x_1, \ldots, x_T\}$ denote a sequence of T consecutive semantic segmentations. The overlap of a segment k with segment j is defined as

$$O_{j,k} = \frac{|\{z \in k\} \cap \{z \in j\}|}{|\{z \in j\}|}. \tag{13}$$

The algorithm is applied sequentially to each segmentation x_t, $t = 1, \ldots, T$, where for each frame, the segments are prioritized based on their segment size. In detail, the algorithm consists of five steps starting with the largest segment $k^{S_{max}} \in \hat{\mathcal{K}}_{x_t}$ in each step. Once a segment $k \in \hat{\mathcal{K}}_{x_t}$ has been matched with a segment from a previous frame, it is ignored in the following steps. Matched segments receive the same tracking id. To this end, we denote a matched segment k in x_t as k_t.

Step 1 matches segments of the same class in x_t which are close to each other, i.e., with a distance less than a constant c_{near}, and thus, are regarded as one segment.

Step 2 matches segments based on their geometric center. If a segment k exists in two consecutive frames, i.e., $k \in \hat{\mathcal{K}}_{x_{t-1}} \cap \hat{\mathcal{K}}_{x_{t-2}}$, segment k_{t-1} is shifted by $(\bar{k}_{t-1} - \bar{k}_{t-2})$ and segments $j \in \hat{\mathcal{K}}_{x_t}$ are matched with the shifted segment $\hat{k}_t$, if the overlap $O_{j,\hat{k}_t}$ is higher than a constant c_{over} or if the distance between the geometric centers $\bar{j}$ and $\bar{\hat{k}}_t$ is smaller than a constant c_{dist}. If segment $k \in \hat{\mathcal{K}}_{x_{t-1}}$ does not exist in two consecutive frames, i.e., $k \notin \hat{\mathcal{K}}_{x_{t-2}}$, segments $j \in \hat{\mathcal{K}}_{x_t}$ are matched based on the distance of the geometric centers $\bar{j}$ and $\bar{k}_{t-1}$.

Step 3 matches segments in consecutive frames based on their overlap, i.e., segments $k \in \hat{\mathcal{K}}_{x_{t-1}}$ and $j \in \hat{\mathcal{K}}_{x_t}$ are matched if $O_{j,k} \geq c_{over}$.

Step 4 accounts for flashing predicted segments due to occlusions or false predictions. It aims at matching segments that are more than one frame apart in temporal direction. To this end, a linear regression model is used to predict the geometric center of segment k in x_t if k was matched in at least two of the last lr segmentations $x_{t-lr}, \ldots, x_{t-1}$. Segments $j \in \hat{\mathcal{K}}_{x_t}$ are matched if the distance between the predicted geometric center $\bar{\hat{k}}_t$ and $\bar{j}$ is less than a constant c_{lin}.

Step 5 assigns a new id to all segments $j \in \hat{\mathcal{K}}_{x_t}$, that have not yet been matched.

5   IoU Prediction

For the task of semantic segmentation, a common measure for predictive quality is the IoU. In our experiments, we use a slight modification proposed in [23], the IoU_{adj}, which is less prone to fragmented objects. We perform segment-wise meta classification, i.e., classifying between $IoU_{adj} = 0$ and $IoU_{adj} > 0$ as well as segment-wise meta regression, that is, predicting the performance of our ConvLSTM semantic segmentation for each segment in terms of IoU_{adj} by means of the metrics defined in Sect. 3. Note that all of these metrics can be calculated from the ConvLSTM's output without any knowledge of the ground truth. An illustration of the meta regression task is given in Fig. 1. We analyze the information gain induced by the temporal metrics for both single frame metrics and time series metrics as proposed in [17]. Those time series metrics are based on the tracking algorithm introduced in Sect. 4. For each segment $k_t \in \hat{\mathcal{K}}_{x_t}$, we obtain single-frame based metrics $V_m^k = V_{m,t}^k$ according to Sect. 3 as well as their history $V_{m,t-1}^k, \ldots, V_{m,t-T}^k$ due to tracking of segment k over T previous frames. In our experiments, we investigate the influence of metric histories for up to $T = 10$ timesteps. In [17], different models for the meta tasks were investigated. We choose the best performing models, i.e., the linear model (LR), the shallow neural network (NN) as well as the gradient boosting model (GB) for our experiments (for implementation details, see [17]). In addition, we investigate the performance of a shallow LSTM neural network (in the following referred to as LSTM) with 50 neurons only for both meta tasks. The number of LSTM cells depends on the respective number of considered timesteps T of the time series metrics.

6   Numerical Results

In this section, we investigate the properties of the temporal metrics defined in Sect. 3. We further investigate the influence of time series metrics as described in the previous section and consider different models for meta classification and regression. To this end, we train a ConvLSTM network with ten ConvLSTM blocks (see Fig. 2), each of them built by five convolutional LSTM cells. We train our model on the synthetic VIPER dataset [21]. The dataset consists of more than 250,000 frames all annotated with ground truth semantic labels with a resolution of 1920×1080 pixels per frame. Since the ground truth annotation has very fine labels, we apply the smoothing algorithm proposed in [24] to generate a coarse ground truth by blurring each class using a normalized box filter. Moreover, we resize the images to 256×512 pixels for computational reasons. The VIPER dataset contains 32 different classes with 23 proposed training ids. Out of these, we further cluster highly underrepresented classes to a misc class which results in a total of 17 training classes. We train our ConvLSTM model on 19 training folders which contain 30,168 images in total and 8 validation folders yielding a total of 7,021 images. In our experiments, we compare two different models from our training procedure: The "strong model" (S) which was trained for 18 epochs yielding a mean IoU ($mIoU$) of 82.82%, as well as the "weak model" (W) which obtained an $mIoU$ of 79.45% after 4 epochs of training. We implement the tracking algorithm from Sect. 4 with parameters $c_{near} = 10$, $c_{over} = 0.35$, $c_{dist} = 100$ and $c_{lin} = 50$.

For the meta tasks, we use 5 validation folders, not yet used during the training procedure of the ConvLSTM model, which sum up to 3,464 images. This results in a total of 46,587,336 segments for the weak model (not yet matched over time) of which 110,739 have non-empty interior. Out of these, 7,649 segments have $IoU_{adj} = 0$. For the strong model, we obtain 42,295,440 segments,

Table 1. Results for meta classification and regression based on temporal metrics for different meta models and the entropy baseline for both the weak (W) and the strong (S) model. The superscript denotes the number of cell state metrics, where the best performance and in particular the given values are reached. The best results are highlighted.

Meta Classification $IoU_{adj} = 0, > 0$					
Entropy Baseline (W): $ACC = 93.40\%(\pm0.20\%)$ $AUROC = 81.63\%(\pm0.78\%)$					
Entropy Baseline (S): $ACC = 95.27\%(\pm0.20\%)$ $AUROC = 80.45\%(\pm0.71\%)$					
		GB	LR	LSTM	NN
ACC	W	$\mathbf{94.72\%(\pm0.22\%)^{7}}$	$94.39\%(\pm0.16\%)^{1}$	$94.01\%(\pm0.16\%)^{6}$	$93.72\%(\pm0.22\%)^{2}$
	S	$\mathbf{95.99\%(\pm0.17\%)^{9}}$	$95.65\%(\pm0.15\%)^{9}$	$95.54\%(\pm0.22\%)^{2}$	$95.35\%(\pm0.21\%)^{6}$
$AUROC$	W	$\mathbf{94.54\%(\pm0.44\%)^{0}}$	$93.69\%(\pm0.47\%)^{2}$	$93.28\%(\pm0.53\%)^{0}$	$92.85\%(\pm0.59\%)^{0}$
	S	$\mathbf{93.87\%(\pm0.43\%)^{2}}$	$92.57\%(\pm0.42\%)^{9}$	$92.25\%(\pm0.44\%)^{9}$	$91.87\%(\pm0.45\%)^{9}$
Meta Regression IoU_{adj}					
Entropy Baseline (W): $\sigma = 0.227(\pm0.002)$ $R^2 = 42.80\%(\pm0.70\%)$					
Entropy Baseline (S): $\sigma = 0.225(\pm0.003)$ $R^2 = 38.58\%(\pm0.81\%)$					
		GB	LR	LSTM	NN
σ	W	$\mathbf{0.154\%(\pm0.002\%)^{8}}$	$0.175\%(\pm0.002\%)^{0}$	$0.162\%(\pm0.001\%)^{0}$	$0.155\%(\pm0.002\%)^{8}$
	S	$0.161\%(\pm0.001\%)^{9}$	$0.175\%(\pm0.002\%)^{0}$	$0.165\%(\pm0.001\%)^{0}$	$\mathbf{0.160\%(\pm0.002\%)^{9}}$
R^2	W	$\mathbf{74.04\%(\pm0.52\%)^{0}}$	$66.85\%(\pm0.43\%)^{9}$	$70.96\%(\pm0.47\%)^{9}$	$73.57\%(\pm0.46\%)^{0}$
	S	$68.95\%(\pm0.61\%)^{1}$	$63.33\%(\pm0.59\%)^{8}$	$67.61\%(\pm0.43\%)^{9}$	$\mathbf{69.19\%(\pm0.47\%)^{3}}$

113,286 with non-empty interior of which 5,622 segments have $IoU_{adj} = 0$. The corresponding naive classification baseline discussed in [23] and [17] yields an accuracy of 93.09% for the weak model and 95.04% for the strong model. This baseline is obtained by random guessing, i.e., randomly assigning a probability to each segment and thresholding on it. The classification accuracy is the number of correct predictions divided by the total number of predictions made. The corresponding $AUROC$ value is 50%. This baseline is clearly outperformed. To this end note that, the stronger the ConvLSTM model, the higher the naive accuracy. We improve the naive accuracy by further $1.63pp$ for the weak model and $0.95pp$ for the strong model.

In all our experiments, we average our results over ten randomly sampled train/val/test (70%/10%/20%) splits using a total of 38,000 segments in each split. In tables, the corresponding standard deviations are given in brackets, whereas, in figures, they are given by shades. All meta models considered yield an inference time for all 38,000 segments together of less than one second. We measure the classification performance of our method in terms of classification accuracy (ACC) and Area Under Receiver Operating Characteristic ($AUROC$), which is obtained by varying the decision threshold between $IoU_{adj} = 0$ and $IoU_{adj} > 0$. For meta regression, we state the results in terms of the regression standard error σ and the R^2 value.

6.1 Evaluation of Temporal Metrics

First, we investigate the influence of single-frame temporal metrics $V_m = V_{m,t}$ by considering the stability of cell states over $m \in \{1, \ldots, 9\}$ ConvLSTM blocks.

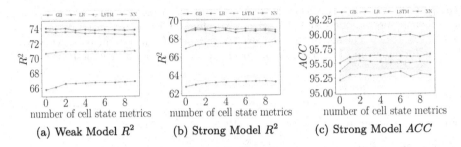

Fig. 4. A selection of results for meta classification in terms of ACC and meta regression in terms of R^2 as functions of the number of considered cell state metrics. Meta regression via the weak model (a), meta regression via the strong model (b), meta classification via the strong model (c).

Table 1 shows the best results for different meta models. The superscript denotes the number of considered cell state metrics, where the best performance and in particular the given values are reached. Note that the superscript being equal to 0 refers to the metric set U_t without any cell state metrics. For the weak model, we achieve test $AUROC$ values of up to $94.54\%(\pm0.44\%)$ and classification accuracies of up to $94.72\%(\pm0.22\%)$. For the strong model, a test accuracy of $95.99\%(\pm0.17\%)$ is reached and $AUROC$ value up to $93.87\%(\pm0.43\%)$. As in [17], GB performs best for meta classification. With regard to meta regression, we obtain R^2 values up to $74.04\%(\pm0.52\%)$ for the weak model and $69.19\%(\pm0.47\%)$ for the strong model. As a baseline, we consider the approach from [23], i.e., the metric set U_t without any cell state metrics. In almost every experiment, best results are obtained when considering temporal metrics. In those cases where the best results are obtained without temporal metrics, we observe vanishing differences between the respective performance metrics for temporal metrics (e.g., see R^2 values for GB and NN in Fig. 4(a)). In [23], the results are compared with the entropy as a single-metric baseline and with the naive baseline introduced above. For the entropy baseline (see Table 1), we use single-frame gradient boosting as suggested in [17]. Both baselines are clearly outperformed. In contrast to the results in [17], the GB meta regression model does not outperform the neural network in all settings, even though it yields the best results in most of the experiments.

Figure 4 shows the influence of temporal metrics with respect to R^2 value and classification accuracy. For the linear meta regression model based on the weak ConvLSTM (Fig. 4(a)), we obtain R^2 values up to $66.85\%(\pm0.43\%)$ when taking account of all $m = 9$ temporal metrics, whereas the baseline metrics U_t (0 considered cell state metrics) only achieve averaged R^2 values of $65.77\%(\pm0.45\%)$. For the stronger ConvLSTM model (Fig. 4(b)), the best results are obtained for 8 cell state metrics, that is, $R^2 = 63.33\%(\pm0.59\%)$, whereas the baseline metrics only obtain R^2 values up to $62.76\%(\pm0.58\%)$. These results are in line with the findings in [23] and [17], that is, stronger segmentation models yield worse meta performance with respect to R^2. Moreover, the analysis of time series metrics in

Table 2. Results for meta classification and regression based on time series temporal metrics for different meta models and the GB baseline from [17] for both the weak (W) and the strong (S) model. The superscript denotes the number of frames, where the best performance and in particular the given values are reached. The best results are highlighted.

Meta Classification $IoU_{adj} = 0, > 0$					
Baseline [17] (W): $ACC = 94.93\%(\pm0.32\%)$ $AUROC = 94.99\%(\pm0.35\%)$					
Baseline [17] (S): $ACC = 96.03\%(\pm0.18\%)$ $AUROC = 94.12\%(\pm0.43\%)$					
		GB	LR	LSTM	NN
ACC	W	$94.95\%(\pm0.24\%)^9$	$94.64\%(\pm0.24\%)^8$	$\mathbf{95.25\%(\pm0.22\%)^1}$	$94.09\%(\pm0.23\%)^6$
	S	$\mathbf{96.15\%(\pm0.17\%)^1}$	$95.88\%(\pm0.23\%)^1$	$96.15\%(\pm0.17\%)^9$	$95.54\%(\pm0.30\%)^1$
$AUROC$	W	$95.00\%(\pm0.28\%)^1$	$94.24\%(\pm0.34\%)^1$	$\mathbf{95.04\%(\pm0.22\%)^1}$	$93.32\%(\pm0.47\%)^1$
	S	$\mathbf{94.23\%(\pm0.42\%)^9}$	$92.85\%(\pm0.39\%)^1$	$93.65\%(\pm0.46\%)^1$	$91.92\%(\pm0.64\%)^0$
Meta Regression IoU_{adj}					
Baseline [17] (W): $\sigma = 0.153(\pm0.002)$ $R^2 = 74.00\%(\pm0.65\%)$					
Baseline [17] (S): $\sigma = 0.161(\pm0.001)$ $R^2 = 68.27\%(\pm0.53\%)$					
		GB	LR	LSTM	NN
σ	W	$\mathbf{0.154\%(\pm0.001\%)^6}$	$0.168\%(\pm0.001\%)^6$	$0.157\%(\pm0.003\%)^6$	$0.157\%(\pm0.003\%)^7$
	S	$\mathbf{0.162\%(\pm0.002\%)^8}$	$0.173\%(\pm0.002\%)^8$	$\mathbf{0.162\%(\pm0.002\%)^8}$	$0.163\%(\pm0.002\%)^8$
R^2	W	$\mathbf{74.31\%(\pm0.33\%)^0}$	$69.15\%(\pm0.46\%)^3$	$73.58\%(\pm0.74\%)^3$	$73.54\%(\pm0.39\%)^0$
	S	$68.97\%(\pm0.81\%)^1$	$64.44\%(\pm0.51\%)^1$	$\mathbf{69.00\%(\pm0.98\%)^6}$	$68.53\%(\pm1.04\%)^6$

[17] showed a performance gain for linear models, whereas the stronger gradient boosting models do not benefit as much from time series metrics. We observe the same effects with regard to temporal metrics. Finally, with regard to meta classification based on the strong model (Fig. 4(c)), we observe that all models benefit from the temporal metrics, while the linear model outperforms the shallow LSTM and neural network by $0.15pp$ and $0.26pp$, respectively. Note that even though the linear model is only slightly better than the shallow network, this result is not in line with the findings of [23] and [17], where the neural networks outperformed the linear models in all experiments.

6.2 Evaluation of Time Series Temporal Metrics

Next, we investigate time series metrics $\{V_{m,t}, V_{m,t-1}, \ldots, V_{m,t-T}\}$ with $m = 9$ and a length of up to $T = 10$ previous timesteps, yielding 11 different sets of metrics. The results are summarized in Table 2. Since the gradient boosting model performs best in [17] as well as in most of our experiments, we consider the gradient boosting model equipped with the metric set $\{U_t, U_{t-1}, \ldots, U_{t-10}\}$ as the baseline model. This baseline is outperformed for both meta tasks and both the strong and the weak model. For the weak model, we achieve classification accuracy up to $95.25\%(\pm0.22\%)$ with our proposed LSTM meta model considering 1 cell state metric. For meta regression, we obtain R^2 values up to $74.31\%(\pm0.33\%)$ for the gradient boosting model. For the strong model, we achieve best results for the classification task by means of the gradient boosting model, while our proposed LSTM meta model outperforms the gradient boosting model in the regression task yielding R^2 values of 69.00%($\pm$0.98%) with 6 considered cell state metrics.

7   Conclusion and Outlook

In this paper, we extended the approach from [23] and [17] for deep ConvLSTM networks. We introduced temporal metrics based on the cell states broadcasted through LSTM cells as additional inputs for meta classification and regression. In our experiments, we studied the influence of different numbers of considered cell state metrics for four meta models, i.e., linear models, gradient boosting, shallow neural networks as well as shallow LSTM models. Moreover, we investigated the influence of LSTM meta models for time series metrics proposed in [17]. In all experiments, our approach slightly improved the state of the art results [23] and [17]. More precisely, we achieve classification accuracy of 96.15%($\pm$0.17%) and $AUROC$ of 95.04% ($\pm$0.22%) using our proposed LSTM meta model with temporal metrics. For meta regression, we obtain R^2 values of 74.31%($\pm$0.33%). We plan to develop further LSTM-based metrics for uncertainty quantification applied to the task of predicting several steps into the future.

Disclaimer. The results, opinions and conclusions expressed in this publication are not necessarily those of Volkswagen Aktiengesellschaft.

References

1. Babenko, B., Yang, M.H., Belongie, S.: Visual tracking with online multiple instance learning. In: 2009 IEEE Conference on Computer Vision and Pattern Recognition, pp. 983–990 (2009). https://doi.org/10.1109/CVPR.2009.5206737
2. Belagiannis, V., Schubert, F., Navab, N., Ilic, S.: Segmentation based particle filtering for real-time 2D object tracking. In: Fitzgibbon, A., Lazebnik, S., Perona, P., Sato, Y., Schmid, C. (eds.) ECCV 2012. LNCS, vol. 7575, pp. 842–855. Springer, Heidelberg (2012). https://doi.org/10.1007/978-3-642-33765-9_60
3. Bergmann, P., Meinhardt, T., Leal-Taixé, L.: Tracking without bells and whistles. In: 2019 IEEE/CVF International Conference on Computer Vision (ICCV), pp. 941–951 (2019). https://doi.org/10.1109/ICCV.2019.00103
4. Blundell, C., Cornebise, J., Kavukcuoglu, K., Wierstra, D.: Weight uncertainty in neural network. In: Bach, F., Blei, D. (eds.) Proceedings of the 32nd International Conference on Machine Learning. Proceedings of Machine Learning Research, vol. 37, pp. 1613–1622. PMLR (2015). https://proceedings.mlr.press/v37/blundell15.html
5. Duvenaud, D., Maclaurin, D., Adams, R.: Early stopping as nonparametric variational inference. In: Gretton, A., Robert, C.C. (eds.) Proceedings of the 19th International Conference on Artificial Intelligence and Statistics. Proceedings of Machine Learning Research, vol. 51, pp. 1070–1077. PMLR (2016). https://proceedings.mlr.press/v51/duvenaud16.html
6. Erdem, C.E., Sankur, B., Tekalp, A.M.: Performance measures for video object segmentation and tracking. IEEE Trans. Image Process. **13**(7), 937–951 (2004). https://doi.org/10.1109/TIP.2004.828427

7. Gal, Y., Ghahramani, Z.: Dropout as a Bayesian approximation: representing model uncertainty in deep learning. In: Balcan, M.F., Weinberger, K.Q. (eds.) Proceedings of The 33rd International Conference on Machine Learning. Proceedings of Machine Learning Research, vol. 48, pp. 1050–1059. PMLR (2016). https:// proceedings.mlr.press/v48/gal16.html

8. Guo, C., Pleiss, G., Sun, Y., Weinberger, K.Q.: On calibration of modern neural networks. In: Precup, D., Teh, Y.W. (eds.) Proceedings of the 34th International Conference on Machine Learning. Proceedings of Machine Learning Research, vol. 70, pp. 1321–1330. PMLR (2017). https://proceedings.mlr.press/v70/guo17a.html

9. Hochreiter, S., Schmidhuber, J.: Long short-term memory. Neural Comput. 9(8), 1735–1780 (1997). https://doi.org/10.1162/neco.1997.9.8.1735

10. Hornauer, J., Belagiannis, V.: Gradient-based uncertainty for monocular depth estimation. In: Avidan, S., Brostow, G., Cissé, M., Farinella, G.M., Hassner, T. (eds) Computer Vision, ECCV 2022. LNCS, vol. 13680, pp. 613–630. Springer, Cham (2022). https://doi.org/10.1007/978-3-031-20044-1_35

11. Huang, P.-Y., Hsu, W.-T., Chiu, C.-Y., Wu, T.-F., Sun, M.: Efficient uncertainty estimation for semantic segmentation in videos. In: Ferrari, V., Hebert, M., Sminchisescu, C., Weiss, Y. (eds.) ECCV 2018. LNCS, vol. 11205, pp. 536–552. Springer, Cham (2018). https://doi.org/10.1007/978-3-030-01246-5_32

12. Hurtado, J.V., Mohan, R., Burgard, W., Valada, A.: MOPT: multi-object panoptic tracking. In: The IEEE Conference on Computer Vision and Pattern Recognition (CVPR) Workshop on Scalability in Autonomous Driving (2020)

13. Jaccard, P.: The distribution of the flora in the alpine zone. New Phytol. 11, 37–50 (1912)

14. Kim, D., Woo, S., Lee, J.Y., Kweon, I.S.: Video panoptic segmentation. In: 2020 IEEE/CVF Conference on Computer Vision and Pattern Recognition (CVPR), pp. 9856–9865 (2020). https://doi.org/10.1109/CVPR42600.2020.00988

15. Kull, M., Perello Nieto, M., Kängsepp, M., Silva Filho, T., Song, H., Flach, P.: Beyond temperature scaling: obtaining well-calibrated multi-class probabilities with dirichlet calibration. In: Wallach, H., Larochelle, H., Beygelzimer, A., Alché-Buc, F.d., Fox, E., Garnett, R. (eds.) Advances in Neural Information Processing Systems, vol. 32. Curran Associates, Inc. (2019). https://proceedings.neurips.cc/ paper_files/paper/2019/file/8ca01ea920679a0fe3728441494041b9-Paper.pdf

16. Lakshminarayanan, B., Pritzel, A., Blundell, C.: Simple and scalable predictive uncertainty estimation using deep ensembles. In: Guyon, I., et al. (eds.) Advances in Neural Information Processing Systems, vol. 30. Curran Associates, Inc. (2017). https://proceedings.neurips.cc/paper_files/paper/2017/file/ 9ef2ed4b7fd2c810847ffa5fa85bce38-Paper.pdf

17. Maag, K., Rottmann, M., Gottschalk, H.: Time-dynamic estimates of the reliability of deep semantic segmentation networks. In: 2020 IEEE 32nd International Conference on Tools with Artificial Intelligence (ICTAI), pp. 502–509 (2020). https:// doi.org/10.1109/ICTAI50040.2020.00084

18. MacKay, D.J.C.: A practical Bayesian framework for backpropagation networks. Neural Comput. 4(3), 448–472 (1992). https://doi.org/10.1162/neco.1992.4.3.448

19. Minderer, M., et al.: Revisiting the calibration of modern neural networks. In: Ranzato, M., Beygelzimer, A., Dauphin, Y., Liang, P.S., Vaughan, J.W. (eds.) Advances in Neural Information Processing Systems, vol. 34, pp. 15682–15694. Curran Associates, Inc. (2021). https://proceedings.neurips.cc/paper_files/paper/ 2021/file/8420d359404024567b5aefda1231af24-Paper.pdf

20. Peng, J., et al.: Chained-tracker: chaining paired attentive regression results for end-to-end joint multiple-object detection and tracking. In: Vedaldi, A., Bischof, H., Brox, T., Frahm, J.-M. (eds.) ECCV 2020. LNCS, vol. 12349, pp. 145–161. Springer, Cham (2020). https://doi.org/10.1007/978-3-030-58548-8_9

21. Richter, S.R., Hayder, Z., Koltun, V.: Playing for benchmarks. In: 2017 IEEE International Conference on Computer Vision (ICCV), pp. 2232–2241 (2017). https://doi.org/10.1109/ICCV.2017.243

22. Riedlinger, T., Rottmann, M., Schubert, M., Gottschalk, H.: Gradient-based quantification of epistemic uncertainty for deep object detectors. In: 2023 IEEE/CVF Winter Conference on Applications of Computer Vision (WACV), pp. 3910–3920 (2023). https://doi.org/10.1109/WACV56688.2023.00391

23. Rottmann, M., et al.: Prediction error meta classification in semantic segmentation: detection via aggregated dispersion measures of softmax probabilities. In: 2020 International Joint Conference on Neural Networks (IJCNN), pp. 1–9 (2020). https://doi.org/10.1109/IJCNN48605.2020.9206659

24. Rottmann, M., Reese, M.: Automated detection of label errors in semantic segmentation datasets via deep learning and uncertainty quantification. In: 2023 IEEE/CVF Winter Conference on Applications of Computer Vision (WACV), pp. 3213–3222 (2023). https://doi.org/10.1109/WACV56688.2023.00323

25. Rottmann, M., Schubert, M.: Uncertainty measures and prediction quality rating for the semantic segmentation of nested multi resolution street scene images. In: 2019 IEEE/CVF Conference on Computer Vision and Pattern Recognition Workshops (CVPRW), pp. 1361–1369 (2019). https://doi.org/10.1109/CVPRW.2019.00176

26. Shi, X., Chen, Z., Wang, H., Yeung, D.Y., Wong, W., Woo, W.: Convolutional LSTM network: a machine learning approach for precipitation nowcasting. In: Proceedings of the 28th International Conference on Neural Information Processing Systems, NIPS 2015, vol. 1, pp. 802–810. MIT Press (2015)

27. Wang, Q., Zhang, L., Bertinetto, L., Hu, W., Torr, P.H.: Fast online object tracking and segmentation: a unifying approach. In: 2019 IEEE/CVF Conference on Computer Vision and Pattern Recognition (CVPR), pp. 1328–1338 (2019). https://doi.org/10.1109/CVPR.2019.00142

28. Wickstrøm, K., Kampffmeyer, M., Jenssen, R.: Uncertainty modeling and interpretability in convolutional neural networks for polyp segmentation. In: 2018 IEEE 28th International Workshop on Machine Learning for Signal Processing (MLSP), pp. 1–6 (2018). https://doi.org/10.1109/MLSP.2018.8516998

Evaluating Explanation Methods
for Multivariate Time Series Classification

Davide Italo Serramazza[(✉)], Thu Trang Nguyen, Thach Le Nguyen,
and Georgiana Ifrim

School of Computer Science, University College Dublin, Dublin, Ireland
{davide.serramazza,thu.nguyen}@ucdconnect.ie,
{thach.lenguyen,georgiana.ifrim}@ucd.ie

Abstract. Multivariate time series classification is an important computational task arising in applications where data is recorded over time
and over multiple channels. For example, a smartwatch can record the
acceleration and orientation of a person's motion, and these signals are
recorded as multivariate time series. We can classify this data to understand and predict human movement and various properties such as fitness
levels. In many applications classification alone is not enough, we often
need to classify but also understand what the model learns (e.g., why was
a prediction given, based on what information in the data). The main
focus of this paper is on analysing and evaluating explanation methods
tailored to Multivariate Time Series Classification (MTSC). We focus on
saliency-based explanation methods that can point out the most relevant
channels and time series points for the classification decision. We analyse
two popular and accurate multivariate time series classifiers, ROCKET
and dResNet, as well as two popular explanation methods, SHAP and
dCAM. We study these methods on 3 synthetic datasets and 2 real-world
datasets and provide a quantitative and qualitative analysis of the explanations provided. We find that flattening the multivariate datasets by
concatenating the channels works as well as using multivariate classifiers
directly and adaptations of SHAP for MTSC work quite well. Additionally, we also find that the popular synthetic datasets we used are not
suitable for time series analysis.

Keywords: Time Series Classification · Explanation · Evaluation

1 Introduction

Real-world time series data are often multivariate, i.e., data collected over a
period of time on different channels. An example is human motion data collected
from participants wearing a tri-axial accelerometer on their dominant wrist. The
tri-variate data can be examined to identify epilepsy convulsions in everyday
life [23]. Another example is traffic data where multiple sensors are set up at
different locations to measure the traffic occupancy in a city[1].

---

[1] https://pems.dot.ca.gov/.

Supplementary Information The online version contains supplementary material
available at https://doi.org/10.1007/978-3-031-49896-1_11.

While univariate time series have been the main research focus, there is a steadily growing interest in multivariate time series (MTS), in particular for the classification task (MTSC). The release of the MTSC benchmark [2], a collaborative effort by researchers from multiple institutions, is an important milestone that has accelerated studies of MTSC methods.

Explainable AI is another important topic due to the explosion of interest in complex machine learning models and deep learning methods. Pioneers in this field have been working mostly on text and image data and, as a result, a number of explanation frameworks including LIME [18], DeepLift [13], Shapley [14] have been introduced. The similarity between image and time series data allows such techniques to be adapted to time series models [24]. Nevertheless, there are some notable differences between images and time series. Firstly, images are usually represented using RGB encoding and all the 3 channels contain necessary information, while for time series it is common to have channels that do not contribute to, or even hinder, the classification decision. Secondly, in images there is a lot of homogeneity in the pixel values while moving between pixels belonging to the same objects and a sharp difference when moving between pixels belonging to different objects. In time series, it is less common to find such a strong locality, especially across all the channels. Furthermore, the data magnitude and pre-processing, such as normalisation, are important factors for time series, but less so for images.

In this work, we focus on methods for explaining MTSC as this is an important open problem that is often as important as the classification itself. In a scenario in which people wear accelerometers on their body while executing a physical exercise, other than classifying the exercise as correctly executed or not, it is also important to provide feedback to users, e.g., an explanation of why the exercise was incorrectly executed by pointing out the relevant data.

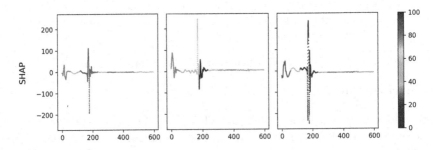

Fig. 1. Sample multivariate time series and explanation heat map. The 3 plots show the x, y, z channels for a jump sample.

In this paper, a *multivariate time series explanation* is a 2D saliency map [3] highlighting the importance of each time series channel and each time point for the classification decision, as illustrated in Fig. 1. A proper MTSC explanation should be able to point out for each channel the relevant time points that may be located at different parts of the time series. For example, CAM [25] was designed for explaining univariate time series thus it can not identify important time points which vary across channels.

In this work we aim to analyse and evaluate a few MTSC explanation methods we found in the literature. Throughout our literature research, the only bespoke MTS explanation methods found are all tailored for deep learning methods (especially CNN), while few others are able to provide a 2D heat map by adapting *univariate time series explanation* to work in a multivariate scenario (most of the time by flattening the dataset and reshaping the 1D heat map into a matrix).

The lack of bespoke multivariate time series explanations, combined with the lack of explanation evaluation methods, is an important gap in the scientific literature. The main aim of this work is to study and evaluate existing MTSC explanation methods in order to start addressing this gap.

Our main contributions in this paper are:

- We analyse the literature on saliency-based explanation methods for MTSC and find very few bespoke methods, all of which are designed for deep learning models. Among these, we select dCAM [3] which extends CAM, a very popular method for time-series and image explanations.
- We conduct experiments using state-of-the-art multivariate time series classifiers ROCKET [6] and dResNet [3] and explanation methods SHAP [14] and dCAM [3]. We study ways to adapt SHAP to work with multivariate time series and compare it to the bespoke MTSC explanation method dCAM.
- We use 3 synthetic datasets and 2 real-world datasets to compare the classifiers and the explanations. We evaluate the explanations both quantitatively, using the methodology proposed in [16], as well as qualitatively. We find that for truly multivariate datasets (i.e., where multiple channels are needed for the correct classification), ROCKET-SHAP works better than dCAM, but is also more computationally expensive. We also find that flattening the datasets by concatenating the channels and using univariate classifiers works as well as using multivariate classifiers directly.

In the rest of the paper, in Sect. 2 we discuss prior work addressing the MTSC explanation task. In Sect. 3 we formally define the problem addressed, the classifiers and the explanation methods used in the experiments. In Sect. 4 we describe the datasets used in our study, in Sect. 5 we describe our experiments and in Sect. 6 we summarise our main findings.

2   Related Work

Explanation Methods Adapted from Univariate to Multivariate TSC. Some multivariate time series explanation methods are simple adaptations of methods developed for univariate data. In [1], the authors explain the adapted classifiers by applying the timeXplain [15] framework on each channel *independently*. The result is a multivariate explanation that highlights the important segments in each channel of the multivariate sample. Nonetheless, it is arguable whether this approach is appropriate since the explained model(s) (univariate) and the model that needs to be explained (multivariate) are not the same. Additionally, it is not clear if the accuracy of the channel-wise univariate model is similar or worse than that of the multivariate model, and this is not discussed in the paper.

Bespoke Explanation Methods for MTSC. Most of the previous explanation methods designed for MTSC are tailored to deep learning methods, which are not state-of-the-art with regard to classification accuracy. In [3], the authors discussed the drawbacks of the CAM explanation method for MTS data. CAM can only produce a univariate saliency map, thus it is unable to identify the important channels. Features that depend on more than one channel are also not detectable. dCAM, proposed in the same paper, addressed these limitations by rearranging the input time series with all the permutations of the channels. The paper shows that this technique can be applied to any architecture with a Global Average Pooling layer (GAP) such as ResNet or InceptionTime. dCAM limitations are discussed by comparing this method with other deep learning explanation methods, as for instance it was shown that dCAM is not the best option when dealing with multivariate datasets that can be classified focusing on just one channel, but there is no comparison against model agnostic methods such as SHAP [14] or LIME [18].

Evaluation of Explanation Methods for MTSC. While explanation methods for MTSC are few, works on evaluating such methods are even fewer. For univariate time series, several approaches have been proposed to compare explanation methods from different angles. The work in [5,11] benchmarks the methods with controllable synthetic datasets. The work of [8] attempted to extract "ground-truth" explanations with a white-box classifier. The "ground-truth" explanation is then used to evaluate post-hoc explanations. AMEE [16] is a recent framework to quantitatively compare explanation methods on a dataset by perturbing input time series and measuring the impact on the classification accuracy of several classifiers. For multivariate time series, recently [22] designed an evaluation framework that is also based on the idea of perturbation, but the work is only limited to evaluating deep learning classifiers and associated explanations. The paper also proposed a synthetic multivariate time series dataset to benchmark explanation methods.

3   Background

A multivariate time series X can be represented as a $d \times L$ matrix, where the d rows are also called channels and the L columns store the values associated with each channel at every time point. Hence X_i^j is the value of the time series at time point i and channel j, with $0 \leq i < L$ and $0 \leq j < d$. We also refer to X^j as the univariate time series at channel j, therefore X can be written as $X = [X^0, X^1, \ldots, X^{d-1}]$.

An explanation of a time series X is a saliency map W that provides an importance weight for each data point (at every time point i and every channel j) in the time series. Hence the saliency map can also be represented by a $d \times L$ matrix. A common visualisation method for the saliency map is a heat map where more important data points are highlighted with warmer colours.

An explanation method for MTSC is a method that, given the input MTS, can produce a saliency map highlighting the relevance of each time point to the classifier decision. Intrinsically explainable models such as Ridge Classifier can also be an explanation method while black-box models such as RestNet (dResNet) and ROCKET need a post-hoc explanation method.

In our experiments we compare three different classifiers and explanation methods: ROCKET [6] coupled with SHAP [14], dResNet coupled with dCAM [3] and the Ridge Classifier [10] which is an intrinsically explainable model. We also use a random explanation (a matrix of random weights) as a sanity check.

3.1   Classification Methods

The first classifier we used is **ROCKET** [6] which was originally designed for UTS, but also has an adaptation for MTS: it applies a large set of random convolution kernels to the time series in order to transform it into tabular data with 20,000 features. It introduced some key concepts such as dilation, proportion of positive values (PPV), etc., starting an algorithm family in which recent members such as Minirocket [7], MultiRocket [21] are improvements of the original idea. All the hyper-parameters for ROCKET were learned from the UCR archive. The authors selected 40 random datasets from the archive and used them as the development set to find the best values for the hyper-parameters. Finally, all the kernel weights are sampled from a distribution $\mathcal{N}(0,1)$. After the transformation step, the authors use classic linear classifiers Ridge or Logistic Regression.

The second classifier is **dResNet** [3] which is a variation of ResNet [9]. This last one, originally designed for image classification, was used for the first time in TSC in [24]. It introduced the key concept of *shortcut connections* to mitigate the gradient vanishing problem. The main architecture of the network is composed of three consecutive blocks which in turn contain three different convolutional layers. These three blocks are followed by a GAP layer and a softmax layer for classification.

The dResNet version uses the same architecture with two differences specifically designed to work alongside dCAM. Firstly, for a multivariate time series X with d channels, i.e., a matrix $X = [X^0, X^1, \ldots, X^{d-1}]$, the input $C(X)$ of the network will be a 3D tensor:

$$
C(X) = \begin{bmatrix} X^{d-1} & X^0 & \ldots & X^{d-3} & X^{d-2} \\ \vdots & \vdots & \vdots & \vdots & \vdots \\ X^1 & X^2 & \ldots & X^{d-1} & X^0 \\ X^0 & X^1 & \ldots & X^{d-2} & X^{d-1} \end{bmatrix}
$$

In other words, the input is turned from a $2D$ matrix into a $3D$ one in which each row contains the d channels in different positions. The second change was to turn the convolution shapes from $1D$ to $2D$ to have the same output shape as ResNet. These changes were made so that the network is able to capture patterns depending on multiple channels while still learning on individual channels.

The third model we used is the well-known **Ridge Classifier** [10], meant to be a baseline in the experiments: we used the scikit-learn [17] package RidgeCV using Cross Validation, leaving the other solver parameters as default. This classifier disregards the time ordering in each time series as it treats each time series as a tabular vector of features.

3.2   Explanation Methods

The first explanation method considered in this paper is **SHAP** [14] which measures feature importance using Shapley values borrowed from game theory. SHAP quantifies the contribution of each feature by examining the differences in the model output when a specific feature is masked, i.e., it is replaced with a specific value and when it is not. SHAP considers every possible masking configuration, thus is computationally expensive. The timeXplain library [15] applies SHAP on the UTSC task by dividing the time series into segments, each is treated as a feature. The segmentation exploits locality in time series and significantly reduces the number of features before applying SHAP. As SHAP is a model-agnostic method, it works with any TSC model. We couple it with ROCKET due to its efficiency and accuracy.

The second explanation method (used along dResNet), is **dCAM** [3]. It computes CAM [25] for each row of the input (described in Sect. 3.1), resulting in a $2D$ matrix $\mathcal{M}$ where all channels are brought back to their original positions to evaluate their contribution. Since the network is trained to compute meaningful predictions regardless of the order in which the channels are provided, dCAM computes k different matrices $\mathcal{M}$ each of them obtained by a different random permutation of the channel order: all these k matrices are then averaged into $\hat{\mathcal{M}}$. The final step to retrieve the explanation W consists in filtering out uninformative time points and uninformative channels using respectively the average value of $\hat{\mathcal{M}}$ in each channel and the variance of all positions for a single channel. dCAM can tell how important a time point was for the classification by taking the differences in $\hat{\mathcal{M}}$ when the time point is present in different positions.

The third explanation method is **Ridge**. As mentioned before, this method is intrinsically explainable because the explanation weights are the weights learned by the classifier. The model is basically a vector of coefficients for each feature, i.e., data point in the time series.

The final explanation method **Random** is a baseline that generates the saliency map W by sampling values randomly from a continuous uniform distribution. The idea is that any good explanation method should provide a better explanation than the random one.

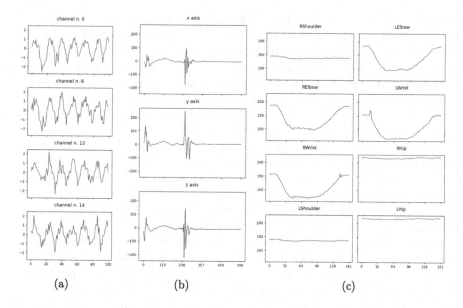

Fig. 2. Sample time series: Fig 2a PesudoPeriodic negative sample. Fig 2b one instance from CMJ Bend. Fig 2c one instance from MP Normal.

4   Datasets

We work with 3 synthetic multivariate time series classification datasets and 2 real-world ones. In Fig. 2 we present one sample from one synthetic dataset and one sample each for the real-world datasets.

4.1   Synthetic Datasets

For the synthetic datasets, we use the multivariate time series classification benchmark by Ismail et al. [11]. We generated three different datasets, using the *Pseudo Periodic, Gaussian* and *Auto Regressive* distributions. Each has 100 samples in both train and test sets, with $L = 100$ and $d = 20$. The two classes for classification are *positive* and *negative*. The discriminative data points are stationary and within a small box, i.e., X_i^j is discriminative if and only if $10 \leq i < 20$ and $0 \leq j < 10$. In other words, 50% of the channels and 10% of the time steps are relevant. Overall, only 5% of the time series matter for predicting the class.

4.2   Real-World Datasets

The first real-world dataset is **Counter Movement Jump** (CMJ) [12]. The data were collected using accelerometer sensors attached on the participants while performing the counter-movement jump exercise. The three classes are: jumps with acceptable form (class 1), with their legs bending during the flight (class 2), and with a stumble upon landing (class 3). The training set has 419 samples while the test set has 179 samples. Each time series has 3 channels ($d = 3$) that record the acceleration in x, y, and z axis. The original data is variable-length thus we resampled every time series to the same length ($L = 596$). From the domain experts, we know that the distinctions between classes are more observable on channel y, thus it makes this channel the most important one.

The second real-world dataset is **Military Press** (MP) [20]. To collect the data, 56 participants were asked to perform the Military Press strength-and-conditioning exercise. Each of them completed 10 repetitions in the normal form and another 30 in induced forms, with 10 repetitions each (simulating 3 types of errors). The time series were extracted from video using the OpenPose library [4]. The dataset has 1452 samples in the training set and 601 in the test set, each time series has 161 time points and 50 channels corresponding to the x, y coordinates of 25 body parts. From the original dataset we have selected 8 channels representing the y coordinates of both left and right Shoulder, Elbow, Wrist and Hip. This dataset has 4 different classes representing the kind of exercise done, namely Normal (N), Asymmetrical (A), Reduced Range (R) and Arch (Arch). We know from domain experts that the importance of channels for this dataset is in decending order: Elbows, Wrists, Shoulders, Hips. High accuracy can be obtained only by using the Elbows and Wrists while it is not possible to achieve a high accuracy by only using one channel. We later show experiments both in Sect. 5 and in the Appendix to document this behaviour.

5   Experiments

In our experiments we aim to understand the strengths and weaknesses of existing methods for explaining multivariate time series classification. As summarised in Table 1, we compared one of the bespoke multivariate method found (dResNet), the popular SHAP, which has the downside of being adapted to provide a 2D heatmap, and Ridge as a sanity check baseline. Some different coupling such as ROCKET paired with dCAM or dResNet paired with SHAP are not possible respectively because dCAM can only explain models having a GAP layer and the timeXplain library (used for ROCKET-SHAP concatenated) is implemented only for 1D-vector instances (univariate time series).

Table 1. Summary of the explanation methods tested in this paper.

Classifier	Explanation Method	MTS Approach
dResNet	dCAM	Bespoke MTSC
ROCKET	SHAP	Concatenated
ROCKET	SHAP	Channel by Channel
Ridge Classifier	Ridge Classifier	Concatenated
n/a	Random	n/a

To make the timeXplain library work with MTS, we apply the following two strategies (Fig. 3): (1) **Concatenated**: Concatenating all the channels to a single univariate time series. As a result, the output saliency map is also univariate and thus needs to be reshaped. (2) **Channel by Channel**: Train and explain one model for each channel independently. The MTSC model in this case is an ensemble of per-channel UTSC models.

For SHAP-channel-by-channel, we assign the number of segments to 10 while, for SHAP-concatenated, the number of segments is set to $d \times 10$. Since Ridge can only work using univariate datasets, we only used the dataset concatenation strategy for this classifier. The output of all explanation methods is a saliency map in the form of either $d \times L$ or $d \times 10$ matrix (reshaped if necessary).

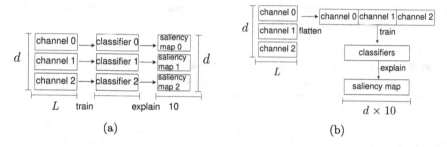

(a)   (b)

Fig. 3. Strategies to use the timeXplain library in a multivariate scenario, for $d = 3$. In Fig 3a, a classifier is trained for each channel: for explaining each classifier, d heat maps of length 10 are produced: stacking these vectors together results in a matrix of dimension $d \times 10$. In Fig 3b the time series are concatenated and one single classifier is trained. We explain the classifier using a number of segments $d \times 10$ and reshape the resulting vector into a 2D matrix having the same shape as in the previous case.

It is important to note that we have only one bespoke method for multivariate time series, dCAM, that computes a saliency map of the same shape as the original time series instance.

All the experiments were done using a machine with 32 GB RAM, Intel i7-12700H CPU and an Nvidia GeForce RTX 350 Ti GPU (the GPU was used only for dResNet/dCAM). All the code used to perform the experiments is available on a Github repository[2].

5.1   Classification Accuracy Analysis

Before diving into the explanations, we first take a look at the accuracy of the classifiers used for producing the explanations. All the classifiers listed in Table 2 were trained 5 different times (for ROCKET we also tried to either normalize the data or not). In this Table are reported the most accurate ones i.e., the models

---

[2] https://github.com/mlgig/Evaluating-Explanation-Methods-for-MTSC.

used in the experiments as well as the accuracy for the univariate concatenated datasets.

Having a look at the table we can notice that all the times both ROCKET and dResNet have high accuracy (with some exceptions for the synthetic datasets): this is an important pre-requisite when comparing explanations methods applied to different classifiers as we did.

We note that RidgeCV does particularly well on the synthetic datasets. On Military Press, the multivariate models are more accurate than the univariate ones (on concatednated data). This is expected since it is difficult to achieve a high accuracy with a single channel for this dataset, so this is a trully multivariate dataset. Concatenating all the channels for Military Press hurts more dResNet which loses 9% points accuracy, while ROCKET loses only 4. For CMJ, the behaviour is reversed, with univariate models being more accurate than the multivariate ones. dResNet has a noticeable 9% points improvement on the concatenated dataset, while ROCKET gains 1% point.

Table 2. Accuracy for the models listed in Table 1 plus dResNet concatenated and ROCKET multivariate: using this table it is possible to appreciate the differences when using multivariate vs univariate datasets.

Classifier/Dataset	PseudoPeriodic	Gaussian	AutoRegressive	CMJ	MilitaryPress
dResNet multivariate	1.0	0.83	0.82	0.82	0.79
dResNet concatenated	1.0	0.89	0.81	0.91	0.68
ROCKET multivariate	1.0	0.93	0.87	0.87	0.87
ROCKET concatenated	1.0	0.72	0.73	0.88	0.83
ROCKET ch-by-ch	0.99	0.72	0.95	0.85	0.65
RidgeCV	1.0	1.0	1.0	0.44	0.61

5.2   Synthetic Data

For the synthetic data, we performed 5-fold cross-validation to train a Logistic Regression classifier for ROCKET, allowing up to 1000 iterations. For dResNet we used 64 filters, and we trained using the Cross-Entropy Loss and Adam optimizer with a learning rate set to 0.0001. Finally for RidgeCV we used the standard scikit-learn parameters for cross-validation using 5 folds.

Regarding the explanation methods we used 10 segments for ROCKET concatenated in the channel-by-channel scenario and 200 segments in the concatenated one; for dCAM the number of permutations to evaluate k was set to 200 (this is the maximum recommended in [3]).

The steps done for syntethic data evaluation are illustrated in Fig. 4. The first step is to reshape all the explanations so that they all have the same dimension. Specifically, the saliency maps we obtained from dCAM and Ridge have a shape

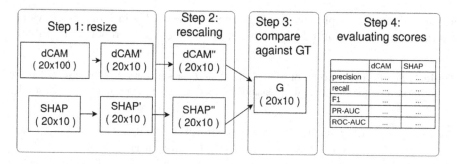

Fig. 4. Steps performed in the synthetic data evaluation when comparing dCAM and SHAP. In Step 1, dCAM is reshaped into $(20, 10)$ averaging 10 consecutive elements in each channel, while SHAP is untouched. In Step 2, the reshaped matrices are rescaled in the range $[0, 100]$. In Step 3, both the explanations achieved so far are compared against the ground truth matrix G and finally in Step 4 the scores computed in the previous step are evaluated.

of $d \times L = 20 \times 100$ while the ones from SHAP concatenated and channel-by-channel have a shape of $d \times$ n. segments $= 20 \times 10$. We chose to average 10 consecutive elements for dCAM and Ridge explanation as we empirically verified that all the metrics had slight improvements. The alternative was to repeat 10 times the same item in SHAP explanations.

After this stage, all explanations have the shape of 20×10.

The second step rescales the explanation weights as they can have different magnitudes among different instances and different methods. First of all, we take the absolute value of each explanation (to also take into consideration variables that have a negative contribution for the classification) and then we rescale by min-max normalization in the range $[0, 100]$.

The third step is to instantiate a ground truth matrix G and compare each explanation against it. For the settings described before, this is a binary matrix having shape 20×10 (same dimension of explanations after Step 2), all the elements are set to 0 except for the ones in G_i^j with $i = 1, 0 \leq j < 10$ that are set to 1. In other words, this is a binary matrix describing whether or not a segment is important for the classification.

To be noted that synthetic dataset parameters such as the number and range of informative time points and channels, and explanation method parameters such as the number of segments were chosen so that the resulting segments are made up either by only informative time points or by only uninformative time points.

The last step is simply to compute the metrics used for the evaluation i.e., Precision, Recall, F1-score, PR-AUC and ROC-AUC [3]. For Precision and Recall we had to fix a threshold dividing the values considered uninformative from the ones considered informative: we have chosen 50 as the medium value between 0 and 100. On the other hand PR-AUC and ROC-AUC do not fix any threshold

as they average multiple scores using different thresholds into one single value.
All these metrics computed for the 3 synthetic datasets are reported in Table 3.

Table 3. Scores and runtime of each XAI method for synthetic datasets: h stands for
hours, m stands for minutes and s stand for seconds; ch-by-ch stands for channel by
channel.

Dataset	XAI Method	Precision	Recall	F1	PR-AUC	ROC-AUC	Time
Pseudo-Periodic	SHAP ch-by-ch	0.73	0.94	0.82	0.99	0.99	6.2 h
Pseudo-Periodic	SHAP concatenated	0.92	0.66	0.77	0.99	0.99	3.5 h
Pseudo-Periodic	dCAM	0.50	0.50	0.50	0.63	0.98	50 m
Pseudo-Periodic	Ridge	1.0	1.0	1.0	1.0	1.0	0 s
Gaussian	SHAP ch-by-ch	0.88	0.63	0.73	0.91	0.99	6.2 h
Gaussian	SHAP concatenated	0.34	0.18	0.24	0.16	0.71	3.5 hr
Gaussian	dCAM	0.36	0.15	0.21	0.35	0.94	50 m
Gaussian	Ridge	0.83	1.0	0.9	1.0	1.0	0 s
Auto-Regressive	SHAP ch-by-ch	0.85	0.60	0.71	0.49	0.77	6.2 h
Auto-Regressive	SHAP concatenated	0.27	0.13	0.18	0.29	0.57	3.5 h
Auto-Regressive	dCAM	0.34	0.15	0.21	0.06	0.57	50 m
Auto-Regressive	Ridge	1.0	1.0	1.0	1.0	1.0	0 s
All	Random	0.05	0.15	0.08	0.05	0.5	0 s

Looking at the table it is possible to note that all the time Ridge has perfect
metrics but for Recall (and consequently F1 score) with the Gaussian dataset.
These results along with the one provided in Table 2 (perfect accuracies of Ridge
for the 3 synthetic datasets), are very strong evidence that these commonly used
benchmarks are not ideal for time series analyses at least using the parameters
described before. We think this is the case due to the way the benchmarks are
created, by adding or subtracting a single value to consecutive time points. This
means that a simple tabular classifier such as Ridge is enough to perfectly classify
these datasets. In conclusion, we recommend against the use of these synthetic
benchmarks for analysing time series classification or explanation methods.

Comparing the other method, most of the time SHAP channel by channel is
the second best model, while comparing dCAM with SHAP concatenated there
is no clear winner as in some metrics the first one has better results while in
some others is the opposite.

The two last points to be noted are that some methods have metrics close
to random, especially for Recall, and the time required for computing the explanations is high, taking into account that these are small datasets: 50 min for
dCAM, 3.5 h for SHAP concatenated, and more than 6 h for SHAP channel by
channel.

5.3 Real-World Data

In this section we used some different hyper-parameters: for dResNet the number of filters is now set to 128 as we found better classification results, the number of dCAM permutations k was set to 6 for dCAM (this dataset has 3 channels so the number of possible channel permutations is just 6) while it is still 200, i.e. the maximum recommended, for MP which has 8 channels. We set the number of timeXplain segments using the concatenated dataset to 30 for CMJ and 80 for MP so that they are still equal to $d \times 10$.

Looking at the classifier accuracy in Table 2 we notice how for the two real-world datasets, the accuracies achieved by dResNet and ROCKET are comparable or even better when using the concatenated dataset versions. This means that analysing the explanation methods for MTSC by turning the multivariate problems into univariate ones could be useful.

The close accuracy between original multivariate and concatenated univariate datasets can arise some questions whether these datasets are truly multivariate (i.e., the necessary information for correct classification is spread among different channels). This seems to be the case for Military Press, but less so for CMJ. We plan to investigate further this point in future work.

In this work we decided to use the concatenated datasets and the methodology developed by [16] to evaluate the explanation methods. For the case of dCAM which produces a matrix as an explanation, we flatten the matrix to a vector by concatenating the rows and using it as any other univariate explanation. So dCAM is obtained in a truly multivariate setting (dResNet is a multivariate classifier and dCAM a multivariate explanation), but reshaped to look like a univariate explanation. The explanations obtained from SHAP and Ridge, on the other hand, are univariate explanations obtained by first concatenating the channels and then running univariate classifiers.

For the real-world datasets we do not have precise explanation ground truth as for the synthetic datasets, but we do have domain knowledge about which channels and parts of the time series are important for the classification.

Finally in this section we didn't include SHAP channel by channel in the MP dataset experiment as the accuracy is low (Table 2) therefore it does not make sense to derive an explanation.

Evaluation of Explanation Methods. We apply AMEE [16], an explanation evaluation method for the univariate time series classification task, on the CMJ and MP univariate datasets obtained through concatenating all channels. This method aims to measure the faithfulness of an explanation by estimating its impact on a set of independent classifiers (the *referee classifiers*). If an explanation correctly points out the important areas of a univariate time series, perturbation of such areas will lead to a drop in accuracies of the referee classifiers. The faithfulness of the explanation is then calculated using the Area Under the Curve (AUC) of the accuracy drop curves of each of the referee classifiers. AMEE is designed to be robust by employing various perturbation strategies (i.e. how an important area is perturbed and replaced with a new value) and a diverse set of high-performing referee classifiers. The main idea is that masking away important parts of the data as pointed out by the explanation, should affect a set of high performing classifiers leading to a drop in accuracy across the board.

Table 4. Accuracy of referee classifiers for the AMEE evaluation of explanation methods for univariate time series classification.

Dataset	MrSEQL	ROCKET	WEASEL 2.0
CMJ-concat	0.76	0.88	0.92
MP-concat	0.82	0.84	0.80

For our task, we use the default perturbation strategies with three classifiers included in the standard referees set: MrSEQL [12] WEASEL 2.0 [19] and ROCKET (for more information and results about this methodology we invite the readers to have a look to the original publication [16]). Table 4 shows the accuracy of these referee classifiers on the evaluated datasets.

The result of the explanation evaluation is presented in Table 5 as well as the methodology and the evaluation running time. The methodology running time is dependent on the number of both perturbation strategies and employed referees. It is specific to our choice of the three mentioned referees and four perturbation types using Mean and Gaussian sample from both time-point dependent (local) and time-point independent (global) statistics of the test samples. Looking at the second one (time for running the explanation methods) we notice the high SHAP computational complexity: this was the main reason why we used only 2 real-world datasets for the experiments. We focused on human motion data because in this case we can rely on domain expertise.

From the quantitative evaluation with AMEE, we note that for the CMJ dataset, SHAP concat is the best method, although it is close to a random explanation. dCAM ranks third for this dataset. We note that this dataset is quite noisy due to quiet parts after the jump, and this could explain why SHAP and Random are so close in ranking.

For the MP dataset, SHAP concatenated is by far the best method, significantly better than dCAM, as well as Random and Ridge. This is an interesting finding considering that dCAM was proposed to deal with datasets where there are clear dependencies between channels, but for MP this method does not seem to perform so well.

We supplement the quantitative ranking with a more detailed qualitative analysis in the Appendix. In short we find that for CMJ, the importance rankings of channels given by SHAP concat and dCAM are the same, while for MP, SHAP provides a ranking more in line with domain knowledge, while dCAM places the least informative channels at the top of the ranking.

Table 5. Results of AMEE to rank XAI methods on CMJ and MP datasets concatenated.

Dataset	XAI method	Explanation Power	Rank	Evaluation Time	Explanation Time
CMJ-concat	SHAP concat	1.00	1	2 h	7.15 h
	Random	0.99	2	2 h	0 s
	dCAM	0.39	3	2 h	30 s
	SHAP ch-by-ch	0.05	4	2 h	7.5 h
	Ridge	0.0	5	2 h	0 s
MP-concat	SHAP concat	1.00	1	4.8 h	24 h
	dCAM	0.33	2	4.8 h	15 m
	Random	0.07	3	4.8 h	0 s
	Ridge	0.0	4	4.8 h	0 s

6 Conclusion

In this paper we have investigated explanation methods for MTSC. We studied two very popular explanation methods, dCAM and SHAP, and have provided a quantitative and qualitative analysis of their behavior on synthetic as well as real-world datasets. We found that adaptations of SHAP for MTSC work quite well, and they outperform the recent bespoke MTSC explanation method dCAM. We have also pointed out that a very popular synthetic MTSC benchmark does not seem suitable for MTSC evaluation, since a simple Ridge classifier outperforms all other methods both in classification accuracy and in explanation quality. Finally, while SHAP seems to work effectively to point out important time series channels and time points, we highlighted the time required to run SHAP and pointed out the open problem of excessive time requirements for this method. In future work we plan to investigate the computation time for SHAP, as well as other frameworks for evaluating bespoke explanation methods for MTSC.

Acknowledgments. This publication has emanated from research supported in part by a grant from Science Foundation Ireland under Grant number 18/CRT/6183. For the purpose of Open Access, the author has applied a CC BY public copyright license to any Author Accepted Manuscript version arising from this submission.

References

1. Babayev, R., Wiese, L.: Interpreting decision-making process for multivariate time series classification. In: Bellatreche, L., et al. (eds.) ADBIS 2021. CCIS, vol. 1450, pp. 146–152. Springer, Cham (2021). https://doi.org/10.1007/978-3-030-85082-1_14
2. Bagnall, A., et al.: The uea multivariate time series classification archive 2018. arXiv preprint arXiv:1811.00075 (2018)
3. Boniol, P., Meftah, M., Remy, E., Palpanas, T.: DCAM: dimension-wise class activation map for explaining multivariate data series classification. In: Proceedings of the 2022 International Conference on Management of Data, pp. 1175–1189 (2022)

4. Cao, Z., Hidalgo Martinez, G., Simon, T., Wei, S., Sheikh, Y.A.: Openpose: real-time multi-person 2D pose estimation using part affinity fields. IEEE Trans. Pattern Anal. Mach. Intell. (2019)
5. Crabbé, J., Van Der Schaar, M.: Explaining time series predictions with dynamic masks. In: Meila, M., Zhang, T. (eds.) Proceedings of the 38th International Conference on Machine Learning. Proceedings of Machine Learning Research, vol. 139, pp. 2166–2177. PMLR (2021). https://proceedings.mlr.press/v139/crabbe21a.html
6. Dempster, A., Petitjean, F., Webb, G.I.: Rocket: exceptionally fast and accurate time series classification using random convolutional kernels. Data Min. Knowl. Disc. 34(5), 1454–1495 (2020)
7. Dempster, A., Schmidt, D.F., Webb, G.I.: Minirocket: a very fast (almost) deterministic transform for time series classification. In: Proceedings of the 27th ACM SIGKDD Conference on Knowledge Discovery & Data Mining, pp. 248–257 (2021)
8. Guidotti, R.: Evaluating local explanation methods on ground truth. Artif. Intell. 291, 103428 (2021)
9. He, K., Zhang, X., Ren, S., Sun, J.: Deep residual learning for image recognition, p. 14. arXiv preprint arXiv:1512.03385 (2015)
10. Hoerl, A.E., Kennard, R.W.: Ridge regression: biased estimation for nonorthogonal problems. Technometrics 12(1), 55–67 (1970)
11. Ismail, A.A., Gunady, M., Corrada Bravo, H., Feizi, S.: Benchmarking deep learning interpretability in time series predictions. In: Larochelle, H., Ranzato, M., Hadsell, R., Balcan, M.F., Lin, H. (eds.) Advances in Neural Information Processing Systems. vol. 33, pp. 6441–6452. Curran Associates, Inc. (2020). https://proceedings.neurips.cc/paper/2020/file/47a3893cc405396a5c30d91320572d6d-Paper.pdf
12. Le Nguyen, T., Gsponer, S., Ilie, I., O'reilly, M., Ifrim, G.: Interpretable time series classification using linear models and multi-resolution multi-domain symbolic representations. Data Min. Knowl. Disc. 33, 1183–1222 (2019)
13. Li, J., Zhang, C., Zhou, J.T., Fu, H., Xia, S., Hu, Q.: Deep-lift: deep label-specific feature learning for image annotation. IEEE Trans. Cybern. 52(8), 7732–7741 (2021)
14. Lundberg, S.M., Lee, S.I.: A unified approach to interpreting model predictions. In: Guyon, I., et al. (eds.) Advances in Neural Information Processing Systems, vol. 30, pp. 4765–4774. Curran Associates, Inc. (2017). http://papers.nips.cc/paper/7062-a-unified-approach-to-interpreting-model-predictions.pdf
15. Mujkanovic, F., Doskoč, V., Schirneck, M., Schäfer, P., Friedrich, T.: timexplain-a framework for explaining the predictions of time series classifiers. arXiv preprint arXiv:2007.07606 (2020)
16. Nguyen, T.T., Nguyen, T.L., Ifrim, G.: Amee: a robust framework for explanation evaluation in time series classification. arXiv preprint arXiv:2306.05501 (2023)
17. Pedregosa, F.: Scikit-learn: machine learning in python. J. Mach. Learn. Res. 12, 2825–2830 (2011)
18. Ribeiro, M.T., Singh, S., Guestrin, C.: "why should i trust you?" explaining the predictions of any classifier. In: Proceedings of the 22nd ACM SIGKDD International Conference on Knowledge Discovery and Data Mining, pp. 1135–1144 (2016)
19. Schäfer, P., Leser, U.: WEASEL 2.0-a random dilated dictionary transform for fast, accurate and memory constrained time series classification. arXiv preprint arXiv:2301.10194 (2023)
20. Singh, A., et al.: Fast and robust video-based exercise classification via body pose tracking and scalable multivariate time series classifiers. CoRR abs/2210.00507 (2022). https://doi.org/10.48550/arXiv.2210.00507

21. Tan, C.W., Dempster, A., Bergmeir, C., Webb, G.I.: Multirocket: multiple pooling operators and transformations for fast and effective time series classification. Data Min. Knowl. Disc. **36**(5), 1623–1646 (2022)
22. Turbé, H., Bjelogrlic, M., Lovis, C., Mengaldo, G.: Evaluation of post-hoc interpretability methods in time-series classification. Nat. Mach. Intell. **5**(3), 250–260 (2023). https://doi.org/10.1038/s42256-023-00620-w
23. Villar, J., Vergara, P., Menéndez González, M., Marín, E., González, V., Sedano, J.: Generalized models for the classification of abnormal movements in daily life and its applicability to epilepsy convulsion recognition. Int. J. Neural Syst. **26**, 1650037 (2016). https://doi.org/10.1142/S0129065716500374
24. Wang, Z., Yan, W., Oates, T.: Time series classification from scratch with deep neural networks: a strong baseline. In: 2017 International Joint Conference on Neural Networks (IJCNN), pp. 1578–1585. IEEE (2017)
25. Zhou, B., Khosla, A., Lapedriza, A., Oliva, A., Torralba, A.: Learning deep features for discriminative localization. In: Proceedings of the IEEE Conference on Computer Vision and Pattern Recognition, pp. 2921–2929 (2016)

tGLAD: A Sparse Graph Recovery Based Approach for Multivariate Time Series Segmentation

Shima Imani and Harsh Shrivastava[✉]

Microsoft Research, Redmond, USA
{shimaimani,hshrivastava}@microsoft.com

Abstract. Segmentation of multivariate time series data is a valuable technique for identifying meaningful patterns or changes in the time series that can signal a shift in the system's behavior. We introduce a domain agnostic framework 'tGLAD' for multivariate time series segmentation using conditional independence (CI) graphs that capture the partial correlations. It draws a parallel between the CI graph nodes and the variables of the time series. Consider applying a graph recovery model uGLAD to a short interval of the time series, it will result in a CI graph that shows partial correlations among the variables. We extend this idea to the entire time series by utilizing a sliding window to create a batch of time intervals and then run a single uGLAD model in multitask learning mode to recover all the CI graphs simultaneously. As a result, we obtain a corresponding temporal CI graphs representation of the multivariate time series. We then designed a first-order and second-order based trajectory tracking algorithm to study the evolution of these graphs across distinct intervals. Finally, an 'Allocation' algorithm is designed to determine a suitable segmentation of the temporal graph sequence which corresponds to the original multivariate time series. tGLAD provides a competitive time complexity of $O(N)$ for settings where number of variables $D << N$. We demonstrate successful empirical results on a Physical Activity Monitoring data. (*Software*: https://github.com/Harshs27/tGLAD).

Keywords: Multivariate time series segmentation · Conditional Independence Graphs · Sparse Graph recovery

1 Introduction

Time series segmentation is the process of dividing a time series into multiple segments, or sub-series, based on certain characteristics or patterns. Segmentation has many benefits, such as reducing a long time series into manageable sections to facilitate labeling by a human or machine annotator, and uncovering unexpected actionable patterns in data through exploration. For example, it can be used in finance to identify trends and patterns in stock prices, in marketing to analyze consumer behavior, and in healthcare to monitor patient vital signs. This helps to understand the underlying dynamics of the data and even make predictions about future events [2,21,37].

© The Author(s), under exclusive license to Springer Nature Switzerland AG 2023
G. Ifrim et al. (Eds.): AALTD 2023, LNAI 14343, pp. 176–189, 2023.
https://doi.org/10.1007/978-3-031-49896-1_12

There are numerous algorithms available for segmenting time series with majority of them primarily designed to handle the univariate case. If N is the length of the time series, most algorithms have an expected time complexity of $O(N^2)$, however, some more recent algorithms have achieved an $O(N \log N)$ time complexity with certain limiting approximations. Some time series segmentation methods are designed for specific domains, limiting their broader application. Additionally, some methods make assumptions about the semantic segments being well-defined, but they may not always align with real-world data and thereby hinder their effectiveness. The extensions suggested for these methods to handle multivariate data are non-trivial and often do not perform well in practice. Related works section covers them in detail.

Consider a small slice of a multivariate time series consisting of D variables, say from T_1 to T_{10} which contains no crucial segmentation points. For this slice, we can expect the correlation between the D variables to be roughly the same throughout $\text{corr}^D(T_1) \sim \text{corr}^D(T_{10})$. Now, let's assume that there is a segmentation point at T_{11}. For instance, if we are monitoring the sensor data of an athlete, we can consider that at time T_{11}, the athlete switched activity from jogging to sprinting. We now expect that the correlations among the variables will change at the segmentation points, $\text{corr}^D(T_{10}) \not\sim \text{corr}^D(T_{11})$. Our proposed framework, called tGLAD, is designed to efficiently detect this change of correlations which indicate segmentation points.

To realize this intuition, we identified a novel cross-domain application of sparse graph recovery for time series analysis. Briefly, given input variables and their samples, sparse graph recovery methods output a graph whose edges capture the direct dependencies among the variables. In our work, we focus on recovering special type of graphs, called the conditional independence (CI) graphs [28]. The CI graphs capture the partial correlations between the variables, which can be either positive or negative. Among the many different algorithms to recover CI graphs, we choose a recently developed state-of-the-art deep model called uGLAD [31,32]. Its multitask learning ability enables a single instance of the model to run on batch input and recover multiple graphs simultaneously, a property that paves way for the high efficiency of tGLAD. Although, one can theoretically utilize any algorithm under the larger umbrella of the sparse graph recovery methods, the methods section will highlight the key reasons which justifies our choice of using the combination of CI graphs and uGLAD.

The process followed by the tGLAD framework for doing multivariate time series segmentation is as follows. We divide the time series into sub-sequences or batches and then run a CI graph recovery model uGLAD that gives a corresponding temporal graphs. The nodes of CI graphs are the variables of the multivariate time series and the edges capture the partial correlation strength between the variables. In essence, we have distilled down some relevant information of the time series in the temporal CI graphs. As per our intuition, the instances where the consecutive CI graphs differ a lot in their correlations, those points of the temporal graphs will correspond to the segmentation points in the time series. We use this insight to develop our multi-step framework tGLAD. Thus, we developed efficient algorithms to capture the dynamics or the evolution pattern of the temporal CI graphs which in turn help us identify the segmentation regions in the original time series.

Listing the key contributions of our work. Please note that we use the terms, time series and sequences, interchangeably throughout.

1. A novel cross-domain approach for multivariate time series segmentation based on using sparse graph recovery algorithms.
2. Efficient method to give linear $O(N)$ time complexity in terms sequence length for cases where the number of variables follow $D^3 << N$
3. Provide explainability and transparency by giving insights into reasons for the segmentation.
4. A domain agnostic framework that can be applied for time series from various domains.

2   Related Works

Our framework is a combination of the literature from time series segmentation and sparse graph recovery. So, we discuss relevant research from both of them to provide background knowledge.

Segmentation Methods . There are several time series segmentation methods available that use different approaches to segment a time series into different classes based on changes in its temporal shape patterns. We divide the existing methods into domain specific and domain agnostic ones.

Domain Specific . If one narrows down the scope for analysing time series to a specific field, specialized methods can be developed by utilizing the domain-specific insights. Survey in [17] did a collective analysis of various such methods and also highlighted one key insight that for almost all the methods some background on the nature of the domain and motion is needed. Although, the recent observed trend is to develop domain agnostic approaches and we can find interesting techniques in this category. For example, Automobile trajectories were studied in [10], electroencephalography data was analysed in [15], electrical power consumption analysis in [23], music sequence analysis in [26], biological time series in [21], human motion segmentation was investigated in [2,3,16] among others.

Domain Agnostic . In attempt to design domain agnostic techniques for wider adaptability, FLOSS (Fast Low-cost Online Semantic Segmentation) [8] was developed. It is a popular method which produces an Arc Curve (AC) that annotates the original time series with information about the likelihood of a regime change at each point in the series. The AC is used to identify segments with similar temporal shape patterns that are likely to belong to the same class and occur within close temporal proximity to each other. Another method called

ESPRESSO (Entropy and ShaPe awaRe timE-Series SegmentatiOn) [5], is a hybrid approach that uses both shape pattern and statistical distribution of time series to segment time series data. ESPRESSO uses a modified version of FLOSS by incorporating the Weighted Chained Arc Curve to capture the density of pattern repetition with time. Recently proposed ClaSP (Classification Score Profile) is a self-supervised time series segmentation method that uses overlapping windows to split time series into hypothetical partitions. For each partition, a binary classifier is trained and evaluated using cross-validation. The degree of self-similarity is recorded for each offset and then the classification score profile is computed, which is ultimately used for segmenting time series data [6]. Other relevant methods include [4, 12, 18, 19].

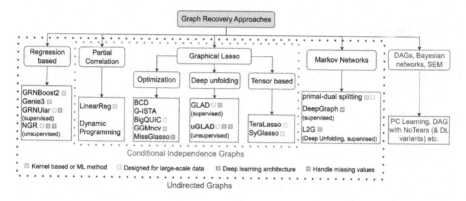

Fig. 1. *Overview of Sparse Graph Recovery methods.* We focus on methods that recover undirected graphs which capture direct dependence among their nodes or features. tGLAD framework utilizes a recently developed deep model, uGLAD, that outputs a conditional independence graph between in the features. Our framework can potentially use other methods and will be interesting topic for future explorations. (partly borrowed from [30])

Sparse Graph Recovery. Given data with D features and M samples as input, the aim of the sparse graph recovery methods is to obtain a probabilistic graphical model [14] that potentially shows sparse connections between the D features. We focus on methods that recover undirected graphical models, refer Fig. 1. Sparse graph recovery methods have been used for various applications like gene regulatory network discovery [1, 11, 20, 34–36], understanding Digester functioning to increase Methane yield [32], extracting insights from an Infant mortality data [29, 30], studying autism by analysing brain sensory signals [22] among many others.

Conditional Independence Graphs. The edges of a CI graph show the partial correlation between the nodes or features. The partial correlation can be considered as capturing direct dependency between the features as it is the conditional probability of the features under consideration given all the other features. Refer inner block in orange of Fig. 1. Popular formulations of recovering CI graph include optimizing the graphical lasso objective [7,25] which include deep models like [27,31–33] or dynamic programming based approach to directly evaluate the expression of partial correlations. Survey [28] formalizes the definition of CI graphs, categorizes various methods that recover such graphs, describe and compares their performance, provide their implementation details and discuss their applications. It is a good entry point to understanding the umbrella of methods that recover CI graphs. The method by [9] they utilized temporal graphs to understand dynamics of systems which is similar idea as ours but was not developed for time series segmentation settings.

3   Methods

We introduce the necessary definitions and notations to facilitate our discussions followed by the steps followed by the tGLAD framework.

3.1   Definitions

A **multivariate time series** T of length N and dimension D is a sequence of real-valued vectors

$$T = t_1, t_2, \ldots, t_N, \text{ where } t_i \in \mathbb{R}^D$$

A **Subsequence** is defined as a local section of a time series that consists of a continuous subset of its values. A subsequence $T_{i,M}$ of a time series T is a continuous subset of the values from T of length M starting from position i. Formally, $T_{i,M} = t_i, t_{i+1}, \ldots, t_{i+M-1}$, where $1 \leq i \leq N - M + 1$.

In order to extract continuous subsequences from time series, we utizlize the **stride length** shifting to determine the next subsequence. In time series data, the stride length is the number of data points by which we shift the starting position of the current subsequence to extract the position of the next subsequence. For example, a stride length s means that if the current subsequence is located at $T_{i,M}$ where i where is the starting position of the subsequence from T with length M, then the next subsequence is $T_{i+s,M}$ with the starting position at $i + s$.

3.2   tGLAD Framework

Figure 2 enumerates the steps followed by tGLAD to do multivariate time-series segmentation. The details for each of these steps are given below.

(A) **Identifying variables and prepare batch input for sparse graph recovery**

For all the variables in the given multivariate time series, basic preprocessing is done which includes missing value imputation using a forward filling algorithm.

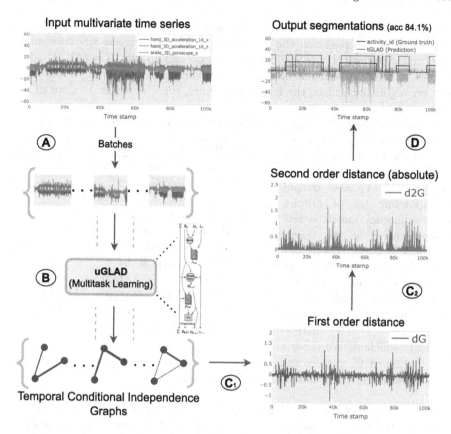

Fig. 2. *tGLAD framework.* (**A**) The time series is divided into multiple intervals by using a sliding window to create a batch of intervals. (**B**) Run a single uGLAD model in multitask learning (or batch) mode setting to recover a CI graph for every input batch. This gives a corresponding set of temporal CI graphs. The entire input is processed in a single step as opposed to obtaining a CI graph for each interval individually. (**C₁**) Get the first order distance, dG sequence, of the temporal CI graphs which captures the distance between the consecutive graphs. This is supposed to give higher values at the segmentation points. (**C₂**) Again take a first order distance of the sequence in the previous step and then its absolute value to get $d2G$ sequence, which further accentuates the values at the segmentation points. (**D**) Apply a threshold to zero out the smaller values of $d2G$ and identify the segmentation blocks using an 'Allocation' algorithm.

The data is now partitioned into small chunks using a fixed window size M and stride length s and runs over the entire time series. The window size determined based on the approach suggested in [13]. We now end up with $B = (N-M+1)/s$ batches, with each having M samples for D variables. The input to the graph recovery algorithm will be the batch of samples, represented as a tensor of size $X \in \mathbb{R}^{B \times M \times D}$.

(B) Obtaining the temporal Conditional Independence graphs

The aim of the sparse graph recovery algorithm is to run on the input from step (A), denoted by X and output corresponding set of graphs, whose adjacency matrix is represented here by the tensor $P \in \mathbb{R}^{B \times D \times D}$. There are 2 key requirements from any such method, namely (1) The resultant graph should capture direct dependencies between the features (2) The method should be efficient. We chose a combination of CI graphs and uGLAD model keeping in mind the desiderata desired.

Algorithm 1: Allocating segments

Function get-segments($d2G$, $Z=5$):
  $B \leftarrow len(\mathbf{d2G})$
  $labels \leftarrow [1] \times B$
  /* Removing noise   */
  $\mathbf{d2G} < 0.5 = 0$
  /* The window size is M   */
  For $i \leftarrow 0$ **to** B **do**
    If $d2G[i] > 0$ **then**
      $start = max(0, i - M \cdot Z)$
      $end = min(B - 1, i + M \cdot Z)$
      $labels[start : end] \leftarrow 0$
  return $labels$

Why CI Graphs? CI graphs capture partial correlations between the features which model direct dependencies between them. The nodes are the features and the edge weights carry the partial correlation value that lies in the range $[-1, 1]$. This additionally provides us with the positive or negative correlation information, which later help us in determining the relevant features that result in a segmentation prediction as well as provide explainability and transparency to our framework.

Why uGLAD? Introduced in [31], uGLAD is a deep-unfolding (or unrolled algorithm) based model which is an unsupervised extension of the GLAD [33] model. These models are based on the optimization of the graphical lasso objective which assumes that the observed data comes from an underlying multivariate Gaussian distribution. Owing to the deep-unfolding done based on the Aternating Minimization updates and then expressiveness provided by the neural network based parameterization, these models are shown to better capture the tail-distribution points and also improve sample complexity results. Apart from the theoretical advantages and performance improvements over the other CI graph recovery methods, uGLAD is efficient as well. The tensor based implementation of uGLAD allows it to do multitask learning. This enables a single model to recover the entire batch of data simultaneously. We want to point out that we consider the sample data within a window size follow i.i.d. setting for the multivariate Gaussian assumption to work.

We run uGLAD in 'batch mode' to obtain all the underlying precision matrices at once, $\theta \leftarrow$ uGLAD(X), where $\theta \in \mathbb{R}^{B \times M \times D}$. The calculation of the partial correlation matrix P is straightforward from Θ, refer [28]. The parameter sharing across these different tasks helps maintain robustness against noisy data and facilitates transfer learning. We thus obtain a series of temporal CI graphs, represented by the adjacency matrices $\mathbf{G} = [G_1, G_2, \cdots, G_B] \in \mathbb{R}^{B \times D \times D}$ using P. Each entry of the adjacency matrix is equal to the partial correlation value, $G_b[p, q] = \rho(D_p, D_q)$ for the bth batch and D_k represent the kth time series variable. The temporal graphs can be seen as distilling some relevant information from the original multivariate time series data in form of graphs.

(C) Towards segmentation of the corresponding temporal CI graphs

Our formulation is based on the assumption that the key signals needed to successfully segment the original time series are captured in the corresponding temporal graphs and that the correlation among the features are informative enough for the task. So, if we are able to segment the temporal graphs, we can map the segmentation to the original time series.

(C_1) We compute the first-order distance sequence $dG \in \mathbb{R}^B$ by finding the distance of the consecutive graphs in the temporal graph series $\mathbf{G}$. For each entry $b \in B$ of dG, we measure the distance between its recovered graph and the next neighbor as

$$dG[b] = \text{distance}(G_b, G_{b+1}) = \sum_{p,q} (G_b[p, q] - G_{b+1}[p, q]) \quad \forall p, q \in \{1, \cdots, D\}$$

where weights are the partial correlation values of the edges of the CI graphs under consideration.

(C_2) Given the sequence dG, next we compute the second-order distance sequence $d2G$ by applying the following distance operation

$$d2G[b] = \text{abs}\,(dG[b] - dG[b-1]), \quad \forall b \in (1, B)$$

The first-order distance measures the change between each recovered graph and its next neighbor, while the second-order distance highlights potential segmentation points. While there are other distance metrics that can potentially be used, in our experiments, we found that the first-order and second-order distances described above worked well for detecting segmentation points. The output of this trajectory tracking step is the $d2G$ sequence.

D. Allocation algorithm for obtaining the final segmentation

We develop an 'Allocation' algorithm to obtain the final segmentation points from the $d2G$ sequence. We first filter out small noises in $d2G$ by applying a conservative threshold. We then traverse the sequence $d2G$ sequentially and mark the start of a segmentation a new block if we observe a non-zero value. We also disregard any changes in behavior or segmentation points that occur in less than Z times the window size (M), otherwise the segmentation size will be significantly smaller than the window size and we will not be able to catch it. We usually choose $Z \sim 5$ in our experiments. The allocation process (Alg. 1) reads the $d2G$ sequence and predict the tGLAD segmentation scores.

3.3 Time Complexity Analysis of tGLAD

We analyse the time complexity of each of the steps followed by the tGLAD framework below.

- *(A)* Creation of batches will require a single full scan of the time series, so complexity is $O(N)$.
- *(B)* the time complexity of this step will consist of the input covariance matrix creation $O(N \cdot D^2)$, and then running uGLAD in batch mode. For a single input, uGLAD runs in $O(D^3 \cdot E)$, so for B batches the sequential runtime will be $O(B \cdot D^3 \cdot E)$. Since, we can process batches in parallel with uGLAD batch mode, in practice we observe significantly less runtime. The worst case scenario will be when $B \to N$, giving time complexity as $O(N \cdot D^3 \cdot E)$.
- *(C_1)* The first order distance function goes through the entire length of the temporal graph sequence and each time enumerate all possible edges between graphs having D nodes. So, it has a time complexity of $O(N \cdot D^2) \sim O(N)$.
- *(C_2)* Creation of $d2G$ will require a single full scan of the dG, so complexity is $O(N)$.
- *(Allocation algorithm)* Scans the $d2G$ array once, so complexity is $O(N)$.

The overall time complexity of the tGLAD framework in cases where the number of variables are not high, $D^3 << N$, is $O(N) + O(N \cdot D^3 \cdot E) + O(N \cdot D^2) \sim O(N)$. The worst case time complexity, where the number of variables are so large that we cannot leverage the power of the multitask learning in batch mode of uGLAD, is $O(N) + O(N \cdot D^3 \cdot E) + O(N \cdot D^2) \sim O(N \cdot D^3)$.

4 Experiments

We evaluate the tGLAD framework on a real world body sensor dataset. Since, it is a novel framework, we conduct several design choices experiments to understand their impact on tGLAD's performance.

4.1 PAMAP2 Dataset

To get a realistic sense about the effectiveness of our approach, we conducted experiments on the PAMAP2 Physical Activity Monitoring dataset [24]. This dataset captures sensor data from multiple participants engaging in a variety of physical activities, making it a valuable resource for activity recognition and algorithm development. Our analysis was primarily based on multi-dimensional time series with the following three signals: the hand acceleration signal in the x-axis and z-axis, and the ankle gyroscope signal in the x-axis, which allowed us to examine the movements and rotations of the hand and ankle during physical activity.

Figure 2 (A & D) shows a three-hour segment of this data collected from one of the participants, highlighting their physical activities such as ironing (44 min), vacuum cleaning (42 min), and stair activity (ascending 15 min, descending 10 min), as well as periods of inactivity (transient). Figure 2 additionally shows all the steps of the tGLAD framework followed in order to segment the data.

4.2   Results

We chose accuracy as the metric to evaluate the segmentation performance. The accuracy is measured as the penalty for mislabeling the segmentation. For the ground truth time series, we put label = 1 whenever an activity occurs and at every segmentation point where there is no activity, we switch the label = 0. For the prediction labels, we consider the $d2G$ sequence obtained from Fig. 2(D) and use the Allocation technique describe in Algorithm 1, with parameter $Z = 5$.

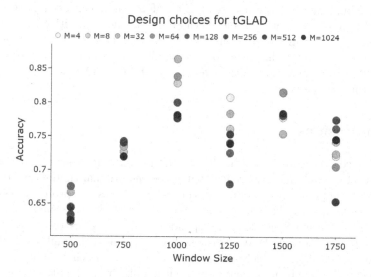

Fig. 3. *Design choices for tGLAD.* Examining the segmentation accuracy on the PAMAP2 dataset which records body sensor data. We vary the window size on the x-axis and for each window size, we evaluate the performance for varying batch sizes (M). The stride length was fixed at 100 for all the experiments.

We achieved an accuracy of 84.1% for the PAMAP2 dataset using a window size of 1000, batch size of 64 and stride length of 100, indicating that the tGLAD framework is effective for physical activity monitoring based time series. The window size is the chunk of the time series considered at a time for processing CI graphs, so it is an important parameter to be chosen while running our framework. The batch size is the number of graphs that are recovered by a single uGLAD model. As we are using multitasking, the parameters of the model are shared among the graphs within a batch, hence this is also an important parameter that can affect tGLAD's performance. Small batch size will lead to increased runtime as more number of batches to process, less robust to noise but more accurate graph recovery, while on the other hand, higher batch size will be efficient in term of runtime and robustness to anomalies, but since it has to recover graphs that are potentially sampled from different underlying distributions, the accuracy might take a hit. So, it is imperative that we do a study on effect of these design choices. Thus, in order to gain insights into the performance of tGLAD with respect to the batch size and window size, we explored the impact on the segmentation accuracy by doing a grid plot over a range of size choices, as illustrated in Fig. 3.

Analysing the results indicate that changes in batch size and window sizes do not significantly affect the accuracy of the segmentation. If we consider any fixed window size, we do not see much variance in the performance over different batch sizes, that suggests a good graph recovery performance of the uGLAD model. Thus, we can potentially increase the batch size for faster runtimes, without compromising much on the accuracy. Lots of research has been done on the choice of window size, with some methods being more sensitive than others. We do see variance in the performance of tGLAD with change in window size, still the results suggest that a reasonable window size can be chosen to achieve a satisfactory segmentation label. The choice of the window size also depends considerably on the type of data as well.

5   Conclusions

We introduce a domain agnostic multivariate time series framework called tGLAD. It is a novel cross-domain approach that maps the original time series to a corresponding temporal graph representation which makes the problem of finding segmentation easier and efficient. The choice of a recently developed deep model uGLAD for recovering conditional independence graphs gives the much needed efficiency to our framework. We identified a unique use of the multitask learning ability of uGLAD model which also makes the case of batch learning in sparse graph recovery models more lucrative. Additionally, from the plethora of graph choices available, this work also narrowed down the type to conditional independence graphs. The CI graphs capture the intuition that correlation among the multivariate timeseries variables will change significantly at the segmentation points. We demonstrate successful segmentation results on the challenging PAMAP2 dataset, with achieving an accuracy of 84.10% along with performing a parameter exploration study.

5.1   Future Work

We have plans to pursue two directions of research for expanding tGLAD. Firstly, we will investigate the potential for segmenting univariate time series data using the tGLAD framework. our approach consists of 'smartly' converting the 1D sequence to multidimensional time series and then use the tGLAD framework. This approach seems promising due to its high efficiency in terms of time complexity and hopefully good segmentation accuracy. Secondly, we aim to extend the tGLAD framework to work in real-time or online settings. This will require adapting the framework and evaluating the trade-offs between computational efficiency and segmentation accuracy. The results of this research could have significant implications for fields such as finance, healthcare, and industrial monitoring.

5.2 Ethical Concerns

Our method does not introduce new ethical issues, but ethical considerations would be important if it were to be applied to sensitive data.

References

1. Aluru, M., Shrivastava, H., Chockalingam, S.P., Shivakumar, S., Aluru, S.: Engrain: a supervised ensemble learning method for recovery of large-scale gene regulatory networks. Bioinformatics **38**, 1312–1319 (2021)
2. Aminikhanghahi, S., Cook, D.J.: A survey of methods for time series change point detection. Knowl. Inf. Syst. **51**(2), 339–367 (2017)
3. Aoki, T., Lin, J.F.S., Kulić, D., Venture, G.: Segmentation of human upper body movement using multiple IMU sensors. In: 2016 38th Annual International Conference of the IEEE Engineering in Medicine and Biology Society (EMBC), pp. 3163–3166. IEEE (2016)
4. Castellini, A., Bicego, M., Masillo, F., Zuccotto, M., Farinelli, A.: Time series segmentation for state-model generation of autonomous aquatic drones: A systematic framework. Eng. Appl. Artif. Intell. **90**, 103499 (2020)
5. Deldari, S., Smith, D.V., Sadri, A., Salim, F.D.: Espresso: entropy and shape aware time-series segmentation for processing heterogeneous sensor data. Proc. ACM Interact. Mob. Wearable Ubiquitous Technol. **4**, 77:1–77:24 (2020)
6. Ermshaus, A., Schäfer, P., Leser, U.: Clasp-parameter-free time series segmentation. arXiv preprint arXiv:2207.13987 (2022)
7. Friedman, J., Hastie, T., Tibshirani, R.: Sparse inverse covariance estimation with the graphical lasso. Biostatistics **9**(3), 432–441 (2008)
8. Gharghabi, S., et al.: Domain agnostic online semantic segmentation for multidimensional time series. Data Min. Knowl. Disc. **33**(1), 96–130 (2019)
9. Hallac, D., Park, Y., Boyd, S., Leskovec, J.: Network inference via the time-varying graphical lasso. In: Proceedings of the 23rd ACM SIGKDD International Conference on Knowledge Discovery and Data Mining, pp. 205–213 (2017)
10. Harguess, J., Aggarwal, J.: Semantic labeling of track events using time series segmentation and shape analysis. In: 2009 16th IEEE International Conference on Image Processing (ICIP), pp. 4317–4320. IEEE (2009)
11. Haury, A.C., Mordelet, F., Vera-Licona, P., Vert, J.P.: TIGRESS: trustful inference of gene regulation using stability selection. BMC Syst. Biol. **6**(1), 1–17 (2012)
12. Imani, S., Abdoli, A., Keogh, E.: Time2cluster: clustering time series using neighbor information (2021)

13. Imani, S., Keogh, E.: Multi-window-finder: domain agnostic window size for time series data (2021)
14. Koller, D., Friedman, N.: Probabilistic Graphical Models: Principles and Techniques. MIT press, Cambridge (2009)
15. Kozey-Keadle, S., Libertine, A., Lyden, K., Staudenmayer, J., Freedson, P.S.: Validation of wearable monitors for assessing sedentary behavior. Med. Sci. Sports Exerc. **43**(8), 1561–1567 (2011)
16. Lan, R., Sun, H.: Automated human motion segmentation via motion regularities. Vis. Comput. **31**, 35–53 (2015)
17. Lin, J.F.S., Karg, M., Kulić, D.: Movement primitive segmentation for human motion modeling: a framework for analysis. IEEE Trans. Human-Mach. Syst. **46**(3), 325–339 (2016)
18. Lu, S., Huang, S.: Segmentation of multivariate industrial time series data based on dynamic latent variable predictability. IEEE Access **8**, 112092–112103 (2020)
19. Machné, R., Murray, D.B., Stadler, P.F.: Similarity-based segmentation of multi-dimensional signals. Sci. Rep. **7**, 12355 (2017)
20. Moerman, T., et al.: Grnboost2 and arboreto: efficient and scalable inference of gene regulatory networks. Bioinformatics **35**(12), 2159–2161 (2019)
21. Omranian, N., Mueller-Roeber, B., Nikoloski, Z.: Segmentation of biological multivariate time-series data. Sci. Rep. **5**(1), 1–6 (2015)
22. Pu, X., Cao, T., Zhang, X., Dong, X., Chen, S.: Learning to learn graph topologies. Adv. Neural Inf. Process. Syst. **34**, 4249–4262 (2021)
23. Reinhardt, A., Christin, D., Kanhere, S.S.: Predicting the power consumption of electric appliances through time series pattern matching. In: Proceedings of the 5th ACM Workshop on Embedded Systems For Energy-Efficient Buildings, pp. 1–2 (2013)
24. Reiss, A., Stricker, D.: Introducing a new benchmarked dataset for activity monitoring. In: 2012 16th International Symposium on Wearable Computers, pp. 108–109. IEEE (2012)
25. Rolfs, B., Rajaratnam, B., Guillot, D., Wong, I., Maleki, A.: Iterative thresholding algorithm for sparse inverse covariance estimation. Adv. Neural. Inf. Process. Syst. **25**, 1574–1582 (2012)
26. Serra, J., Müller, M., Grosche, P., Arcos, J.L.: Unsupervised music structure annotation by time series structure features and segment similarity. IEEE Trans. Multimedia **16**(5), 1229–1240 (2014)
27. Shrivastava, H.: On Using Inductive Biases for Designing Deep Learning Architectures. Ph.D. thesis, Georgia Institute of Technology (2020)
28. Shrivastava, H., Chajewska, U.: Methods for recovering conditional independence graphs: a survey. arXiv preprint arXiv:2211.06829 (2022)
29. Shrivastava, H., Chajewska, U.: Neural graphical models. arXiv preprint arXiv:2210.00453 (2022)
30. Shrivastava, H., Chajewska, U.: Neural graph revealers. arXiv preprint arXiv:2302.13582 (2023)
31. Shrivastava, H., Chajewska, U., Abraham, R., Chen, X.: A deep learning approach to recover conditional independence graphs. In: NeurIPS 2022 Workshop: New Frontiers in Graph Learning (2022). https://openreview.net/forum?id=kEwzoI3Am4c
32. Shrivastava, H., Chajewska, U., Abraham, R., Chen, X.: uGLAD: sparse graph recovery by optimizing deep unrolled networks. arXiv preprint arXiv:2205.11610 (2022)
33. Shrivastava, H., et al.: GLAD: learning sparse graph recovery. arXiv preprint arXiv:1906.00271 (2019)

34. Shrivastava, H., Zhang, X., Aluru, S., Song, L.: Grnular: gene regulatory network reconstruction using unrolled algorithm from single cell rna-sequencing data. bioRxiv (2020)
35. Shrivastava, H., Zhang, X., Song, L., Aluru, S.: Grnular: a deep learning framework for recovering single-cell gene regulatory networks. J. Comput. Biol. **29**(1), 27–44 (2022)
36. Vân Anh Huynh-Thu, A.I., Wehenkel, L., Geurts, P.: Inferring regulatory networks from expression data using tree-based methods. PloS One **5**(9) (2010)
37. Yeh, C.C.M., et al.: Matrix profile i: all pairs similarity joins for time series: a unifying view that includes motifs, discords and shapelets. In: 2016 IEEE 16th International Conference on Data Mining (ICDM), pp. 1317–1322. IEEE (2016)

Designing a New Search Space for Multivariate Time-Series Neural Architecture Search

Christopher MacKinnon[✉] and Robert Atkinson

University of Strathclyde, Glasgow, Scotland
{christopher.mackinnon,robert.atkinson}@strath.ac.uk

Abstract. With the rise of edge computing and the Internet of Things (IoT), there is an increasing demand for models with low memory footprints. These models must be adaptable to embedded system applications, while being able to leverage the large quantities of data recorded in these systems to produce superior performance.

Automatic Neural Architecture Search (NAS) has been an active and successful area of research for a number of years. However, a significant proportion of effort has been aimed at finding architectures which are able to effectively extract and transform the information in image data. This has lead to search space design which is heavily influenced by the heuristics of image classifiers.

We review and incorporate the characteristics of successful time-series methods, while seeking to address traits of conventional NAS search-space design which may be detrimental to performance on time-series.

This paper provides an in-depth look at the effects of each of our design choices with an analysis of time-series network design spaces on two benchmark tasks: Human Activity Recognition (HAR) using the UniMib-SHAR dataset and Electroencephalography (EEG) data from the BCI Competition IV 2a dataset.

Guided by these design principles and the results of our experimental procedure, we produce a search space tailored specifically to time-series tasks. This achieves excellent performance while producing architectures with significantly fewer parameters than other deep learning approaches.

We provide results on a collection of datasets from the UEA Multivariate time-series Classification Archive and achieve comparable performance to both deep learning and state-of-the-art machine learning time-series classification methods, using a simple random search.

1 Introduction

Neural Architecture Search (NAS) is a method of automatic architecture discovery and has been an active area of research for a number of years. Through this process, a large space of possible models is traversed and evaluated in an attempt to discover the optimal network architecture for a given domain task. While automated architecture design is well studied with regard to image data, its application to time-series problems has only recently begun to be investigated.

© The Author(s), under exclusive license to Springer Nature Switzerland AG 2023
G. Ifrim et al. (Eds.): AALTD 2023, LNAI 14343, pp. 190–204, 2023.
https://doi.org/10.1007/978-3-031-49896-1_13

NAS search spaces have evolved over time to contain a high density of strong models. This has been achieved by adopting the principles that guide manual architecture design and applying them to search space design. These choices are easily seen when looking at cell-based search spaces such as NasNet [1] and DARTS (Differentiable Architecture Search) [2], where repeating cells are stacked often with residual connections between cells. When applying these methods to a new domain, however, the heuristics which guided search space design in one application may not be useful in another.

NAS search spaces can be considered restrictive in the diversity of models contained within them. While these spaces are "large" (DARTS for example is of order 10^{18}), many design choices are made to remove poor models from the space, reducing its overall diversity. While this likely improves the convergence speed and anytime performance of an architecture search, it limits the discovery of truly novel architectures which do not conform to traditional architecture design rules [3].

While deep learning approaches have begun to show promising results, particularly in multivariate time-series classification, the fidelity of these approaches is still dependent on the quality of manually designed architectures. In the domain of image classification NAS has achieved great success discovering architectures which outperform human designed architectures. This is the case despite the fact that top-performing architectures - and even parameterisations - often exhibit greater transfer-ability across tasks as evidenced by the relative ease of transfer learning compared with time-series classification [4]. The wide variety of problem characteristics in time-series tasks - such as dataset size, signal length, or discriminatory features - makes designing an optimal 'one-size-fits-all' architecture a challenging proposition. This highlights the opportunities for automatic architecture design methods which can discover architectures tuned to the specific characteristics of a dataset.

This paper introduces a novel search space for time-series NAS, which achieves competitive results compared with state-of-the-art (SOTA) time-series classification methods across a diverse set of multivariate time-series classification challenges, with only the most rudimentary search algorithm. We draw on concepts from successful time-series classification methods, as well as incorporating the characteristics of modern convolutional vision networks, integrating them into the design of a deep learning search space which produces highly efficient architectures with strong performance for time-series classification.

2   Related Work

2.1   Time-Series Classification

Time-series classification tasks are dominated by models which can generate a multitude of representations. A representation being a transform or encoding of the raw time-series which may reveal useful patterns or information. Unlike image classification models which often use deep repeating structures to extract complex features, successful time-series models - whether they are deep learning or more traditional machine learning methods - are frequently characterised by an emphasis on the 'breadth' of representations. The Hierarchical Vote Collective of Transformation-based Ensembles (HIVE-COTE) [5] is a good example of this, achieving SOTA performance by ensembling the predictions of a broad range of classifiers. Rocket [6] and Canonical Interval Forest (CIF) [7] are other examples of a focus on a diverse set of representations. These feature based methods, apply a large collection of randomly generated transforms to produce features. These features can then be used by a relatively simple classifier to achieve impressive results.

2.2 Deep Learning for Time-Series

The application of deep learning techniques to time-series classification has gained increasing attention in recent years. One of the earliest works in this area is the study by *Wang et al.* [8] who proposed a deep learning framework for time-series classification and compared convolutional neural networks (CNN) with Multi-Layer Perceptrons (MLP), specifically looking at a ResNet architecture and Fully Convolutional Networks (FCN). The authors demonstrated the effectiveness of their proposed method on the set of UCR uni-variate time-series problems.

In the study by Fawaz, Lucas, Forestier, et al. [9], the authors proposed the use of InceptionTime, a modification of the Inception architecture designed specifically for time-series classification. This achieved strong performance in multivariate time-series classification tasks. The novel feature of InceptionTime is its use of parallel 1D convolutional filters. The kernels of these convolutions vary in length from 10 to 40, allowing the model to capture and extract patterns at various time scales in the signal.

The success of this approach shows again the importance of a broad set of representations but also the value in extracting information at different time scales for successful performance across diverse problems. We aim to leverage these insights in the application of NAS to discover effective architectures tailored to specific problems.

2.3 Neural Architecture Search

NAS can be considered as a subset of the general problem of hyperparameter optimisation. In a general sense, it frames any machine learning task as a bi-level optimisation problem, wherein both a set of parameters weights and hyperparameters settings are optimised w.r.t to the training and validation losses respectively. This is given by Eqs. 1 and 2, where θ is the parameters of a model and λ is the architecture configuration, with θ^* and λ^* being the optimal value of each respectively.

$$\lambda^* = \arg\min_{\lambda} \mathcal{L}_{validation}(\theta^*(\lambda), \lambda) \tag{1}$$

$$\text{s.t. } \theta^*(\lambda) = \arg\min_{\theta} \mathcal{L}_{train}(\theta, \lambda) \tag{2}$$

Initial approaches to architecture search within deep learning typically optimised the number of layers and the operation on each layer using a fixed model topology. This formulation is easily mapped to general hyperparameter optimisation methods with the number of layers, channels or kernels sizes being individual hyperparameters.

Although some early work in neuro-evolution searched for simple models in topological spaces such as NEAT [10], a significant innovation in the development of NAS was to search for models in a topological space. Many of these approaches used 'factorised' spaces such as hierarchical spaces or more famously cell-based spaces and achieved significant success [1,11]. In this type of approach architectures are constructed from repeating blocks which follows the characteristics of successful human designed architectures. The overall aim of this is to remove a large quantity of poorly performing architectures from the space while retaining the majority of strong networks, which conform to these heuristics.

3   Designing a New Search Space

In this section, we introduce a novel search space designed specifically for the characteristics of time-series data, which aims to effectively handle a wide range of signal lengths and produce a diverse set of transforms akin to what we see in

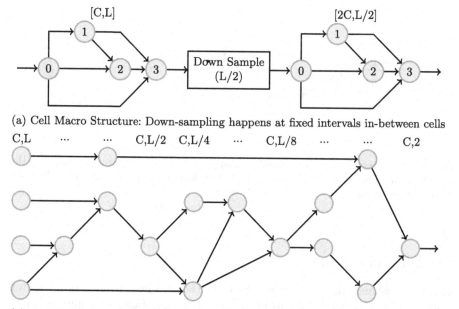

(a) Cell Macro Structure: Down-sampling happens at fixed intervals in-between cells

(b) Our Graph Space Macro Structure: Dynamic down-sampling through-out model.

Fig. 1. Comparison of down-sampling and network structure in a cell-based search space and in our graph space.

other successful time-series methods. Figure 1 shows the traditional cell-based space compared with our approach.

In conventional cell-based network structure, down-sampling of the input signal is coupled to the network depth occurring at fixed intervals between cells. In contrast, our approach incorporates this down-sampling into the architecture search. The advantages of this are twofold: firstly, it allows for the extraction of features at multiple signal resolutions in parallel, where computation can be performed at the most effective granularity for different discriminatory features. Secondly, it avoids the need for very deep networks when dealing with long signal lengths or manual tweaks to the down-sampling operations for specific tasks.

We define a model topology where configurations are described in terms of a Directed Acyclic Graph (DAG) that defines the edges and connectivity of an architecture, as well as a set of operations with one corresponding to each of the defined edges. A valid architecture can be constructed from any DAG where the start and end nodes are connected via all paths. In order to generate a wide range of topologies, which conform to this specification, we propose an iterative method. Starting with a simple DAG containing 3 vertices (S,1,T) each connected by a single edge, we randomly apply one of two operations, "edge insertion" or "edge split". Algorithm 1 describes a single iteration of this process with Fig. 2 showing this process over multiple iterations.

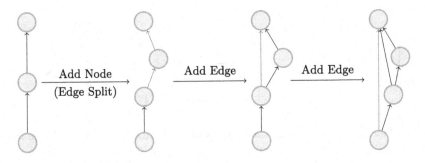

Fig. 2. Three iterations of the graph generation algorithm adding a new node in the first step, and a new edge in the subsequent iterations. Changes are highlighted in red. (Color figure online)

3.1   Operation Chain

To further enhance the range of architectures that can be expressed in the search space, aspects that are often part of the primitive operations or simply built into a fixed macro architecture are brought into the search space. This work innovates on the standard DAG representations of neural architectures, with the inclusion of node attributes.

Previous implementations like DARTS or NasNet primarily focused on edge attributes, i.e., the primitive operations. Our approach expands on this by associating attributes such as the normalisation, activation function, channel width (number of channels) and down-sampling (stride) to the node rather than an edge. An example of this is an edge (1,3) and (2,3), which will have the same node attributes, due to their common destination at node 3.

Figure 3 provides a visualisation of this operation chain and the assignment of attributes to edges or nodes.

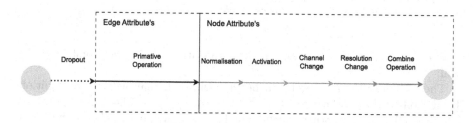

Fig. 3. Chain of operations in a compiled edge

Adjustments in the number of channels or resolution are implemented through the use of point-wise and depth-wise convolutions, respectively. Where the latter has a kernel size equal to its stride. These changes in resolution and channel width are propagated downstream to all subsequent edges and nodes. Figure 4 shows an example, if node A contains a down-sample of signal length L by a factor of two, and there exists an edge (A, B), then the operation of this edge will act on and produce data of size $(C, L/2)$ assuming no changes to the channel width. This means that B will be of size $(C, L/2)$. If another node C connects to B and has a signal length of L, then a down-sample operation will be added here also to produce two signals of the same length. This feature increases the flexibility of the generated architecture, allowing it to adapt to signals of varying lengths.

4   Benchmarking Tasks

In order to draw broadly useful conclusion about NAS search spaces for time-series problems we look at two time-series classification tasks from disparate domains.

4.1   Human Activity Recognition (HAR)

Human Activity Recognition is the task of classifying actions such as walking, running, jumping, as well as falls through the use of gyroscopic data. Among members of the population who are over 65, falls are a common risk and can have severe consequences with the frequency only becoming larger with age.

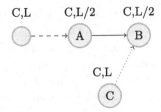

Fig. 4. Example of down-sampling operations and the propagation of signal length to subsequent nodes. Dashed lines indicate where a node contains a down-sample operation, dotted line indicates when a down-sample operation is induced.

Undetected these falls can result in hospitalisation or, in the worst case, be fatal.

The *UniMib-SHAR* dataset is a benchmark for human activity recognition (HAR) collected by the University of Milano-Bicocca [12]. The dataset contains data from 30 subjects, both male and female aged 18–60, performing activities of daily living (ADL), such as standing, walking and sitting, as well as a collection of falls, while wearing a smartphone on their waist. The smartphone's accelerometer and gyroscope sensors capture three-axial linear acceleration and three-axial angular velocity, respectively. This dataset can be used for 4 classification tasks:

- (AF-17) - Distinguishing all 17 fine-grained classes from the ADL and FALL categories
- (AF-2) - Binary classification of ADLs and FALLs
- (A-9) - Classifying the 9 ADL fine-grained classes
- (F-8) - Classifying the 8 FALL fine-grained classes

In this paper we look specifically at the AF-17 scheme which is considered the most challenging task, with data being split based on subjects unless specifically stated otherwise.

4.2 Electroencephalography (EEG)

The *BCI Competition IV 2a* dataset [13] is a widely used electroencephalography (EEG) dataset, collected as part of the Brain-Computer Interface (BCI) Competition IV. It comprises EEG recordings from 9 subjects, each performing 4 different motor imagery tasks: left hand, right hand, both feet and tongue movements. The dataset contains 22 EEG channels and 3 electrooculography (EOG) channels, sampled at 250 Hz, with each trial lasting approximately 8 s. In this paper we use only the 22 EEG channels.

Algorithm 1. Generate Graph Iteration

```
procedure GEN_ITER(edges, rate)
    g ← DiGraph(edges)
    if random() > rate then                                    ▷ Add an edge
        sorted_nodes ← TopologicalSort(g)
        number_valid ← len(sorted_nodes) − 1
        source_index ← RandInt(0, number_valid)
        new_source ← sorted_nodes[source_index]
        existing ← Neighbors(g, new_source)
        valid ← sorted_nodes[source_index + 1 :]
        valid ← valid.remove([existing, "S"])
        new_end ← RandomChoice(valid)
        edges.append((new_source, new_end))
    else                                                       ▷ Add a node (Edge split)
        edge ← random.choice(edges)
        new_id ← len(edges) + 1
        idx ← edges.index(edge)
        edges[idx] ← (edge[0], new_id)
        edges.append((new_id, edge[1]))
    end if
    return list(set(edges))
end procedure
```

Table 1. Summary of the dataset properties

Dataset	Samples	Dimensions	Timesteps
EEG Train Data	2328	22	1750
EEG Test Data	2368	22	1750
SHAR Train Data	10541	3	151
SHAR Test Data	1230	3	151

5   Method

In order to make comparisons of different search spaces we adopt a method utilised in the analysis of design spaces for image classifiers [14,15]. We perform a random sampling of architectures (Random Search) in each search space on a set of tasks, comparing the Cumulative Distribution Function (CDF) - which gives the probability that a random observation will be less than or equal to a certain value. This gives us a more robust comparison between two spaces than a single point estimate, such as the single best performing model. By performing a series of experiments following this methodology, the goal is to find a search space of strong performing architectures for time-series classification by iteratively improving the search space at each step.

This is conducted as a random search evaluating 500 models over our two datasets. Each model has a fixed stem size of 32 channels, with a Global Average Pooling (GAP) and fully connected linear layer as the output. We define both spaces, the cell-based and graph search-spaces to have 32 edges for which operations are searched. Each model is trained with a batch size of 256 for 200 epochs, with the learning rate decaying from 0.01 to 1×10^{-5} throughout the training process, based on the cosine annealing strategy.

5.1 Experiment 1: Understanding the Role of Width Multipliers During Down Sampling in Graph and Cell-Based Topologies

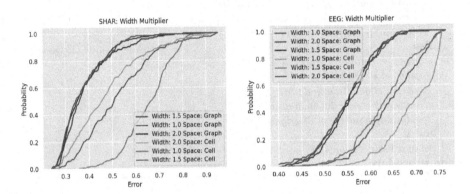

Fig. 5. Effects of different width multipliers on graph and cell based topologies across search spaces

As we have seen in Sect. 2.1, in comparison with Image tasks, time-series models generally make use of shallower networks favoring a wide variety of representations. However, time-series tasks can also have a large variety of signal lengths, adding an additional challenge to architecture design. Cell-based NAS architectures down samples the resolution or signal length at the end of specific 'reduction cells', increasing the number of channels to maintain the capacity. This approach however can lead to challenges in the context of time-series data, due to the coupling of signal down-sampling and network depth. We compare the effects on a cell based search space, based on implementation of [2] with our graph based search space. We use 4 cells, with down-sampling occurring after each cell, maintaining the same number of operations (32) in both search spaces.

Figure 5 shows the CDF of architecture error of the DARTS search space compared with our graph based search space over a range of down-sample width multipliers. We can see that in the case of the cell search space the optimal width multiplier seems to vary according to dataset, with a constant width performing consistently poorly. In contrast, this setting seems to have little effect on the graph search space.

The effect of these settings on the number of model parameters is also significant with a difference of around 1 order of magnitude between models of different width multipliers.

Moving forward we use the graph based architecture with a wide multiplier of 1 as the basis for further experiments.

5.2 Experiment 2: Breaking Out of the Separable Convolution (Depth-Wise and Point-Wise Operations)

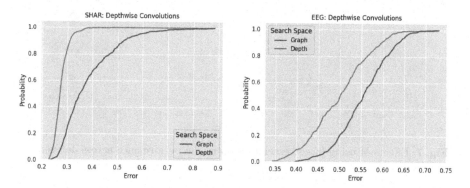

Fig. 6. Effects of breaking out the separable convolution operation across datasets

While depth-wise and point-wise convolutions are commonly used in NAS as constituent parts of the separable convolution to build more efficient architectures, we propose breaking the fundamental convolution operation down to the depth-wise and point-wise convolution. These operations are significantly less computationally demanding as each operation now contains a single convolution operation rather than the 4 convolutions in a separable convolution. In ViT architectures, we also see a separation of spatial and channel-wise information mixing, which may be a beneficial trait. Specifically in the context of multivariate time-series data, the input features may contain information which is not temporally aligned across channels, which could make channel mixing to be counter productive at certain stages in the model.

In order to have this approach be effective we also break out the activation and normalisation functions from the primitive operations. Taking inspiration for the ConvNeXt [16] results, we include 2 'none' operations for each activation and normalisation function, to produce networks with roughly 1 activation and normalisation in every 3 primitive operations.

We can adjust for the reduction in model capacity by increasing the number of edges in our architecture, allowing for a more diverse set of architectures at the same or lower computational cost. We also maintain the same distribution of operations for random sampling by introducing each of the depth-wise and point-wise convolutions into the operation pool four times for each kernel. The dropout rate was also reduced by a factor of 4 to maintain the same total dropout across each network.

Figure 6 shows the effects of these changes on the two datasets. Here we can see improvements across the board.

5.3   Experiment 3: Kernel Size and Dilation

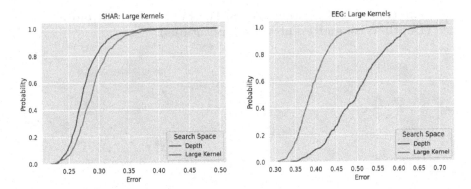

Fig. 7. Effects of using large kernel sizes on model performance across datasets

The use of dilation in convolutional networks for time-series is well established as an effective method of increasing the receptive field without exploding the number of parameters. This has shown success in a broad range of tasks and model types pertaining to time-series, with WaveNet [17] showing its application to deep learning and more recently ROCKET showing the effectiveness of dilated convolution kernels as feature extractors for more traditional machine learning approaches. We introduce kernels with a set of exponential dilation's (2,4,8,16,32) to the search space.

To further expand the search space we also add larger kernel sizes which has shown success in both image and time-series applications. We again add kernels of exponential sizes (reduced by one for padding) at 15,31,63. We also add pooling at these kernel sizes. Again we maintain the proportion of pooling, skip and convolution operations when adding the new operations to the pool of primitives.

Figure 7 shows the results of these large kernels on our datasets. Unlike with the previous change the results here are more mixed with a significant improvement on one dataset and a slight deterioration in another. These results are understandable due to the significantly shorter signal length of the SHAR dataset. This means a significant number of the kernels are larger than the entire signal even before down-sampling.

6   Results

We now show the performance of our new search space across a number of datasets. We randomly partition the dataset into a train, validation and test dataset. We use the simple random search algorithm [18], run for 500 iterations to select the architecture for each task. Each architecture is evaluated twice to improve quality of the evaluation, with the hyperparameters described in Sect. 5. The results of the final architecture on a holdout test set is reported as the mean accuracy of 10 training runs. Each search was run across 4 GPUs with all the architectures trained from scratch. Each search took between 3 and 24 h to complete, depending on the characteristics and size of the dataset. Note that the search algorithm itself is intentionally rudimentary without any proxy evaluation methods to produce baseline performance estimates.

6.1   UniMib-SHAR

Table 2 presents the results obtained from two different schema: a 'subject-based split' and a 'random split'. In the 'subject-based split', no subject appears in more than one of the train, validation, or test sets. The random split is a standard random division of the data. The search was run for each approach separately.

The results compare the state of the art methods on this task with the discovered architecture. An improvement in both categories can be seen in terms of accuracy. A new SOTA is achieved with 95.7% accuracy in the random split, improving the accuracy by over 3% on the previous best, as well as a more modest 77.6% accuracy in the subject-based split. This was achieved while also producing models with a significantly lower number of parameters than reported by other approaches.

Table 2. UniMib-SHAR: Discovered architecture vs SOTA

Method	Subject-Based Split	Random Split	Parameters
Gao, Zhang, Teng, et al. [19]	–	79.03	2.40M
Mukherjee, Mondal, Singh, et al. [20]	–	92.60	–
Al-qaness, Dahou, Elaziz, et al. [21]	77.29	84.99	2.40M
Helmi, Al-qaness, Dahou, et al. [22]	–	86.08	–
Teng, Wang, Zhang, et al. [23]	–	78.07	0.55M
New Search Space	**77.63**	**95.70**	0.10M

6.2   EEG

Next, we look at the EEG dataset; here we look at a random split, looking for general accuracy over the entire dataset. In the literature, it is more common to use subject-specific models as they tend to provide improved performance on the particular subject, however, this involves the training of many different specialised models. We compare our approach with ResNet [8] and InceptionTime [9], both providing a strong baseline performance for deep learning models on time-series classification. These are implemented with 32 channels and an additional 64 channel version for InceptionTime. Table 3 shows the accuracy of our approach compared with the benchmark models. We see a significant disparity in performance here, with ResNet in particular struggling to find a good solution.

Table 3. EEG: Discovered architecture vs Deep Learning Approaches

Method	Random Split	Parameters
ResNet	35.89	0.95M
InceptionTime (32)	49.08	0.48M
InceptionTime (64)	50.22	1.89M
New Search Space	66.98	0.12M

6.3   UEA Multivariate Time-Series Classification Archive

We compare our search space to the SOTA time-series classification methods on a subset of the time-series classification archive. Due to the additional complications involved with performing NAS with small dataset sizes - which is out of scope for this paper - we look specifically at the 4 largest datasets in terms of number of samples. These are specifically the four largest multivariate datasets with equal length in the time-series classification archive to allow for comparison with the baseline experiments [24]. We conduct a search on each dataset separately. Table 4 shows the results of our new search space compared with SOTA time-series methods evaluated in Middlehurst, Large, Flynn, et al. [5] as well as deep learning approaches from Ruiz, Flynn, Large, et al. [24]. Our search space produces models which perform well compared with current state of the art, losing in average rank to only InceptionTime.

Table 4. UEA (Resamples) - Multivariate time-series Classification Archive: SOTA methods compared random sampling of new search space

Method	FaceDetection	LSST	PenDigits	PhonemeSpectra	Average Rank
HC2	71.35	**63.70**	99.56	29.43	3
ROCKET	69.38	61.85	99.57	27.03	4.25
HC1	69.17	53.84	97.19	32.87	4.25
ResNet	62.97	42.94	99.64	30.86	5.25
InceptionTime	**77.24**	33.97	**99.68**	**36.74**	2.5
TapNet	52.87	46.33	93.65	–	6.33
New Search Space	75.01	**63.68**	99.6	29.84	2.75

7   Further Work

This work outlines a new search-space for NAS which is both performant and adaptable to the diverse set of characteristics presented in time-series classification problems. We present results based on a simple random search of architectures. This gives an indication of baseline performance, which can be build upon in subsequent research. One main direction for further work is the design of optimisation algorithms for this space. Another avenue for future research is the discovery of efficient proxies for evaluation. Common methods such as super-networks are challenging to apply due to the unbounded nature of the search-space, as well as the low-data environments common to this domain.

8 Conclusion

We introduce a search space specifically designed for time-series classification tasks, which not only achieves competitive results compared with the SOTA but also produces highly efficient architectures with fewer parameters than other deep learning approaches. We search a more granular space than previous approaches, describing a larger diversity of models, which are dynamic to the task signal length. We introduce the use depth-wise and point-wise convolution as the primitive convolution operations in NAS and show that very large kernels with extensive dilation are effective for some problems.

Without the use of an advanced search algorithm or efficient proxy evaluations we achieve strong results on a range of problems. We set a benchmark for further work showing that with a well designed search-space NAS has strong potential as a time-series classification approach.

References

1. Zoph, B., Vasudevan, V., Shlens, J., Le, Q.V.: Learning transferable architectures for scalable image recognition (2018). https://doi.org/10.48550/ARXIV. 1707.07012. arXiv: 1707
2. Liu, H., Simonyan, K., Yang, Y.: DARTS: Differentiable architecture search. arXiv: 1806.09055 (2019)
3. Schrodi, S., Stoll, D., Ru, B., Brox, T., Hutter, F.: Towards discovering neural architectures from scratch, Rhea Sukthanker (2022)
4. Ismail Fawaz, H., Forestier, G., Weber, J., Idoumghar, L., Muller, P.-A.: Transfer learning for time series classification. In: 2018 IEEE International Conference on Big Data (Big Data), pp. 1367–1376 (2018). https://doi.org/10.1109/BigData. 2018.8621990
5. Middlehurst, M., Large, J., Flynn, M., Lines, J., Bostrom, A., Bagnall, A.: Hivecote 2.0:aA new meta ensemble for time series classification. Mach. Learn. **110**(11-12), 3211–3243 (2021)
6. Dempster, A., Petitjean, F., Webb, G.I.: Rocket: exceptionally fast and accurate time series classification using random convolutional kernels. Data Mining Knowl. Dis. **34**(5), 1454–1495 (2020)
7. Middlehurst, M., Large, J., Bagnall, A.: The canonical interval forest (cif) classifier for time series classification. In: 2020 IEEE International Conference on Big Data (Big Data), pp. 188–195 (2020). https://doi.org/10.1109/BigData50022.2020. 9378424
8. Wang, Z., Yan, W., Oates, T.: Time series classification from scratch with deep neural networks: A strong baseline. In: 2017 International Joint Conference on Neural Networks (IJCNN), pp. 1578–1585 (2017). https://doi.org/10.1109/IJCNN. 2017.7966039
9. Fawaz, H.I., Lucas, B., Forestier, G., et al.: InceptionTime: finding AlexNet for time series classification. Data Mining Knowl. Dis. **34**(6), 1936–1962 (2020). https://doi.org/10.1007/s10618-020-00710-y.
10. Stanley, K.O., Miikkulainen, R.: Evolving neural networks through augmenting topologies. Evol. Comput. **10**(2), 99–127 (2002). https://doi.org/10.1162/ 106365602320169811

11. Miikkulainen, R., Liang, J., Meyerson, E., et al.: Evolving Deep Neural Networks (2017)
12. Micucci, D., Mobilio, M., Napoletano, P.: Unimib shar: a dataset for human activity recognition using acceleration data from smartphones. Appli. Sci. **7**(10) (2017). https://doi.org/10.3390/app7101101. https://www.mdpi.com/2076-3417/7/10/1101, ISSN: 2076-3417
13. Brunner, C., Leeb, R., Müller-Putz, G., Schlögl, A., Pfurtscheller, G.: Bci competition 2008-graz data set a. In: Institute for Knowledge Discovery (Laboratory of Brain-Computer Interfaces), Graz University of Technology, vol. 16, pp. 1–6 (2008)
14. Radosavovic, I., Kosaraju, R.P., Girshick, R., He, K., Dollar, P.: Designing network design spaces. In: Proceedings of the IEEE/CVF Conference on Computer Vision and Pattern Recognition (CVPR) (2020)
15. Radosavovic, I., Johnson, J., Xie, S., Lo, W.-Y., Dollár, P.: On network design spaces for visual recognition (2019). arXiv: 1905.13214
16. Liu, Z., Mao, H., Wu, C.-Y., Feichtenhofer, C., Darrell, T., Xie, S.: A convnet for the 2020s. In: Proceedings of the IEEE/CVF Conference on Computer Vision and Pattern Recognition, pp. 11 976–11 986 (2022)
17. Oord, A. v. d., Dieleman, S., Zen, H., et al.: Wavenet: A generative model for raw audio, arXiv preprint arXiv:1609.03499 (2016)
18. Bergstra, J., Bengio, Y.: Random search for hyper-parameter optimization. J. Mach. Learn. Res. **13**(1), 281–305 (2012)
19. Gao, W., Zhang, L., Teng, Q., He, J., Hao, W.: Danhar: dual attention network for multimodal human activity recognition using wearable sensors. Appl. Soft Comput. **111**, 107728 (2021)
20. Mukherjee, D., Mondal, R., Singh, P.K., Sarkar, R., Bhattacharjee, D.: Ensemconvnet: a deep learning approach for human activity recognition using smartphone sensors for healthcare applications. Multimedia Tools Appli. **79**, 31663–31690 (2020)
21. Al-qaness, M.A.A., Dahou, A., Elaziz, M.A., Helmi, A.M.: Multiresatt: multilevel residual network with attention for human activity recognition using wearable sensors. IEEE Trans. Industrial Inform. **19**(1), 144–152 (2023). https://doi.org/10.1109/TII.2022.3165
22. Helmi, A.M., Al-qaness, M.A., Dahou, A., Abd Elaziz, M.: Human activity recognition using marine predators algorithm with deep learning. Future Generation Comput. Syst. **142**, 340–350 (2023)
23. Teng, Q., Wang, K., Zhang, L., He, J.: The layer-wise training convolutional neural networks using local loss for sensor-based human activity recognition. IEEE Sens. J. **20**(13), 7265–7274 (2020)
24. Ruiz, A.P., Flynn, M., Large, J., Middlehurst, M., Bagnall, A.: "The great multivariate time series classification bake off: a review and experimental evaluation of recent algorithmic advances. Data Mining Knowl. Dis. **35**(2), 401–449 (2021)

Back to Basics: A Sanity Check on Modern Time Series Classification Algorithms

Bhaskar Dhariyal$^{(\boxtimes)}$, Thach Le Nguyen, and Georgiana Ifrim

School of Computer Science, University College Dublin, Dublin, Ireland
bhaskar.dhariyal@ucdconnect.ie, {thach.lenguyen,georgiana.ifrim}@ucd.ie

Abstract. The state-of-the-art in time series classification has come a long way, from the 1NN-DTW algorithm to the ROCKET family of classifiers. However, in the current fast-paced development of new classifiers, taking a step back and performing simple baseline checks is essential. These checks are often overlooked, as researchers are focused on establishing new state-of-the-art results, developing scalable algorithms, and making models explainable. Nevertheless, there are many datasets that look like time series at first glance, but classic algorithms such as tabular methods with no time ordering may perform better on such problems. For example, for spectroscopy datasets, tabular methods tend to significantly outperform recent time series methods. In this study, we compare the performance of tabular models using classic machine learning approaches (e.g., Ridge, LDA, RandomForest) with the ROCKET family of classifiers (e.g., Rocket, MiniRocket, MultiRocket). Tabular models are simple and very efficient, while the ROCKET family of classifiers are more complex and have state-of-the-art accuracy and efficiency among recent time series classifiers. We find that tabular models outperform the ROCKET family of classifiers on approximately 19% of univariate and 28% of multivariate datasets in the UCR/UEA benchmark and achieve accuracy within 10% points on about 50% of datasets. Our results suggest that it is important to consider simple tabular models as baselines when developing time series classifiers. These models are very fast, can be as effective as more complex methods and may be easier to understand and deploy.

Keywords: Time series · Classification · Evaluation · Baselines

1 Introduction

Time series classification is a challenging task that has attracted significant research interest recently. The ever-evolving computational capabilities and abundant applications and use cases have led to the development of a wide range of time series classification methods, from simple distance-based methods (1-NN-DTW [1]) to complex deep learning models (Inception Time [2]).

Most of the research in time series classification is focused on establishing state-of-the-art results, developing scalable algorithms, and making models

© The Author(s), under exclusive license to Springer Nature Switzerland AG 2023
G. Ifrim et al. (Eds.): AALTD 2023, LNAI 14343, pp. 205–229, 2023.
https://doi.org/10.1007/978-3-031-49896-1_14

explainable. However, in this quest, it is often possible to forget the first principle of research, which is to compare with existing simpler methods.

Historically, there have been many instances where traditional models have outperformed deep learning methods on some tasks. For example, a recent study [3] showed that linear models can be more effective than deep learning networks for forecasting. Similarly, the work of [4] showed that linear models can outperform other complex models for classification tasks in spectroscopy data. However, there is less empirical work investigating the performance of classic tabular models on time series classification tasks.

In this study, we take a step back from the pursuit of providing yet another state-of-the-art method and perform some simple sanity checks, which are often missed. We compare the performance of tabular models with the ROCKET [5–7] family of classifiers, which are currently considered state-of-the-art for time series classification. In this paper, the main contributions are:

- We empirically compared tabular and time series methods on the established UCR/UEA benchmarks for univariate and multivariate time series classification.
- We analysed the accuracy-time tradeoffs for all the methods on both benchmarks and found that on about 50% of datasets in both benchmarks, the tabular methods perform within 10% points accuracy of state-of-the-art time series classification methods, while being two orders of magnitude faster.
- We discussed the performance of tabular versus time series methods for different data and problem types and the potential implications for how the very popular UCR/UEA benchmarks are formed and used by the community. In particular, if tabular methods significantly outperform time series methods on some problem types, we raise the question of whether these datasets should be included in a time series benchmark.

2   Related Work

The UCR and UEA Benchmarks. Univariate Time Series Classification (UTSC). State-of-the-art UTS classifiers are classifiers that have been shown to be the most accurate methods on the UCR/UEA benchmark. The most notable ones are ROCKET [5] and its variants (MiniROCKET, Multi-ROCKET and HYDRA [8]), due to their high accuracy and efficiency. These classifiers follow a two-step approach: transforming the time series into tabular features and classifying these transformations using linear models such as logistic regression. While deep learning methods (e.g., FCN, ResNet, InceptionTime [2]) or ensembles (e.g., HIVE-COTE [9], TDE [10]) are also as accurate, they often demand significantly more computing resources (time, CPU, GPU, etc.). Other notable classifiers include symbolic-classifiers such as WEASEL [11] and MrSQM [12] and shapelet-classifiers such as RDST [13]. The UCR/UEA time series archive is a public collection of time series datasets that has been used extensively as the unified benchmark by researchers in this area. The archive is the result of a massive collaborative effort lead by research groups from the

University California Riverside (UCR) and the University of East Anglia (UEA), hence the name of the benchmark. Starting with 85 univariate datasets in 2015, the archive was expanded to 128 datasets in 2018. The expansion also introduced a classification benchmark for multivariate time series which includes 30 datasets. The dedicated website[1] for the archive contains not only the downloadable datasets but also pointers to code, publications, and other information that can be useful to any interested party. Without a doubt, the archive is a major resource that pushes forward research in TSC. However, while extremely useful for providing an overview and comparing against existing work, it potentially creates a pitfall where new works only focus on "beating the benchmark" and neglect what makes a classifier useful in real-life applications.

Multivariate Time Series Classification (MTSC). In general, it can be said that the MTSC literature is less developed when compared to UTSC. The benchmark for MTSC was introduced later with fewer datasets. Most state-of-the-art MTSC methods are UTSC methods that are adapted for MTS data. The most straightforward approach is to learn from each channel independently (e.g., HIVE-COTE, WEASEL-MUSE [14]). On the other hand, some classifiers actually utilize channel dependency, and thus are called bespoke MTS classifiers. For example, the multivariate variants of ROCKET (and MiniROCKET, MultiROCKET) replace the 1D kernels with 2D kernels to produce multi-channel dependent features (see [6,7] for details).

Tabular Methods. Classic machine learning models such as Random Forest, Logistic Regression, Linear Regression, seem to have been largely ignored in recent time series literature. Such methods often assume independence between values at different time points and thus are deemed unsuitable for time series data. The work in [15] employs tabular models, however, the models are trained on transformed data after applying techniques such as PCA, Spectral approaches and auto-correlation. Nonetheless, outside of the time series literature, these methods are still favourable choices in some communities. In particular, the work of [4,16] investigated several approaches for modelling milk spectroscopy data and found that tabular methods significantly outperformed time series methods. While these datasets are not inherently time series data, spectroscopy data have been part of the UCR/UEA benchmark since its inception and have been widely accepted by the community as time series data. This finding suggests that not all datasets in the benchmark are suitable for time series methods. We further investigate this issue in the next sections.

3 Background

A **time series** is a sequence of numbers representing some measurements over time. For example, a time series could represent a person's heartbeat variation on a 30-minute morning run. Each value in a time series usually has significance with respect to the previous and next values.

---

[1] http://www.timeseriesclassification.com.

A typical mathematical representation of time series is $T : \{x_0, x_1, x_2, \ldots x_n\}$ where $x \in \Re$ and n is the length of the time series. When we assign a discrete label to the time series, we can perform time series classification. We discuss two types of time series tasks in this paper, i.e., univariate time series classification (UTSC) and multivariate time series classification (MTSC). In univariate time series classification, data is recorded from a single source, meaning only one observed variable exists. On the other hand, multivariate time series classification involves recording data from multiple sources, resulting in the presence of multiple observed variables. A mathematical representation of multivariate time series can take the form:

$$T : \{< x_0^0, x_1^0, \ldots x_n^0 > < x_0^1, x_1^1, \ldots x_n^1 > \ldots < x_0^{m-1}, x_1^{m-1}, \ldots x_n^{m-1} >\}$$

where m is the number of channels. If the time series is univariate, $m = 1$. It is common in some applications to convert multivariate time series to univariate time series by concatenating all the channels into a single univariate time series. After this transformation, univariate classifiers can be trained with this data.

Tabular data is the most ubiquitous data type. It is a data structure that organizes data into rows and columns. Each row represents a single record, and each column represents a single attribute of that record. It has no concept of temporality. This means that the previous value has no impact on the current value. A time series can be considered a tabular vector and used as input to a tabular method, e.g., linear regression.

4   Experiments

4.1   Datasets

The UEA/UCR [17] benchmark datasets are mostly used in the empirical evaluation and comparison of various algorithms. Since the benchmark contains both univariate and multivariate datasets, it is popular for testing new algorithms on. Table 8 and 9 in the appendix provide the data dictionary for both types of datasets. As it is common in recent time series literature, we run experiments on 109 univariate datasets and 25 equal-length multivariate datasets. We make our code available on github[2].

4.2   Univariate Time Series Classification

Before comparing tabular versus time-series models, we compared a few popular methods within each group separately.

Tabular Methods Results. For tabular methods we select three linear methods known for their efficiency and effectiveness in real-world applications [4], as well as Random Forest to have an effective non-linear classifier. We run these methods using the sklearn implementation[3] with default parameters. Later in

---

[2] https://github.com/mlgig/TabularModelsforTSC.
[3] https://scikit-learn.org/stable/supervised_learning.html.

the paper we also discuss parameter tuning and its impact on accuracy and runtime. In Fig. 1, we compare the accuracy of four tabular models on univariate datasets: Random Forest, Logistic Regression, Ridge Regression (RidgeCV) and Linear Discriminant Analysis (LDA). The critical difference diagram [18] captures the average accuracy rank over all the datasets. The accuracy gain is evaluated using a Wilcoxon signed-rank test with Holm correction and visualised with the critical difference (CD) diagram with significance value $(\alpha) = 0.05$. The figure illustrates Random Forest significantly outperforms the other three models and Logistic Regression outperforms the other linear models Table 1 illustrates the mean accuracy and total training and test computation time in minutes. The tabular results correspond to the tabular CD diagram, where Random Forest is the best classifier.

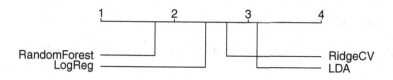

Fig. 1. Accuracy comparison of tabular methods on UTSC datasets.

Table 1. Mean accuracy and total computation time taken by tabular models on UTSC datasets.

	Mean Accuracy	Total Time (minutes)
RandomForest	0.74	0.886
LogReg	0.69	0.31
RidgeCV	0.67	0.09
LDA	0.63	0.09

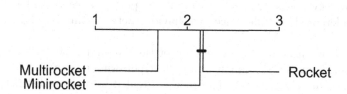

Fig. 2. Accuracy comparison of time-series methods on UTSC datasets.

Time Series Methods Results. Similarly, in Fig. 2 and Table 2, we compare the accuracy of three time series classification models: Multirocket, MiniRocket, and Rocket. We use the implementation in the aeon-toolkit library[4] with default

---

[4] https://www.aeon-toolkit.org/en/latest/api_reference/classification.html.

Table 2. Mean accuracy and total computation time taken by time-series models on UTSC datasets.

	Mean Accuracy	Total Time (minutes)
Minirocket	0.86	34.56
Multirocket	0.86	73.46
Rocket	0.85	158.76

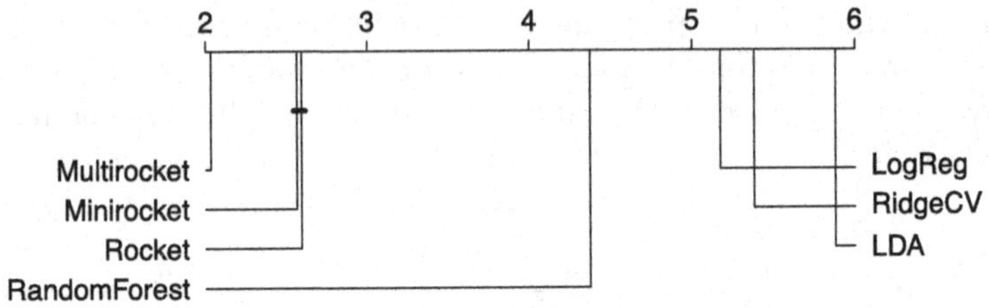

Fig. 3. Accuracy comparison of tabular and time series models on UTSC datasets.

parameters. From the critical difference diagram (Fig. 2) we note that Multi-Rocket is significantly more accurate than MiniRocket and Rocket.

Time Series Methods vs Tabular Methods. In Fig. 3, we compare the accuracy of time-series and tabular models. We can see that the time-series models have a higher mean accuracy rank than the tabular models. Multirocket is significantly more accurate than all other models, and Random Forest is the closest tabular model to the time-series models.

Detailed Analysis. Figure 3 provides a summary overview of the performance of classifiers using their average accuracy ranking across the datasets analysed. Average behaviour with respect to accuracy or rank is a common and useful summary to get an overview of the performance of multiple classifiers over multiple datasets. However, it is crucial to examine the performance of models at a finer level to understand the difference in behaviour between tabular and time-series models.

In Fig. 4, we illustrate the accuracy of tabular and time series models on each dataset, focusing on comparing the best-performing tabular with the best-performing time series model. The plot is divided into three distinct regions: green, grey, and red.

- The green region illustrates the datasets where the tabular models outperform the time series models or where both models achieve the same accuracy.
- The grey region represents datasets where the two models have performance within a fixed threshold. It is crucial to consider the accuracy-time trade-off in this region when deciding the better model. Datasets in this region are highlighted when the difference between the best-performing time-series model and the best-performing tabular model ranges from 1 to 9% points.

– The red region represents the datasets where time series models outperform tabular models. The time series models in these datasets are at least 10% points better than tabular models.

For the UEA benchmark, surprisingly, 19.2% of the datasets performed better with tabular models (green region), 31.1% performed within 10% points with both tabular and time series models (grey region), and 49.5% performed better than 10% points with time series models (red region).

The above numbers imply that on about 19% of the benchmark, there are only weak temporal patterns, and tabular methods that disregard time ordering are very competitive when compared with time series methods. As a result, for many of those datasets in the green and grey region, using a complex time series model would be like using a sledgehammer to crack a nut. We of course acknowledge that time series methods work very well for the datasets in the red region, but these account for slightly less than half of the benchmark. We also acknowledge that the Rocket algorithms have been tested outside of this benchmark with good results in many real time series applications [19–22]. The question remains though: should we include the datasets in the green and grey areas into a time series benchmark at all, given that tabular methods have similar accuracy to the best time series methods on those datasets.

Computation Time Analysis. Traditionally, tabular models are known for their computational speed. This is also evident from Tables 1 and 2, which show that tabular models are an order of magnitude faster than time series models. Figure 4 illustrates the various regions for accuracy, but it is worth highlighting that tabular models in the green and grey regions are faster and almost as accurate, or even more accurate than time series methods.

Figure 5 shows the tradeoff between the mean accuracy and total computation time for the various time-series and tabular models in grey region datasets. Multirocket and Random Forest are the most accurate models among time series and tabular models, respectively. The difference in accuracy between Multirocket and Random Forest is approximately 5% points. However, Multirocket takes an average of 30 min longer to train.

Domain-Wise Analysis. Table 3 shows the mean accuracy of different classifiers on datasets from various domains (as annotated by the meta-data in UCR/UEA). The benchmark is highly dominated by three domains: Image, Sensor, and Motion. About 63% of the benchmark comprises these three domains out of a total of 13 domains in the benchmark.

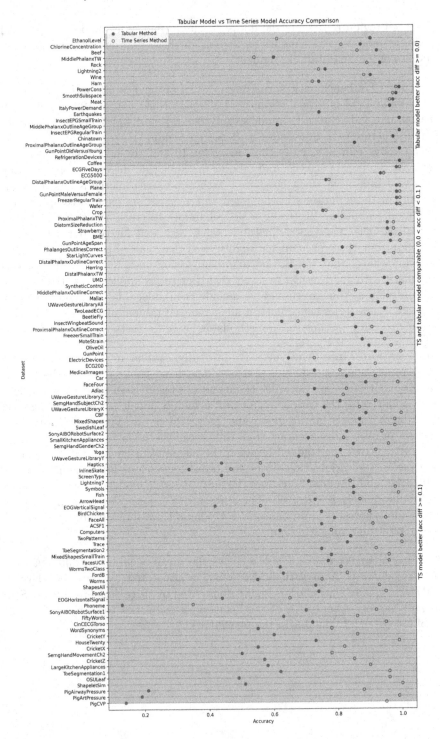

Fig. 4. Accuracy comparison of the best time series model with the best tabular model on univariate time series datasets. Red circles represent the tabular models, and blue circles represent the time series models. Each marker shows the maximum accuracy achieved by the tabular models versus the time series models. (Color figure online)

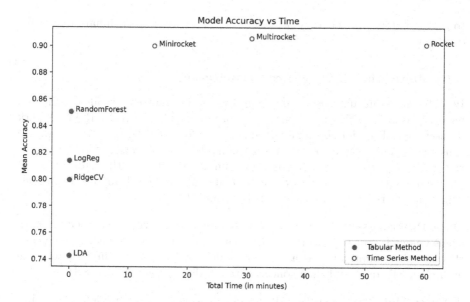

Fig. 5. Accuracy-Time tradeoff for datasets in the **grey region** shown in Fig. 4. We observe a mean accuracy difference of about 5% points, but at least an order of magnitude difference in computation time, between tabular and time series methods. (Color figure online)

Table 3. Mean accuracy of classifiers by problem types on UCR univariate datasets.

Domain (#datasets)	Tabular Models				Time Series Models		
	RidgeCV	LDA	LogReg	RandomForest	Rocket	Minirocket	Multirocket
Image(31)	0.66	0.62	**0.71**	0.75	0.85	0.85	**0.85**
Sensor(20)	0.73	0.69	0.72	**0.76**	0.86	0.86	**0.87**
Motion(17)	0.58	0.46	0.58	**0.70**	0.84	0.84	**0.85**
Device(8)	0.48	0.44	0.48	0.62	0.76	0.74	**0.77**
Simulated(8)	0.78	0.82	0.81	**0.88**	**0.99**	0.98	**0.99**
Spectro(8)	0.86	**0.90**	0.86	0.82	0.84	0.86	**0.86**
ECG(4)	**0.92**	0.84	0.92	0.82	0.97	0.97	**0.97**
Spectrum(4)	**0.75**	0.67	0.74	0.67	0.83	0.82	**0.88**
Hemodynamics(3)	0.05	**0.16**	0.12	0.13	0.66	**0.94**	0.81
EOG(2)	0.3	0.28	0.37	**0.43**	0.59	0.57	**0.60**
EPG(2)	0.82	**1.00**	**1.00**	1.00	0.99	1.00	1.00
Power(1)	0.98	0.73	0.99	**1.00**	0.92	**0.99**	0.98
Traffic(1)	**0.98**	0.95	0.98	0.98	0.98	0.98	**0.98**

As expected, with regard to average accuracy in a specific domain, as also shown in Fig. 3, time series models performed better than tabular models in most of the domains. However, we note that the tabular models performed especially well in the Spectro domain. This could be because the Spectro domain does not have strong temporal features. Also, as we have seen in Fig. 4, average behaviour can be misleading and we need to look at the accuracy on individual datasets to get a good idea of accuracy behaviour across the entire benchmark or specific domains.

4.3 Multivariate Time Series Classification

In addition to our analysis of univariate time series datasets, we also conducted an analysis on multivariate time series datasets. The UEA/UCR benchmark dataset we utilized for this analysis consisted of 26 datasets. However, to ensure consistency and comparability among the models, we narrowed down our focus to the 25 datasets that all models could run on. We filtered the datasets based on equal length, and one dataset (Pen Digits) was removed due to Minirocket, which cannot run on datasets with lengths less than 8.

Data Preprocessing: Unlike univariate time series, which have data from a single channel, multivariate time series data have multiple channels. To convert this data into a format that a tabular model can process, we first standardize each channel's data and then concatenate the data across all channels.

Tabular Methods Results. After preprocessing the data, we followed a similar approach to our univariate analysis. We selected the same tabular models: Random Forest, LDA, Logistic Regression, and RidgeCV. The critical difference diagram (Fig. 6) illustrates that Random Forest performed significantly better than the other three models, and Logistic Regression outperformed the other two linear models.

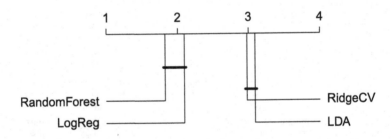

Fig. 6. Accuracy comparison of tabular methods on MTSC datasets.

Table 4 shows the total time taken by tabular models and their corresponding mean accuracy. The table corroborates the results of the critical difference diagram, which showed that Random Forest is the most accurate tabular model, closely followed by LogisticRegression and RidgeCV. RidgeCV is also the most time-efficient method.

Time Series Methods Results. Similar to the tabular methods, we ran the multivariate time series methods, namely Minirocket, Multirocket, and Rocket, on the MTSC datasets. Since the implemented algorithm works well with multivariate time series, there was no need to preprocess the data in this case.

Table 4. Mean accuracy and total computation time taken by tabular models on MTSC datasets.

	Mean Accuracy	Total Time (minutes)
RandomForest	0.61	6.40
LogisticRegression	0.59	6.20
RidgeCV	0.56	5.27
LDA	0.52	6.70

Figure 7 and Table 5 illustrate the performance of time series methods on the benchmark datasets. Both the figure and table show that Minirocket outperforms the other two classifiers. Additionally, Minirocket is also the fastest method among the three methods.

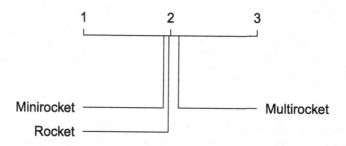

Fig. 7. Accuracy comparison of time-series methods on MTSC datasets.

Table 5. Mean accuracy and total computation time taken by time series models on MTSC datasets.

	Mean Accuracy	Total Time (minutes)
Minirocket	0.71	49.33
Multirocket	0.70	67.10
Rocket	0.70	129.05

Time Series Methods vs Tabular Methods. Finally, we compared tabular and time series models, as shown in Fig. 8. As expected, the time series models outperformed the tabular models in terms of average accuracy. However, we conducted a more detailed analysis to investigate the reasons for this difference. We discuss our findings below.

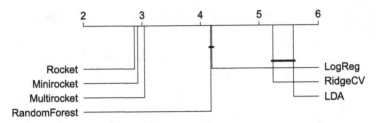

Fig. 8. Accuracy comparison time-series and tabular methods on MTSC datasets.

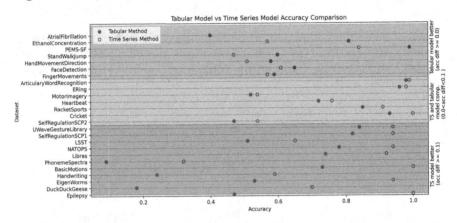

Fig. 9. Accuracy comparison of time series models with tabular models on multivariate time series datasets. Red circles represent tabular models, and blue circles represent time series models. Each marker shows the maximum accuracy achieved by the tabular models versus the time series models. Detailed results are provided with the code. (Color figure online)

Figure 9 shows the difference in performance between the best-performing tabular model and the best-performing time series model. The performance of each model is highlighted in a different region, as defined above in Sect. 4.2. Approximately 28% of the datasets are represented in each green and grey region (56% total), indicating that the tabular model performs better or within 10% points in these cases. Another 44% of the datasets fall within the red region, indicating that the time series models outperform the tabular models in those instances.

Computation Time Analysis. For the same reasons as for the univariate time series classification task, we perform the time-accuracy tradeoff analysis for multivariate time series classification. Figure 10 illustrates the performance of various time-series and tabular models on the datasets in the grey region of Fig. 9. Rocket is the most accurate among time-series models, and Random Forest is the most accurate model among tabular models. The difference between

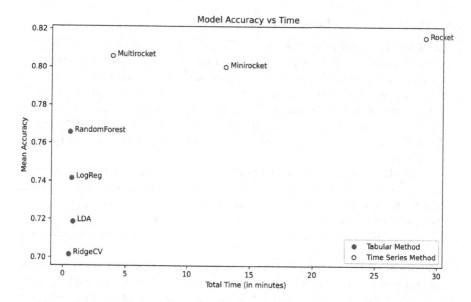

Fig. 10. Accuracy-Time tradeoff for datasets in the **grey region** in Fig. 9. (Color figure online)

the mean accuracy of Rocket and the mean accuracy of Random Forest is about 5% point, while the difference in total computation time is about 4 min.

In addition to considering the trade-off between time and accuracy, we also analyzed the domain-wise performance of tabular and time series models in multivariate datasets in Table 6. The datasets consisted of 6 domains, with 60% of the data coming from two domains (HAR and EEG). Time series models generally performed well, but tabular models performed better in the ECG and EEG/MEG domains.

Table 6. Mean accuracy of classifiers by problem types on UCR multivariate datasets.

Domain (#datasets)	Tabular Models				Time Series Models		
	RidgeCV	LDA	LogReg	RandomForest	Rocket	Minirocket	Multirocket
HAR(9)	0.67	0.53	0.74	**0.78**	0.92	**0.94**	0.94
EEG/MEG(6)	0.55	0.54	**0.58**	0.50	**0.55**	0.55	0.54
Audio Spectra(3)	**0.18**	0.16	0.18	0.18	0.46	**0.70**	0.52
Other(3)	0.52	0.58	0.65	**0.74**	**0.84**	0.83	0.80
ECG(2)	**0.46**	0.20	**0.46**	0.40	**0.27**	0.26	0.24
Motion(2)	0.59	0.65	0.65	**0.72**	0.99	**1.00**	1.00

4.4 Discussion and Lessons Learned

– **Redefining baselines:** Most previous research has considered 1NN-DTW as the baseline for time series classification. This is a reasonable choice, as 1NN-DTW is a simple and effective algorithm that is often competitive with more complex time series methods. However, our study suggests that simple tabular models can perform significantly well on some datasets, even when compared to recent state-of-the-art TSC algorithms. This finding suggests that there is a need to rethink how we do baseline comparisons for time series classification.

– **Not all that looks time series is a time series:** Our study demonstrated that tabular methods outperformed time series methods on some domains, specifically Spectro (Table 3), EEG or ECG (Table 6). This could be because the Spectro datasets did not contain strong temporal information. Either way, we need to ask whether it makes sense to have these datasets in a time series classification benchmark.

– **Considering trade-offs:** In our study we observed that time series models outperformed tabular models by a few percentage points on the red datasets. However, tabular models outperformed time series methods in the green datasets and were significantly faster to train and test. Therefore, especially for datasets in the grey region, where tabular and time series methods are close in accuracy, we recommend carefully considering whether tabular models are preferable to time series methods, especially if time is a constraint.

4.5 Improving Tabular Models

Since the above-mentioned experiments were conducted using the default hyperparameters, we wanted to investigate whether we could improve the performance of tabular models by tuning the hyperparameters. To do this, we performed hyperparameter tuning on Random Forest and Logistic Regression, since they were the best performing models in both univariate (Fig. 5) and multivariate (Fig. 10) experiments.

We performed hyperparameter tuning with a combination of scaling and regularization. Table 7 shows the results of the hyperparameter tuning and the improvement for the best tabular model. We found that hyperparameter tuning can increase accuracy, but it also takes a significant amount of time to find the best hyperparameters.

Table 7. Improvement on accuracy on univariate and multivariate datasets and mean computation time in minutes.

	Mean Accuracy		Mean Computation Time (minutes)	
	Before	After	Before	After
Univariate	0.86	0.87	0.47	13.41
Multivariate	0.74	0.75	0.91	43.10

5   Conclusion

In this study, we compared the performance of tabular models with state-of-the-art time series models on the UCR/UEA univariate and multivariate time series classification benchmarks. We found that tabular models performed surprisingly well on many datasets, outperforming the recent Multirocket classifier on a significant percentage of the datasets. On many other datasets, the accuracy was comparable, but tabular models were more efficient in terms of computation time. Overall, in about half of the datasets in either the univariate or the multivariate benchmarks, tabular methods were within 10% points accuracy of the time series methods.

Our findings suggest that tabular models should be considered as baselines for evaluating improvements in time series classifiers, and even for considering whether a dataset should be included in the time series classification benchmarks. Furthermore, tabular methods can be a viable alternative to time series models for some classification tasks. Tabular models are easier to train and deploy, and they are more efficient in terms of computation time. The performance of tabular models does vary depending on the characteristics of the dataset. In future work, we plan to further investigate the factors that contribute to the performance of tabular models on time series data, and include more tabular models and parameter tuning.

Acknowledgement. This publication has emanated from research supported in part by a grant from Science Foundation Ireland through the VistaMilk SFI Research Centre (SFI/16/RC/3835) and the Insight Centre for Data Analytics (12/RC/2289 P2). For the purpose of Open Access, the author has applied a CC BY public copyright licence to any Author Accepted Manuscript version arising from this submission. We would like to thank the reviewers for their constructive feedback. We would also like to thank all the researchers that have contributed open source code and datasets to the UEA MTSC Archive and especially, we want to thank the groups at UEA and UCR who continue to maintain and expand the archive.

Appendix

(See Tables 10, 11 and 12).

Table 8. Data dictionary for Multivariate time series classification.

Domain	Datasets	Train Size	Test Size	#Channels	TS-len	#Classes
Audio Spectra	DuckDuckGeese	50	50	1345	270	5
Other	PEMS-SF	267	173	963	144	7
EEG/MEG	FaceDetection	5890	3524	144	62	2
EEG/MEG	MotorImagery	278	100	64	3000	2
Audio Spectra	Heartbeat	204	205	61	405	2
EEG/MEG	FingerMovements	316	100	28	50	2
Human Activity Recogntion	NATOPS	180	180	24	51	6
Audio Spectra	PhonemeSpectra	3315	3353	11	217	39
EEG/MEG	HandMovementDirection	160	74	10	400	4
Motion	ArticularyWordRecognition	275	300	9	144	25
EEG/MEG	SelfRegulationSCP2	200	180	7	1152	2
EEG/MEG	SelfRegulationSCP1	268	293	6	896	2
Human Activity Recogntion	BasicMotions	40	40	6	100	4
Human Activity Recogntion	Cricket	108	72	6	1197	12
Human Activity Recogntion	EigenWorms	128	131	6	17984	5
Human Activity Recogntion	LSST	2459	2466	6	36	14
Human Activity Recogntion	RacketSports	151	152	6	30	4
ECG	StandWalkJump	12	15	4	2500	3
Human Activity Recogntion	ERing	30	270	4	65	6
Human Activity Recogntion	Handwriting	150	850	3	152	26
Human Activity Recogntion	UWaveGestureLibrary	120	320	3	315	8
Motion	Epilepsy	137	138	3	206	4
Other	EthanolConcentration	261	263	3	1751	4
ECG	AtrialFibrillation	15	15	2	640	3
Motion	PenDigits	7494	3498	2	8	10
Other	Libras	180	180	2	45	15

Table 9. Data dictionary for Univariate time series classification.

Data	Train Size	Test Size	TS-Len	#Classes	Domain
ACSF1	100	100	1460	10	DEVICE
Adiac	390	391	176	37	IMAGE
ArrowHead	36	175	251	3	IMAGE
Beef	30	30	470	5	SPECTRO
BeetleFly	20	20	512	2	IMAGE
BirdChicken	20	20	512	2	IMAGE
BME	30	150	128	3	SIMULATED
Car	60	60	577	4	SENSOR
CBF	30	900	128	3	SIMULATED
Chinatown	20	345	24	2	Traffic
ChlorineConcentration	467	3840	166	3	SIMULATED
CinCECGTorso	40	1380	1639	4	ECG

(continued)

Table 9. (*continued*)

Data	Train Size	Test Size	TS-Len	#Classes	Domain
Coffee	28	28	286	2	SPECTRO
Computers	250	250	720	2	DEVICE
CricketX	390	390	300	12	MOTION
CricketY	390	390	300	12	MOTION
CricketZ	390	390	300	12	MOTION
Crop	7200	16800	46	24	IMAGE
DiatomSizeReduction	16	306	345	4	IMAGE
DistalPhalanxOutlineAgeGroup	400	139	80	3	IMAGE
DistalPhalanxOutlineCorrect	600	276	80	2	IMAGE
DistalPhalanxTW	400	139	80	6	IMAGE
Earthquakes	322	139	512	2	SENSOR
ECG200	100	100	96	2	ECG
ECG5000	500	4500	140	5	ECG
ECGFiveDays	23	861	136	2	ECG
ElectricDevices	8926	7711	96	7	DEVICE
EOGHorizontalSignal	362	362	1250	12	EOG
EOGVerticalSignal	362	362	1250	12	EOG
EthanolLevel	504	500	1751	4	SPECTRO
FaceAll	560	1690	131	14	IMAGE
FaceFour	24	88	350	4	IMAGE
FacesUCR	200	2050	131	14	IMAGE
FiftyWords	450	455	270	50	IMAGE
Fish	175	175	463	7	IMAGE
FordA	3601	1320	500	2	SENSOR
FordB	3636	810	500	2	SENSOR
FreezerRegularTrain	150	2850	301	2	SENSOR
FreezerSmallTrain	28	2850	301	2	SENSOR
GunPoint	50	150	150	2	MOTION
GunPointAgeSpan	135	316	150	2	MOTION
GunPointMaleVersusFemale	135	316	150	2	MOTION
GunPointOldVersusYoung	135	316	150	2	MOTION
Ham	109	105	431	2	SPECTRO
Haptics	155	308	1092	5	MOTION
Herring	64	64	512	2	IMAGE
HouseTwenty	34	101	3000	2	DEVICE
InlineSkate	100	550	1882	7	MOTION
InsectEPGRegularTrain	62	249	601	3	EPG
InsectEPGSmallTrain	17	249	601	3	EPG
ItalyPowerDemand	67	1029	24	2	SENSOR
LargeKitchenAppliances	375	375	720	3	DEVICE
Lightning2	60	61	637	2	SENSOR
Lightning7	70	73	319	7	SENSOR
Mallat	55	2345	1024	8	SIMULATED
Meat	60	60	448	3	SPECTRO
MedicalImages	381	760	99	10	IMAGE
MiddlePhalanxOutlineAgeGroup	400	154	80	3	IMAGE
MiddlePhalanxOutlineCorrect	600	291	80	?	IMAGE
MiddlePhalanxTW	399	154	80	6	IMAGE
MixedShapes	500	2425	1024	5	IMAGE
MixedShapesSmallTrain	100	2425	1024	5	IMAGE

(*continued*)

Table 9. (*continued*)

Data	Train Size	Test Size	TS-Len	#Classes	Domain
MoteStrain	20	1252	84	2	SENSOR
OliveOil	30	30	570	4	SPECTRO
OSULeaf	200	242	427	6	IMAGE
PhalangesOutlinesCorrect	1800	858	80	2	IMAGE
Phoneme	214	1896	1024	39	SOUND
PigAirwayPressure	104	208	2000	52	HEMODYNAMICS
PigArtPressure	104	208	2000	52	HEMODYNAMICS
PigCVP	104	208	2000	52	HEMODYNAMICS
Plane	105	105	144	7	SENSOR
PowerCons	180	180	144	2	DEVICE
ProximalPhalanxOutlineAgeGroup	400	205	80	3	IMAGE
ProximalPhalanxOutlineCorrect	600	291	80	2	IMAGE
ProximalPhalanxTW	400	205	80	6	IMAGE
RefrigerationDevices	375	375	720	3	DEVICE
Rock	20	50	2844	4	SPECTRO
ScreenType	375	375	720	3	DEVICE
SemgHandGenderCh2	300	600	1500	2	SPECTRO
SemgHandMovementCh2	450	450	1500	6	SPECTRO
SemgHandSubjectCh2	450	450	1500	5	SPECTRO
ShapeletSim	20	180	500	2	SIMULATED
ShapesAll	600	600	512	60	IMAGE
SmallKitchenAppliances	375	375	720	3	DEVICE
SmoothSubspace	150	150	15	3	SIMULATED
SonyAIBORobotSurface1	20	601	70	2	SENSOR
SonyAIBORobotSurface2	27	953	65	2	SENSOR
StarLightCurves	1000	8236	1024	3	SENSOR
Strawberry	613	370	235	2	SPECTRO
SwedishLeaf	500	625	128	15	IMAGE
Symbols	25	995	398	6	IMAGE
SyntheticControl	300	300	60	6	SIMULATED
ToeSegmentation1	40	228	277	2	MOTION
ToeSegmentation2	36	130	343	2	MOTION
Trace	100	100	275	4	SENSOR
TwoLeadECG	23	1139	82	2	ECG
TwoPatterns	1000	4000	128	4	SIMULATED
UMD	36	144	150	3	SIMULATED
UWaveGestureLibraryAll	896	3582	945	8	MOTION
UWaveGestureLibraryX	896	3582	315	8	MOTION
UWaveGestureLibraryY	896	3582	315	8	MOTION
UWaveGestureLibraryZ	896	3582	315	8	MOTION
Wafer	1000	6164	152	2	SENSOR
Wine	57	54	234	2	SPECTRO

Table 10. Accuracy of tabular and time series methods on UTSC datasets.

Name	RidgeCV	LDA	LogRegCV	RandomForest	Rocket	Minirocket	Multirocket
ACSF1	0.42	0.41	0.62	0.75	0.90	0.91	0.88
Adiac	0.44	0.53	0.73	0.65	0.79	0.83	0.83
ArrowHead	0.73	0.67	0.73	0.70	0.82	0.84	0.87
Beef	0.87	0.93	0.87	0.77	0.83	0.87	0.77
BeetleFly	0.85	0.75	0.85	0.85	0.90	0.90	0.85
BirdChicken	0.50	0.55	0.70	0.75	0.90	0.90	0.90
BME	0.91	0.95	0.91	0.97	1.00	1.00	1.00
Car	0.80	0.80	0.83	0.67	0.90	0.92	0.92
CBF	0.83	0.84	0.85	0.89	1.00	1.00	1.00
Chinatown	0.98	0.95	0.98	0.98	0.98	0.98	0.98
ChlorineConcentration	0.85	0.88	0.78	0.71	0.82	0.77	0.79
CinCECGTorso	0.39	0.45	0.45	0.72	0.83	0.87	0.95
Coffee	1.00	1.00	1.00	0.96	1.00	1.00	1.00
Computers	0.51	0.49	0.48	0.62	0.75	0.70	0.78
CricketX	0.27	0.13	0.27	0.55	0.82	0.81	0.81
CricketY	0.37	0.15	0.39	0.60	0.86	0.83	0.85
CricketZ	0.31	0.15	0.28	0.57	0.85	0.82	0.84
Crop	0.56	0.63	0.69	0.76	0.75	0.75	0.77
DiatomSizeReduction	0.96	0.96	0.95	0.90	0.98	0.92	0.96
DistalPhalanxOutlineAgeGroup	0.66	0.60	0.69	0.77	0.76	0.75	0.78
DistalPhalanxOutlineCorrect	0.66	0.66	0.65	0.76	0.76	0.79	0.79
DistalPhalanxTW	0.61	0.58	0.60	0.68	0.72	0.70	0.69
Earthquakes	0.75	0.65	0.68	0.75	0.75	0.75	0.75
ECG200	0.80	0.59	0.84	0.83	0.91	0.91	0.92
ECG5000	0.93	0.93	0.94	0.94	0.95	0.95	0.95
ECGFiveDays	0.99	0.94	0.97	0.80	1.00	1.00	1.00
ElectricDevices	0.44	0.46	0.47	0.65	0.73	0.73	0.73
EOGHorizontalSignal	0.34	0.27	0.39	0.44	0.64	0.59	0.65
EOGVerticalSignal	0.25	0.28	0.35	0.42	0.54	0.56	0.54
EthanolLevel	0.66	0.91	0.72	0.48	0.57	0.61	0.62
FaceAll	0.79	0.79	0.77	0.79	0.95	0.81	0.80
FaceFour	0.89	0.85	0.86	0.75	0.97	0.99	0.94
FacesUCR	0.70	0.62	0.73	0.77	0.96	0.96	0.96
FiftyWords	0.43	0.32	0.56	0.63	0.83	0.84	0.86
Fish	0.82	0.73	0.85	0.77	0.98	0.99	0.98
FordA	0.52	0.53	0.49	0.74	0.94	0.95	0.95
FordB	0.50	0.50	0.49	0.63	0.79	0.81	0.83
FreezerRegularTrain	0.99	0.98	0.98	0.95	1.00	1.00	1.00
FreezerSmallTrain	0.86	0.94	0.81	0.75	0.95	0.97	0.99
GunPoint	0.85	0.81	0.85	0.92	1.00	0.99	1.00
GunPointAgeSpan	0.87	0.57	0.89	0.97	1.00	0.99	1.00
GunPointMaleVersusFemale	0.97	0.68	0.99	0.97	1.00	1.00	1.00
GunPointOldVersusYoung	1.00	0.88	1.00	1.00	0.99	1.00	1.00
Ham	0.71	0.66	0.65	0.75	0.71	0.69	0.73
Haptics	0.43	0.35	0.38	0.44	0.52	0.53	0.56
Herring	0.59	0.58	0.63	0.66	0.70	0.66	0.67
HouseTwenty	0.73	0.72	0.72	0.71	0.97	0.97	0.99
InlineSkate	0.19	0.23	0.27	0.34	0.46	0.45	0.47
InsectEPGRegularTrain	0.82	1.00	1.00	1.00	1.00	1.00	1.00

(*continued*)

Table 10. (continued)

Name	RidgeCV	LDA	LogRegCV	RandomForest	Rocket	Minirocket	Multirocket
InsectEPGSmallTrain	0.83	1.00	1.00	1.00	0.98	1.00	1.00
InsectWingbeatSound	0.62	0.26	0.58	0.63	0.66	0.67	0.68
ItalyPowerDemand	0.97	0.94	0.96	0.97	0.97	0.96	0.97
LargeKitchenAppliances	0.44	0.38	0.39	0.58	0.90	0.87	0.88
Lightning2	0.77	0.66	0.72	0.75	0.75	0.74	0.69
Lightning7	0.64	0.55	0.67	0.71	0.84	0.79	0.82
Mallat	0.76	0.86	0.82	0.91	0.96	0.95	0.92
Meat	0.98	0.98	0.93	0.92	0.95	0.97	0.93
MedicalImages	0.55	0.49	0.63	0.73	0.80	0.80	0.81
MiddlePhalanxOutlineAgeGroup	0.60	0.48	0.60	0.62	0.60	0.60	0.62
MiddlePhalanxOutlineCorrect	0.62	0.58	0.59	0.81	0.83	0.84	0.86
MiddlePhalanxTW	0.61	0.53	0.53	0.56	0.55	0.53	0.54
MixedShapes	0.79	0.71	0.82	0.87	0.97	0.97	0.98
MixedShapesSmallTrain	0.77	0.69	0.78	0.78	0.94	0.95	0.96
MoteStrain	0.86	0.72	0.86	0.88	0.91	0.93	0.95
OliveOil	0.90	0.90	0.90	0.90	0.90	0.93	0.97
OSULeaf	0.40	0.32	0.46	0.49	0.93	0.96	0.96
PhalangesOutlinesCorrect	0.67	0.66	0.67	0.82	0.83	0.84	0.85
Phoneme	0.11	0.08	0.10	0.13	0.28	0.27	0.35
PigAirwayPressure	0.02	0.21	0.08	0.09	0.09	0.88	0.60
PigArtPressure	0.10	0.12	0.17	0.19	0.95	0.99	0.95
PigCVP	0.04	0.14	0.10	0.11	0.93	0.95	0.88
Plane	0.98	0.99	0.98	0.98	1.00	1.00	1.00
PowerCons	0.98	0.73	0.99	1.00	0.92	0.99	0.98
ProximalPhalanxOutlineAgeGroup	0.84	0.83	0.85	0.86	0.85	0.85	0.86
ProximalPhalanxOutlineCorrect	0.84	0.84	0.85	0.86	0.90	0.91	0.91
ProximalPhalanxTW	0.75	0.75	0.76	0.80	0.81	0.82	0.82
RefrigerationDevices	0.35	0.35	0.37	0.53	0.53	0.48	0.50
Rock	0.88	0.94	0.84	0.66	0.90	0.80	0.86
ScreenType	0.44	0.40	0.39	0.42	0.49	0.47	0.57
SemgHandGenderCh2	0.85	0.76	0.82	0.85	0.92	0.90	0.96
SemgHandMovementCh2	0.50	0.39	0.50	0.50	0.62	0.71	0.78
SemgHandSubjectCh2	0.78	0.59	0.81	0.68	0.89	0.87	0.92
ShapeletSim	0.49	0.51	0.48	0.51	1.00	1.00	1.00
ShapesAll	0.50	0.11	0.63	0.73	0.91	0.92	0.93
SmallKitchenAppliances	0.54	0.35	0.41	0.71	0.81	0.82	0.82
SmoothSubspace	0.80	0.83	0.86	0.99	0.98	0.94	0.98
SonyAIBORobotSurface1	0.69	0.70	0.68	0.67	0.92	0.89	0.89
SonyAIBORobotSurface2	0.83	0.81	0.81	0.81	0.91	0.92	0.94
StarLightCurves	0.85	0.81	0.92	0.95	0.98	0.98	0.98
Strawberry	0.93	0.95	0.95	0.96	0.98	0.98	0.98
SwedishLeaf	0.66	0.72	0.83	0.87	0.97	0.97	0.98
Symbols	0.77	0.82	0.82	0.85	0.97	0.98	0.98
SyntheticControl	0.80	0.93	0.91	0.96	1.00	0.98	1.00
ToeSegmentation1	0.57	0.55	0.58	0.62	0.96	0.96	0.95
ToeSegmentation2	0.55	0.54	0.56	0.75	0.92	0.92	0.92
Trace	0.61	0.70	0.76	0.83	1.00	1.00	1.00
TwoLeadECG	0.94	0.89	0.95	0.73	1.00	1.00	1.00
TwoPatterns	0.79	0.84	0.84	0.83	1.00	1.00	1.00
UMD	0.82	0.79	0.84	0.95	0.99	0.99	0.99

(continued)

Table 10. (*continued*)

Name	RidgeCV	LDA	LogRegCV	RandomForest	Rocket	Minirocket	Multirocket
UWaveGestureLibraryAll	0.85	0.28	0.81	0.93	0.98	0.97	0.98
UWaveGestureLibraryX	0.63	0.51	0.63	0.76	0.86	0.85	0.87
UWaveGestureLibraryY	0.53	0.42	0.58	0.68	0.77	0.78	0.80
UWaveGestureLibraryZ	0.51	0.45	0.55	0.71	0.79	0.80	0.82
Wafer	0.94	0.94	0.94	0.99	1.00	1.00	1.00
Wine	0.83	0.91	0.89	0.78	0.81	0.83	0.89
WordSynonyms	0.38	0.23	0.46	0.55	0.75	0.76	0.78
Worms	0.38	0.42	0.34	0.55	0.74	0.75	0.75
WormsTwoClass	0.55	0.62	0.52	0.62	0.81	0.77	0.78
Yoga	0.65	0.59	0.67	0.81	0.91	0.91	0.92

Table 11. Computation time (in minutes) for univariate datasets.

Name	RidgeCV	LDA	LogReg	RandomForest	Rocket	Minirocket	Multirocket
ACSF1	0.03	0.04	0.29	0.19	0.83	0.12	0.26
Adiac	0.03	0.02	0.12	0.40	0.38	0.07	0.17
ArrowHead	0.01	0.01	0.03	0.11	0.14	0.02	0.07
Beef	0.01	0.01	0.05	0.10	0.08	0.02	0.04
BeetleFly	0.01	0.01	0.02	0.09	0.06	0.01	0.04
BirdChicken	0.01	0.01	0.04	0.09	0.06	0.02	0.04
BME	0.01	0.00	0.01	0.09	0.07	0.01	0.04
Car	0.01	0.01	0.06	0.11	0.19	0.04	0.09
CBF	0.01	0.00	0.01	0.09	0.31	0.05	0.18
Chinatown	0.01	0.00	0.01	0.09	0.03	0.01	0.03
ChlorineConcentration	0.02	0.02	0.04	0.40	1.85	0.28	1.08
CinCECGTorso	0.03	0.03	0.15	0.14	5.69	0.90	2.35
Coffee	0.01	0.01	0.02	0.09	0.04	0.02	0.03
Computers	0.03	0.05	0.04	0.28	0.87	0.21	0.37
CricketX	0.04	0.03	0.11	0.36	0.57	0.13	0.31
CricketY	0.03	0.03	0.11	0.34	0.57	0.15	0.31
CricketZ	0.03	0.03	0.13	0.37	0.57	0.13	0.31
Crop	0.08	0.05	0.53	2.98	4.23	1.86	5.57
DiatomSizeReduction	0.01	0.01	0.04	0.09	0.29	0.05	0.12
DistalPhalanxOutlineAgeGroup	0.01	0.01	0.03	0.18	0.13	0.04	0.09
DistalPhalanxOutlineCorrect	0.01	0.01	0.02	0.26	0.20	0.05	0.13
DistalPhalanxTW	0.01	0.01	0.03	0.18	0.12	0.04	0.08
Earthquakes	0.03	0.04	0.02	0.29	0.58	0.13	0.35
ECG200	0.01	0.01	0.01	0.11	0.05	0.02	0.04
ECG5000	0.02	0.02	0.05	0.26	1.66	0.32	0.83
ECGFiveDays	0.01	0.00	0.01	0.09	0.28	0.05	0.14
ElectricDevices	0.24	0.10	0.15	6.60	6.03	2.79	6.49
EOGHorizontalSignal	0.09	0.14	0.47	0.51	2.19	0.44	0.94
EOGVerticalSignal	0.06	0.14	0.44	0.53	2.18	0.42	0.95
EthanolLevel	0.16	0.30	0.41	0.86	4.29	0.81	1.66
FaceAll	0.02	0.02	0.13	0.40	0.69	0.13	0.36
FaceFour	0.02	0.01	0.04	0.11	0.10	0.02	0.06

(continued)

Table 11. (*continued*)

Name	RidgeCV	LDA	LogReg	RandomForest	Rocket	Minirocket	Multirocket
FacesUCR	0.02	0.01	0.06	0.20	0.67	0.14	0.34
FiftyWords	0.05	0.04	0.46	0.73	0.58	0.13	0.24
Fish	0.02	0.03	0.15	0.21	0.38	0.08	0.16
FordA	0.58	0.45	0.19	5.25	6.03	1.44	2.77
FordB	0.78	0.34	0.23	5.80	5.51	1.34	2.62
FreezerRegularTrain	0.02	0.03	0.02	0.16	2.03	0.34	0.98
FreezerSmallTrain	0.01	0.01	0.03	0.12	1.93	0.31	0.92
GunPoint	0.01	0.01	0.03	0.11	0.08	0.02	0.04
GunPointAgeSpan	0.01	0.01	0.02	0.13	0.16	0.03	0.08
GunPointMaleVersusFemale	0.01	0.01	0.01	0.12	0.16	0.03	0.08
GunPointOldVersusYoung	0.01	0.01	0.01	0.11	0.16	0.03	0.08
Ham	0.02	0.03	0.02	0.14	0.22	0.05	0.10
Haptics	0.03	0.05	0.14	0.24	1.17	0.21	0.44
Herring	0.02	0.02	0.03	0.13	0.16	0.03	0.07
HouseTwenty	0.04	0.06	0.07	0.14	0.74	0.13	0.35
InlineSkate	0.06	0.08	0.40	0.25	2.79	0.45	1.18
InsectEPGRegularTrain	0.02	0.02	0.03	0.11	0.43	0.07	0.21
InsectEPGSmallTrain	0.01	0.02	0.04	0.12	0.36	0.06	0.18
InsectWingbeatSound	0.03	0.02	0.09	0.23	1.26	0.21	0.48
ItalyPowerDemand	0.01	0.01	0.01	0.11	0.07	0.02	0.06
LargeKitchenAppliances	0.08	0.10	0.21	0.44	1.27	0.24	0.45
Lightning2	0.01	0.02	0.03	0.12	0.18	0.04	0.10
Lightning7	0.02	0.01	0.05	0.14	0.11	0.02	0.06
Mallat	0.03	0.04	0.15	0.17	5.47	0.94	1.77
Meat	0.01	0.01	0.04	0.11	0.13	0.03	0.06
MedicalImages	0.02	0.01	0.04	0.25	0.27	0.06	0.14
MiddlePhalanxOutlineAgeGroup	0.01	0.01	0.03	0.20	0.12	0.04	0.08
MiddlePhalanxOutlineCorrect	0.01	0.01	0.02	0.29	0.19	0.05	0.12
MiddlePhalanxTW	0.01	0.01	0.04	0.22	0.11	0.04	0.08
MixedShapes	0.11	0.17	0.24	0.67	6.73	1.20	2.49
MixedShapesSmallTrain	0.04	0.04	0.14	0.20	5.77	1.01	2.06
MoteStrain	0.01	0.00	0.01	0.11	0.24	0.05	0.13
OliveOil	0.03	0.01	0.06	0.11	0.09	0.03	0.04
OSULeaf	0.06	0.03	0.16	0.22	0.44	0.09	0.19
PhalangesOutlinesCorrect	0.04	0.02	0.03	0.97	0.56	0.19	0.37
Phoneme	0.05	0.08	0.93	0.77	4.86	0.93	1.98
PigAirwayPressure	0.08	0.08	1.96	0.63	1.43	0.27	0.61
PigArtPressure	0.07	0.08	2.12	0.60	1.43	0.27	0.54
PigCVP	0.06	0.08	1.98	0.62	1.44	0.30	0.62
Plane	0.01	0.01	0.03	0.13	0.08	0.02	0.04
PowerCons	0.02	0.01	0.01	0.13	0.13	0.03	0.07
ProximalPhalanxOutlineAgeGroup	0.01	0.01	0.03	0.19	0.13	0.05	0.08
ProximalPhalanxOutlineCorrect	0.01	0.01	0.02	0.28	0.18	0.05	0.12
ProximalPhalanxTW	0.01	0.01	0.03	0.20	0.13	0.03	0.08
RefrigerationDevices	0.05	0.09	0.08	0.44	1.26	0.27	0.59
Rock	0.05	0.05	0.35	0.14	0.46	0.10	0.19
ScreenType	0.09	0.08	0.13	0.43	1.25	0.30	0.49
SemgHandGenderCh2	0.06	0.12	0.13	0.42	3.09	0.68	1.57
SemgHandMovementCh2	0.11	0.20	0.33	0.77	3.14	0.78	1.63
SemgHandSubjectCh2	0.14	0.19	0.29	0.72	3.13	0.79	1.62

(*continued*)

Table 11. (*continued*)

Name	RidgeCV	LDA	LogReg	RandomForest	Rocket	Minirocket	Multirocket
ShapeletSim	0.01	0.01	0.01	0.11	0.23	0.05	0.13
ShapesAll	0.16	0.13	0.86	1.71	1.42	0.34	0.60
SmallKitchenAppliances	0.05	0.08	0.10	0.40	1.25	0.29	0.46
SmoothSubspace	0.01	0.01	0.01	0.11	0.02	0.01	0.02
SonyAIBORobotSurface1	0.01	0.00	0.01	0.10	0.10	0.03	0.06
SonyAIBORobotSurface2	0.01	0.00	0.01	0.10	0.15	0.04	0.09
StarLightCurves	0.39	0.56	0.35	1.04	21.16	4.04	6.29
Strawberry	0.04	0.03	0.04	0.34	0.55	0.14	0.25
SwedishLeaf	0.02	0.02	0.09	0.34	0.35	0.09	0.18
Symbols	0.01	0.01	0.05	0.11	0.90	0.20	0.34
SyntheticControl	0.01	0.01	0.03	0.17	0.09	0.03	0.07
ToeSegmentation1	0.01	0.01	0.02	0.11	0.17	0.04	0.08
ToeSegmentation2	0.01	0.01	0.02	0.11	0.13	0.03	0.07
Trace	0.01	0.01	0.04	0.13	0.13	0.04	0.08
TwoLeadECG	0.01	0.01	0.01	0.10	0.22	0.05	0.11
TwoPatterns	0.05	0.03	0.05	0.69	1.46	0.33	0.84
UMD	0.01	0.01	0.02	0.11	0.07	0.02	0.04
UWaveGestureLibraryAll	0.38	0.34	0.42	1.13	9.54	1.97	3.71
UWaveGestureLibraryX	0.10	0.08	0.13	0.79	3.17	0.70	1.19
UWaveGestureLibraryY	0.08	0.06	0.17	0.83	3.18	0.69	1.21
UWaveGestureLibraryZ	0.13	0.06	0.13	0.82	3.15	0.63	1.20
Wafer	0.03	0.03	0.03	0.66	2.44	0.48	1.18
Wine	0.01	0.01	0.02	0.11	0.07	0.02	0.04
WordSynonyms	0.02	0.02	0.18	0.33	0.56	0.12	0.22
Worms	0.03	0.05	0.14	0.27	0.55	0.13	0.25
WormsTwoClass	0.03	0.05	0.06	0.24	0.55	0.13	0.25
Yoga	0.03	0.04	0.06	0.31	3.10	0.55	1.18
Sum	5.88	5.75	18.38	53.16	158.77	34.56	73.47

Table 12. Computation time (in minutes) for multivariate datasets.

Dataset	RidgeCV	RandomForest	LogRegCV	LDA
DuckDuckGeese	0.18	0.18	0.18	0.16
PEMS-SF	0.87	0.99	0.84	0.58
FaceDetection	0.57	0.61	0.65	0.57
MotorImagery	0.47	0.50	0.47	0.52
cre Heartbeat	0.65	0.72	0.67	0.72
cre FingerMovements	0.58	0.49	0.59	0.56
NATOPS	0.73	0.78	0.74	0.76
PhonemeSpectra	0.05	0.09	0.05	0.04
HandMovementDirection	0.54	0.47	0.58	0.49
ArticularyWordRecognition	0.87	0.98	0.97	0.97
SelfRegulationSCP2	0.43	0.47	0.44	0.46
BasicMotions	0.63	0.73	0.63	0.35
Cricket	0.82	0.89	0.92	0.93
EigenWorms	0.50	0.52	0.53	0.44
LSST	0.30	0.51	0.25	0.26
RacketSports	0.72	0.85	0.76	0.55
SelfRegulationSCP1	0.73	0.82	0.77	0.73
ERing	0.95	0.95	0.96	0.88
StandWalkJump	0.60	0.47	0.53	0.20
Epilepsy	0.31	0.47	0.33	0.33
EthanolConcentration	0.48	0.43	0.65	0.81
Handwriting	0.17	0.20	0.24	0.15
UWaveGestureLibrary	0.67	0.84	0.78	0.53
AtrialFibrillation	0.33	0.33	0.40	0.20
Libras	0.52	0.74	0.63	0.51

References

1. Sakoe, H., Chiba, S.: Dynamic programming algorithm optimization for spoken word recognition. IEEE Trans. Acoust. Speech Signal Process. **26**(1), 43–49 (1978)
2. Fawaz, H.I., et al.: Inceptiontime: finding alexnet for time series classification. Data Min. Knowl. Disc. **34**(6), 1936–1962 (2020)
3. Zeng, A., Chen, M., Zhang, L., Xu, Q.: Are transformers effective for time series forecasting? (2023)
4. Frizzarin, M., et al.: Classification of cow diet based on milk mid infrared spectra: a data analysis competition at the "international workshop on spectroscopy and chemometrics 2022". Chemometr. Intell. Lab. Syst. **234**, 104755 (2023)
5. Dempster, A., Petitjean, F., Webb, G.I.: ROCKET: exceptionally fast and accurate time series classification using random convolutional kernels. Data Min. Knowl. Disc. **34**(5), 1454–1495 (2020)

6. Tan, C.W., Dempster, A., Bergmeir, C., Webb, G.I.: MultiRocket: multiple pooling operators and transformations for fast and effective time series classification. Data Min. Knowl. Disc. **36**(5), 1623–1646 (2022)

7. Dempster, A., Schmidt, D.F., Webb, G.I.: Minirocket: a very fast (almost) deterministic transform for time series classification. In: Proceedings of the 27th ACM SIGKDD Conference on Knowledge Discovery & Data Mining, pp. 248–257 (2021)

8. Dempster, A., Schmidt, D.F., Webb, G.I.: Hydra: competing convolutional kernels for fast and accurate time series classification. Data Min. Knowl. Disc. (2023)

9. Middlehurst, M., Large, J., Flynn, M., Lines, J., Bostrom, A., Bagnall, A.: HIVE-COTE 2.0: a new meta ensemble for time series classification. Mach. Learn. **110**(11), 3211–3243 (2021)

10. Middlehurst, M., Large, J., Cawley, G., Bagnall, A.: The temporal dictionary ensemble (TDE) classifier for time series classification. In: Hutter, F., Kersting, K., Lijffijt, J., Valera, I. (eds.) ECML PKDD 2020. LNCS (LNAI), vol. 12457, pp. 660–676. Springer, Cham (2021). https://doi.org/10.1007/978-3-030-67658-2_38

11. Schäfer, P., Leser, U.: Weasel 2.0 - a random dilated dictionary transform for fast, accurate and memory constrained time series classification (2023)

12. Nguyen, T.L., Ifrim, G.: Fast time series classification with random symbolic subsequences. In: Guyet, T., Ifrim, G., Malinowski, S., Bagnall, A., Shafer, P., Lemaire, V. (eds.) Advanced Analytics and Learning on Temporal Data: 7th ECML PKDD Workshop, AALTD 2022, Grenoble, France, 19–23 September 2022, Revised Selected Papers, pp. 50–65. Springer, Heidelberg (2023). https://doi.org/10.1007/978-3-031-24378-3_4

13. Guillaume, A., Vrain, C., Elloumi, W.: Random dilated shapelet transform: a new approach for time series shapelets. In: El Yacoubi, M., Granger, E., Yuen, P.C., Pal, U., Vincent, N. (eds.) Pattern Recognition and Artificial Intelligence, pp. 653–664. Springer, Cham (2022). https://doi.org/10.1007/978-3-031-09037-0_53

14. Schäfer, P., Leser, U.: Multivariate time series classification with weasel+ muse. arXiv preprint arXiv:1711.11343 (2017)

15. Bagnall, A., Davis, L., Hills, J., Lines, J.: Transformation based ensembles for time series classification. In: Proceedings of the 2012 SIAM International Conference on Data Mining, pp. 307–318. SIAM (2012)

16. Frizzarin, M., et al.: Mid infrared spectroscopy and milk quality traits: a data analysis competition at the "international workshop on spectroscopy and hemometrics 2021". Chemometr. Intell. Lab. Syst. **219**, 104442 (2021)

17. Dau, H.A., et al.: The UCR time series archive. IEEE/CAA J. Automatica Sinica **6**(6), 1293–1305 (2019)

18. Demšar, J.: Statistical comparisons of classifiers over multiple data sets. J. Mach. Learn. Res. **7**, 1–30 (2006)

19. Singh, A., et al.: Fast and robust video-based exercise classification via body pose tracking and scalable multivariate time series classifiers. Data Min. Knowl. Disc. **37**(2), 873–912 (2023)

20. Dhariyal, B., Le Nguyen, T., Ifrim, G.: Scalable classifier-agnostic channel selection for multivariate time series classification. Data Min. Knowl. Disc. **37**(2), 1010–1054 (2023)

21. Bagnall, A.J., Bostrom, A., Large, J., Lines, J.: The great time series classification bake off: an experimental evaluation of recently proposed algorithms. extended version. CoRR arxiv:1602.01711 (2016)

22. Ruiz, A.P., Flynn, M., Large, J., Middlehurst, M., Bagnall, A.J.: The great multivariate time series classification bake off: a review and experimental evaluation of recent algorithmic advances. Data Min. Knowl. Disc. **35**(2), 401–449 (2021)

Do Cows Have Fingerprints? Using Time Series Techniques and Milk Flow Profiles to Characterise Cow Milking Performance and Detect Health Issues

Changhong Jin[1,2](✉) ⓘ, John Upton[2,3] ⓘ, and Brian Mac Namee[1,2] ⓘ

[1] School of Computer Science, University College Dublin, Dublin, Ireland
changhong.jin@ucdconnect.ie
[2] VistaMilk SFI Research Centre, Teagasc Moorepark, Fermoy, Co. Cork, Ireland
[3] Animal and Grassland Research and Innovation Centre, Teagasc Moorepark, Fermoy, Co. Cork, Ireland

Abstract. On modern dairy farms technologies that are capable of measuring high frequency indicators (e.g. milk yield, milk flow-rates, and electrical conductivity) at every milking can play an important role in helping farmers manage animal health. The most modern dairy farms use milk meters that provide detailed, high-frequency data about the flow of milk during every milking (cows are typically milked twice daily). This forms a time series that we call a *milk flow profile*. As cows are milked twice per day, every day this data forms a series of time series collected in a relatively controlled way that offers detailed insights into cow milking performance and cow health. In this paper we show that milk flow profiles act as a finger print for cows in a herd and offer opportunities for extracting useful insights about cow health that are unexplored. We demonstrate that unsupervised time series clustering approaches, particularly those that utilize the shape of time series, can be used to characterize a herd and that supervised approaches applied to milk flow profiles can be used for automated mastitis detection. In the latter case it is interesting that approaches using standard machine learning methods applied to features extracted from milk flow profiles, out-perform approaches specifically designed for time series.

Keywords: precision agriculture · dairy farming · mastitis detection · time series classification

1 Introduction

Managing animal health protocols to ensure high-quality milk supply to dairies is a significant challenge facing dairy farms today. Modern precision dairy farming technology that is capable of measuring high frequency indicators (e.g. milk yield, milk flow-rates, and electrical conductivity) at every milking can play an important role in this. Automated detection of mastitis in dairy cows is one

G. Ifrim et al. (Eds.): AALTD 2023, LNAI 14343, pp. 230–242, 2023.
https://doi.org/10.1007/978-3-031-49896-1_15

of the best examples. Mastitis is a health problem afflicting dairy cows that causes inflamed and painful udders leading to reduced milk yield, and is the most economically damaging disease on modern dairy farms [34]. Automated mastitis detection systems based on the milk yield at each milking, data on the composition of the milk collected at each milking[1] [28], genetic data, the electrical conductivity of milk collected [20,32], and cow medical history data have all been described in the literature [6,30,38].

On farms that have installed more advanced sensing technology known as milk meters[2], detailed data about the flow of milk during every milking (cows are typically milked twice per day, once in the morning and once in the afternoon) has become available. Data relating to milk flow rates have been shown to be useful for a variety of health indications [15,16,40]. More detailed measurement of milk flow throughout milking allows a milk flow profile that shows the cumulative amount of milk that flows during milking to be constructed. Examples of milk flow profiles for the morning and afternoon milking of four different cows on a single day are shown in Fig. 1. Each curve shows the cumulative milk yield (measured in kilograms) over time (measured at intervals of 10 s) from each milking. Milk flow profiles offer a rich and currently unexplored time series data source for monitoring cow health, and are the subject of this paper.

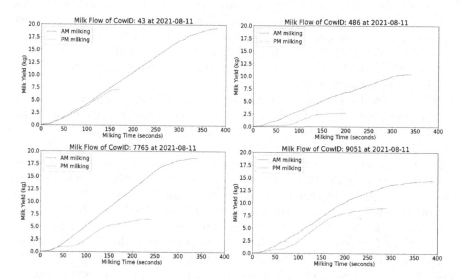

Fig. 1. Examples of milk flow profiles for the morning and afternoon milking of two different cows on a single day.

---

[1] This is typically known as milk recording data and includes information such as the percentage of fat and lactose contained in the milk.

[2] A milk meter is a device inserted into the milk pipeline that records the individual animal milk yield during milking.

In this paper we introduce milk flow profiles as a rich source of information about cow health and explore how they can be used to characterise cows in a herd—essentially providing a fingerprint for each animal. We also explore the use of milk flow profiles for the task of mastitis detection—this can be framed as a time series classification problem. Interestingly we find that distance based approaches—specifically 1-nearest neighbour classifiers using dynamic time warping—do not work well for this, while feature-based approaches give good results. The paper is organised as follows: Sect. 2 describes related work; Sect. 3 introduces milk flow profiles and illustrates how they can be used to profile a herd; Sect. 4 describes how milk flow profiles can be used for detecting mastitis (framed as a time series classification problem); and Sect. 5 concludes the paper and suggests directions for future work.

2   Related Work

Precision agriculture [39], or the application of data science to decision making on farms, has brought significant changes to how modern farms are managed. Farms now generate masses of data about crops, animals, inputs, outputs, and activities that can be stored and analysed to help farmers make better decisions. One of the most promising uses of data on farms is managing animal health [27]. Data describing animal bio-metrics and behaviours can aid farmers in better identifying and managing health problems, especially on larger farms. On modern dairy farms mastitis is the most significant udder health issue on modern dairy farms, and there are good examples of data-driven approaches to detecting and managing mastitis in the literature.

The mastitis detection problem can be framed in different ways. Some studies, for example [7,29], build models that detect both clinical mastitis and subclinical mastitis; while others, for example [9,19], focus only on one of these. Other studies, like [2,37], do not address mastitis directly but instead attempt to predict values for cows that are expensive to measure, in particular Somatic Cell Count (SCC) which requires sending samples to a lab for analysis, for cows based other more easily available data. Other studies, for instance [10,33], do not attempt to build prediction models but instead investigate factors that are good indicators of mastitis and which may be useful in building prediction models.

Analysis of time series in machine learning is a well studied area with applications in agriculture widely studied [1,12,18,21]. While milk flow profiles themselves have not been studied widely before, there are other time series that are similar—for example undersea valves in oil and gas mining [3]. The remainder of this paper explores how milk flow profiles can be used to understand cow behaviours and to predict cow health issues.

3   Milk Flow Profiles

A milk flow profile captures detailed data about the cumulative milk yield harvested during milking. A milk meter installed in the milking machine measures the yield (kilograms) at regular intervals (typically every 10 s)—the average cow milking takes between 5 and 7 min. Figure 2a shows examples of milk flow profiles from the same cow on her morning milkings on multiple days, referred to as the *internal milk flow distance* (IMFD). Figure 2b shows flow profiles from morning milkings for all cows in the herd for a single milking day, referred to as *external milk flow distance* (EMFD).

These images clearly show the way that the milk flow profile can act as a finger print for a cow. All of the milk flow profiles for the single cow in Fig. 2a show a similar pattern with a very tight distribution—the milk flow profile for each milking is essentially the same. On the other hand the milk flow profiles in Fig. 2b have much higher variation with quite different patterns evident.

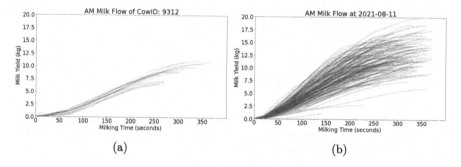

Fig. 2. A comparison of milk flow profiles for (a) all morning milking for one cow over the 4 month study period (IMFD) and (b) morning milkings for all cows in the herd for one single day (EMFD).

To formally measure this difference we calculate the distance, using dynamic time warping [26], between the milk flow profiles for all cows on a single day, EMFD, (shown in Fig. 2a) and all milkings of a single cow in the dataset (shown in Fig. 2b). Figure 3 compares the distributions of these distances. A permutation test [14] yields a p-value of 0.0007 indicating a statistically significant difference. It is clear that the distances between milk flow profiles for the single cow are much smaller than those calculated across the herd. Moreover, the permutation test provides evidence supporting the notion that the two groups exhibit statistically distinct distributions.

Although normal milk flow profiles are characterised by a common upward sloping curve, as milk yield increases with milking time, different cows can have dramatically different milk flow profiles. One cow may complete the entire milking process in a short time, resulting in a milk curve with a steep gradient, while another cow may take a long time to complete its milking and the corresponding milk curve would be relatively flat. It could even be the case that in both instances the peak flow rates are the same. Not only does milk flow profile data provide greater detail about individual milking events of each cow, but changes in a cow's milk flow profiles could also help in the diagnosis of health problems such as mastitis.

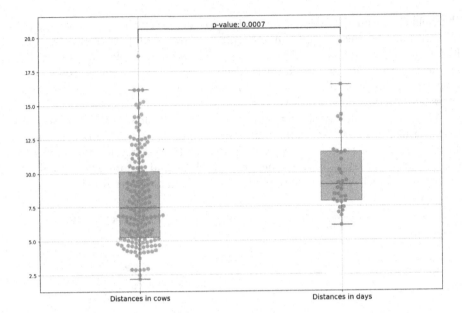

Fig. 3. Box plots showing the distribution of distances between all milk flow profiles from a single cow across the full dataset (IMFD) and distances between milk flow profiles of all cows in a herd on a single day (EMFD).

To further explore the use of milk flow profiles as a finger print for different cows we use a dataset collected from milking equipment and laboratory analysis at Teagasc Dairy Research Centre at Moorepark, Ireland[3]. The milking parlour software was modified to record the milk flow-rate from each cow at every milking at 10 s intervals. Cows were managed in a pasture-based system and were milked twice per day, once in the morning and once in the afternoon.

The dataset covered 9 months from March 2021 to November 2021 and included 18,662 milk flow profiles at SCC measurement days from 293 dairy cows[4]. The cows were electronically identified on entering the milking parlor and data from each milking session was linked to a specific cow. Cumulative milk yield, and conductivity were collected simultaneously as milking began, and then recorded at 10 s intervals until the end of the milking. A sample of

---

[3] A midi-line 30 unit Dairymaster herringbone, swing-over milking system (Dairymaster, Ireland) was used to milk the cows twice per day. The milking system utilised simultaneous pulsation and was fitted with automatic cluster removers and weigh-all milk meters (Dairymaster, Ireland). The standard farm milk flow rate switch-point of the automatic cluster removers was 0.2 kg/min.

[4] The majority of cows were from the Holstein-Friesian breed. 92 of the cows were at parity of 1 (meaning they had given birth to just one calf, or were primiparous) and the remaining 201 were at parity of 2 or greater (meaning they had given birth to just one calf, or were multiparous).

milk was also taken from each cow on one occasion per week for composition and somatic cell count (SCC) analysis[5].

To explore the different groups that exist within the dataset based on the milk flow profiles we performed a series of clustering exercises. Figure 4 shows the clusters found using k-means clustering with $k = 8$ (we experimented with different values and found that 8 clusters gave a good mix between achieving a high silhouette score and usefulness determined by domain experts) compared to other and dynamic time warping as the distance measure. In each case the blue lines represent the milk flow profile for a single milking and the red lines show the average milk flow profile for a cluster.

Examining the different clusters we see interesting sub-groups within the herd emerge. Clusters 0, 4, and 6 illustrate an almost linear milk profile where the rate of milking remains largely constant throughout milking indicating a relatively consistent flow of milk from the udder during the period of milking unit attachment. Clusters 1 and 3 show a pronounced curve illustrating rapid let down of milk fallowed by a relatively high and sustained peak milk flow period. These curves then tail off to an elongated low flow period, this typically indicates that one quarter of the udder is still producing milk at a low level until the milking unit is removed. Clusters 2 and 5 sit somewhere between these two, for example they have an identifiable peak milk flow period followed by an elongated low flow tail. Cluster 7 is a typical *other* cluster, and contains a broad spread of milk flow curve types that did not fit well with clusters 0 to 6.

The value of using milk flow profiles for this clustering, is illustrated by the scatter plots shown in Fig. 5. Figure 5a shows a scatter plot of the dataset used for clustering where the vertical axis shows total milk yielded from the milking and the horizontal axis shows total time taken for milking. The colours of the points indicate cluster membership for clustering performed using non-standardised data and Euclidean distance. It is clear from this that clustering using the milk profile in a non-standardised format and Euclidean distance captures no more information from the milk flow profiles than clustering simply using total yield and total milking time. Essentially we can see that cluster membership is determined by milk yield and milking time by the colour bands showing that each cluster is clearly separated from the others in this scatter plot.

In Fig. 5b showing the same plot after clustering using standardised data and DTW distance, however, we see no distinction between cluster memberships showing that the milk flow profiles provide distinctions between cows and milkings beyond what is evident from simply looking at total yield and milking time.

---

[5] Milk composition analysis, often know as milk recording, is used to analyse the content of milk. Typically the percentage of fat, protein, and lactose in the milk is measured as well as the amount of casein and urea (both important in cheese making) present. The number of somatic cells, usually white blood cells, is also measured and typically referred to as somatic cell count (SCC). SCC is the most used and studied indicator in mastitis detection research, especially for sub-clinical mastitis detection [36]. A Fossomatic machine (Foss, Denmark) was used to measure SCC and other indicators of milk composition.

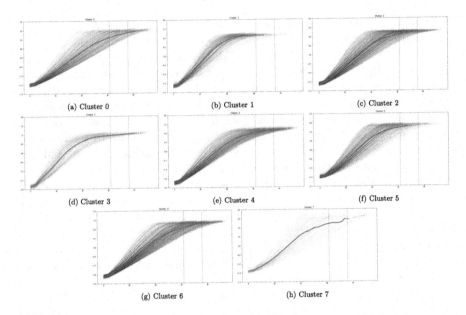

(a) Cluster 0   (b) Cluster 1   (c) Cluster 2

(d) Cluster 3   (e) Cluster 4   (f) Cluster 5

(g) Cluster 6   (h) Cluster 7

Fig. 4. The results of clustering the milk flow profiles in the dataset into 8 clusters using k-means clustering based on DTW distances. The blue lines show milk flow profiles and the red lines show the average for each cluster. (Color figure online)

This is a compelling illustration of the value of milk flow profiles. In the next section we explore how these profiles can be used to predict health problems in cows.

4   Using Milk Flow Profiles for Mastitis Detection

Mastitis is recognised as the most significant health problem on modern dairy farms [34]. Elevated levels of SCC are recognised as indicating sub-clinical mastitis—the early stages of mastitis, before symptoms (such as inflamed udders or clots in milk) are visible [13].

Detecting the onset of sub-clinical mastitis gives farmers the opportunity to intervene before cows progress to clinical mastitis or an infection spreads further to other cows in the herd. Although high SCC recordings are considered a reliable indicator of sub-clinical mastitis [36], recording SCC is a time-intensive process, typically only performed once per month on dairy farms. For this reason automated detection of sub-clinical mastitis using machine learning methods applied to data more routinely available from milking machines are attractive and have been widely studied (e.g. [2,28]). However, milk flow profiles have not been widely used for this before. In this section we describe an experiment to use time series classification techniques to classify milk flow profiles as belonging to days on which a cow had a high SCC value, and so likely sub-clinical mastitis, versus days when they did not. This illustrates the value of the milk flow profile time series as an indicator of cow health.

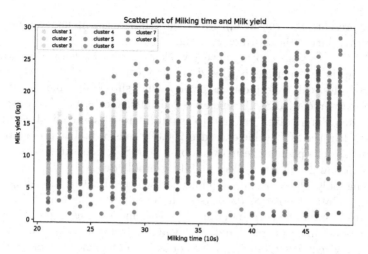

(a) Non-standardised data Euclidean distances

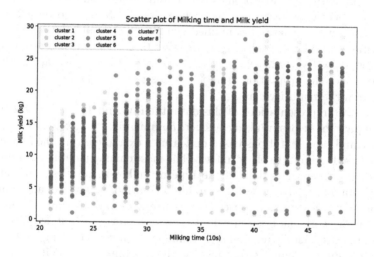

(b) Standardised data DTW distances

Fig. 5. Scatter plots of milk yield versus milking time for the cow dataset with points coloured based on cluster membership for (a) clusters found using non-standardised data and Euclidean distance, and (b) standardised data and DTW distance. (Color figure online)

4.1   Dataset

The dataset described in Sect. 3 was used in this study. This includes milk flow profiles for morning and afternoon milkings for each cow in the herd, and details of weekly laboratory testing of each cows' milk characteristics (including the percentage of fat, protein, and lactose in the milk, as well as the amount of casein and urea present, and the SCC). Milk characteristic sampling was performed every 7 days, during the morning milking.

The SCC recordings captured every week were used to define the target feature used in these experiments. Based on the recommendation of [17], for cows having their first calf (referred to as primiparous) sub-clinical mastitis was indicated when the recorded SCC value exceeded 150,000 cells/mL. For cows having their second or later calves (referred to as multiparous) sub-clinical mastitis was indicated when the SCC value exceeded 250,000 cells/mL. The prediction problem then was to replicate the information in the SCC measurements using the much cheaper and easier to collect milk flow profile data.

Keeping only the morning milkings for which an SCC recording existed results in a dataset with 8,703 rows each containing a milk flow profile and an SCC reading for the corresponding day. To remove outliers, records containing values exceeding $\pm$ three standard deviations from the mean were removed. Similarly, any records containing values outside the technical parameters of the data collection devices were removed (e.g. SCC values above 10 million cells/ml). Also, records with milk flow profiles not starting from 0 and negative values for milk characteristics were treated as outliers. These steps removed 5.2% of the original dataset. The dataset contained significant class-imbalance, with many more instances where the sub-clinical mastitis target feature was negative than when it was positive (7225 versus 1478). Under-sampling was applied in this study to reduce the proportion of majority classes by randomly removing observations from the majority class.

We use two representations of this data: the raw milk flow profiles which are used as inputs to the best ranked classifiers for univariate time series classification problems, and representations based on features extracted from the flow profiles which are used as input to other models. The most common method of extracting features from time series data of the type of milk flow profiles is to calculate summary statistics, such as mean, standard deviation, maximum, and minimum from the values in the time series. The features extracted from the milk flow profiles in this work can be grouped into three categories[6]. First, statistical time domain features such as maximum and minimum values, and lengths. Secondly, univariate temporal features that provide the dynamics of the milk flow profile, for example, auto-correlation, entropy, and total energy. Finally, spectral time-frequency features, representing changes in the frequency domain over time. In our experiments we also use the Catch-22 feature set [23], a small set of derived features shown to be effective for time series classification problems.

4.2 Experimental Setup

In this section we describe the setup of experiments to evaluate the effectiveness of using milk flow profiles to predict the presence of sub-clinical mastitis. First

---

[6] All features were extracted from flow profile data using the tsfresh package in Python [5].

we describe the models used, the experimental methodology, and finally the performance measures employed.

To demonstrate the ability of machine learning methods based on raw time series representations and representations based on features extracted from time series data, we use four machine learning algorithms in our experiments: 1-*nearest neighbor* using *dynamic time warping* as a distance measure (1NN-DTW) [4,26,35,41], *random convolutional kernel transform* (ROCKET) [8], *the hierarchical vote collective of transformation-based ensembles* (HIVE-COTE 2.0) [24] and *gradient boosting machines* (GBMs) [11] that use a combination of many weak learning models to create a strong predictive model.

To evaluate the performance of each model type for the mastitis detection problem we perform a 5-fold cross-validation. For each machine learning algorithm we evaluate performance on the original dataset and on an under sampled version (under-sampling is only applied to the training partition for each experiment). Accuracy fails to effectively represent model performance for imbalanced data sets. For this reason, the area under the receiver operating characteristic curve (AUC) [22] is more appropriate.

4.3   Results and Discussion

Table 1 shows the results of experiments completed. The AUC scores show that it is possible to train effective mastitis prediction models using milk flow profiles as input. The AUC scores shown are in line with similar results in the literature based on other data type inputs. It is particularly interesting to note that the feature based approaches were more effective than the approaches based on raw time series representations. This is contradictory to other benchmark results which typically indicate the success of ROCKET and HIVE-COTE 2.0 [25,31]. It is also interesting to note that the models trained using the larger feature set are more effective than those trained on the set of Catch-22 features.

Table 1. Experimental results for model comparison.

Modelling	AUC Score
1NN-DTW	0.513
ROCKET	0.607
HIVE-COTE 2.0	0.622
GBM with Catch-22	0.659
GBM with tsfresh	**0.677**

5   Conclusions and Future Work

This paper has introduced milk flow profiles. These are enabled by the use of milk meters in modern dairy parlours and allow the use of time series techniques for analysis. We have shown how the milk profiles themselves can be used as a cow finger-print offering insights into cow milking performance and cow health. Clustering techniques show how a herd can be partitioned according to these profiles. We also demonstrate that milk flow profiles can be used for predicting health problems faced by cows, in this case sub-clinical mastitis (one of the most significant health issues faced on dairy farms).

This work introduces this new data representation and in the future we intend developing this work to build better health prediction models by integrating milk flow profiles with other data sources. We also intend to take advantage of the interpretable nature of milk flow profiles to build explainable prediction models.

Acknowledgements. This publication has emanated from research conducted with the financial support of Science Foundation Ireland (SFI) and the Department of Agriculture, Food and Marine on behalf of the Government of Ireland under Grant Number [16/RC/3835]. Further financial and technical support was provided by Dairymaster.

References

1. Abdoli, A., Murillo, A.C., Yeh, C.C.M., Gerry, A.C., Keogh, E.J.: Time series classification to improve poultry welfare. In: 2018 17TH IEEE International Conference on Machine Learning and Applications (ICMLA), pp. 635–642. IEEE (2018)
2. Anglart, D., Hallén-Sandgren, C., Emanuelson, U., Rönnegård, L.: Comparison of methods for predicting cow composite somatic cell counts. J. Dairy Sci. **103**(9), 8433–8442 (2020)
3. Atif Qureshi, M., Miralles-Pechuán, L., Payne, J., O'Malley, R., Namee, B.M.: Valve health identification using sensors and machine learning methods. In: Gama, J., et al. (eds.) ITEM/IoT Streams -2020. CCIS, vol. 1325, pp. 45–60. Springer, Cham (2020). https://doi.org/10.1007/978-3-030-66770-2_4
4. Berndt, D.J., Clifford, J.: Using dynamic time warping to find patterns in time series. In: KDD Workshop, Seattle, WA, USA, vol. 10, pp. 359–370 (1994)
5. Christ, M., Braun, N., Neuffer, J., Kempa-Liehr, A.W.: Time series feature extraction on basis of scalable hypothesis tests (tsfresh-a Python package). Neurocomputing **307**, 72–77 (2018)
6. Cogato, A., Brščić, M., Guo, H., Marinello, F., Pezzuolo, A.: Challenges and tendencies of automatic milking systems (AMS): a 20-years systematic review of literature and patents. Animals **11**(2), 356 (2021)
7. De Mol, R., Kroeze, G., Achten, J., Maatje, K., Rossing, W.: Results of a multivariate approach to automated oestrus and mastitis detection. Livest. Prod. Sci. **48**(3), 219–227 (1997)
8. Dempster, A., Petitjean, F., Webb, G.I.: Rocket: exceptionally fast and accurate time series classification using random convolutional kernels. Data Min. Knowl. Disc. **34**(5), 1454–1495 (2020)
9. Ebrahimi, M., Mohammadi-Dehcheshmeh, M., Ebrahimie, E., Petrovski, K.R.: Comprehensive analysis of machine learning models for prediction of sub-clinical mastitis: deep learning and gradient-boosted trees outperform other models. Comput. Biol. Med. **114**, 103456 (2019)
10. Ebrahimie, E., Ebrahimi, F., Ebrahimi, M., Tomlinson, S., Petrovski, K.R.: A large-scale study of indicators of sub-clinical mastitis in dairy cattle by attribute

weighting analysis of milk composition features: highlighting the predictive power of lactose and electrical conductivity. J. Dairy Res. **85**(2), 193–200 (2018)

11. Friedman, J.H.: Greedy function approximation: a gradient boosting machine. Ann. Stat. **29**, 1189–1232 (2001)

12. Frizzarin, M., et al.: Classification of cow diet based on milk Mid Infrared Spectra: a data analysis competition at the "International Workshop on Spectroscopy and Chemometrics 2022". Chemometr. Intell. Lab. Syst. **234**, 104755 (2023)

13. Frössling, J., Ohlson, A., Hallén-Sandgren, C.: Incidence and duration of increased somatic cell count in Swedish dairy cows and associations with milking system type. J. Dairy Sci. **100**(9), 7368–7378 (2017)

14. Good, P.: Permutation Tests: A Practical Guide to Resampling Methods for Testing Hypotheses. Springer Science & Business Media, New York (2013). https://doi.org/10.1007/978-1-4757-2346-5

15. Grindal, R.J., Hillerton, J.E.: Influence of milk flow rate on new intramammary infection in dairy cows. J. Dairy Res. **58**(3), 263–268 (1991)

16. Japertiene, R., Juozaitiene, V., Kriauziene, J., Rudejeviene, J., Japertas, S.: The interrelationships between milkability traits and subclinical mastitis in cows. Pol. J. Vet. Sci. **10**(4), 255–261 (2007)

17. Jensen, D.B., van der Voort, M., Hogeveen, H.: Dynamic forecasting of individual cow milk yield in automatic milking systems. J. Dairy Sci. **101**(11), 10428–10439 (2018)

18. Kamilaris, A., Prenafeta-Boldú, F.X.: Deep learning in agriculture: a survey. Comput. Electron. Agric. **147**, 70–90 (2018)

19. Khatun, M., et al.: Development of a new clinical mastitis detection method for automatic milking systems. J. Dairy Sci. **101**(10), 9385–9395 (2018)

20. Khatun, M., et al.: Early detection of clinical mastitis from electrical conductivity data in an automatic milking system. Anim. Prod. Sci. **57**(7), 1226–1232 (2017)

21. Liu, G., Zhong, K., Li, H., Chen, T., Wang, Y.: A state of art review on time series forecasting with machine learning for environmental parameters in agricultural greenhouses. Inf. Process. Agric. (2022)

22. Lobo, J.M., Jiménez-Valverde, A., Real, R.: AUC: a misleading measure of the performance of predictive distribution models. Glob. Ecol. Biogeogr. **17**(2), 145–151 (2008)

23. Lubba, C.H., et al.: catch22: CAnonical Time-series CHaracteristics: selected through highly comparative time-series analysis. Data Min. Knowl. Disc. **33**(6), 1821–1852 (2019)

24. Middlehurst, M., et al.: HIVE-COTE 2.0: a new meta ensemble for time series classification. Mach. Learn. **110**(11–12), 3211–3243 (2021)

25. Middlehurst, M., Schäfer, P., Bagnall, A.: Bake off redux: a review and experimental evaluation of recent time series classification algorithms. arXiv preprint arXiv:2304.13029 (2023)

26. Müller, M.: Dynamic time warping. In: Information Retrieval for Music and Motion, pp. 69–84. Springer, Heidelberg (2007). https://doi.org/10.1007/978-3-540-74048-3_4

27. Neethirajan, S.: The role of sensors, big data and machine learning in modern animal farming. Sens. Bio-Sens. Res. **29**, 100367 (2020)

28. Pakrashi, A., et al.: Early detection of subclinical mastitis in lactating dairy cows using cow-level features. J. Dairy Sci. **106**(7), 4978–4990 (2023). https://doi.org/10.3168/jds.2022-22803, https://www.sciencedirect.com/science/article/pii/S0022030223002977

29. Panchal, I., Sawhney, I., Sharma, A., Dang, A.: Classification of healthy and mastitis Murrah buffaloes by application of neural network models using yield and milk quality parameters. Comput. Electron. Agric. **127**, 242–248 (2016)
30. Pyörälä, S.: Indicators of inflammation in the diagnosis of mastitis. Vet. Res. **34**(5), 565–578 (2003)
31. Ruiz, A.P., Flynn, M., Large, J., Middlehurst, M., Bagnall, A.: The great multivariate time series classification bake off: a review and experimental evaluation of recent algorithmic advances. Data Min. Knowl. Disc. **35**(2), 401–449 (2021)
32. Rutten, C.J., Velthuis, A., Steeneveld, W., Hogeveen, H.: Invited review: sensors to support health management on dairy farms. J. Dairy Sci. **96**(4), 1928–1952 (2013)
33. Santman-Berends, I., Riekerink, R.O., Sampimon, O., Van Schaik, G., Lam, T.: Incidence of subclinical mastitis in Dutch dairy heifers in the first 100 days in lactation and associated risk factors. J. Dairy Sci. **95**(5), 2476–2484 (2012)
34. Seegers, H., Fourichon, C., Beaudeau, F.: Production effects related to mastitis and mastitis economics in dairy cattle herds. Vet. Res. **34**(5), 475–491 (2003)
35. Senin, P.: Dynamic time warping algorithm review. Information and Computer Science Department University of Hawaii at Manoa Honolulu, USA, vol. 855, no. 1-23, p. 40 (2008)
36. Sharma, N., Singh, N., Bhadwal, M.: Relationship of somatic cell count and mastitis: an overview. Asian Australas. J. Anim. Sci. **24**(3), 429–438 (2011)
37. Sitkowska, B., Piwczynski, D., Aerts, J., Kolenda, M., Özkaya, S.: Detection of high levels of somatic cells in milk on farms equipped with an automatic milking system by decision trees technique. Turkish J. Vet. Anim. Sci. **41**(4), 532–540 (2017)
38. Slob, N., Catal, C., Kassahun, A.: Application of machine learning to improve dairy farm management: a systematic literature review. Prev. Vet. Med. **187**, 105237 (2021)
39. Stafford, J.V.: Implementing precision agriculture in the 21st century. J. Agric. Eng. Res. **76**(3), 267–275 (2000)
40. Upton, J., Penry, J., Rasmussen, M., Thompson, P., Reinemann, D.: Effect of pulsation rest phase duration on teat end congestion. J. Dairy Sci. **99**(5), 3958–3965 (2016)
41. Xi, X., Keogh, E., Shelton, C., Wei, L., Ratanamahatana, C.A.: Fast time series classification using numerosity reduction. In: Proceedings of the 23rd International Conference on Machine Learning, pp. 1033–1040 (2006)

Exploiting Context and Attention Using Recurrent Neural Network for Sensor Time Series Prediction

Rashmi Dutta Baruah[1,2]([✉]) [iD] and Mario Muñoz-Organero[1] [iD]

[1] Department of Telematic Engineering, Universidad Carlos III de Madrid,
Avda. de la Universidad, 30, Leganés, Madrid 28911, Spain
{rdutta,munozm}@it.uc3m.es
[2] Department of Computer Science and Engineering, Indian Institute of Technology
Guwahati, Guwahati 781039, Assam, India

Abstract. In the current era of Internet of Things, typically data from multiple sources are captured through various sensors yielding Multivariate Time Series (MTS) data. Sensor MTS prediction has several real-life applications in various domains such as healthcare, manufacturing, and agriculture. In this paper, we propose a novel Recurrent Neural Network (RNN) architecture that leverages contextual information and attention mechanism for sensor MTS prediction. We adopt the notion of primary and contextual features to distinguish between the features that are independently useful for learning irrespective of other features, and the features that are not useful in isolation. The contextual information is represented through the contextual features and when used with primary features can potentially improve the performance of the model. The proposed architecture uses the contextual features in two ways. Firstly, to weight the primary input features depending on the context, and secondly to weight the hidden states in the alignment model. The latter is used to compute the dependencies between hidden states (representations) to derive the attention vector. Further, integration of the context and attention allows visualising temporally and spatially the relevant parts of the input sequence which are influencing the prediction. To evaluate the proposed architecture, we used two benchmark datasets as they provide contextual information. The first is NASA Turbofan Engine Degradation Simulation dataset for estimating Remaining Useful Life, and the second is appliances energy prediction dataset. We compared the proposed approach with the state-of-the-art methods and observed improved prediction results, particularly with respect to the first dataset.

Keywords: Recurrent Neural Network · Gated Recurrent Unit · Context · Attention · Multivariate Sensor Time Series · Remaining Useful Life · Appliance energy prediction

This work is supported by CONEX-Plus programme funded by Universidad Carlos III de Madrid and the European Union's Horizon 2020 research and innovation programme under the Marie Sklodowska-Curie grant agreement No. 801538.

G. Ifrim et al. (Eds.): AALTD 2023, LNAI 14343, pp. 243–259, 2023.
https://doi.org/10.1007/978-3-031-49896-1_16

1   Introduction

The Internet of Things (IoT), driven by advanced sensors, computing and communication technologies, has enabled capturing data from various sources and utilise them to realise various 'smart' environments such as smart homes, smart cities, smart factories. The data captured through various sensors can be considered as Multivariate Time Series (MTS) [25]. Sensor MTS can be used for learning predictive models, thereby innovating various applications for such environments. These data rich environments often provide contextual information that can be leveraged while learning the predictive models to improve the performance [26]. For example, an automated fault detection and diagnosis agent for a HVAC system in a smart building can utilise the environmental factors such as indoor and outdoor temperature and humidity (contextual information) along with the current and voltage data from the HVAC system [11]. However, most of the machine learning algorithms do not explicitly take into account the available contextual information [13].

We adopt the definitions of *primary* and *contextual* features to distinguish between the features that are independently useful for learning irrespective of other features, and the features that are not useful in isolation [26]. The contextual data available in terms of contextual features may influence the performance by improving the model but may not be involved directly in learning. We also emphasize that the contextual data is available from the environment where primary data is captured and is a MTS itself. Over the past decade, Recurrent Neural Networks (RNNs) including Long Short-Term Memory (LSTM) and Gated Recurrent Units (GRU) have been widely used for sequential or time series data modeling. They are well known for capturing temporal contexts implicitly due to their internal memory. It is worth mentioning here that in this paper, the focus is not on the temporal context or the contexts that are generated within the network from input and/or output signals. Here, the focus is on *explicit* contexts, which is in the form of additional data available from the problem domains. The current RNN architectures do not explicitly exploit the contextual data. Recently, in [8,9], a context integrated RNN (CiRNN) which uses GRU as basic unit is proposed. CiRNN, takes both primary and contextual features as input. The contextual features are used to weight the primary features depending on the context such that the input to hidden layer weights are function of contextual features. With CiRNN, a significant improvement in performance is observed when compared to state-of-the-art methods for the task of remaining useful life prediction in machine prognostics.

On the other hand, recently, attention mechanism has received a great deal of attention mainly due to the work of Bahdanau et al. [1] in the area of neural machine translation (NMT). Typically, NMT models are based on encoder-decoder approach where the encoder is for the source language and the decoder is for the target language. For the source language encoder, usually RNNs are used where the necessary information of the source sentence is compressed in to a fixed length vector. For longer sentences, this conventional approach, gives poor performance. Attention mechanism allows to capture the information from all or few source positions in the encoder thereby alleviating the problem with conventional encoder-decoder approach.

In this paper, we propose a novel RNN architecture that exploits context and attention for sensor MTS prediction. The architecture primarily consists of CiRNN with attention layer and finally a fully connected (FCN) layer. In addition to CiRNN, attention layer uses the contextual features to weight the hidden sates of the alignment model [18]. The alignment model is used to compute the dependencies among the hidden states or representations to derive the attention vector. Further, adding contextual attention to CiRNN, provides interpretations at two levels. First, the input features weighted by the context indicates which of the features are relevant in a given context for prediction. Second, the attention weights show which parts of the time series, apart from the last time step, the network is attending to prior to the prediction.

To demonstrate the effectiveness of the proposed approach, it is applied to two benchmark datasets. The first task is in the domain of engine health prognostics where we considered the widely used NASA Turbofan Engine Degradation Simulation dataset (C-MAPSS dataset) for estimating RUL [21]. The dataset contains information from 21 sensors and 3 operational settings. The operational settings have a substantial effect on engine performance and represent the contextual information required for the proposed model. The second task is to predict household appliance energy usage where Appliances energy prediction (AEP) dataset from UCI repository is used [2]. The results of the proposed model is compared with baseline models and also state-of-the-art methods. The results show an improvement in performance in prediction results.

The rest of the paper is organised as follows. In the next section, we briefly present the related work. In Sect. 3, we discuss the architecture and learning in the proposed architecture. Section 4, first describes the datasets and then discusses the experiments and results. Finally, Sect. 5 concludes the paper.

2 Related Work

Considering the increase in amount and dimensionality of time series data, particularly data from ubiquitous sensors, deep learning methods have been applied to a great extent to extract features and to recognize complex latent patterns [10]. In this paper, we limit the scope of related work to prediction models that use RNNs and attention mechanism for MTS prediction. The work related to context integration to RNN is largely done in the area of natural language processing (NLP) domain and it has been discussed in [8,9].

In [5], three extensions of content attention [1] are provided that use the relative positions in input and output to capture the pseudo-periods in time series. Several experiments with MTS data showed that for multi-horizon forecasting the proposed approach is significantly better than RNN with attention and baseline methods based on ARIMA and Random Forests (RF). In [20], a dual-stage attention-based recurrent neural network (DA-RNN) is proposed which consists of an encoder with an input attention mechanism and a decoder with a temporal attention mechanism. It is tested for predicting indoor temperature and for predicting the index value of the NASDAQ 100 using stock dataset. A temporal pattern attention mechanism for multivariate time series is presented in [23]. The focus is on extracting relevant input features rather than time steps through attention. CNN filters are applied to the row vectors of RNN (encoder) hidden units before deriving the attention vector. They tested the approach with six MTS datasets that include various domains such as energy, music, traffic, and finance, and achieved good results. In [7], temporal attention-based encoder-decoder model is proposed for MTS multi-step forecasting tasks. It uses a Bidirectional-LSTM (Bi-LSTM) with attention mechanism to encode the hidden representations of MTS data as the temporal context vector. Another LSTM is used to decode the hidden representation for prediction. Experiments on five MTS datasets showed that the proposed model is effective in multi-step forecasting. Cheng et al. [3] proposed a model that uses dual stage attention with Bi-LSTM as encoder and LSTM decoder. The experimental results with MTS data related to energy and finance showed better performance for single step and multi-step prediction. However, for longer time steps, the prediction performance of the model reduces.

To summarise, the existing approaches discussed here leverage attention mechanism to deal with longer time sequences which LSTM or GRU alone is not able to handle. Also, the attention mechanism is tailored for MTS data such that relevant input features is taken into consideration while computing the attention vector. None of the previous studies, to the best of our knowledge, investigated the possibility of utilizing contextual information to weight the hidden states as well as the input features through CiRNN to realise a context sensitive attention based model for improving sensor MTS prediction.

3 Proposed Approach

In this section, we first present the overall framework and finally the details of each of the units is provided[1]

3.1 Proposed Framework

Figure 1 shows the proposed context sensitive attention-based RNN model for the prediction of sensor MTS. It consists of Context Integrated Gated Recurrent Units (CiGRU) [8] which have recurrent connections and takes the primary and contextual input. The learned sequential features (hidden states of CiGRU) are provided as input to the attention layer. The output of the attention layer is an attention vector ($\mathbf{a}_t$) which is computed using the temporal context vector (TCV). Note that, conventionally the TCV is referred to as *context vector*. Here, to make a distinction between temporal context and explicit context we are using the term TCV. The TCV ($\mathbf{c}_t$) is computed using the attention weights

---

[1] The code is available at https://github.com/rduttabaruah/CiRNN.

computed in the attention layer. The target hidden state (h_t) is concatenated with the TCV through a concatenation layer to produce the attention vector. Finally, the attention vector is passed as input to fully connected layers (FCLs) in the network to predict the target at time step $(t + 1)$.

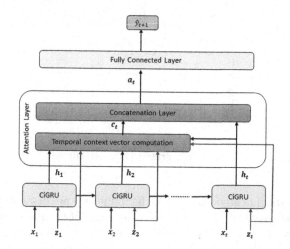

Fig. 1. Proposed framework with CiGRU and attention.

3.2   Context Integrated Gated Recurrent Unit

The RNN is composed of CiGRU units [8,9], which are fundamentally GRUs [4] with an additional context input. In CiGRU, the input to hidden unit connection weights are dependent on the context variables. Figure 2 shows the architecture of a single CiGRU. The output $(\hat{\mathbf{y}}_t \in \Re^{n_y \times 1})$ at time step t in CiGRU is computed in similar manner as in GRU. However, the candidate hidden state $(\tilde{\mathbf{h}}_t \in \Re^{n_h \times 1})$, update gate $(\mathbf{s}_t \in \Re^{n_h \times 1})$, and reset gate $(\mathbf{r}_t \in \Re^{n_h \times 1})$ values are determined based on context $\mathbf{z}_t$ as shown below:

$$\hat{\mathbf{y}}_t = f(\mathbf{V}\mathbf{h}_t + \mathbf{b}_y)$$
$$\mathbf{h}_t = \mathbf{s}_t \odot \mathbf{h}_{t-1} + (1 - \mathbf{s}_t) \odot \tilde{\mathbf{h}}_t$$
$$\tilde{\mathbf{h}}_t = tanh(\mathbf{W}^h(\mathbf{z}_t)\mathbf{x}_t + \mathbf{U}^h(\mathbf{r}_t \odot \mathbf{h}_{t-1})) \qquad (1)$$
$$\mathbf{s}_t = \sigma(\mathbf{W}^s(\mathbf{z}_t)\mathbf{x}_t + \mathbf{U}^s\mathbf{h}_{t-1})$$
$$\mathbf{r}_t = \sigma(\mathbf{W}^r(\mathbf{z}_t)\mathbf{x}_t + \mathbf{U}^r\mathbf{h}_{t-1})$$

where n_x, n_y, n_z, n_h are the input, output, context, and hidden unit dimensions, $\mathbf{h}_t \in \Re^{n_h \times 1}$ is the hidden unit activation at time step t, $\mathbf{U} \in \Re^{n_h \times n_h}$, $\mathbf{V} \in \Re^{n_y \times n_h}$, $\mathbf{W} \in \Re^{n_h \times n_x}$ are the parameter (weight) matrices, and $\mathbf{b}_y \in \Re^{n_y \times 1}$ is the bias vector.

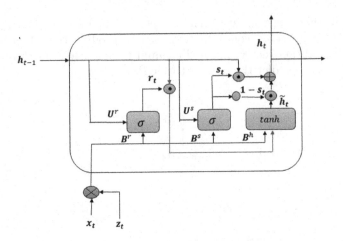

Fig. 2. A Context Integrated Gated Recurrent Unit.

In Eq. 1, the weights associated with the input $(\mathbf{x}_t)$ are dependent on the vector of contextual variables $(\mathbf{z}_t)$. Let us consider one of the parameters, $\mathbf{W}^h(\mathbf{z}_t)$. The parameters $\mathbf{W}^s(\mathbf{z}_t)$ and $\mathbf{W}^r(\mathbf{z}_t)$ can be expressed in a similar way. The matrix $\mathbf{W}^h(\mathbf{z}_t)$ is of dimension $n_h \times n_x$ and each of the components can be given as:

$$\mathbf{W}^h(\mathbf{z}_t) = \begin{bmatrix} w_{11}^h(\mathbf{z}_t) & w_{12}^h(\mathbf{z}_t) & \cdots & w_{1n_x}^h(\mathbf{z}_t) \\ w_{21}^h(\mathbf{z}_t) & w_{22}^h(\mathbf{z}_t) & \cdots & w_{2n_x}^h(\mathbf{z}_t) \\ \vdots & \vdots & \cdots & \vdots \\ w_{n_h1}^h(\mathbf{z}_t) & w_{n_h2}^h(\mathbf{z}_t) & \cdots & w_{n_hn_x}^h(\mathbf{z}_t) \end{bmatrix} \tag{2}$$

where each element of the matrix can be expressed as:

$$\begin{aligned} w_{ki}^h(\mathbf{z}_t) &= \mathbf{B}_{ki}^h \mathbf{G}(\mathbf{z}_t), \quad k = 1, .., n_h, \quad i = 1, .., n_x \\ \mathbf{B}_{ki}^h &= [b_{ki1}^h, b_{ki2}^h, \cdots, b_{kim}^h] \end{aligned} \tag{3}$$

where $\mathbf{G}(\mathbf{z}_t) = [g_1(\mathbf{z}_t), g_2(\mathbf{z}_t), ..., g_m(\mathbf{z}_t)]^T$ is a vector of basis functions that can be chosen at the time of design. $\mathbf{B}_{ki}^h$ is a vector of coefficients that specify the dependence of weights on context variables. We can define a matrix $\mathbf{B}^h$ where each row $\mathbf{B}_k^h$ can be formed by concatenating coefficient vectors $\mathbf{B}_{ki}^h$ as shown below. Therefore, $\mathbf{B}^h$ is of dimension $(n_h \times n_x m)$.

$$\mathbf{B}_k^h = [\mathbf{B}_{k1}^h, \mathbf{B}_{k2}^h, \cdots, \mathbf{B}_{kn_x}^h], \quad k = 1, 2, ..., n_h \tag{4}$$

Using $\mathbf{B}^h$ and similarly $\mathbf{B}^s$ and $\mathbf{B}^r$, the candidate hidden state $\tilde{\mathbf{h}}_t$, the update gate $\mathbf{s}_t$, and reset gate $\mathbf{r}_t$ in equation (1) can be expressed as:

$$\tilde{\mathbf{h}}_t = tanh[\mathbf{B}^h(\mathbf{x}_t \otimes \mathbf{G}(\mathbf{z}_t)) + \mathbf{U}^h(\mathbf{r}_t \odot \mathbf{h}_{t-1})]$$
$$\mathbf{s}_t = \sigma[\mathbf{B}^s(\mathbf{x}_t \otimes \mathbf{G}(\mathbf{z}_t)) + \mathbf{U}^s\mathbf{h}_{t-1}] \qquad (5)$$
$$\mathbf{r}_t = \sigma[\mathbf{B}^r(\mathbf{x}_t \otimes \mathbf{G}(\mathbf{z}_t)) + \mathbf{U}^r\mathbf{h}_{t-1}]$$

where the symbol $\otimes$ represents Kronecker product.

Learning of the vector of coefficients $\mathbf{B}^h_{ki}$ with m elements is similar to RNN. For RUL estimation, L2 loss function and back propagation through time (BPTT) is used. Finally, the parameters can be optimized using any suitable optimization algorithm such as stochastic gradient descent (SGD), Adam or RMSProp. The details are available in [9].

3.3 Attention Mechanism

The attention used here is global attention [18], at each time step t, the hidden states of CiGRU is used to compute the TCV ($\mathbf{c}_t$) which captures relevant information about the next target $\mathbf{y}_t$. The vector $\mathbf{c}_t$ is defined as:

$$\mathbf{c}_t = \sum_{i=1}^{t} \alpha_{ti}\mathbf{h}_i \qquad (6)$$

where α_{ti} is the attention weight. So, the context vector considers all the hidden states of the CiGRU weighted by attention weights. The attention weight is given as:

$$\alpha_{ti} = \frac{exp(f(\mathbf{h}_t, \mathbf{h}_i))}{\sum_{i=1}^{t} exp(f(\mathbf{h}_t, \mathbf{h}_i))} \qquad (7)$$

The function f is given by, $f(\mathbf{h}_t, \mathbf{h}_i) = \mathbf{h}_t^T \mathbf{W}^a(\mathbf{z}_t)\mathbf{h}_i$. Here, the weight matrix $\mathbf{W}^a \in \Re^{n_h \times n_h}$ depends on the context $\mathbf{Z}$. As discussed in Sect. 3.2, f can further be expressed as,

$$f(\mathbf{h}_t, \mathbf{h}_i) = \mathbf{h}_t^T[\mathbf{B}^a(\mathbf{h}_i \otimes \mathbf{G}(\mathbf{z}_t))] \qquad (8)$$

where $\mathbf{B}^a$ is of dimension $(n_h \times n_h m)$.

Finally, the TCV and the hidden state $\mathbf{h}_t$ is combined in the concatenation layer through a fully connected layer to get the attention vector as given by the following equation.

$$\mathbf{a}_t = tanh(\mathbf{W}^c[\mathbf{c}_t, \mathbf{h}_t]) \qquad (9)$$

4 Experiments and Results

In this section, we first describe the datasets, and then discuss the experiments and the results achieved with the proposed model. The results from the proposed model are compared with baseline models and also with the state-of-the-art methods.

4.1 Dataset Description

For evaluation of the proposed model, we considered two benchmark datasets where contextual information is available. The first dataset is the widely used, NASA Turbofan Engine Degradation Simulation Data Set (TEDS) [21]. The dataset is generated using Commercial Modular Aero-Propulsion System Simulation (C-MAPSS) tool. The dataset consists of four distinct datasets that contain information from 21 sensors (such as Total temperature at fan inlet, Total temperature at Low Pressure Compressor outlet), 3 operational settings (flight altitude, Mach number, and throttle resolver angle). In addition to these, engine identification number, and cycles of each engine is also available. We considered the dataset (FD002) which has six operating conditions. Due to the presence of different working conditions, it is suitable for the proposed model. The operating working conditions can be treated as contextual features while training the model. The dataset provides separate training and test sets. In the training set, the sensor data is captured until the system fails. Whereas in the test set it is captured up to a certain time prior to the failure. The test sets also provide true Remaining Useful Life (RUL) values. The FD002 dataset has 260 and 259 number of engines, 53759 and 33991 data samples in train and test set, respectively, and has one fault mode.

The second dataset is Appliance Energy Prediction (AEP) dataset [2]. The dataset comprises of measurements of house temperature and humidity with a 10 min interval for a period of 4.5 months. The indoor data was merged with weather data from the nearest airport weather station (Chievres Airport, Belgium) using date and time column. The weather data was retrieved from a public data set from Reliable Prognosis (rp5.ru). Two random variables are also included in the data set for testing the regression models and to filter out non-predictive attributes (parameters). It consists of 19735 data samples and 29 features including the random variables. The dataset has features like, energy use of light fixtures in the house, Temperature in kitchen area (T1), Humidity in kitchen area (RH_1), Appliances energy usage, and weather data such as outside temperature, humidity, pressure, wind speed etc.

4.2 Data Preprocessing

For TEDS dataset, the data from the 21 sensors are analysed. First, univariate and bivariate analyses are performed and the trend of sensor data is also analyzed. We selected 6 sensors $(s_1, s_2, s_8, s_{13}, s_{14}, s_{19})$ considering scatter plot observations and correlation analysis [8]. As the training data does not have the true RUL values, piece-wise degradation model [6,16] is used to get the values. With this degradation model, initially for a specific period, the RUL values remain constant and after that as the number of time cycles progress, the RUL values reduces linearly [12]. For our experiments, 125 is selected as the initial constant RUL based on existing works that have used C-MAPSS dataset. The data is normalized using min-max normalization and then it is clustered into

6 clusters based on operational regimes and then normalized again using cluster mean and range. Finally, the data is smoothed using moving average with window size of 3 while excluding the target. The target variable is RUL.

For AEP dataset, first the two random variables are removed and then the data is normalized using min-max normalization. The outside temperature, pressure, humidity, wind speed and hour of the day is considered as context variable and the remaining indoor variables are used as primary features. The target variable is Appliances energy usage.

4.3   Performance Metrics

The performance of the proposed model is measured using three metrics, RMSE (Root Mean Squared Error), MAE (Mean Absolute Error), and score from a asymmetric scoring function.

The scoring function is specific to the problem of RUL estimation and was proposed by by Saxena et al. [21]. The score metric given in equation (10) is formulated in such a way that late predictions (positive errors) draw more penalty compared to early predictions (negative errors). In either case, the penalty increases exponentially with error.

$$
score = \begin{cases} \sum_{i=1}^{n} e^{-\frac{d_i}{a_1}} - 1, & \text{if } d_i < 0 \\ \sum_{i=1}^{n} e^{\frac{d_i}{a_2}} - 1, & \text{if } d_i \geq 0 \end{cases} \tag{10}
$$

where $a_1 = 10$, $a_2 = 13$, and $d_i = R\hat{U}L_i - RUL_i$ is the difference between predicted RUL and actual RUL values, n is the number of samples in the test data .

4.4   Training and Validation

To train the models, a validation set is created from the available training dataset of TEDS. From each engine unit the last l samples, where l is multiple of sequence length, are kept for validation. Thus, the validation set consists of samples from each engine unit as in the test set. For the experiments, l is set to 2. The AEP dataset is split into 80% training and 20% testing and for another set of experiments it is divided as 75% training and 25% testing. From the training set, 10% data is used as validation set. This ratio is selected to compare the results with existing works. The following hyperparameters are used for tuning the model, number of hidden units (RNN): 15–30, step 5, number of hidden units (FCL): 5–30, step 5, sequence (window) length: {10, 15, 20}, learning rate: $loguniform(1e-5, 1e-3)$, oprimizer: SGD, Adam, RMSProp. The number of CiGRU layers is fixed to 1 and the batch size is set to 128. For the contextual inputs, polynomial basis functions of degree 2 are used. The proposed model is implemented using Python 3.10 with PyTorch 1.12 library in a Dell Precision 3650 workstation with Ubuntu 20.04 OS. The hyperparameters are optimized using Optuna with Tree-Structured Parzen Estimater sampler (TPESampler) and Median Pruner.

We considered two models as baseline to compare with the proposed model, for which we use the acronym as CiGRU + CxA (CiGRU with contextual attention). The first baseline model is RNN with GRUs, and the second is RNN with CiGRU and attention (CiGRU + A). All the models are trained with primary as well as contextual features, however, in the first model (GRU) contextual features are concatenated with primary features. The latter way of using contextual features with primary features is also referred to as contextual expansion [26]. The models and the best hyperparameter values achieved after tuning the models using TEDS (FD002) dataset and AEP dataset is presented in Table 1. The hyperparameters shown in the Table 1 are: number of hidden units (GRU/CiGRU), number of hidden units in fully connected layer of CiGRU with attention, sequence length, batch-size, and learning rate.

Table 1. Model configurations and Hyperparameters

Dataset	Model	Hyperparameter	Optimizer
TEDS (FD002)	GRU [9]	$15, 10, 64, 9 \times 10^{-3}$	RMSProp
	CiGRU [9]	$20, 15, 64, 5 \times 10^{-3}$	RMSProp
	CiGRU + A	$30, 5, 15, 128, 3 \times 10^{-3}$	Adam
	CiGRU + CxA (Proposed)	$20, 20, 10, 128, 6 \times 10^{-3}$	RMSProp
AEP	GRU	$15, 15, 128, 2 \times 10^{-3}$	RMSProp
	CiGRU	$10, 15, 128, 5 \times 10^{-5}$	RMSProp
	CiGRU + A	$25, 10, 20, 128, 2 \times 10^{-3}$	Adam
	CiGRU + CxA (Proposed)	$15, 15, 20, 128, 1 \times 10^{-3}$	Adam

4.5 Results

Table 2 presents the results obtained from CiGRU + CxA and the baseline models with the test dataset of TEDS and AEP. For TEDS, the testing is performed for each engine unit separately and the average RMSE and average score is reported. It is apparent from Table 2 that CiGRU, CiGRU + A, and CiGRU + CxA performed similar in terms of RMSE with CiGRU + CxA model's RMSE marginally better. On the other hand, the scores of CiGRU + A and CiGRU + CxA are comparable and significantly better than CiGRU. So, CiGRU + CxA is able to lower the number of late predictions. Figure 3 shows the predicted RUL values versus actual RUL values for a selected engine from the test data. It can be observed from the figure that for the constant part, the error is negative which is contributing towards low score. Similar trend is observed in other engines as well.

Table 2. Comparison of proposed model with baseline models

Dataset	TEDS-FD002		AEP	
Model	RMSE	Score	RMSE	MAE
GRU [9]	25.83	4122.89	75.81	38.42
CiGRU [9]	11.97	363.03	76.40	40.30
CiGRU + A	12.57	**299.75**	60.11	30.58
CiGRU + CxA (Proposed)	**11.80**	306.23	**59.11**	**26.55**

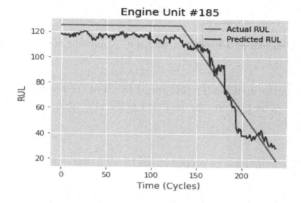

Fig. 3. Actual and Predicted RUL values.

For AEP dataset, CiGRU + CxA performance is better than all other models in terms of MAE. Considering RMSE metric, CiGRU + CxA performed slightly better than CiGRU + A but significantly better than other models. Figure 4 shows the predicted and actual Appliance energy usage for first 300 samples in the test data which is almost 2 days of data. It can be observed from the figure that the model can predict appliance energy but underestimates the peaks. One of the reasons could be that for certain days of the week the energy consumption is higher compared to the other days which is not captured by the model. Incorporating additional features such as day of the week and holidays potentially can improve the model. It is to be noted here, CiGRU + CxA is CiGRU + A and context in attention, CiGRU + A is CiGRU with attention, and CiGRU is GRU with context as separate input. The results show that adding context and attention to the baseline GRU provides a significant improvement in terms of given performance metrics.

A comparison of results achieved from CiGRU + CxA and results from state-of-the-art deep learning models applied to TEDS dataset is presented in Table 3. The models that are selected for comparison are sequential models based on LSTM, sequential models with attention, and additionally CNN-based models are considered. The best values from the existing approaches and the values from the proposed model is highlighted in bold. It is evident from the table that

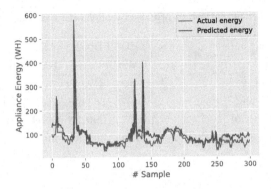

Fig. 4. Actual and Predicted values of Appliance energy usage.

CiGRU + CxA performed better compared to all other models both in terms of RMSE and score. The percentage decrease is 25.41% and 69.62% in RMSE and score, respectively.

Table 3. Comparison of proposed model with state-of-the-art -TEDS

Model	RMSE	Score
LSTM + FNN [32]	24.49	4,450.00
CNN + FNN [15]	22.36	10,412.00
RBM + LSTM [16]	22.73	3,366.00
LSTM + Attention [6]	17.65	2,102.00
MS-DCNN [14]	19.35	3,747.00
DA-CNN [24]	16.95	1,842.38
Attention Bi LSTM [22]	16.59	1,223.00
DA architecture [17]	17.08	1,575.00
Transformer Encoder + Attention [28]	**15.82**	**1,008.08**
CiGRU + CxA (this paper)	**11.80**	**306.23**

Table 4 shows the comparison of CiGRU + CxA with existing approaches for AEP dataset. It is to be noted that there are several other approaches [30] that used the AEP dataset, however, only three approaches are compared here. The reason is that there is inconsistency in selection of test data in the existing approaches. The original paper [2] that published the dataset used 25% of the data as test set and showed that Gradient Boosting Machines (GBM) achieved the best results. Similarly, [31] used a 25% data as test set with XGBoost. Finally, [19] considered 20% data for testing with Adaptive Input Selection RNN (AIS-RNN). As shown in the Table 4, we tested CiGRU + CxA with two test sets one is 25% of available data and the other is 20% of the data for comparison.

It is apparent from the results that CiGRU + CxA performed better or at par with existing approaches in terms of RMSE. However, the MEA is comparatively little higher than other models.

Table 4. Comparison of proposed model with state-of-the-art-AEP

Model	RMSE	MAE
GBM [2]	66.21	35.24
XGBoost [31]	59.69	**26.67**
CiGRU + CxA (this paper)	**58.82**	29.33
AIS-RNN [19]	59.81	**23.42**
CiGRU + CxA (this paper)	**59.11**	26.55

The experimental results show that RNN model with CiGRU and contextual attention performed significantly better than other models in presence of context, particularly in case of TEDS dataset where multiple operating conditions are explicitly present. Also, in comparison to other models, the proposed model achieved the given performance with relatively simpler model with 1 layer, 20 hidden units in RNN and 20 in FCL for TEDS and 1 layer 15 hidden units in RNN and 15 in FCL for AEP dataset. For TEDS dataset, the results are also influenced by selected features and normalization based on clustering. It is also worth mentioning here that each of the existing approaches had considered the operating conditions (contextual features) in a different way. For example, Zheng et al. [32], in their approach, clustered the operating conditions and use one-hot encoding for their representation and then it is included as a primary feature. On the other hand, for AEP dataset, the existing approaches consider both the weather and indoor conditions as primary inputs.

Next, we analyse the attention weights and contextual weights. For RUL prediction model, Fig. 5 shows the attention weights for the same engine unit as in Fig. 3. It can be seen that prediction at time steps 25 to 190 mainly relied on early as well as recent time windows (5–15) whereas during the last time steps the network focuses at the last time window. In Fig. 6 the contextual weights ($\mathbf{B}^s$) associated with only one primary feature (demanded corrected fan speed) is shown which has mostly positive values. Similarly, two other features, for which heatmaps are not shown here, associated with fan speed have higher weights compared to other primary features. This indicates that the fan speed has more impact in prediction of RUL compared to other features. We performed similar analysis with AEP dataset. However, we are not providing the heatmaps for the weights due to space constraint. We observed that the heatmaps for the primary features are not significantly different except two heatmaps, temperature in the kitchen area and temperature in laundry room. In comparison to these two features, other features have more positive weights. Thus, the attention and contextual weights allow understanding the impact of features and time steps on the predicted output. However, as the size of this weight matrices grow the interpretation becomes challenging.

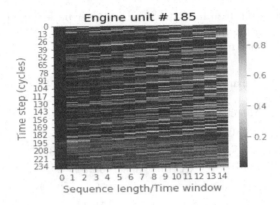

Fig. 5. Attention weights at each time step.

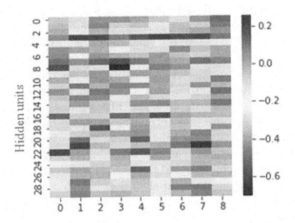

Fig. 6. Contextual input-hidden weights (part of matrix $\mathbf{B}^s$ associated with one input, *demanded corrected fan speed*, with dimension $n_h \times m$)

5   Conclusion and Future Work

In this paper, we proposed a novel RNN architecture which has CiGRU as basic units and additionally incorporates the contextual attention mechanism. CiGRU allows integrating explicit contexts available from the problem domain and attention mechanism helps in retaining information from long sequences. Further, attention weights are learnt in a way that they are influenced by the context. The contextual weights in CiGRU and attention weights can be utilized for interpreting the model by visualising which feature and time steps are affecting the predictions. The experimental results with two benchmark datasets showed that the architecture achieves better performance or at par with the existing approaches. In future, we intend to perform more experiments and analysis with other benchmark datasets, and also apply it to the applications for smart environments where context data can be acquired. Recently, the success of transformers [27] in NLP and computer vision has attracted researchers and practitioners from time series community and there is a surge in transformer-based solutions for time series forecasting [29]. Investigating the pertinence of transformers to sensor MTS prediction and also the relevance of external contextual information for such models will further be considered in future.

Ethical Statement. This research work does not involve any human subjects or personal information pertaining to them. It neither has potential policing or military use.

References

1. Bahdanau, D., Cho, K., Bengio, Y.: Neural machine translation by jointly learning to align and translate (2014). https://arxiv.org/abs/1409.0473
2. Candanedo, L.M., Feldheim, V., Deramaix, D.: Data driven prediction models of energy use of appliances in a low-energy house. Energy Build. **140**, 81–97 (2017)
3. Cheng, Q., Chen, Y., Xiao, Y., Yin, H., Liu, W.: A dual-stage attention-based Bi-LSTM network for multivariate time series prediction. J. Supercomput. **78**(14), 16214–16235 (2022)
4. Cho, K., et al.: Learning phrase representations using RNN encoder-decoder for statistical machine translation. In: Proceedings of the 2014 Conference on Empirical Methods in Natural Language Processing (EMNLP), pp. 1724–1734. Association for Computational Linguistics, Doha, Qatar (2014)
5. Cinar, Y., Mirisaee, H., Goswami, P., Gaussier, E., Aït-Bachir, A., Strijov, V.: Position-based content attention for time series forecasting with sequence-to-sequence RNNs. In: International Conference on Neural Information Processing, pp. 533–544 (2017). https://doi.org/10.1007/978-3-319-70139-4_54
6. da Costa, P., Akçay, A.E., Zhang, Y., Kaymak, U.: Attention and long short-term memory network for remaining useful lifetime predictions of turbofan engine degradation. IJPHM Special Issue PHM Appl. Deep Learn. Emerging Anal. **10**(4), 1–12 (2019)
7. Du, S., Li, T., Yang, Y., Horng, S.J.: Multivariate time series forecasting via attention-based encoder-decoder framework. Neurocomputing **388**, 269–279 (2020)
8. Dutta Baruah, R., Muñoz Organero, M.: Integrating explicit contexts with recurrent neural networks for improving prognostic models. In: IEEE Aerospace Conference (2023), accepted
9. Dutta Baruah, R., Organero, M.M.: Explicit context integrated recurrent neural network for sensor data applications (2023). https://arxiv.org/abs/2301.05031
10. Han, Z., Zhao, J., Leung, H., Ma, K.F., Wang, W.: A review of deep learning models for time series prediction. IEEE Sens. J. **21**(6), 7833–7848 (2021)
11. Haruehansapong, K., Roungprom, W., Kliangkhlao, M., Yeranee, K., Sahoh, B.: Deep learning-driven automated fault detection and diagnostics based on a contextual environment: a case study of HVAC system. Buildings **13**(1) (2023)
12. Heimes, F.O.: Recurrent neural networks for remaining useful life estimation. In: 2008 International Conference on Prognostics and Health Management, pp. 1–6 (2008)
13. Kinch, M.W., Melis, W.J., Keates, S.: The benefits of contextual information for speech recognition systems. In: 2018 10th Computer Science and Electronic Engineering (CEEC), pp. 225–230 (2018)

14. Li, H., Zhao, W., Zhang, Y., Zio, E.: Remaining useful life prediction using multiscale deep convolutions neural network. Appl. Soft Comput. **89**, 106113 (2020)
15. Li, X., Ding, Q., Sun, J.Q.: Remaining useful life estimation in prognostics using deep convolution neural networks. Reliabil. Eng. Syst. Safety **172**, 1–11 (2018)
16. Listou Ellefsen, A., Bjørlykhaug, E., Æsøy, V., Ushakov, S., Zhang, H.: Remaining useful life predictions for turbofan engine degradation using semi-supervised deep architecture. Reliabil. Eng. Syst. Safety **183**, 240–251 (2019)
17. Liu, L., Song, X., Zhou, Z.: Aircraft engine remaining useful life estimation via a double attention-based data-driven architecture. Reliabil. Eng. Syst. Safety **221**, 108330 (2022)
18. Luong, T., Pham, H., Manning, C.D.: Effective approaches to attention-based neural machine translation. In: Proceedings of the 2015 Conference on Empirical Methods in Natural Language Processing, pp. 1412–1421. Association for Computational Linguistics, Lisbon, Portugal (2015)
19. Munkhdalai, L., et al.: An end-to-end adaptive input selection with dynamic weights for forecasting multivariate time series. IEEE Access **7**, 99099–99114 (2019). https://doi.org/10.1109/ACCESS.2019.2930069
20. Qin, Y., Song, D., Cheng, H., Cheng, W., Jiang, G., Cottrell, G.W.: A dual-stage attention-based recurrent neural network for time series prediction. In: Proceedings of the 26th International Joint Conference on Artificial Intelligence, pp. 2627–2633. IJCAI'17, AAAI Press (2017)
21. Saxena, A., Goebel, K., Simon, D., Eklund, N.: Damage propagation modeling for aircraft engine run-to-failure simulation. In: 2008 International Conference on Prognostics and Health Management, pp. 1–9 (2008)
22. Shah, S.R.B., Chadha, G.S., Schwung, A., Ding, S.X.: A sequence-to-sequence approach for remaining useful lifetime estimation using attention-augmented bidirectional LSTM. Intell. Syst. Appl. **10**, 200049 (2021)
23. Shih, S.Y., Sun, F.K., Lee, H.Y.: Temporal pattern attention for multivariate time series forecasting. Mach. Learn. **108**(8), 1421–1441 (2019)
24. Song, Y., Gao, S., Li, Y., Jia, L., Li, Q., Pang, F.: Distributed attention-based temporal convolutional network for remaining useful life prediction. IEEE Internet Things J. **8**(12), 9594–9602 (2020)
25. Sun, L., Zhong, Z., Zhang, C., Zhang, Y., Wu, D.: TESS: multivariate sensor time series prediction for building sustainable smart cities. ACM Trans. Sens. Netw. (2022), just Accepted
26. Turney, P.D.: The management of context-sensitive features: a review of strategies (2002). https://arxiv.org/abs/cs/0212037
27. Vaswani, A., et al.: Attention is all you need. In: Guyon, I., et al. (eds.) Advances in Neural Information Processing Systems, vol. 30. Curran Associates, Inc. (2017)
28. Wang, X., Li, Y., Xu, Y., Liu, X., Zheng, T., Zheng, B.: Remaining useful life prediction for aero-engines using a time-enhanced multi-head self-attention model. Aerospace **10**(1) (2023)
29. Wen, Q., et al.: Transformers in time series: a survey (2023)
30. Yang, Y., Jinfu, F., Zhongjie, W., Zheng, Z., Yukun, X.: A dynamic ensemble method for residential short-term load forecasting. Alex. Eng. J. **63**, 75–88 (2023)

31. Zhang, T., Liao, L., Lai, H., Liu, J., Zou, F., Cai, Q.: Electrical energy prediction with regression-oriented models. In: Krömer, P., Zhang, H., Liang, Y., Pan, J.-S. (eds.) ECC 2018. AISC, vol. 891, pp. 146–154. Springer, Cham (2019). https://doi.org/10.1007/978-3-030-03766-6_16
32. Zheng, S., Ristovski, K., Farahat, A., Gupta, C.: Long short-term memory network for remaining useful life estimation. In: 2017 IEEE International Conference on Prognostics and Health Management (ICPHM), pp. 88–95 (2017)

Rail Crack Propagation Forecasting Using Multi-horizons RNNs

Sara Yasmine Ouerk[1](✉), Olivier Vo Van[2], and Mouadh Yagoubi[1]

[1] IRT SystemX, Palaiseau, France
`sara-yasmine.ouerk@irt-systemx.fr`
[2] SNCF, Saint-Denis, France

Abstract. The prediction of rail crack length propagation plays a crucial role in the maintenance and safety assessment of materials and structures. Traditional methods rely on physical models and empirical equations such as Paris' law, which often have limitations in capturing the complex nature of crack growth. In recent years, machine learning techniques, particularly Recurrent Neural Networks (RNNs), have emerged as promising methods for time series forecasting. They allow to model time series data, and to incorporate exogenous variables into the model. The proposed approach involves collecting real data on the French rail network that includes historical crack length measurements, along with relevant exogenous factors that may influence crack growth. First, a preprocessing phase was performed to prepare a consistent data set for learning. Then, a suitable Bayesian multi-horizons recurrent architecture was designed to model the crack propagation phenomenon. Obtained results show that the Multi-horizons model outperforms state-of-the-art models such as LSTM and GRU.

Keywords: Crack propagation · Machine Learning · Time series

1 Introduction

The French rail network has over 100,000 km of rail, including around 10,000 km for high-speed lines (LGV). The passage of rolling stock over these rails generates stresses in the rail, on the wheel-rail contact zone, which eventually leads to rolling contact fatigue. Defects resulting from this fatigue are monitored, and crack propagation is periodically checked, as a defect can propagate over several decades or a few months. When the length or depth of the crack becomes critical, it is imperative to correct the defect, otherwise there is a risk of rail break and potential derailment. Rolling contact fatigue is thus separated into two distinct phases, first the crack initiation, and then the crack propagation. In this paper, we focus on the latter and propose to build a predictive model that allows to evaluate the residual life of an already existing crack before reaching the critical threshold. This phenomenon can be partially explained by physical models and many studies have been led to understand the impact of various parameters.

© The Author(s), under exclusive license to Springer Nature Switzerland AG 2023
G. Ifrim et al. (Eds.): AALTD 2023, LNAI 14343, pp. 260–275, 2023.
https://doi.org/10.1007/978-3-031-49896-1_17

Bonniot et al. showed that the crack propagation in the rail is complex and follow mixed non proportional propagation modes [1]. Crack propagation speed depends on Stress Intensity Factor (SIF) identified from laboratory experiment, plastic deformation, friction between crack lips, its wear and corrosion and many other geometrical parameters such as initial crack width and direction, as shown by Fang et al. [2]. Moreover, other parameters in-situ are known to have an impact, such as track flexibility or acceleration and breaking and others still not quantified such as material decay over time. To deal with the lack of representativity of physical simulation in crack propagation modeling, we need to consider other parameters and phenomena that can lead to a more and more computationally expensive simulations, prohibiting thus their use to solve real world problems. At the same time, the mass of real data collected on various characteristics such as "infrastructure" and "traffic" makes it possible to investigate the potential of data-driven models. The problem can be seen as a time series forecasting of the crack length. In this paper, we propose a multi-horizon approach to predict the propagation of rail crack based on historical data that we compare with state of the art time series machine learning methods. The remainder of this paper is organized as follows. In Sect. 2 we present some recent related works. Section 3 describes the data processing analysis required to build the different models that are presented in Sect. 4. The comparative results are discussed in Sect. 5, and as usual Sect. 6 summarizes the contribution of this work and suggests directions for future research.

2   Related Work

Time series forecasting is a fundamental task in various domains, encompassing finance, weather prediction, demand forecasting, and more. Over the years, traditional and deep learning models have played a pivotal role in advancing the accuracy and effectiveness of time series forecasting.

Traditional approaches for time series forecasting have been widely used especially for univariate time series forecasting. Holt et al. introduced a method commonly employed for time series forecasting, Exponential Smoothing (ES) [3]. They involve recursively updating the forecasted values by assigning exponentially decreasing weights to past observations. Simple Exponential Smoothing [4], Holt's Linear Exponential Smoothing [5], and Holt-Winters' Seasonal Exponential Smoothing [6] are variations of this approach.

Autoregressive Integrated Moving Average (ARIMA) [7] is also a popular method for time series forecasting. It models the time series as a combination of autoregressive (AR), differencing (I), and moving average (MA) components. ARIMA models are widely used for stationary time series data.

These traditional approaches have been widely used in time series forecasting and have provided valuable insights in various domains. However, they have certain limitations that can impact their effectiveness and accuracy. In fact, many traditional time series forecasting methods assume that the underlying data follows a stationary process, where the statistical properties remain constant over time. However, real-world data often exhibits non-stationarity, such as trends, seasonality, and changing statistical properties. Failing to account for non-stationarity can lead to inaccurate forecasts. Moreover, these methods primarily focus on historical time series data and may not naturally incorporate external factors. However, many forecasting problems benefit from including additional variables, such as weather data.

While traditional time series forecasting approaches have their limitations, recent advancements in machine learning, such as deep learning models aim to address some of these challenges and provide more accurate and flexible forecasting capabilities.

Neural Networks (NN) have been widely used for time series forecasting and have achieved state-of-the-art performance in many applications. Neural networks, especially recurrent neural networks (RNNs) and their variants, have proven to be effective in capturing temporal dependencies and patterns in time series data. Moreover, there have been efforts to incorporate external factors or exogenous variables into time series forecasting models. These factors can include contextual information or additional time series that may influence the target variable.

One of the most popular RNN architectures for time series forecasting is the Long Short-Term Memory (LSTM) network [8]. LSTMs are designed to address the vanishing gradient problem and are capable of learning long-term dependencies in sequential data. They have been successfully applied to various time series forecasting tasks, including stock market prediction, energy load forecasting, and weather forecasting.

In recent years, other advanced variants of RNNs, such as Gated Recurrent Units (GRUs) [9] and Transformers [10], have also shown promising results in time series forecasting. GRUs are similar to LSTMs but have a simpler architecture, which makes them computationally more efficient.

Transformers, originally introduced for natural language processing tasks, have been adapted for time series forecasting by leveraging self-attention mechanisms. Transformers have the advantage of parallel processing and have shown competitive performance in several domains.

3   Data Description and Processing

Collected real data can be divided in four different categories. Each time it was possible, categorical data were converted to numerical data.

- **Infrastructure data**: These data correspond to the network description. The interesting features to consider are all parameters that can change the vehicle dynamic, namely the rail linear mass, to take into account rail profile and vertical flexibility, sleeper type, rail grade, radius of curvature, cant, slope and side of the rail (left or right);
- **Traffic data**: These data correspond to the use of network. The dynamic impact of rolling stock is considered by maximal velocity allowed and quantity and number of acceleration and breaking. The rail loading is considered using

annual tonnage (number of ton of vehicle seen by the rail) and number and type of vehicle (passenger or goods);

- **Environment data**: These are data not related to railway environment. The only environment data used here are temperatures and rain classified by type (low rain, strong storm, ice, snow, ...)
- **Defect**: These data correspond to the state of the network. Here, three different defects were selected, which represent most of rail defects in french railway, namely squats (in three different parts of the rail). Each defect is discovered at a recorded date and regularly visited to check its evolution. Each time, parameters such as crack length and measurement date are recorded.

One last parameter is considered and called "UIC Group". It is strongly correlated with speed limit and tonnage and defines maintenance conditions. Through this parameter are thus included other unavailable data at the time of the study such as grinding works. These data present a number of anomalies (inconsistent format, missing values, etc.), which necessitated a data preprocessing phase to obtain a consistent database to train the Machine Learning models.

Note that crack data was the most challenging to process for several reasons:

- Crack length values also present anomalies linked to database filling errors (negative values, exceeding certain thresholds, or considerable falls in values);
- Discovery date happened between 2008 and 2018 and crack life before it is removed can vary from several months to several years;
- Visit dates at which the crack length is measured are manually and empirically planed, the duration between two visits can thus vary from one week to a couple of years;
- The perceived high risk cracks are frequently visited and lead to sequence length (the time series) longer than others;
- Abrupt propagation have been observed for some defects. This behavior may be physically explained (caused by an extremely cold day), or simply based on a human judgement to merge two spatially close defects;
- Abrupt reduction of the crack length, which can be due to rail grinding;
- Measurement uncertainty, which is a known issue and led to approximate the measured length to the closest multiple of 5.

Data Processing

All the above information have been crossed to create a single training dataset containing all the information. The anomalies mentioned above were also addressed based on experts knowledge on the data. To overcome the problem of irregular time steps in the time series, an interpolation was performed. A frequency of 3 months was chosen and a linear average was computed on all series, resulting in 3-month time-step series with a maximum length of 59 time steps. After this step, defects with a fall in values greater than 15 mm were removed from the database, to avoid introducing errors into the learning model. Drops in values of less than 15 mm are tolerated, as it is possible to have variations in measurement conditions such as temperature variation that can lead to crack closure and reduce the size measured as explained in [11]. The measurement is also subject to operator interpretation of the observed signal and can thus vary with operators.

Feature Extraction

In the collected data, defect discovery dates vary widely, with some defects being more recent than others. To consider this information in the learning process, we set up an input variable that calculates the elapsed time since the defect was discovered.

The crack propagation speed was also calculated between time steps, which can give an indication of how fast the crack length propagates in a given context for the learning model. This information can only be used in the past horizon (the notion of horizon will be introduced in Sect. 4.2) and not in the future horizon, to avoid giving information on the lengths to be predicted. This feature extraction and selection resulted in 37 exogenous features for each time step in the time series.

4   Modeling Approaches

4.1   Feature Based Modeling

Initially, crack length values are considered unknown to the model. Only exogenous variables will be taken into account by the model to predict the corresponding crack lengths. As mentioned in the previous section, several variables are available. The time series are therefore multivariate, with several dynamic (evolving over time) or static features for the different time steps. For this configuration, sequences were created using a sliding window of size t.

The goal is to model the distribution of the crack length sequence, knowing its current context $X_{1:t}$, as

$$P(Y_{1:t}|X_{1:t}). \tag{1}$$

Were $X_{1:t}$ represents the exogenous feature (static and dynamic) by time step, and $Y_{1:t}$ their corresponding crack length values to be predicted.

Static features are encoded using Fully Connected (FC) layers, the dynamical features are encoded also using Fully Connected (FC) layers and then passed to one type of recurrent layers (RNN, LSTM or GRU) which can handle the time dependency between time steps. These models are respectively called **RNN-FC**, **LSTM-FC** and **GRU-FC**.

4.2   Considering the Historical Crack Length Values

For this new setup, a dataset containing crack length sequences was created using a sliding window of length $t + k$ over our time series. Each position of the sliding window contains a sample in our dataset with the first t values of crack lengths (the history), and their corresponding contextual features being the input of the past horizon and the last k values (the forecasting horizon) being the output.

The goal in this case is to model the distribution of the crack length sequence, knowing its historical features $X_{1:t}$ and measurements $Y_{1:t}$, as

$$P(Y_{t+1:t+k}|Y_{1:t}, X_{1:t}). \tag{2}$$

As mentioned above, interpolation is used to deal with the problem of irregular time series. The interpolated values are calculated using a linear average. For some time series, the past horizon may contain interpolated length values after the last measured value. These values are calculated using crack length values from the prediction horizon, as explained in Fig. 1. So, introducing them to the learning model will give information about the future values that are supposed to be unknown for the model, and thus may introduce a bias for the learning process.

To avoid this problem, only interpolated values before the last measured value are included. For time steps interpolated after this step, the last measured value is used to replace the interpolated steps. As an example in Table 1, we assume that crack length values of the defect corresponding to the past horizon are the values in the first row. The "Last measured value" variable indicates the last measured crack value (not an interpolated value), the "Step is interpolated" variable indicates whether the time step corresponds to an interpolated or non-interpolated (measured) crack length value.

The fifth time step is interpolated, and is the last time step before the prediction horizon, so its value can give information about the first value in the prediction horizon. Consequently, this value is replaced by the last measured crack length value. The model input for the "historical crack length values" feature will then be the "model input" variable in the table.

It should be noted that the model will be less accurate with this modification, but at least it will avoid biasing it with information it is not supposed to know. Some variables have been added to indicate whether the time step is interpolated and, if so, the number of time steps since the last measurement. This will reduce the effect of this replacement on performance.

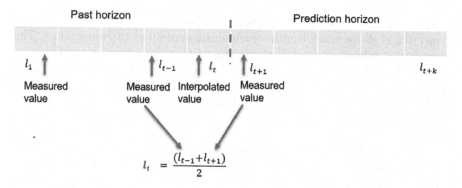

Fig. 1. Example of interpolation for the last step before the prediction horizon

Table 1. Example of model input of crack length values in the past horizon with last crack length value replacement

Crack length	30	32.5	35	35	**38.125**
Last measured value	30	30	35	35	**35**
Time step is interpolated	No	Yes	No	No	**Yes**
Model input	30	32.5	35	35	**35**

Simple Recurrent Model

For this model, only historical exogenous characteristics and corresponding crack length values are considered. These variables are passed on to the recurrent layer (LSTM/GRU), then their latent representation is passed on to some fully connected layers in order to infer crack length values in the future. These models are called **LSTM-FC-LH and GRU-FC-LH**, where LH refers to the historical crack lengths.

Multi-horizons Recurrent Model

In a second step, a model was implemented to consider both historical context $X_{1:t}$ and lengths $Y_{1:t}$, as well as the current context $X_{t+1:t+k}$. The aim is to model the distribution,

$$P(Y_{t+1:t+k}|Y_{1:t}, X_{1:t}, X_{t+1:t+k}). \tag{3}$$

This model is a recurrent neural network with multiple time horizons. It consists of a past horizon which takes as input exogenous variables and historical crack length measurements, and a future prediction horizon which takes as input the encoded output from the past horizon as well as current contextual variables in order to infer future crack length values, as described in Fig. 2.

The general architecture of the multi-horizon model is shown in Fig. 3.

For all the described models above, a customized Mean Squared Errors (MSE) has been used for learning. This loss is an MSE loss that ignores the padded time steps in order to avoid introducing bias to the model.

Bayesian Multi-horizons Recurrent Model

As mentioned above, crack length measurements are subject to uncertainty. This uncertainty is related to the data quality that cannot be reduced by adding more data, but it can be quantified. This type of uncertainty is called *Aleatoric* uncertainty and captures inherent noise in the observations. The learning model itself may be also uncertain regarding its predictions, due to a lack of learning data for example. This is called *epistemic* uncertainty and can be reduced by observing more data.

The multi-horizons model described above has been adapted, based on a Bayesian approach suggested by Kendall et al. [12], to allow uncertainty estimation in parallel with model prediction. This model is called the Bayesian Multi-horizons model (B-MH).

The B-MH model output, is composed of predictive mean $\hat{y}$ as well as predictive variance $\hat{\sigma}^2$.

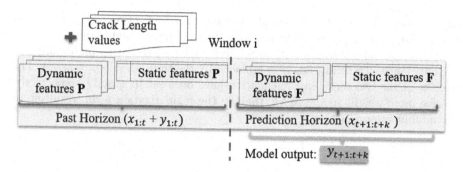

Fig. 2. Scheme of the prediction model

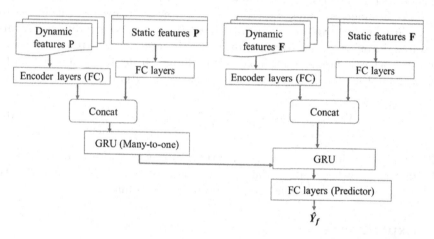

Fig. 3. Architecture of the multi-horizons recurrent model

The general architecture of the model remains unchanged, with only the last fully connected layers duplicated in order to output both $\hat{y}$ and $\hat{\sigma}^2$. $\hat{y}$ represents the predictive mean crack length and $\hat{\sigma}^2$ its predictive variance.

A Gaussian likelihood is used to model the aleatoric uncertainty, as the available crack length values follow a Gaussian distribution. This induces the minimization loss function for a given sequence x_i,

$$L_{\text{B\_MH}} = \frac{1}{N_i} \sum_{j=1}^{N_i} \frac{1}{2\hat{\sigma}(x_{ij})^2} ||y_{ij} - \hat{y}_{ij}||^2 + \frac{1}{2} log(\hat{\sigma}(x_{ij})^2), \qquad (4)$$

were $\hat{\sigma}(x_{ij})^2$ is the predictive variance for the time step j of the sequence x_i, $\hat{y}_{ij}$ its predictive mean and N_i the number of time steps in the sequence x_i.

The variance $\hat{\sigma}^2$ is implicitly learnt from the loss function. The division of the residual loss $||y_{ij} - \hat{y}_{ij}||^2$ (which represent the MSE loss) by $\hat{\sigma}(x_{ij})^2$ makes the model more robust to noisy data. In fact, data for which the model has learned to predict a high uncertainty will have lower effect on loss. The second regularization term prevents the network from predicting infinite uncertainty.

For numerical stability, and to avoid dividing by zero or either predicting negative variance, the term $\hat{\sigma}(x_{ij})^2$ is replaced by the term $s_{ij} = log(\hat{\sigma}(x_{ij})^2)$. The weights of the two terms in the equation have been set to $\frac{2}{3}$ and $\frac{1}{3}$ respectively, to give more weight to the MSE than to the regularization term, resulting in the minimization function,

$$L_{\text{B\_MH}} = \frac{1}{N_i} \sum_{j=1}^{N_i} \frac{2}{3} exp(-s_{ij}) \|y_{ij} - \hat{y}_{ij}\|^2 + \frac{1}{3} s_{ij}. \tag{5}$$

To quantify the uncertainty, a dropout approach [13] is used as Bayesian approximation. The model is trained with dropout before every weight layer. Contrary to what is usually done for a network trained with dropout layers, dropout remains activated during inference to generate stochastic rather than deterministic outputs. T stochastic prediction samples are performed using Dropout, allowing to approximate the predictive uncertainty for one observation as

$$\text{Var}(y) \approx \left(\frac{1}{T}\sum_{t=1}^{T}\hat{y}_t - \left(\frac{1}{T}\sum_{t=1}^{T}\hat{y}_t\right)^2\right) + \frac{1}{T}\sum_{t=1}^{T}\hat{\sigma}_t^2, \tag{6}$$

with $\{\hat{y}_t, \hat{\sigma}_t^2\}_{t=1}^{T}$ the set of T sampled outputs after each forward pass.

The first term of this total variance corresponds to the epistemic uncertainty and the second one corresponds to the aleatoric uncertainty.

5   Experiments

5.1   Data Preparation for Learning

Whatever the model used for learning, the generated time series have been preprocessed to ensure that the learning models function correctly.

By choosing a maximum size for the prediction horizon at a given value, not all the series generated have the same length. As some are shorter than the maximum length, these series have been completed by adding zeros at the end, so that they all have the same length. These completed time steps will be ignored when calculating the cost functions by implementing custom functions that ignore these time steps for backpropagation.

After this step, the dataset is divided into three parts: 60% training set for the learning procedure, 20% validation set for hyperparameter optimization and convergence control, and 20% test set for performance evaluation. The division strategy adopted ensures that the subsequences of a given defect series belong to only one of the three previous sets.

The time series are then normalized using a custom time series standard scaler, so that their mean is 0 and their standard deviation is 1. This makes the model much more robust to outliers. Min-max normalization has also been tested, but gives slightly poorer results.

5.2   Settings

The work has been implemented in Python using Pytorch. All the experiments are conducted using an NVIDIA A40 GPU.

Adam optimizer is used to perform the gradient descent minimization of the loss function. The activation function used is the $Tanh$ function for all hidden layers.

The convergence of the models is checked on learning rates from 10^{-1} to 10^{-4}, and on different batch sizes. The models perform best with the learning rate of 0.001 and batch size of 128. The models are also fitted over a variable number of epochs, the classical recurrent models converge after about 25 epochs, and the multi-horizons models converge after 10 epochs.

To benchmark the different models, many ML and physical metrics are used to compare their performances. MAE and $RMSE$ errors are used as machine learning metrics. Other physical criteria are considered to avoid some physical constraints violations such as the drop in the crack length, a phenomenon that should not occur physically (the crack can either progress or remain constant). These physical criteria are:

- **MSQNS**, for Mean SeQuence Negative Slope, is the percentage of sequences that contains at least one fall in the predicted values;
- **MSTNS**, for Mean STeps Negative Slope, is the percentage of steps that contains at least one fall in the predicted values.
- **MLNS**, for Mean Length Negative Slope, is the mean value of the fall in predicted length values. As a reminder, the observation time series themselves contain drops in values of up to 15 mm.

The computation of evaluation criteria for all reported experiments in this paper is performed using the recently proposed LIPS Framework for benchmarking learned physical systems [14].

5.3   Experiments with Simple Configuration (Without Historical Crack Length Values)

For this modeling, there is no notion of horizons in the generation of sequences. Generated sequences are of size 4 (we need to anticipate crack lengths values over a period of one year with a time step of 3 months). As previously stated, only exogenous variables are considered for prediction. Recurrent models were compared using the various ML and physical criteria defined above. This comparison is made in particular for the average score over the 4 time steps to be predicted (mean MAE and mean RMSE), as well as for the scores linked to the prediction of the first time step (MAE 1st and RMSE 1st) as shown in Table 2. The results show that the GRU-FC model outperforms LSTM-FC and RNN-FC in terms of machine learning criteria. The LSTM-FC and RNN-FC models have quite similar ML results, but the LSTM-FC model gives the best results in terms of physical criteria.

Table 2. ML and Physical results for the recurrent models without using historical crack length values

Model	MAE 1st	Mean MAE	RMSE 1st	Mean RMSE	MLNS	MSQNS	MSTNS
RNN-FC	10.48	10.47	13.67	13.66	1.72	29%	8%
GRU-FC	**9.65**	**9.45**	**12.60**	**12.38**	2.59	24%	6%
LSTM-FC	10.54	10.53	13.75	13.72	**1.18**	**3%**	**1%**

5.4 Experiments Considering Historical Crack Length Values

Experiments with Recurrent Models

For this modeling, time series were created using a sliding window of size 9: with a past horizon of size 5 and a prediction horizon of size 4. The size of the past horizon containing historical crack values was chosen at 5 time steps, inspired by [15] which suggests that a past horizon of size $1.25 \times k$ (k being the size of the prediction horizon) gives the best prediction results.

Table 3 shows ML and physical criteria for the recurrent models that considers historical crack length values. ML scores include the MAE for the different time steps in the prediction horizon (from $t+1$ to $t+4$) and their average value, and the RMSE score for the first time step in the prediction horizon and the average score over the entire prediction horizon. The LSTM-FC-LH model gives slightly better results than the GRU-FC-LH. For the physical criteria, this time it is the GRU-FC-LH model that gives slightly better results.

Table 3. ML and Physical results for the recurrent models considering historical crack length values

Model	MAE 1	MAE 2	MAE 3	MAE 4	Mean MAE	RMSE 1st	Mean RMSE	MLNS	MSQNS	MSTNS
LSTM-FC-LH	**2.37**	**3.05**	**3.85**	**4.51**	**3.45**	**4.72**	**6.01**	1.16 mm	1%	0.15%
GRU-FC-LH	**2.37**	3.11	**3.85**	4.58	3.49	4.77	6.06	**1.07**	**0.5%**	**0.13%**

Experiments with the Multi-horizons and Bayesian Multi-horizons Models

For this modelling, a number of past horizon sizes were tested to see their effect on the various criteria to be minimized.

Tables 4 and 5 show the results of the different ML and physical criteria of the multi-horizons model and the Bayesian multi-horizons model with different past horizon sizes. Good results can already be obtained from a single measurement in the past horizon. The size of the training set decreases as the size of the past horizon increases, due to the filtering of sequences to respect the minimum size. The choice of the size of the past horizon is conditioned both by the criteria to be minimized as far as possible and by industrial use. Indeed, information on

Table 4. ML and physical criteria results for the multi-horizons model considering different past horizons lengths for prediction

dim_hp	nb_sequences train	MAE 1st	Mean MAE	RMSE 1st	Mean RMSE	MSQNS %	MSTNS %	MLNS mm
1	294018	1.22	2.41	2.50	4.38	2.95	0.79	1.14
2	265519	1.15	2.29	2.39	4.22	2.85	0.76	1.13
3	238222	1.51	2.58	2.82	4.54	4.58	1.20	1.18
4	216021	1.28	2.26	2.50	4.26	14.09	3.61	1.11
5	193901	1.54	2.64	2.62	4.33	2.87	0.74	1.13
6	173598	1.27	2.29	2.43	4.13	6.58	1.69	1.08
7	158040	1.39	2.31	2.58	4.13	4.80	1.22	1.17
8	141407	1.33	2.17	2.43	4.05	8.61	2.22	1.08
9	126847	1.33	2.10	2.39	3.91	6.78	1.74	1.16
10	113175	1.23	2.15	2.33	3.96	14.91	3.80	1.14

Table 5. ML and physical criteria results for the Bayesian multi-horizons model (B-MH) considering different past horizons lengths for prediction

dim_hp	nb_sequences train	MAE 1st	Mean MAE	RMSE 1st	Mean RMSE	MSQNS %	MSTNS %	MLNS mm
1	294018	0.86	2.21	2.40	4.28	1.99	0.52	1.09
2	265519	0.94	2.26	2.32	4.22	1.51	0.39	1.14
3	238222	0.90	2.21	2.44	4.30	1.05	0.29	1.13
4	216021	1.20	2.23	2.63	4.29	3.56	0.91	1.05
5	193901	0.94	2.19	2.44	4.19	1.30	0.35	1.09
6	173598	0.98	2.13	2.37	4.06	2.87	0.73	1.04
7	158040	1.28	2.31	2.58	4.13	1.41	0.37	1.07
8	141407	1.13	2.15	2.38	4.00	9.83	2.49	1.04
9	126847	1.13	2.06	2.31	3.87	6.20	1.58	1.02
10	113175	1.02	1.96	2.34	3.93	2.94	0.78	1.09

historical measurements is sometimes available for just 1 or 2 time steps, which corresponds to three months or less, but we still want to predict crack lengths in the future because some cracks might have exceeded the security threshold before 6 months. The model must therefore be able to make predictions even with a limited past horizon size.

Figures 4 and 5 show ML scores (MAE and RMSE) for both the multi-horizons and Bayesian multi-horizons models using different past horizons lengths, these scores are presented in detail over the entire prediction horizon. Models errors increase with distance from the past horizon. The Bayesian multi-

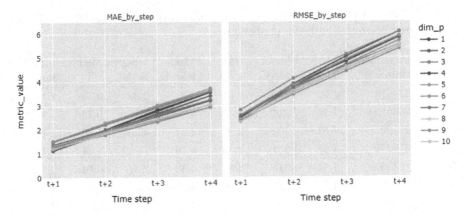

Fig. 4. MAE and RMSE scores for the prediction horizon using the multi-horizons model with different past horizon lengths.

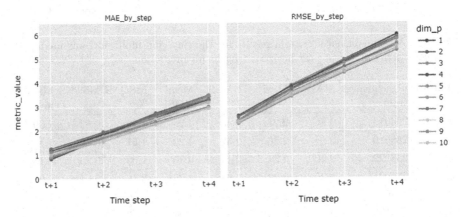

Fig. 5. MAE and RMSE scores for the prediction horizon using the Bayesian multi-horizons model with different past horizon lengths

horizons model outperforms the multi-horizons model over the entire forecast horizon.

Figure 6 shows the scatter plots for each time step in the prediction horizon. The x-axis and the y-axis correspond to the measured and predicted values of crack length respectively. There is a high density around the $y = x$ line which explains the good prediction scores. There are, however, some miss-predicted values, especially when crack lengths become large, where the model tends to underestimate them. This result is mainly due to the small percentage of large crack length values in the dataset.

Uncertainty Quantification Using the Bayesian Multi-horizons Model
As described above, uncertainty quantification is performed after the training of the model using Monte Carlo dropout sampling. Dropout is set after each

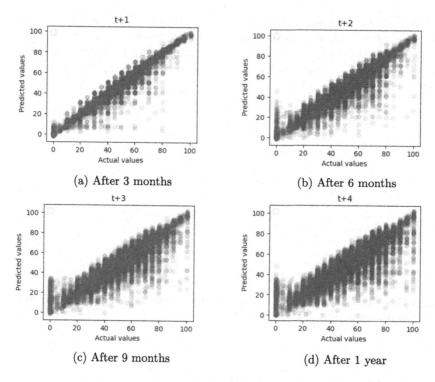

Fig. 6. Actual vs predicted crack length values over the prediction horizon

layer (except the last one) and 50 Monte Carlo samples were generated for each time series. Then, the sum of the two types of uncertainty is calculated using Eq. 6. The dropout rate was varied from 10% to 50%. Aleatoric uncertainty does not vary widely, as it is linked to the inherent noise of the data. Epistemic uncertainty, on the other hand, increases as the dropout rate is increased, since it is linked to the learning model. As a result, total uncertainty increases, as does the size of the confidence interval, resulting in higher coverage. For the rest of this study, a dropout rate of 10% is set after each layer, and an approximate 95%-level prediction confidence interval is constructed. Results show that only 48% of time steps are covered by this confidence interval. Indeed, as mentioned above, all the measured length values were approximated to the closest multiple of 5, which led us to add threshold of 5 to the confidence interval. This time, about 93% of time steps are covered by the new confidence interval.

Figure 7 shows some example of crack length propagation, the corresponding predicted values and uncertainty estimated values. Example 1 is a case of a crack whose final value becomes significant (around 80 mm). The predicted values are very close to the measurements but the corresponding epistemic uncertainty is quite high. This can be explained by the fact that the training set contains less than 3% of measurements ≥ 80 mm.

Example 2 is an example of propagation with decreasing values. The model underestimates crack lengths for the first few predicted values, then converges to the measured values at the end. However, falling values can be considered as inherent data noise or measurement errors, resulting in a high aleatoric uncertainty for this example.

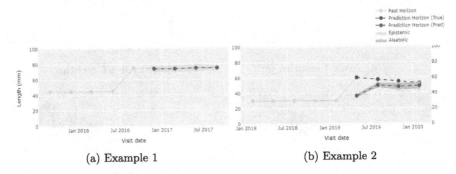

(a) Example 1   (b) Example 2

Fig. 7. Crack length propagation example with corresponding uncertainty estimation using the Bayesian Multi-horizons model

6   Conclusion and Future Works

Predicting the propagation of cracks in rails is a critical issue for optimizing the maintenance operations across the rail network. This task is intrinsically complex, and cannot be handled simply with physical simulations. In this paper, we proposed a deep learning approach based on real data collected on the rail. Obtained results show that the multi-horizons model outperforms conventional recurrent models such as GRU. The Bayesian multi-horizons model performs even better, and allows to quantify both aleatoric and epistemic uncertainties. Several avenues of improvement can be investigated in future work, in particular the calibration of models to predict more accurate uncertainties, as proposed in [16]. We aim also at combining recurrent layers with attention layers that assign different weights to the hidden states based on their significance for forecasting the crack lengths. Finally, the hybridization of ML methods and physical simulations is also part of the work in progress. Indeed, information provided from physical simulation can contribute in enriching the variables of the learned model such as the wheel load of the vehicle rolling on the rail, and thus improving the prediction performance.

References

1. Bonniot, T., Doquet, V., Mai, S.H.: Mixed mode II and III fatigue crack growth in a rail steel. Int. J. Fatigue **115**, 42–52 (2018)

2. Fang, X.-Y., Zhang, H.-N., Ma, D.-W.: Influence of initial crack on fatigue crack propagation with mixed mode in U71Mn rail subsurface. Eng. Failure Anal. **136**, 106220 (2022)

3. Holt, C.C.: Forecasting trends and seasonals by exponentially weighted moving averages. ONR Memorandum **52**(52), 5–10 (1957)

4. Gardner Jr., E.S.: Exponential smoothing: the state of the art. J. Forecasting **4**(1), 1–28 (1985)

5. Kalekar, P.S., et al.: Time series forecasting using holt-winters exponential smoothing. In: Kanwal Rekhi school of information Technology 4329008.13, pp. 1–13 (2004)

6. Gardner Jr., E.S., McKenzie, E.: Note–Seasonal exponential smoothing with damped trends. Manage. Sci. **35**(3), 372–376 (1989)

7. Bartholomew, D.J.: Time Series Analysis Forecasting and Control (1971)

8. Hochreiter, S., Schmidhuber, J.: Long short-term memory. Neural Comput. **9**(8), 1735–1780 (1997)

9. Cho, K., et al.: Learning phrase representations using RNN encoderdecoder for statistical machine translation. In: arXiv:1406.1078 (2014)

10. Vaswani, A., et al.: Attention is all you need. In: Advances in Neural Information Processing Systems 30 (2017)

11. Kou, X., Pei, C., Chen, Z.: Fully noncontact inspection of closed surface crack with nonlinear laser ultrasonic testing method. Ultrasonics **114**, 106426 (2021)

12. Kendall, A., Gal, Y.: What uncertainties do we need in bayesian deep learning for computer vision? In: Advances in Neural Information Processing Systems 30 (2017)

13. Srivastava, N., et al.: Dropout: a simple way to prevent neural networks from overfitting. J. Mach. Learn. Res. **15**(1), 1929–1958 (2014)

14. Leyli-Abadi, M., et al.: LIPS-Learning Industrial Physical Simulation benchmark suite. Adv. Neural. Inf. Process. Syst. **35**, 28095–28109 (2022)

15. Lara-Benitez, P., Carranza-Garcia, M., Riquelme, J.C.: An experimental review on deep learning architectures for time series forecasting. Int. J. Neural Syst. **31**(03), 2130001 (2021)

16. Kuleshov, V., Fenner, N., Ermon, S.: Accurate uncertainties for deep learning using calibrated regression. In: International Conference on Machine Learning. PMLR, pp. 2796–2804 (2018)

Electricity Load and Peak Forecasting: Feature Engineering, Probabilistic LightGBM and Temporal Hierarchies

Nicolò Rubattu[✉], Gabriele Maroni, and Giorgio Corani

Dalle Molle Institute for Artificial Intelligence (IDSIA), USI-SUPSI, 6962 Lugano, Switzerland
{nicolo.rubattu,gabriele.maroni,giorgio.corani}@idsia.ch

Abstract. We describe our experience in developing a predictive model that placed a high position in the BigDEAL Challenge 2022, an energy competition of load and peak forecasting. We present a novel procedure for feature engineering and feature selection, based on cluster permutation of temperatures and calendar variables. We adopted gradient boosting of trees and we enhanced its capabilities with trend modeling and distributional forecasts. We also included an approach to forecasts combination known as temporal hierarchies, which further improves the accuracy.

Keywords: Load Forecasting · Feature engineering · Gradient Boosting · Hierarchical Forecasting · Forecast Reconciliation

1 Introduction

Load forecasting is the problem of predicting the future profile of power demand, while *peak forecasting* is the problem of predicting the maximum (e.g. daily) value of demand and the time of its occurrence. Peak forecasting is important because often decisions are made based on the forecast of the peak rather than on the forecast of the entire load profile.

In this work, we present an approach that successfully competed in the BigDEAL Challenge 2022, which was about energy load and peak forecasting. The competition was held in October-December 2022; 121 contestants took part, divided into 78 teams. The forecasts were assessed using different indicators and the competition was split into a qualifying match and a final match. We achieved the 3rd position in the qualifying match, gaining access to the final match, where we ended 6th [16].

For the qualifying match, we used Gradient Boosting (GB) of trees, coupled with an original method for feature engineering and feature selection. For the final match, we developed a more sophisticated approach. In particular, we adopted a recent probabilistic version of LightGBM [28] and used temporal hierarchies [3] in order to improve the forecasts by combining predictions at different temporal scales. Even though the competition only scored the point forecasts,

G. Ifrim et al. (Eds.): AALTD 2023, LNAI 14343, pp. 276–292, 2023.
https://doi.org/10.1007/978-3-031-49896-1_18

our approach is probabilistic and thus quantifies the uncertainty of the forecasts. This is indeed needed to support decision-making.

We present our approach in this paper, which is organized as follows. In Sect. 2.1 an outlook of long-term load forecasting and our motivations are given. We introduce Gradient Boosting (GB) of trees and probabilistic extensions in Sect. 2.2. We present our approach for feature engineering for load forecasting in Sect. 2.3, and feature selection in Sect. 2.4. Temporal hierarchies are presented in Sect. 2.5. In Sect. 3 we detailed review our pipeline with technical insights, and competition results. We end this work with a critical conclusion in Sect. 4.

2 Methodology

2.1 Long-Term Load Forecasting

Load forecasting is the problem of predicting the electricity demand of the next H time steps, denoted by $[y_{T+1}, \ldots, y_{T+H}]$. When the order of magnitude of H is a few hundred or more, we talk about *long-term* forecasting. For instance, forecasting a year ahead at an hourly scale implies producing $24 \times 365 = 8760$ forecasts. Classical forecasting strategies [4] condition the forecast on the last observations of the time series. However, this is not viable for long-term forecasting, since in this case y_{T+H} is independent of y_T. Long-term forecasting is better addressed as a regression problem, adopting a rich set of explanatory variables (*features*) regarding calendar effects, temperatures, etc. [7]. This approach allows adopting regression methods such as Gradient Boosting (GB) of trees [11], which is indeed successful in long-term energy forecasting [32].

2.2 Gradient Boosting and Distributional Forecasts

In fact, GB achieved top positions in the Global Energy Forecasting Competitions (GEFCom) of 2012, 2014, and 2017 [18–20], in the M5 forecasting competition [23], and competitions on tabular data [6]. The most popular implementations are XGBoost, LightGBM, and CatBoost.

GB can be trained with different loss functions besides the traditional least squares. For instance, GB trained to perform quantile regression won the GEFCom2014 probabilistic competition [12]. Yet, even quantile regression only returns point forecasts without a predictive distribution. It is possible to train different GB models, one for each desired quantile; but if the predicted quantiles cross, the predictive distribution is invalid [29,30]. The recent versions of probabilistic GB of trees constitute a sounder approach [9,27,28] to probabilistic forecasting. In this work, we adopt the LightGBM extended model of März et al. [28], which returns the moments of the predictive distribution.

A successful implementation of GB requires anyway paying attention to some possible issues. For instance, GB is generally unable to model a long-term trend. If the time series is trendy, it is recommended to detrend it, fit the GB model, and then add the predicted trend to the GB forecast [34]. Another pre-processing step that is sometimes helpful is a logarithmic transformation which stabilizes the variance of the target time series [31]. Moreover, GB is subject to overfitting. The DART algorithm [33] solves the problem by introducing Dropout regularization analogously to Neural Networks.

2.3   Feature Engineering

The exogenous variables that are frequently used in load forecasting are related to calendars and temperatures.

Calendar Features. Calendar variables allow to capture the seasonal patterns. They are commonly modeled by categorical variables. For example, the day of the week is represented by a categorical variable with seven levels. Holidays are represented by a binary variable: 1 for holidays and 0 for non-holiday.

Lagged and Rolling Temperatures. Temperature impacts energy consumption, by driving the use of heating, ventilation, and air conditioning (HVAC) systems. However, there is generally a delay between the change in temperature and the change in energy consumption. We thus consider the lagged hourly temperatures:

$$T(t - h), \qquad h = 1, 2, \dots, L \tag{1}$$

where L is the maximum lag; and the rolling temperature's statistics:

$$T_f^w(t) = f(T(t - 1), \dots, T(t - w)) \tag{2}$$

where $f(\cdot)$ is some statistical function and w indicates the width of the window of past values of hourly temperatures considered. For example, the moving average of the last 24 h of temperature values is $T_{avg}^{24}(t) = \frac{1}{24} \sum_{h=1}^{24} T(t - h)$.

Aggregated Indicators of Temperature. Aggregated features can capture the long-term effect of temperature on energy load. They can be expressed as $\tilde{T}_f^g(t)$ where g is the aggregation period and $f(\cdot)$ is the aggregation function. These features include, for example, the daily maximum and minimum values of the temperature or the monthly standard deviation of the temperature.

In this paper, we propose additional aggregation functions (Table 1) borrowed from signal processing [10, 36], which to the best of our knowledge have not yet been used in energy forecasting. They should be computed on the time series of temperature, and provide insights about the variability and shape within the aggregation period. For example, the crest factor measures the peak-to-average ratio of a signal; a high daily crest factor corresponds to large variations of temperature during the day, which generally increase energy demand; a low daily crest factor corresponds to stable temperatures during the day, which generally decreases energy demand.

Table 1. Signal Processing features for load forecasting.

RMS	$x_{RMS} = \sqrt{\frac{1}{N} \sum_{i=1}^{N} x_i^2}$
Peak value	$x_p = \max(|x_i|)$
Crest factor	$x_{crest} = \frac{x_p}{x_{RMS}}$
Impulse factor	$x_{if} = \frac{x_p}{\frac{1}{N} \sum_{i=1}^{N} |x_i|}$
Margin factor	$x_{mf} = \frac{x_p}{\left(\sum_{i=1}^{N} |x_i|^{1/2}\right)^2}$
Shape factor	$x_{sf} = \frac{x_{RMS}}{\frac{1}{N} \sum_{i=1}^{N} |x_i|}$
Peak to peak value	$x_{pp} = \max(x_i) - \min(x_i)$

2.4   Feature Selection

Feature engineering generates a large set of features, after which feature selection is needed [22,25]. We perform feature selection based on hierarchical clustering and pairwise correlation of the features. The core of our approach is Permutation Feature Importance (PFI), which measures the drop in performance when a feature is randomly shuffled [5]. The size of the drop in performance shows how much the model relies on that feature for prediction. PFI is appealing since it can be applied to any model; it is easy to implement (Algorithm 1); it can measure feature importance on the metric of the competition; it can be computed out-of-sample.

Algorithm 1. Permutation Feature Importance

Require: A trained model and recorded score s on an evaluation dataset.
   for feature $x_j, j = 1, \ldots, d$ **do**
      for each repetition $k, k = 1, \ldots, K$ **do**
         Randomly shuffle column j of the original evaluation set.
         Compute the new score $s_{k,j}$ of the model on the perturbed set.
      end for
      Compute the importance of feature x_j as $I_j = s - \frac{1}{K} \sum_{k=1}^{K} s_{k,j}$
   end for

However, shuffling a single feature can produce unrealistic results if features are dependent. Furthermore, correlated features share importance, therefore their relevance may be underestimated (substitution effect, [15]).

Clustered Permutation Feature Importance. To solve such issues we propose a novel approach, which we call Clustered Permutation Feature Importance (CPFI). The method works as follows.

At first, groups of highly correlated features are identified by applying hierarchical clustering on the correlation matrix of the features. For that, a measure of dependence between each feature pair is computed using a correlation index,

Pearson's or Spearman's for instance. Then, all the variables of the same cluster are shuffled, and the subsequent performance drop is computed. The more orthogonal the information contained in different clusters, the more reliable the estimate of importance. Finally, non-informative feature clusters are dropped. Also, only one or few features can be selected from each relevant cluster based on some measure of explanation with respect to the target, or some expert advice. We propose a criterion for informativeness in Sect. 3.

2.5   Temporal Hierarchies

As a further tool to improve forecasting accuracy, we consider temporal hierarchies [3]. For instance, assume that we want to generate forecasts at the hourly scale (referred to as the *bottom* level). A temporal hierarchy creates and combines forecasts also at coarser temporal scales (e.g., 2-hourly and 4-hourly), referred to as the *upper* levels. The smoothness of the upper time series enables enhanced modeling of long-term patterns. This process generally improves forecasting accuracy at all levels [3,24].

A temporal hierarchy works as follows. First, forecasts are independently created at different temporal scales (*base forecasts*). For instance, Fig. 1 shows a temporal hierarchy aimed at forecasting 4-hours ahead. It contains 4 forecasts computed at hourly frequency ($\hat{h}_1, ..., \hat{h}_4$, bottom level); two forecasts computed at 2-hour frequency ($\hat{h}_{12}, ..., \hat{h}_{34}$, intermediate level); one forecast computed at 4-hour frequency ($\hat{h}_{1234}$, top level). Generally, the base forecasts do not sum up correctly and they are referred to as *incoherent*. For instance: $\hat{h}_{12} \neq \hat{h}_1 + \hat{h}_2$, $\hat{h}_{34} \neq \hat{h}_3 + \hat{h}_4$, etc. *Reconciliation* [35] is the process of adjusting the base forecast so that they become *coherent*, i.e., they sum up correctly. The reconciled forecasts are denoted with a tilde and thus in the example of Fig. 1 after reconciliation, we have: $\tilde{h}_{12} = \tilde{h}_1 + \tilde{h}_2$, $\tilde{h}_{34} = \tilde{h}_3 + \tilde{h}_4$, $\tilde{h}_{1234} = \tilde{h}_{12} + \tilde{h}_{34}$.

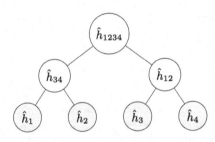

Fig. 1. Temporal hierarchy for forecasting 4-hours ahead, using hourly forecasts (bottom level), 2-hourly forecasts, and 4-hourly forecasts.

Temporal hierarchies require the mean and the variance of the base forecasts. The original algorithm [3] provides only the reconciled point forecast, while the approach of [8] yields also a reconciled predictive distribution.

3   Experiments

The BigDEAL Challenge 2022 was divided in a qualifying match and a final match. The *qualifying match* provided hourly load and hourly temperature statistics (mean, median, min, max) of four weather stations for the period 2002–2006; see Fig. 2 for an example. It required forecasting the year 2007 given the actual temperatures. This is referred to as *ex-post* setting. The *final match* provided three years (2015–2017) of hourly load of three U.S. local distribution companies (LDC), and hourly temperatures from six weather stations. The forecasted (*ex-ante* setting) 1-day ahead temperatures for 2018 were released on a rolling basis, two months at a time. The forecasts for these periods were to be delivered, in a total of six consecutive rounds. Both matches required forecasts at hourly scale for the 24 h, the values of the peak for each day, and its time of occurrence (i.e. a discrete number between 1 and 24).

The qualifying match served as a support for participants to validate their forecasting approach. Its ex-post setting is optimistic as *actual* temperatures for the forecasting horizon are used. The ex-ante setting of the final match instead represents a realistic scenario as forecasts are obtained from *forecasted* temperatures. In the literature, the comparison of the two settings is used to measure the effectiveness of the forecasting models [21], i.e. the influence of the forecast errors is isolated in the input variables.

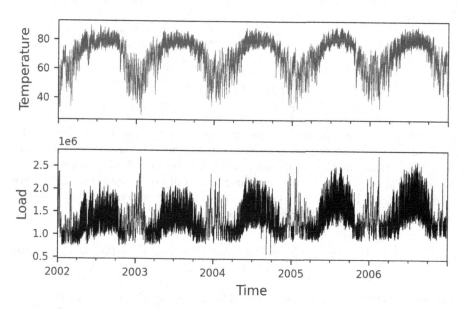

Fig. 2. Load (MW) and temperature T_{avg} (°F) of the qualifying match of the BigDEAL challenge. For readability, we show data aggregated over 12 h.

3.1   Performance Measures

The organizers evaluated the forecasts of each match with three different tracks.

In the qualifying match the hourly forecasts ($24 \times 365 = 8760$) were scored using the *Mean Absolute Percentage Error* (MAPE):

$$\text{MAPE} = \frac{1}{H} \sum_{t=T+1}^{T+H} \frac{|y_t - \hat{y}_t|}{|y_t|} \times 100, \tag{3}$$

where y_t and $\hat{y}_t$ denote the actual and the forecasted value for time t. The second metric was the *Magnitude* (M); it is the MAPE between the actual and forecasted daily peak values (i.e., it refers to 365 forecasts with a one-year horizon). We recall that MAPE has been criticized in the forecasting literature: it penalizes over-estimation errors more than under-estimation ones [2] and it is numerically unstable when dealing with values close to 0. To score the prediction of peak hours the organizers used a third metric, called *Timing* (T), which computes the *Mean Absolute Error*. For example, if the actual peak is at 6 pm, and the forecasted peak time is at 8 pm, the error for that day is $|6 - 8| = 2$.

The final match scored the forecasts using *Magnitude* (M) and *Timing* (T), plus an additional metric called *Shape* (S). However, the definition of Timing was modified introducing a non-uniform cost for the error. Let us denote by T_d and $\hat{T}_d$ the actual and the forecasted peak hour for a day d. Timing was then defined as:

$$T = \frac{1}{|days|} \sum_{d\,in\,days} w(T_d, \hat{T}_d),\,\text{with}$$

$$w(T_d, \hat{T}_d) = \begin{cases} |T_d - \hat{T}_d|, & \text{if } |T_d - \hat{T}_d| = 1, \\ 2|T_d - \hat{T}_d|, & \text{if } 2 \le |T_d - \hat{T}_d| \le 4, \\ 10, & \text{if } |T_d - \hat{T}_d| \ge 5 \end{cases} \tag{4}$$

Shape (S) scored the shape of the forecast around the peak. To compute it, the 24h load forecasts of a day are normalized by the peak forecast of that day, and the same is done for the actual load. Then the sum of absolute errors during the 5-hour peak period (actual peak hour $\pm 2\,\text{h}$) of every day is calculated. We denote by $\bar{y}_d$ and $\bar{\hat{y}}_d$ the normalized actual and forecasted load for a day d; $\bar{y}_d = \frac{y_d}{\max y_d}, \bar{\hat{y}}_d = \frac{\hat{y}_d}{\max \hat{y}_d}$. Shape is defined as:

$$S = \frac{1}{|days|} \sum_{d\,in\,days} \sum_{t\,in\,\{T_d, T_d\pm1, T_d\pm2\}} |\bar{y}_d(t) - \bar{\hat{y}}_d(t)| \tag{5}$$

Scoring the Predictive Distribution. While the competition only assessed the point forecasts, we also scored the distributional forecasts obtained from our probabilistic models. In particular, we compared the probabilistic forecast of our GB model (based on [28]) with those obtained after the application of the temporal hierarchy. We scored the predictive distributions of the model using the *Continuous Ranked Probability Score* (CRPS) [14]. Let us denote by $\hat{\mathbf{F}}$ the predictive cumulative distribution function and by y the actual value:

$$\mathrm{CRPS}(\hat{\mathbf{F}}, y) = \int_{-\infty}^{\infty} (\hat{\mathbf{F}}(x) - \mathbb{1}(x \geq y))^2 \, dx \tag{6}$$

With Gaussian $\hat{\mathbf{F}}$, the integral can be computed in closed form [14]. We then scored the prediction intervals using the *Interval Score* (IS) [13]. Let us denote by $1 - \alpha$ the nominal coverage of the interval (assumed 0.9 in this paper), by $\mathbf{l}$ and $\mathbf{u}$ its lower and upper bound. We thus computed with the models, for each hour, a 90% prediction interval and the score:

$$\mathrm{IS}(\mathbf{l}, \mathbf{u}, y) = (\mathbf{u} - \mathbf{l}) + \frac{2}{\alpha}(\mathbf{l} - y)\mathbb{1}(y < \mathbf{l}) + \frac{2}{\alpha}(y - \mathbf{u})\mathbb{1}(y > \mathbf{u}). \tag{7}$$

We also report the proportion of cases in which the interval $(\mathbf{l}, \mathbf{u})$ contains y.

Skill score. Let m_{origin} and m_{new} be the results obtained by two different models on a certain metric to be minimized. We denote the positive or negative percentage improvement by the Skill score defined as:

$$\mathrm{Skill}_\%(m_{origin}, m_{new}) = \frac{m_{origin} - m_{new}}{(m_{origin} + m_{new})/2} \times 100 \tag{8}$$

3.2   Qualifying Match

Here, we detail the building blocks of our implementation.

Baseline. We started by modeling essential calendar features (`Year`, `Month`, `Week`, `Day`, `Weekday`, `Hour`) and temperatures at the current time (T_{avg}, T_{med}, T_{min}, T_{max}). We applied a logarithmic transformation to the target variable to stabilize its variance. Moreover, since the target variable has a long-term increasing trend, we performed detrending. We fitted a Linear Regression (LR) model ($y_i = \beta_0 + \beta_1 x_i$, where x_i are progressive time indices with $i = 1, \ldots, T$) to the training data. We then subtracted the linear trend before fitting the LightGBM model. At prediction, we added the extrapolated trend to the out-of-sample predictions, followed by an exponential transformation, to obtain the final forecast. With detrending: the residuals have a mean of 0, otherwise, they are severely biased; we reduced the MAPE (H) of the baseline model from 6.18 to 4.81.

Cross-validation. We used time series cross-validation to evaluate the performance of each model, hyper-parameter tuning, and feature selection. The size of the time window is typically chosen equal to the size of the test set on which the final prediction is to be made. Hence, for the qualifying phase, the years 2004, 2005, and 2006 were used as out-of-sample folds.

Feature Engineering. Feature engineering was performed *incrementally* by adding related feature blocks one step at a time. We found the following features to be predictive for this competition:

- Additional calendar features: `Holiday, Holiday name, Weekend, Week of month, Season, Day of year, Days since last/until next holiday.` We transform the `Holiday name` string feature with label encoding.
- Lagged hourly temperatures: for each temperature variable (T_{avg}, T_{med}, T_{min}, T_{max}) lagged hourly temperatures were incorporated into the model, ranging from a minimum lag of 1 h to a maximum lag of 48 h, for a total of 192 new features.
- Temperature-based rolling statistics: for each temperature variable, and 4 different values of window widths (3 h, 1 day, 1 week, 1 month), 5 statistical functions (*mean, max, min, median, std*) were computed, for a total of 80 new features.
- Aggregated temperature statistics: for each temperature variable, for 2 different aggregation periods (Year-Month-Day, Month-Hour), 11 aggregation functions (*mean, max, min, median,* and centered *RMS, crest factor, peak value, impulse factor, margin factor, shape factor, peak to peak value*) coupled with the differences between the current temperature values and the aggregated values were computed for a total of $88 \times 2 = 176$ new features. For example, we denote by $\tilde{T}_{max}^{Year,Month,Day}(t)$ the daily maximum, where Year-Month-Day is the aggregation period, to be read from left to right.

Feature selection. To evaluate our feature selection strategy, we carried out multiple experiments. First, we assessed the model performance without any feature selection (experiment **a**). Then, we applied the feature selection strategy described in Sect. 2.4 after completing all feature engineering, on the entire set of features added to the baseline model (experiment **b**). Finally, we performed *step-by-step* feature selection whenever we added a new block of features to the model, i.e. after adding lagged variables, after adding rolling variables, and so on (experiment **c**).

Cluster permutations were executed 100 times, and mean values and standard deviations of performance drops were calculated against all the out-of-sample folds. We consider a cluster of features *informative* if the importance value fall within three standard deviations of the mean, above 0. Results are presented in Table 2. Specifically, the columns for MAPE, Magnitude, and Timing present the results based on the respective competition metrics, whereas columns **a**, **b**, and **c** correspond to the 3 experimental strategies employed. It is important to note that, unlike experiment **a**, where the results were obtained in a single training run, the results for experiments **b** and **c** were derived from three different training runs, each one maximizing the metric of interest.

Table 2. Out-of-fold qualification results with feature selection methods.

	MAPE (H)			Magnitude			Timing		
	a	b	c	a	b	c	a	b	c
Baseline	4.81	-	-	4.43	-	-	1.42	-	-
Calendar	4.83	-	4.78	4.48	-	4.46	1.39	-	1.39
Lags	3.33	-	3.24	3.29	-	3.20	0.94	-	0.92
Roll lags	3.28	-	3.16	3.22	-	3.20	1.06	-	0.94
Agg stats	3.24	3.16	3.09	3.21	3.10	3.08	0.91	0.95	0.91

For illustration purposes, in Fig. 3, we present the feature selection results obtained after incorporating lagged hourly temperatures into the model. Figure 3a presents the dendrogram obtained from hierarchical clustering computed on the Spearman correlation matrix, which is shown in Fig. 3b. With a threshold value of 0.1, we identified 36 clusters. The cluster rankings that maximize, respectively, the performance of MAPE, Magnitude, and Timing are visible in Fig. 3c. For all the metrics, cluster 8 proved to be the most significant, followed by clusters 31, 7, 2, and 12. This suggests that most informative lags are at t-$\{1, 2, 3, 4, 5, 6\}$, t-$\{11, 12\}$, and t-$\{25, 26\}$. Table 3 shows the clusters associated feature set.

Table 3. Clustered Permutation Feature Importance: Top-5 clusters of lagged temperatures that maximize performance indicators.

Cluster ID	Feature Set
8	$T_{avg,med,min}(t-1)$, $T_{avg,med,min}(t-2)$
31	$T_{avg,med,min}(t-11)$, $T_{avg,med,min}(t-12)$
7	$T_{avg,med,min}(t-3)$, $T_{avg}(t-4)$
2	$T_{avg,med,min}(t-5)$, $T_{avg,med}(t-6)$
12	$T_{max}(t-1)$, $T_{max}(t-2)$, $T_{max}(t-25)$, $T_{max}(t-26)$

Hyper-parameter optimization We used the Optuna framework [1] to tune the learning control parameters of LightGBM, primarily: the max number of leaves in one tree, the minimal number of data in one leaf, L1 and L2 regularization, bagging and feature fractions, the number of estimators, and the learning rate. The parameters are optimized for the best cross-validation performance, also considering the standard deviation of the different folds. Optuna implements time-budget optimization which was useful given the short deadlines of the competition.

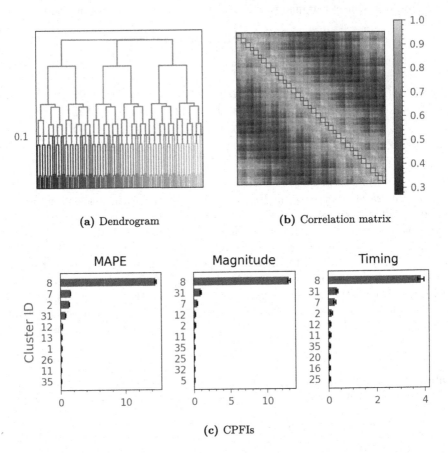

(a) Dendrogram   (b) Correlation matrix

(c) CPFIs

Fig. 3. Hierarchical clustering (threshold of 0.1) (a) and Spearman's correlation matrix (b). The blue squares highlight the 36 clusters. In (c) Clustered Permutation Feature Importance (CPFI) values are reported for each track. (Color figure online)

Results. Our team was named "swissknife"; as reported in Tab. 4, we ranked 8th on the hourly forecast (H), 3rd on the Magnitude (M), 3rd on the Timing (T).

3.3 Final Match

For the final match, we followed the same pipeline tuned in the qualification phase, with the exception of target transformation, which was not required as the target variable was already stationary. Additionally, three LDC loads were required to be forecasted (LDC1, LDC2, LDC3), and the temperature variables come from six weather stations (T1, T2, T3, T4, T5, T6), without aggregate statistics and geographical references. To further enhance performance, we incorporated several techniques, including DART, probabilistic LightGBM, and temporal hierarchies.

Table 4. Leaderboard of Qualifying Match [17].

Team	Rank H.	Team	Rank M.	Team	Rank T.
X-Mines	1	Amperon	1	RandomForecast	1
Amperon	2	Team SGEM KIT	2	Amperon	2
Yike Li	3	swissknife	3	swissknife	3
peaky-finders	4	peaky-finders	4	freshlobster	4
KIT-IAI	5	KIT-IAI	5	peaky-finders	5
Overfitters	6	EnergyHACker	6	*Recency Benchmark*	
BelindaTrotta	7	BelindaTrotta	7	X-Mines	6
swissknife	8	Overfitters	8	BrisDF	7
Recency Benchmark		VinayakSharma	9	BelindaTrotta	8
RandomForecast	9	SheenJavan	10	KIT-IAI	9
Team SGEM KIT	10			SheenJavan	10
· · ·		*Recency Benchmark*	13	· · ·	
Tao's Vanilla Benchmark	27	*Tao's Vanilla Benchmark*	25	*Tao's Vanilla Benchmark*	30

Feature Selection. The most important lagged temperatures were found at time t-$\{1, 2, 3, 4, 5\}$, and t-$\{10, 11, 12\}$, and the most important rolling lag temperatures were found with $w = \{3\,hours, 1\,day\}$. Figure 4 shows that within the six weather stations, temperatures {T1, T2, T5} better explain LDC1. Analogously, LDC2 is better explained by {T3, T4}, and LDC3 by {T5, T6, T1}. To save space, we do not present the Out-of-fold Top-20 features for LDC2 and LDC3 in this paper, but the results are in line with those of LDC1. Hence, even if according to the guidelines of the competition it was not necessary to rely on the location of the data, our method nicely handles datasets with multiple weather stations.

Regularization. Using Dropout, the DART booster reduced the overfitting that affects LightGBM with the standard booster. It also reduced the prediction error, but training became slower since it required more boosting iterations. We tested DART on the qualification data only when it was over. With 30'000 iterations, the MAPE (H) went from 3.24 to 2.83, and the Magnitude from 3.21 to 3.09. Hence, we included DART in the final match models.

Temporal Hierarchies. We built temporal hierarchies by summing the hourly load and temperatures at the following scales: *2-hours*, *4-hours*, *6-hours*, and *12-hours*. We trained an independent probabilistic LightGBM-LSS [28] model at each time scale. The model minimizes the Negative Log-Likelihood loss function. Gaussian distributional base forecasts were obtained at each temporal scale for the same forecasting horizon H. We implemented probabilistic reconciliation as formulated in [8]. In Table 5 (load profile) and Table 6 (peak), we compare base and reconciled forecasts, using skill scores ($S_\%$); in Fig. 5 we show some forecasts. Temporal hierarchy improves only slightly the point forecasts, but more importantly the predictive distribution, with a skill score of about 5% on CRPS and 10% on IS. We also tested 1-day aggregation without further improvement for the bottom time series. As the previous feature importance analyses showed,

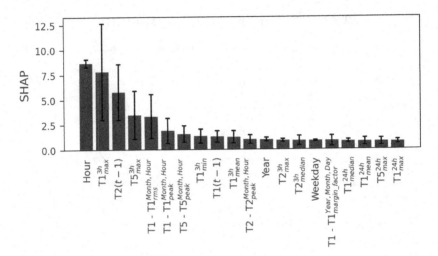

Fig. 4. Out-of-fold Top-20 Features Importance obtained after the last incremental step of feature engineering (*aggregated features*) and feature selection, for LDC1 at Round 1. On the y-axis, we reported SHAP (SHapley Additive exPlanations) [26] values of the LightGBM model.

Table 5. Reconciliation metrics for the *load profiles*; base ($\hat{y}$) and reconciled ($\tilde{y}$) forecasts, with skill scores ($S_\%$). Temporal hierarchy for forecasting using hourly (bottom level), 2-hourly, 4-hourly, 6-hourly, and 12-hourly aggregations.

	MAPE			CRPS			$IS_{90\%}$			$IC_{90\%}$ (%)	
	$\hat{y}$	$\tilde{y}$	$S_\%$	$\hat{y}$	$\tilde{y}$	$S_\%$	$\hat{y}$	$\tilde{y}$	$S_\%$	$\hat{y}$	$\tilde{y}$
LDC1	4.87	**4.84**	0.75	6.35	**6.03**	5.16	61.62	**55.01**	11.34	99.24	98.81
LDC2	5.02	**4.99**	0.52	10.92	**10.44**	4.49	101.35	**90.39**	11.43	99.07	98.49
LDC3	4.51	**4.5**	0.05	45.99	**43.84**	4.78	446.49	**398.37**	11.39	98.85	98.14

past values close to the conditioning time are the most important variables for prediction. We came to the explanation that a high-scale aggregation (empirically greater than 1 day) makes these variables vanish. Instead, small hierarchies also improved peaks, as shown in Table 6 and Fig. 5. Given the availability, the metrics we present for the final match refer to actual competition values of Round 1–5 (Jan-Oct 2018).

Table 6. Reconciliation metrics for the *peaks*; base ($\hat{y}$) and reconciled ($\tilde{y}$) forecasts, with skill scores ($S_{\%}$). Temporal hierarchy for forecasting using hourly (bottom level), 2-hourly, 4-hourly, 6-hourly, and 12-hourly aggregations.

	Magnitude			Timing			Shape			$\text{CRPS}_{\text{peak}}$		
	$\hat{y}$	$\tilde{y}$	$S_{\%}$	$\hat{y}$	$\tilde{y}$	$S_{\%}$	$\hat{y}$	$\tilde{y}$	$S_{\%}$	$\hat{y}$	$\tilde{y}$	$S_{\%}$
LDC1	4.97	**4.90**	1.34	1.22	**1.13**	7.93	0.088	**0.086**	2.16	8.33	**7.89**	5.46
LDC2	5.51	**5.48**	0.52	1.26	**1.23**	1.87	0.102	**0.101**	1.11	15.73	**15.13**	3.85
LDC3	4.83	**4.79**	0.95	1.19	**1.09**	8.80	0.079	**0.078**	1.56	60.83	**57.97**	4.82

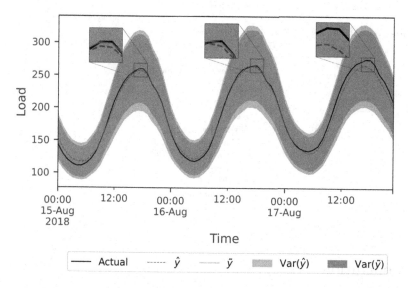

Fig. 5. Comparison of probabilistic forecasts, before and after the application of the temporal hierarchy. The temporal hierarchy slightly improves the point forecasts. It also shortens the prediction intervals without compromising their reliability. The sample refers to three days (15–17 Aug 2018) for LDC1.

Results. We placed 6th (M), 6th (T), and 7th (S) [16], see Table 7.

Table 7. Leaderboard of Final Match [16].

Team	Rank M.	Team	Rank T.	Team	Rank S.
Amperon	1	KIT-IAI	1	KIT-IAI	1
Overfitters	2	Amperon	2	Amperon	2
peaky-finders	3	BelindaTrotta	3	Overfitters	3
Team SGEM KIT	4	Overfitters	4	X-mines	4
KIT-IAI	5	X-mines	5	SheenJavan	5
swissknife	6	swissknife	6	Rajnish Deo	6
Recency Benchmark	7	peaky-finders	7	swissknife	7
Energy HACker	8	Rajnish Deo	8	*Recency Benchmark*	8
Rajnish Deo	9	Team SGEM KIT	9	RandomForecast	8.5
X-mines	10	SheenJavan	10	Yike Li	8.5
...		...		peaky-finders	10
Tao's Vanilla Benchmark	17.5	*Recency Benchmark*	14	...	
		Tao's Vanilla Benchmark	18	*Tao's Vanilla Benchmark*	16

Team	Final Rank
Amperon	1
KIT-IAI	2
Overfitters	3
peaky-finders	4
X-mines	5
swissknife	6
Rajnish Deo	7
Team SGEM KIT	9
Recency Benchmark	10
...	
Tao's Vanilla Benchmark	14

4   Conclusion

We described our experience in an international energy forecasting competition. We introduced features borrowed from the literature of signal processing, a novel strategy for feature selection, and we pointed out the improvement that the DART booster allowed us to achieve over the traditional Gradient Boosting (GB) of trees. Furthermore, we adopted a recent probabilistic extension of LightGBM. A predictive distribution, instead of the point forecast solely, is of great impact because the decision-making processes can rely on the uncertainty inherent in the forecast. To the limits of our knowledge, these models have not yet been adopted in energy forecasting. Moreover, with distributional forecasts, we applied temporal hierarchies and further improved the results.

For future work, we intend to evaluate our method on other datasets and improve the capabilities of other models, specifically Deep learning models for energy forecasting.

Acknowledgments. Work partially funded by the Swiss National Science Foundation (grant 212164), and the ERA-NET Smart Energy Systems program (grant 883973, project Digicities).

References

1. Akiba, T., Sano, S., Yanase, T., Ohta, T., Koyama, M.: Optuna: a next-generation hyperparameter optimization framework. In Proceedings of the 25th ACM SIGKDD International Conference on Knowledge Discovery & Data Mining, pp. 2623–2631 (2019)
2. Armstrong, J.S., Collopy, F.: Error measures for generalizing about forecasting methods: empirical comparisons. Int. J. Forecast. **8**(1), 69–80 (1992)
3. Athanasopoulos, G., Hyndman, R.J., Kourentzes, N., Petropoulos, F.: Forecasting with temporal hierarchies. Eur. J. Oper. Res. **262**(1), 60–74 (2017)
4. Bontempi, G., Ben Taieb, S., Le Borgne, Y.-A.: Machine learning strategies for time series forecasting. Business Intelligence: Second European Summer School, eBISS 2012, Brussels, Belgium, July 15–21, 2012, Tutorial Lectures, pp. 62–77 (2013)
5. Breiman, L.: Random forests. Mach. Learn. **45**, 5–32 (2001)
6. Carlens, H.: State of competitive machine learning in 2022 (2022). mlcontests.com/state-of-competitive-machine-learning-2022/. Accessed 01 Apr 2023
7. Charlton, N., Singleton, C.: A refined parametric model for short term load forecasting. Int. J. Forecast. **30**(2), 364–368 (2014)
8. Corani, G., Azzimonti, D., Augusto, J.P., Zaffalon, M.: Probabilistic reconciliation of hierarchical forecast via bayes' rule. In: Machine Learning and Knowledge Discovery in Databases: European Conference, ECML PKDD 2020, Ghent, Belgium, September 14–18, 2020, Proceedings, Part III, pages 211–226. Springer, 2021
9. Duan, T., Anand, A., Ding, D.Y., Thai, K.K., Basu, S., Ng, A., Schuler, A.: Ngboost: Natural gradient boosting for probabilistic prediction. In International Conference on Machine Learning, pp. 2690–2700. PMLR (2020)
10. Erişti, H., Uçar, A., Demir, Y.: Wavelet-based feature extraction and selection for classification of power system disturbances using support vector machines. Electric Power Syst. Res. **80**(7), 743–752 (2010)
11. Friedman, J.H.: Stochastic gradient boosting. Comput. Stat. Data Anal. **38**(4), 367–378 (2002)
12. Gaillard, P., Goude, Y., Nedellec, R.: Additive models and robust aggregation for gefcom2014 probabilistic electric load and electricity price forecasting. Int. J. Forecast. **32**(3), 1038–1050 (2016)
13. Gneiting, T.: Quantiles as optimal point forecasts. Int. J. Forecast. **27**(2), 197–207 (2011)
14. Gneiting, T., Raftery, A.E., Westveld, A.H., Goldman, T.: Calibrated probabilistic forecasting using ensemble model output statistics and minimum crps estimation. Mon. Weather Rev. **133**(5), 1098–1118 (2005)
15. Gregorutti, B., Michel, B., Saint-Pierre, P.: Correlation and variable importance in random forests. Stat. Comput. **27**, 659–678 (2017)
16. Hong, T.: BigDeal Challenge 2022, Final Match. blog.drhongtao.com/2022/12/bigdeal-challenge-2022-final-leaderboard.html. Accessed 09 Apr 2023
17. Hong, T.: BigDeal Challenge 2022, Qualifying Match. blog.drhongtao.com/2022/11/bigdeal-challenge-2022-qualifying-match.html. Accessed 09 Apr 2023
18. Hong, T., Pinson, P., Fan, S.: Global energy forecasting competition 2012 (2014)
19. Hong, T., Pinson, P., Fan, S., Zareipour, H., Troccoli, A., Hyndman, R.J.: Probabilistic energy forecasting: Global energy forecasting competition 2014 and beyond (2016)

20. Hong, T., Xie, J., Black, J.: Global energy forecasting competition 2017: hierarchical probabilistic load forecasting. Int. J. Forecast. **35**(4), 1389–1399 (2019)
21. Hyndman, R.J., Fan, S.: Density forecasting for long-term peak electricity demand. IEEE Trans. Power Syst. **25**(2), 1142–1153 (2009)
22. James, G., Witten, D., Hastie, T., Tibshirani, R.: An introduction to statistical learning (2013)
23. Januschowski, T., Wang, Y., Torkkola, K., Erkkilä, T., Hasson, H., Gasthaus, J.: Forecasting with trees. Int. J. Forecast. **38**(4), 1473–1481 (2022)
24. Kourentzes, N., Athanasopoulos, G.: Elucidate structure in intermittent demand series. Eur. J. Oper. Res. **288**(1), 141–152 (2021)
25. Li, J., Cheng, K., Wang, S., Morstatter, F., Trevino, R.P., Tang, J., Liu, H.: Feature selection: a data perspective. ACM Comput. Surv. (CSUR) **50**(6), 1–45 (2017)
26. Lundberg, S.M., Lee, S.-I.: A unified approach to interpreting model predictions. Advances in neural information processing systems, 30 (2017)
27. März, A.: Xgboostlss-an extension of xgboost to probabilistic forecasting. arXiv preprint arXiv:1907.03178 (2019)
28. März, A., Kneib, T.: Distributional gradient boosting machines. arXiv preprint arXiv:2204.00778 (2022)
29. Meinshausen, N., Ridgeway, G.: Quantile regression forests. J. Mach. Learn. Res. **7**(6) (2006)
30. Nespoli, L., Medici, V.: Multivariate boosted trees and applications to forecasting and control. J. Mach. Learn. Res. **23**(246), 1–47 (2022)
31. Smyl, S., Hua, N.G.: Machine learning methods for gefcom2017 probabilistic load forecasting. Int. J. Forecast. **35**(4), 1424–1431 (2019)
32. Taieb, S.B., Hyndman, R.J.: A gradient boosting approach to the kaggle load forecasting competition. Int. J. Forecast. **30**(2), 382–394 (2014)
33. Vinayak, R.K., Gilad-Bachrach, R.: Dart: dropouts meet multiple additive regression trees. In: Artificial Intelligence and Statistics, pp. 489–497. PMLR (2015)
34. Wang, Y., Sun, S., Chen, X., Zeng, X., Kong, Y., Chen, J., Guo, Y., Wang, T.: Short-term load forecasting of industrial customers based on svmd and xgboost. Int. J. Electr. Power Energy Syst. **129**, 106830 (2021)
35. Wickramasuriya, S.L., Athanasopoulos, G., Hyndman, R.J.: Optimal forecast reconciliation for hierarchical and grouped time series through trace minimization. J. Am. Stat. Assoc. **114**(526), 804–819 (2019)
36. Yu, J.: Bearing performance degradation assessment using locality preserving projections and gaussian mixture models. Mech. Syst. Signal Process. **25**(7), 2573–2588 (2011)

Time-Aware Predictions of Moments of Change in Longitudinal User Posts on Social Media

Anthony Hills[1]([✉]), Adam Tsakalidis[1,2], and Maria Liakata[1,2,3]

[1] Queen Mary University of London, London, UK
{a.r.hills,a.tsakalidis,m.liakata}@qmul.ac.uk
[2] The Alan Turing Institute, London, UK
[3] University of Warwick, Coventry, UK

Abstract. Capturing changes in an individual's language is an important aspect of personalised mental health monitoring. A key component is modelling the influence of time, as contextual information both in the recent or distant past/future carries varying semantic weight. We capture and contrast this information by identifying neural, time-sensitive, bi-directional representations of individuals – modelling time-intervals in their social-media posts inspired by the Hawkes process. We demonstrate that our approach helps identify whether an individual's mood is changing drastically, or smoothly on two social media datasets – yielding superior performance compared to time-insensitive baselines and outperforming the state-of-the-art on the CLPsych 2022 shared task.

Keywords: Social Media · Mental Health · Longitudinal Modelling

1 Introduction

Mental health has rapidly become one of the most prevalent public health problems worldwide. A recent large-scale longitudinal study [13] on identifying changes in mental health showed that the prevalence of likely mental health problems in the UK increased from 24.3% between 2017-19 to 37.8% in April 2020 during the COVID-19 pandemic, claiming large health and economic costs and highlighting the timeliness and need for developing scalable tools for monitoring changes in mental health in an automated, real-time manner.

Social media provide a rich resource for addressing this challenge. However, most related work based on longitudinal social media data typically ignore the time-varying nature of an individual's mental state and instead make aggregate user- [2, 4, 14, 26] or post-level predictions – e.g. identifying posts with suicidal ideation indicators [9, 25, 31] or mental health symptoms [8, 20, 23].

https://github.com/Maria-Liakata-NLP-Group/time-aware-predictions-of-mocs.

© The Author(s), under exclusive license to Springer Nature Switzerland AG 2023
G. Ifrim et al. (Eds.): AALTD 2023, LNAI 14343, pp. 293–305, 2023.
https://doi.org/10.1007/978-3-031-49896-1_19

Task Definition. This work focuses on **predicting moments of change in mood** (MoCs) in individuals on the basis of textual content shared online. Following the definitions by [34], we work with *user timelines* (sequences of chronologically ordered individual user posts), aiming at classifying each post as a: (1) *switch* – sudden, abrupt change in mood, from positive to negative, or vice versa; (2) *escalation* – gradual change, where the user's mood progressively becomes more positive/negative; or (3) *none* – user's baseline mood, no MoC. The task formed the basis of the latest CLPsych shared task [33], where neural networks, such as LSTMs, were employed by nearly all teams [1,3,5,6,10,24]. While such approaches help in modelling the sequence dynamics in posts, they lack the ability to account for the significant changes and heterogeneity in time-intervals between posts.

Temporal Point Processes (TPPs) [11,12] are designed for modelling variable-length, asynchronous event sequences spaced irregularly in continuous-time (e.g. posts on social media). The self-exciting **Hawkes process** [21] is a popular TPP that has been frequently applied to social media data [27]. It models the probability of an event occurring, where recent events spike the probability of future events occurring, followed by a (typically exponential) decay, making the probability of future events less likely in the absence of recent ones. Neural TPPs (NTTPs) [30] leverage neural networks (typically RNNs [16]) to learn a highly complex, flexible representation of an event history, which is then used to parameterize the conditional distribution of the probability of a next event occurring.

In this paper, rather than predicting the probability of post events occurring, we instead aim to enrich learned dynamics of individuals by taking advantage of the parameterizations for modelling time in the Hawkes process. We thus model BiLSTM hidden states over post embeddings of a given user to learn the basic sequence dynamics of a user's linguistic posting context, and aggregate these with a transformation similar to a Hawkes process – to combine the learned dynamics of the sequence information captured by LSTMs with the time-sensitive information in the representations, modelled with exponential decay. Specifically we make the following contributions:

- We propose a time-aware approach for modelling textual posts of individuals, by transforming their respective LSTM hidden states over previous/future posts with self-excitation and exponential decay that varies with time.
- We extend the time-aware approach to the bi-directional setting and work on two social media datasets, showcasing that this combination outperforms non-time-aware baselines, and all teams from the CLPsych 2022 shared task.
- We demonstrate the effectiveness of our approach, in an ablation study investigating (1) time-aware features and (2) bi-directionality.

2 Method

Notation. A user's u timeline $T^{(u)}$ consists of chronologically ordered posts $p^{(u,i)} = \{v^{(u,i)}, t^{(u,i)}, y^{(u,i)}\}$ ($0 \leq i < |T^{(u)}|$), where the ith post is represented by its post-level embeddings $v^{(u,i)}$, associated posting timestamp $t^{(u,i)}$ and ground-truth label $y^{(u,i)} \in \{S, E, O\}$ (switch, escalation or none respectively). Our aim is to predict each label $\hat{y}^{(u',i)}$ in a test user's u' timeline $T^{(u')}$, given the sequence of $\{v^{(u',i)}, t^{(u',i)}\}$.

2.1   Model

Here we outline our model for incorporating temporally contextual information for identifying MoCs in a timeline. We model historical, time-sensitive information about the user (**HEAT**) and extend our model to operate over trainable hidden representations (**Modelling sequence dynamics**) as well as contextual future information (**Bi-directionality**).

Compared to prior work for this task [33,34], we note that we are first to approach the problem with a sequence-based, bi-directional, and time-sensitive approach that considers the time-stamps of historical and future posts to predict moments of change in mood. Most prior approaches fail to model the influence of time [1,3,5–7,18,19,24], neglect the importance of bi-directionality [1,5–7,10,24] or fail to model sequence dynamics [7,24] for predicting moments of change.

HEAT. To aggregate historical posts of a user into a temporally-informed embedding, [29] proposed to model the influence of time on an individual's historical post representations $v^{(i)}$ in a timeline via the Historical Emotional AggregaTion (HEAT), comparing each post at index i, with each historical post in the timeline at index j:

$$v^{(i)}_{\text{HEAT}} = \sum_{j:\Delta\tau_j > 0} v^{(j)} + \epsilon e^{-\beta \Delta \tau_j} \max(v^{(j)}, 0), \qquad (1)$$

where $\Delta\tau_j = t^{(i)} - t^{(j)}$ (measured in days), and ϵ and β are fixed hyper-parameters reflecting the amount of self-excitation and exponential time-decay to apply to each post respectively when building an aggregate representation at each time-step. As such, HEAT encodes the dynamics of historical post representations in a time-aware manner.

Modelling Sequence Dynamics. [28] model raw post representations $v^{(i)}$ via Eq. 1. By contrast we model BiLSTM hidden state representations $h^{(i)}$ of posts, to better capture sequence dynamics. We thus apply Eq. 1 by substituting v with h at each timestep to model aggregate representations of u's historical posts.

Bi-directionality. Motivated by the notion that changes are better identified by comparing the current post in relation to previous *and* future posts made by u, and by the recent work of [32] who explored bi-directional neural ordinary differential equations for classifying posts on social media, we further extend the HEAT representations to be bi-directional: we learn a HEAT representation over historical posts with timestamps $t < t^{(i)}$, which is then concatenated with another HEAT representation that is learned over future posts with timestamps $t > t^{(i)}$.

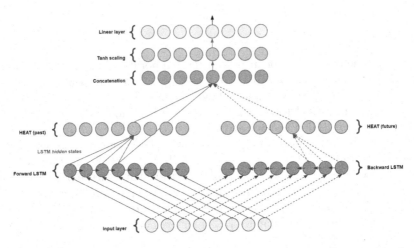

Fig. 1. Architecture of our proposed BiLSTM-HEAT model. Forward and backward LSTM hidden states are aggregated using HEAT (Eq. 1), in the past and future directions respectively. Future and past HEAT representations are then concatenated for each post index, along with the associated original BiLSTM hidden representation at each post index. After scaling the concatenated representation, this is passed into the final linear layer to predict the label of each post in a given timeline.

Final Model. We concatenate the HEAT representations with the original hidden representations of the BiLSTM learned at i. This is to preserve the sequence information captured by the BiLSTM, and linguistic information in the original post embeddings, and to contrast these to the temporal information in the historical and future post representations that are concatenated. We scale all 3 concatenated representations by passing them through a tanh activation function before feeding them as input to the final linear layer, making one prediction per time-step (post) for an entire timeline (see Fig. 1).

3   Experimental Setting

Datasets. We work with two datasets containing timelines of longitudinal user posts in English annotated for MoCs (see Table 1). We note that these are the only two such datasets available for this task. These datasets include (a) Reddit, from the CLPsych 2022 shared task [33]; and (b) TalkLife [34], a social network for mental health support. Both datasets were annotated using annotation

Table 1. Summary of the datasets used in our work.

	Reddit	TalkLife
Users	186	500
Timelines (posts)	255 (6,195)	500 (18,702)
Label distr. % (O/E/S)	77.6/15.8/6.6	84.5/10.8/4.7
Timeline Length	~ 2 months	≤ 2 weeks

guidelines introduced in [34], which are also summarized in our appendix A. (a) was annotated by 4 English (2 native) speakers and (b) by 3 English speaking (1 native) university educated annotators. We keep the train/test split used by [33] for (a); for (b) we perform the same 5-fold cross-validation as in [34].

Models, Baselines and Metrics. We represent each post in a timeline as its [CLS] representation extracted from BERT [15] fine-tuned for identifying MoCs at the post-level on our training data, using focal loss [22]. On **Reddit**, we contrast our performance against state-of-the-art (SOTA) from the CLPsych 2022 shared task: (a) UoS [3] is an attention-based BiLSTM operating on different input representations of each post of a timeline; (b) WResearch [5] is a XGBoost classifier, fed with emotionally-informed and abnormality seq2seq-based vectors for each post. On **TalkLife**, we compare against SOTA from [34]: (a) BERT(f) is a post-level BERT-based classifier, trained using focal loss; (b) BiLSTM-bert is a timeline-level BiLSTM operating on the posts, which are represented as the [CLS] token of (a). We report (per-class/macro-averaged) precision, recall and F1 scores (i) on the test set of Reddit, and (ii) on the 5 folds of TalkLife (macro-averaged). The grid-searched hyper-parameters and training details are provided in Appendix B.

4   Results

4.1   Comparison Against SOTA

Results of our model (BiLSTM-HEAT) and baselines in Reddit and TalkLife are shown in Table 3. BiLSTM-HEAT surpasses all models on Reddit in nearly all evaluation metrics and classes, offering a 5.7% relative improvement on macro-F1 compared to current SOTA – UoS [3]. Importantly, it achieves a large performance gain of 17.6% relative on F1 over UoS – also a BiLSTM-based model – on the most challenging class (switch), highlighting the importance of time-aware modelling for capturing rare cases (see Table 1).

On TalkLife, BiLSTM-HEAT fails to outperform the SOTA BiLSTM-bert in most cases, which could be due to the difference in temporal granularity between the TalkLife and Reddit datasets – where Reddit consists of much longer timelines with much larger time-intervals between posts. As a result, modelling the heterogeneity in the time-differences between posts may be more important for identifying MoCs for this dataset – whereas modelling sequence dynamics alone is sufficient for timelines with shorter time-intervals between posts, which we investigate further in our ablation study, presented next (Table 2).

Table 2. Per-class and macro-averaged results on each dataset (Reddit, TalkLife). **Best** scores are highlighted.

Reddit	macro-avg			S			E			O		
	P	R	F1	P	R	F1	P	R	F1	P	R	F1
Majority	âĂŞ	.333	.280	âĂŞ	.000	.000	âĂŞ	.000	.000	.724	**1.000**	.840
WResearch	.625	.579	.598	.362	.256	.300	.646	.553	.596	.868	.929	.897
UoS	.689	.625	.649	**.490**	.305	.376	.697	.630	.662	.881	.940	.909
BiLSTM-HEAT	**.706**	**.670**	**.686**	.475	**.415**	**.442**	**.741**	**.654**	**.694**	**.902**	.942	**.921**

TalkLife	macro-avg			S			E			O		
	P	R	F1	P	R	F1	P	R	F1	P	R	F1
Majority	âĂŞ	.333	.280	âĂŞ	.000	.000	âĂŞ	.000	.000	.845	**1.000**	.916
BERT(f)	.520	.554	.534	.260	**.321**	.287	.401	**.478**	.436	.898	.864	.881
BiLSTM-bert	**.621**	**.553**	**.580**	**.397**	.264	**.316**	**.568**	.461	**.508**	**.898**	.936	**.917**
BiLSTM-HEAT	.584	.552	.566	.329	.290	.308	.524	.448	.483	.897	.920	.908

4.2 Ablation Analysis

To study the contribution of each component in our model, we ablate each of the components presented in Sect. 2 and train and evaluate the resulting models on both datasets: (a) we keep HEAT but remove the bidirectionality component, so that HEAT operates on the previous hidden states of an LSTM (-**BDR**); (b) we remove the 'modelling sequence dynamics' component (-**MSD**), so that HEAT operates on our raw input embeddings instead of the hidden states – concatenating past and future HEAT representations of $v^{(u,a,i)}$ only.

Table 3 summarises our results. Removing the LSTM component (-MSD) has the worst performance by a large margin, highlighting the importance of sequential modelling for our task. This further illustrates the benefit of applying HEAT over LSTM hidden states, rather than on raw posts – as we are able to take advantage of the dynamics learned by these sequence based models.

Bi-directionality (i.e. applying HEAT both on historical and future directions, compared to only applying HEAT in the historical direction) seems to benefit our model most for predicting escalations, and less so for switches. We attribute this due to escalations being more gradual and smoother changes over several future posts, as opposed to switches which are more abrupt and can be more immediately seen just by considering a shift from the previous context – and as such may benefit less from considering the context in a user's future posts.

Table 3. Ablation study: Scores when removing/altering parts of our model. Results are averaged over 3 different random seeds. **Best** scores are highlighted.

Reddit	macro-avg			S			E			O		
	P	R	F1	P	R	F1	P	R	F1	P	R	F1
BiLSTM-HEAT	.706	.670	.686	.475	.415	.442	**.741**	**.654**	**.694**	**.902**	.942	.921
-BDR	**.722**	**.673**	**.693**	**.533**	**.439**	**.480**	.735	.630	.677	.899	**.950**	**.924**
-MSD	.571	.565	.566	.182	.228	.201	.655	.591	.621	.877	.875	.876

TalkLife	macro-avg			S			E			O		
	P	R	F1	P	R	F1	P	R	F1	P	R	F1
BiLSTM-HEAT	.584	**.552**	**.566**	**.329**	**.290**	**.308**	.524	**.448**	**.483**	**.897**	.920	.908
-BDR	**.585**	.528	.551	.325	.257	.286	**.540**	.397	.457	.890	**.930**	**.910**
-MSD	.480	.442	.455	.200	.139	.161	.368	.272	.312	.872	.915	.893

Sequence Length. We analyse the performance of our model and its variants introduced in our ablation study, investigating the ability of our model to account for the heterogeneity in time-intervals between posts, as well as being able to model sequences of varying lengths.

Figure 2 shows our full model BiLSTM-HEAT is able to best capture sequences of varying lengths, being best suited for capturing moments of change in timelines with both few and many longitudinal posts. Removing the component which models sequence dynamics (-MSD) leads to the largest performance drop across all sequence lengths, suggesting that modelling LSTM hidden states with exponential time-decay provided by HEAT provides the largest performance gain compared to modelling the raw posts without considering the sequential dynamics. Indeed for TalkLife, we see a large 23.9% and 10.1% relative performance gain when averaging the macro-average F1 scores from using BiLSTM-HEAT over -MSD for both long ($80 \leq$ posts ≤ 100) and short ($0 \leq$ posts ≤ 20) sequences. Modelling posts in a bi-directional manner also leads to another performance gain of 1.5% and 6.6% when comparing BiLSTM-HEAT to -BDR by averaging the macro-average F1 scores for the same long and short sequences. This further suggests that considering the user's representations of their future and past together is well suited for identifying changes in a user.

For Reddit a much higher relative performance gain over -BDR occurs for shorter sequence lengths, and a lower relative gain for longer sequences is observed – whereas for TalkLife the opposite is true. Furthermore, we also see that performance decreases with sequence length for all models on Reddit, but conversely performance increases for all models (except -MSD) on TalkLife. We attribute these due to differences in the domains of the datasets, where posts on Reddit are specifically made on mental health related subreddits which might be more indicative of a MoC, whereas posts on TalkLife are more general – discussing day-to-day-life. This is also supported by the easier nature of the task on Reddit based on our results in Table 3.

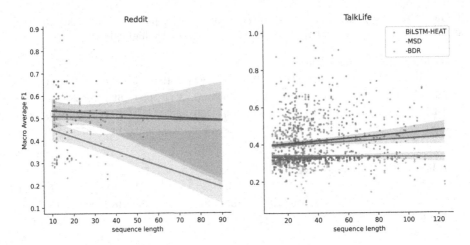

Fig. 2. Performance of models when assessing posts in timelines of varying sequence lengths.

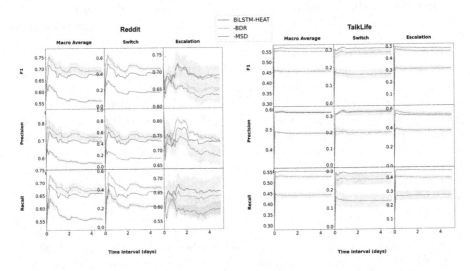

Fig. 3. Effect of time-intervals when assessing posts for MoCs, with the models presented in our ablation study. We evaluate the performance on posts that have a time-interval of less than or equal to what is presented on the x-axis.

Time-Intervals. Figure 3 demonstrates BiLSTM-HEAT outperforms all metrics for varying time intervals relative to previous posts, for nearly all classes and metrics on TalkLife – slightly under performing -BDR only in macro-average precision and precision for escalations. On Reddit, BiLSTM-HEAT achieves the best macro average F1 score for capturing the rare class "escalation" overall across varying time-intervals, with a relative performance gain in F1 of 1.4% and 9.0% on larger timer intervals (≤5 days). On Reddit our model struggles to model switches effectively – being outperformed by -BDR, which only considers the forward direction when modelling sequence dynamics and performing aggregation with HEAT. -BDR observed a gain in F1 over BiLSTM of 28.9% on smaller time intervals and a lower relative gain of 14.1% on larger time intervals. This further suggests that for Reddit, the more abrupt class (switch) is better captured by only considering the immediate previous context rather than the rest of the user's distant future posts with bi-directionality, as discussed earlier from analysing Table 3. Compared to -MSD, we see a high 81.4% relative performance gain in F1-score for BiLSTM-HEAT on Reddit for smaller time-intervals ($\leq$1 day) and a significantly higher 240.0% relative gain on longer time-intervals ($\leq$5 days), for assessing "switches" – demonstrating the effectiveness of modelling BiLSTM hidden states with HEAT in a bi-directional manner.

5 Conclusion

In this paper we have presented a time-sensitive approach for building representations of users at different points in time, based on linguistic and temporal context in social media posts in a bi-directional manner. By modelling a user's timeline of posts with a BiLSTM parametrized by time-dependent exponential decay with a Hawkes process, we demonstrate superior performance over prior approaches which did not consider temporality and bi-directionality together when assessing changes in mood of individuals – outperforming the best performing systems on the CLPsych 2022 shared task, which targets the same objective.

6 Limitations

Our model is trained to predict the presence of MoCs on the basis of content shared online by social media users. As such, it cannot generalise to detect changes in mood unless these are reflected in an individuals' posts. This fact has a further downstream effect in sample bias, since our datasets consist of users who have (a) certain demographic characteristics as social media users who post in English and (b) have *selected* to self-disclose their well-being online, which has been shown to lack generalisability in related (user-level) mental-health tasks [17].

The limitation of generalisability is also present in the ability of our models to effectively predict MoCs in datasets of different characteristics. For example, the BERT(f) model trained on TalkLife, which achieved the second-best results in [34] on this dataset, was easily outperformed when applied on Reddit by a simple post-level logistic regression trained with in-domain tfidf feature vectors [33]. This highlights the importance of the different characteristics of each platform (e.g., length/content of messages) as well as of the different time intervals used to define what constitutes a 'user timeline' in the pre-annotation stage (e.g. 2 weeks in TalkLife *vs* 2 months on Reddit).

Finally, the definitions of MoC that we have followed in our work has been established on the basis of *mood changes in social media*. A well-established model performance on other related types of NLP-based MoC identification tasks, such as detecting changes during psychotherapy sessions, cannot be safely hypothesised from the findings of this work.

Ethics Statement. Ethics IRB approval was obtained from the IRB Committee of the lead University prior to engaging in this research study. Our work involves ethical considerations around the analysis of user generated content shared on social media (TalkLife and Reddit). A license was obtained to work with the user data from TalkLife and a project proposal was submitted to them in order to embark on the project. Potential risks from the application of our work in being able to identify moments of change in individuals' timelines are akin to the identification of those in earlier work on personal event identification from social media and the detection of suicidal ideation. Potential mitigation strategies include restricting and regulating access to the code base and annotation labels used for evaluation.

A   Annotation Guidelines

The two datasets of longitudinal user posts annotated for MoCs that we make use of in this paper were sourced by [33,34] for TalkLife and Reddit respectively. Both datasets were annotated using the same annotation guidelines and annotation interface proposed [34].

Annotators were provided with timelines to view, containing chronologically ordered posts by users, along with their associated comments and timestamps. They were then asked to label posts for MoCs.

The first type of label, "Switch" was defined in the guidelines as a "drastic change in mood, in comparison with the recent past". Annotators were also tasked to label how long the Switch in mood persists (i.e. label its beginning and end). The second type of label "Escalation" was defined in their guidelines as a "gradual change in mood, which should last for a few posts". Similarly, annotators were also instructed to label the associated range of posts for how long this change persists: where a peak of the escalation must be labelled, and the beginning and end of the gradual mood change also provided. Finally, a label of "None" was provided by default where no mood change was identified for that given post.

B   Hyper-parameters Searched

We perform a grid-search over the HEAT parameters (Eq. 1): both β (decay rate) and α (self-excitation) in the range $[0.00001, 0.001, 0.1]$ for both datasets. All models are searched with learning rates in the range $[0.0001, 0.001, 0.01]$ on Reddit and $[0.001, 0.01]$ for TalkLife. All models are trained with 100 epochs with early stopping using a patience of 5 for all models and both datasets. For the BiLSTM module, we perform a grid-search over all layers using output dimensions of $[128, 256, 512]$ and $[128, 256]$ for Reddit and Talklife respectively. All models were implemented with PyTorch, and were trained using K-Fold cross validation over 5 folds using training, validation, and testing sizes of 60%, 20%, 20% respectively.

References

1. Alhamed, F., Ive, J., Specia, L.: Predicting moments of mood changes overtime from imbalanced social media data. In: Proceedings of the Eighth Workshop on Computational Linguistics and Clinical Psychology, pp. 239–244. Association for Computational Linguistics, Seattle, USA, July 2022. https://doi.org/10.18653/v1/2022.clpsych-1.23. https://aclanthology.org/2022.clpsych-1.23
2. Amir, S., Coppersmith, G., Carvalho, P., Silva, M.J., Wallace, B.C.: Quantifying mental health from social media with neural user embeddings. In: Machine Learning for Healthcare Conference, pp. 306–321. PMLR (2017)
3. Azim, T., Gyanendro Singh, L., Middleton, S.E.: Detecting moments of change and suicidal risks in longitudinal user texts using multi-task learning. In: Proceedings of the Eighth Workshop on Computational Linguistics and Clinical Psychology, pp. 213–218. Association for Computational Linguistics, Seattle, USA, July 2022. https://doi.org/10.18653/v1/2022.clpsych-1.19. https://aclanthology.org/2022.clpsych-1.19
4. Bagroy, S., Kumaraguru, P., De Choudhury, M.: A social media based index of mental well-being in college campuses. In: Proceedings of the 2017 CHI Conference on Human factors in Computing Systems, pp. 1634–1646 (2017)
5. Bayram, U., Benhiba, L.: Emotionally-informed models for detecting moments of change and suicide risk levels in longitudinal social media data. In: Proceedings of the Eighth Workshop on Computational Linguistics and Clinical Psychology, pp. 219–225. Association for Computational Linguistics, Seattle, USA, July 2022. https://doi.org/10.18653/v1/2022.clpsych-1.20. https://aclanthology.org/2022.clpsych-1.20
6. Boinepelli, S., Subramanian, S., Singam, A., Raha, T., Varma, V.: Towards capturing changes in mood and identifying suicidality risk. In: Proceedings of the Eighth Workshop on Computational Linguistics and Clinical Psychology, pp. 245–250 (2022)
7. Bucur, A.M., Jang, H., Liza, F.F.: Capturing changes in mood over time in longitudinal data using ensemble methodologies (2022)
8. Coppersmith, G., Dredze, M., Harman, C., Hollingshead, K., Mitchell, M.: CLPsych 2015 shared task: Depression and PTSD on Twitter. In: Proceedings of the 2nd Workshop on Computational Linguistics and Clinical Psychology: From Linguistic Signal to Clinical Reality, pp. 31–39. Association for Computational Linguistics, Denver, Colorado, 5 June 2015. https://doi.org/10.3115/v1/W15-1204. https://aclanthology.org/W15-1204
9. Coppersmith, G., Ngo, K., Leary, R., Wood, A.: Exploratory analysis of social media prior to a suicide attempt. In: Proceedings of the Third Workshop on Computational Linguistics and Clinical Psychology, pp. 106–117 (2016)
10. Culnan, J., Diaz, D.R., Bethard, S.: Exploring transformers and time lag features for predicting changes in mood over time. In: Proceedings of the Eighth Workshop on Computational Linguistics and Clinical Psychology, pp. 226–231 (2022)
11. Daley, D.J., Vere-Jones, D.: An Introduction to the Theory of Point Processes. Volume II: General Theory and Structure. Springer (2008)

12. Daley, D.J., Vere-Jones, D., et al.: An introduction to the theory of point processes: volume I: elementary theory and methods. Springer (2003)
13. Daly, M., Sutin, A.R., Robinson, E.: Longitudinal changes in mental health and the COVID-19 pandemic: evidence from the UK Household Longitudinal Study. Psychological Medicine, pp. 1–10, November 2020. https://doi.org/10.1017/S0033291720004432. https://www.cambridge.org/core/product/identifier/S0033291720004432/type/journal_article
14. De Choudhury, M., Gamon, M., Counts, S., Horvitz, E.: Predicting depression via social media. In: Proceedings of the International AAAI Conference on Web and Social Media, vol. 7 (2013)
15. Devlin, J., Chang, M.W., Lee, K., Toutanova, K.: BERT: pre-training of Deep Bidirectional Transformers for Language Understanding, pp. 4171–4186, June 2019. https://doi.org/10.18653/v1/N19-1423. https://www.aclweb.org/anthology/N19-1423
16. Du, N., Dai, H., Trivedi, R., Upadhyay, U., Gomez-Rodriguez, M., Song, L.: Recurrent marked temporal point processes: embedding event history to vector. In: Proceedings of the 22nd ACM SIGKDD International Conference on Knowledge Discovery and Data Mining, pp. 1555–1564 (2016)
17. Ernala, S.K., et al.: Methodological gaps in predicting mental health states from social media: triangulating diagnostic signals. In: Proceedings of the 2019 chi Conference on Human Factors in Computing Systems, pp. 1–16 (2019)
18. Gamaarachchige, P.K., Orabi, A.H., Orabi, M.H., Inkpen, D.: Multi-task learning to capture changes in mood over time. In: Proceedings of the Eighth Workshop on Computational Linguistics and Clinical Psychology, pp. 232–238 (2022)
19. Ganesan, A.V., et al.: Wwbp-sqt-lite: multi-level models and difference embeddings for moments of change identification in mental health forums. In: Proceedings of the Eighth Workshop on Computational Linguistics and Clinical Psychology, pp. 251–258 (2022)
20. Gkotsis, G., et al.: Characterisation of mental health conditions in social media using informed deep learning. Sci. Rep. 7(1), 1–11 (2017)
21. Hawkes, A.G.: Point spectra of some mutually exciting point processes. J. Roy. Stat. Soc.: Ser. B (Methodol.) 33(3), 438–443 (1971)
22. Lin, T.Y., Goyal, P., Girshick, R., He, K., Dollar, P.: Focal Loss for Dense Object Detection, pp. 2980–2988 (2017). https://openaccess.thecvf.com/content_iccv_2017/html/Lin_Focal_Loss_for_ICCV_2017_paper.html
23. Loveys, K., Crutchley, P., Wyatt, E., Coppersmith, G.: Small but mighty: affective micropatterns for quantifying mental health from social media language. In: Proceedings of the Fourth Workshop on Computational Linguistics and Clinical Psychology-From Linguistic Signal to Clinical Reality, pp. 85–95 (2017)
24. Marcos, H.F., et al.: Approximate nearest neighbour extraction techniques and neural networks for suicide risk prediction in the clpsych 2022 shared task. In: Proceedings of the Eighth Workshop on Computational Linguistics and Clinical Psychology, pp. 199–204 (2022)
25. Masuda, N., Kurahashi, I., Onari, H.: Suicide ideation of individuals in online social networks. PLoS ONE 8(4), e62262 (2013)
26. Preoţiuc-Pietro, D., et al.: The role of personality, age, and gender in tweeting about mental illness. In: Proceedings of the 2nd Workshop on Computational Linguistics and Clinical Psychology: From Linguistic Signal to Clinical Reality, pp. 21–30 (2015)
27. Rizoiu, M.A., Lee, Y., Mishra, S., Xie, L.: A tutorial on hawkes processes for events in social media. arXiv preprint arXiv:1708.06401 (2017)

28. Sawhney, R., Agarwal, S., Wadhwa, A., Shah, R.: Exploring the scale-free nature of stock markets: hyperbolic graph learning for algorithmic trading. In: Proceedings of the Web Conference 2021, pp. 11–22. ACM, Ljubljana Slovenia, April 2021. https://doi.org/10.1145/3442381.3450095. https://dl.acm.org/doi/10.1145/3442381.3450095

29. Sawhney, R., Joshi, H., Shah, R.R., Flek, L.: Suicide ideation detection via social and temporal user representations using hyperbolic learning. In: Proceedings of the 2021 Conference of the North American Chapter of the Association for Computational Linguistics: Human Language Technologies, pp. 2176–2190. Association for Computational Linguistics, Online (2021). https://doi.org/10.18653/v1/2021.naacl-main.176. https://www.aclweb.org/anthology/2021.naacl-main.176

30. Shchur, O., Türkmen, A.C., Januschowski, T., Günnemann, S.: Neural temporal point processes: a review. arXiv preprint arXiv:2104.03528 (2021)

31. Shing, H.C., Nair, S., Zirikly, A., Friedenberg, M., Daumé III, H., Resnik, P.: Expert, crowdsourced, and machine assessment of suicide risk via online postings. In: Proceedings of the Fifth Workshop on Computational Linguistics and Clinical Psychology: From Keyboard to Clinic, pp. 25–36 (2018)

32. Tamire, M., Anumasa, S., Srijith, P.K.: Bi-directional recurrent neural ordinary differential equations for social media text classification. In: Proceedings of the 2nd Workshop on Deriving Insights from User-Generated Text, pp. 20–24. Association for Computational Linguistics, (Hybrid) Dublin, Ireland, and Virtual, May 2022. https://doi.org/10.18653/v1/2022.wit-1.3. https://aclanthology.org/2022.wit-1.3

33. Tsakalidis, A., et al.: Overview of the CLPsych 2022 shared task: Capturing moments of change in longitudinal user posts. In: Proceedings of the Eighth Workshop on Computational Linguistics and Clinical Psychology, pp. 184–198. Association for Computational Linguistics, Seattle, USA, July 2022. https://doi.org/10.18653/v1/2022.clpsych-1.16. https://aclanthology.org/2022.clpsych-1.16

34. Tsakalidis, A., Nanni, F., Hills, A., Chim, J., Song, J., Liakata, M.: Identifying moments of change from longitudinal user text. In: Proceedings of the 60th Annual Meeting of the Association for Computational Linguistics (Volume 1: Long Papers), pp. 4647–4660. Association for Computational Linguistics, Dublin, Ireland, May 2022. https://doi.org/10.18653/v1/2022.acl-long.318. https://aclanthology.org/2022.acl-long.318

Author Index

G. Ifrim et al. (Eds.): AALTD 2023, LNAI 14343, pp. 307–308, 2023.
https://doi.org/10.1007/978-3-031-49896-1

Printed in the United States
by Baker & Taylor Publisher Services

Printed in the United States
by Baker & Taylor Publisher Services